DATE DUE

AG 9'01			
DE - 7 '02			
OC 10 '19			

DEMCO 38-296

GLOBAL
DEVELOPMENT

A Reference Handbook

R

G L O B A L
DEVELOPMENT

A Reference Handbook

William Savitt and Paula Bottorf

**CONTEMPORARY
WORLD ISSUES**

ABC-CLIO

Santa Barbara, California
Denver, Colorado
Oxford, England

Library of Congress Cataloging-in-Publication Data

Savitt, William, 1962–
   Global Development : a reference handbook / William Savitt,
  Paula Bottorf
     p. cm.— (Contemporary World Issues)
    Includes bibliographical references and index.
    1. Developing countries—Economic policy. 2. Economic
  development. 3. International economic relations. I. Bottorf, Paula.
  II. Title. III. Series.
  HC59.7.S283 1995 338.9—dc20 95-40213

ISBN 0-87436-774-3

02 01 00 99 98 97 96 95   10 9 8 7 6 5 4 3 2 1

ABC-CLIO, Inc.
130 Cremona Drive, P.O. Box 1911
Santa Barbara, California 93116-1911

This book is printed on acid-free paper ∞ ·

Manufactured in the United States of America

Contents

Preface

We'd like to thank a number of people who contributed to this book and made its realization possible. We are very grateful to Aoife O'Reilly who assisted in drafting two chapters and made an important research contribution to the volume. Vigorous thanks also to Sarah L. White, the coeditor of *Hunger TeachNet*, who is responsible for much of the gender analysis that appears in the Overview. Mario Hyacinth worked with us in the early stages of research, and we greatly appreciate his substantial effort on this project, as well as his continuing hard work on behalf of Interfaith Hunger Appeal. Sheila Weigert was a splendid summer intern, and her feedback, suggestions, and overall enthusiasm helped shape the book. In the last stages of the project, Adina Batnitzky contributed to the manuscript with careful and critical reading, while Francesca Crispino helped us along with her competence and collegiality. Thanks, too, to Todd Hallman of ABC-CLIO, who shepherded the project from conception through publication with patience and considerable skill. Finally, we would like to express our appreciation to the agencies of Interfaith Hunger Appeal: Catholic Relief Services, Church World Service, Lutheran World Relief, and

The American Jewish Joint Distribution Committee. Our collaboration with these agencies has informed our commitment to, and belief in, the promise of contemporary global development.

Global Development: An Overview

I n its modern sense, the idea of global development is a creature of the post–World War II era. Like much of the ideology born in the decade following that conflict, "development" betrayed an intensely optimistic, perhaps naive, confidence in the red ressability of an inequitable world order. Standing right alongside the tension of the cold war, development—a cluster of ideas collectively committed to the end of poverty, disease, and ignorance—was a beatific and peaceful ideological cousin. The world's wealthier nations pledged to collaborate with the poorer to distribute the earth's riches more universally; no longer were there to be different standards for the treatment of different races and peoples. The invasive institution of colonialism was to be swept aside by independence, sovereignty, and national empowerment. Human rights graduated from gentle dream to political fact with the 1948 adoption of the United Nations Declaration of Universal Human Rights. A world of technical prowess, political freedom, and goodwill declared itself poised to take on the most ancient, persistent ills of human society, and win.

Such were the broad strokes of "development" as it emerged as a massive international enterprise in the late 1940s. The drive for development soon gave rise to a global industry, fueled by the large-scale assistance programs of Northern and Western governments, and ongoing relief and development programs implemented by nonprofit organizations.[1] By some yardsticks, the results of these efforts have been remarkable: In the half-century since World War II, rich and poor nations have enjoyed unprecedented economic growth. And notwithstanding countless disasters of human and natural origin, the basic indices of human development—literacy, longevity, health—have recorded major gains throughout the global South. So pervasive and compelling was the ideology that Pope Paul VI was moved to declare that "development is the new name for peace."

Despite important progress, however, the genial consensus with which the development enterprise was launched was beginning to fracture, by at least the 1960s. Much of the most important criticism came from the global South itself, where important voices denounced the whole development undertaking as rooted in an inherently inegalitarian international structure. The result, they concluded, was that even the best and most generously conceived efforts would perpetuate inequality. Truly just development could only happen within a new international economic order.

Development also came under attack in the developed world, where frustrated donors overlooked substantial incremental progress the world over to conclude that the poverty problem was insoluble. The 1970s and 1980s yielded increasing distrust of large-scale government programs, fueled by the rise of neoclassical economics and greater economic insecurity in industrialized countries. Even before the fall of the Berlin Wall, development was a suspect idea, in North and South, East and West alike.

The end of the cold war has provoked still more profound reflection about the nature and direction of international development. Even when the optimism and humanitarian imperative to facilitate development had waned, the West's competition with the Soviet Union and its allies had ensured global engagement in the poorest parts of the world. But with the end of the incessant competition with the East, the geopolitical motivation for international assistance crumbled as quickly as the Berlin Wall. The development enterprise, now unmoored from its strategic rationale, will herein be evaluated on its merits and on its significance to the countries on either side of the equation. Not surprisingly, the prevailing sentiment in the United States is less than encouraging:

The U.S. government's lead agency dedicated to international development faces absorption into the State Department, and U.S. appropriations for overseas assistance, already the lowest among all industrialized countries, are primed for far-reaching reduction by an inward-looking Congress. Commitment to development is under similar attack elsewhere in the West.

Born in great, perhaps giddy, hope at mid-century, development was a binding, defining force in the post–World War II international order. But development has yet to be invited to join the new order that is incoherently, inevitably emerging to replace that of the cold war. Whither development on the eve of the twenty-first century?

The present volume does not endeavor to resolve that difficult and uncertain question. What we do aspire to provide, however, are the tools that the interested citizen requires to think critically about the state of the international development enterprise and the role and potential of humanitarian engagement and cooperation in the years to come. The moral impulse that undergirded the emergence of the development movement remains as compelling now as it was a half-century ago; so too does the potential for achieving even the greatest promises of development. Our conviction is that development will continue to figure prominently on the world's agenda. The forces of interdependence—economic, environmental, human—are sufficiently powerful that we all, from practical or moral motivations, will perforce engage the whole world and have a stake in its development.

The chapters that follow provide a brief history of the global development movement, outline the key organizations and individuals in the field, survey the literature and scholarship of development, and define terms essential to the subject. This overview reflects on a variety of key subfields, so that readers may turn to the reference material with a proper perspective on the breadth of development studies.

Historical Backdrop of Development—Imperialism

The historical backdrop against which global development emerged is the legacy of imperialism, which even today weighs heavily on the countries of the global South. With few exceptions, all the developing countries were at one time colonies of European imperial powers: Britain, France, Spain, the Netherlands, Portugal, and Germany. And it is important for readers to remember that the colonial experience for tropical nations was much different than pre-1776 development in North America. Settler populations in the global South remained extremely small in comparison with native populations, and economic life emphasized the evacuation of raw materials for the benefit of the mother country. There was no reciprocal transplant of European social or economic institutions; economic development was designed to enhance the colonial powers, to the great detriment of the self-sufficiency of the colonized.

The colonial experience varied substantially from region to region. Latin America was the first area to be colonized (as early as the sixteenth century) and among the first areas to achieve political independence (in the early nineteenth century, for most countries), although European capital continued to dominate the economies of Latin America well into the twentieth century. Asian colonization occurred later and involved much more industrialized economies—indeed, Asia was more industrially advanced than Europe until the late eighteenth century. The colonial era in Africa began in the late nineteenth century and was characterized by ferocious competition among the European powers for territory. Decolonization in Asia took place mainly in the years just after World War II, while most African countries achieved independence in the 1950s and 1960s.

However, the many common political and economic developments in Latin America, Africa, and Asia are for some purposes more important than the considerable historical differences. Throughout today's developing world, the colonial experience meant the transformation and often the destruction of native economic systems, as self-sufficiency and manufacturing were discouraged and the production of agricultural goods for export was encouraged. Productive and diverse economies had flourished from East Africa to East Bengal (now Bangladesh), but the European intrusion introduced a range of calamities—ranging from new livestock diseases to low-priced Lancashire textiles—that devastated indigenous economies. For example, India before colonial rule had been an exporter of manufactured textiles, but afterward became an importer of British textiles and an exporter of raw cotton. In many cases, colonial economic and settlement policies forced people into labor migrations, contributing to depopulation, low levels of agricultural development, infrastructural impoverishment, and reduced economic self-sufficiency. One part of the colonial legacy, then, are economies geared toward producing agricultural commodities and buying finished goods, to the detriment of local economic development.

A second result of the colonial experience was abrupt change in landownership and distribution. This process was facilitated according to different models depending on location and colonial power, but had the effect everywhere in today's Third World of eroding indigenous land tenure patterns. Usually this resulted in the concentration of wealth in the hands of a small, largely urban elite and insecurity for rural farming communities. In this process, we see the origin of what some scholars call "the dual economy"—the stark division of wealth and power in Third World countries and the attendant pursuit of often distorted policies that benefit the elite but imperil the great majority of the population.

A third critical outcome of the colonial intervention, especially in Africa, was the erosion of organic governing units and the imposition of artificial national boundaries. Frontiers drawn up in London, Paris, and Berlin in the nineteenth century survived the decolonization process, such that national groups were often indiscriminately assembled in new independent states in the 1960s. Young nations sometimes inherited a tenuous bureaucracy, sometimes an incumbent ruler favored by the departing colonial power, but frequently little else in the way of national identity and solidarity. One consequence has been the instability of many African political regimes and the difficult process of state building that has confronted two generations of leaders on that continent. In this, as in so many ways, the imperial intrusion saddled the developing world with a burden that it still labors to overcome.

Development Economics

As the colonial era closed in the years following World War II, modern global development efforts began. In these first years of Southern independence, development was synonymous with economic growth: Developing countries were those in which income was growing rapidly, measured initially by real per capita income. As will be outlined below, this basic yardstick of development has been considerably refined and challenged in recent years, but per capita income remains the most common measurement of development performance. The principal question, however, has remained constant: How can nations boost their income? Our introduction thus begins with a survey of the four major economic development strategies of the post–World War II period.[2]

Import Substitution Industrialization (ISI)

ISI, the first widely implemented development strategy, was launched in the 1950s. This approach endeavored to spur domestic production of goods that might otherwise be imported, thus nurturing infant industries in major sectors and promoting local employment and industrial capacity. Protected industries were provided with special subsidies such as lower interest rates, subsidized electricity, discount building sites, and important tax incentives; meanwhile, imports in these industries were squelched by restrictive quotas and high tariffs.

The ISI tactic yielded impressive gains for less-developed countries such as Korea, Brazil, and Chile in the 1950s and 1960s. But after remarkable growth, countries that relied on ISI began to suffer stagnation. National economies proved too small to justify domestic production of all or most durable goods; insufficient markets, the absence of competitive pressure, and an inability to benefit fully from economies of scale constituted fundamental flaws that limited the ability of the ISI approach to deliver sustained growth. Today, near-consensus exists among economists that ISI policies cannot alone sustain necessary development.

State-Led Export Promotion

Several nations that adopted ISI in the 1950s gravitated to an export-led growth model in the 1960s. The export promotion approach requires governments to guide, if not completely plan, the economy, selecting industries for support, and to encourage export in these chosen domains by subsidizing interest rates and enforcing inter-firm cooperation and effective discipline of the workforce. Industries guided in this way will be well positioned to compete in the international market, bringing more foreign currency home. An ongoing trade surplus allows steadily rising wages and standards of living and encourages a cycle of better training and enhanced competitiveness.

This strategy has been particularly successful in East Asia, where so-called tigers such as Korea and Taiwan experienced massive growth in the 1960s notwithstanding a near-complete absence of valuable natural resources.[3] Growth here has been sustained over decades, so that these countries have themselves becomes models of development. Note, however, a logical problem at the core of the export promotion tactic: For every exporter, there must be an importer; for every unit of trade surplus, there must be, somewhere, a corresponding unit of trade deficit. Not all countries can employ this strategy simultaneously. And the very success of the approach has tilted developed economies such as the United States toward protectionism and a search for trade surpluses, while other developing nations attempt to copy the East Asian model. Export promotion might still be a valuable tool, but only if the world economy grows, markets remain open, and rational decisions are made by governments as to which industries ought be promoted in the context of the global economy. The continuing utility of export promotion hinges on the happy resolution of these uncertain questions.

Growth with Equity

The important development successes of the 1950s and 1960s masked disturbing side effects. Research in the early 1970s found that alongside growth for nations in the aggregate was increasing inequality in income distribution. While poorer societies as a whole were becoming richer, the benefits within societies flowed disproportionately to the wealthy. Moreover and more vexing, some research demonstrated that absolute poverty was increasing: The poor were not only getting a smaller share, they were getting absolutely poorer.

In response to these data, major development organizations such as the World Bank launched broad campaigns to guarantee that the world's poorest benefited fairly from the broader development effort, and so a new strategy, "growth with equity," was born. To deliver equitable growth, development agencies implemented a variety of programs, including employment creation, integrated rural development, and the "basic needs" approach which endeavored to ensure the provision of necessities of life. Unfortunately, these efforts unfolded against the backdrop of two oil shocks, disastrous weather patterns, and major dislocations in the international economy. While massive external borrowing permitted developing nations to sustain respectable growth rates in the face of these difficulties, there was no measurable improvement in equity.[4]

Back to the Future

Underlying each of these approaches was the assumption that developing economies did not have markets sufficient to sustain traditional capitalist development. As a result, development economists had insisted that government planning and state-owned enterprises were fundamental to rapid growth. In the 1980s, however, development theory rediscovered the market and returned to laissez-faire principles ignored since World War II.

Under this approach, governments should limit their activities to those which governments alone can perform. Government is properly charged with maintaining the national defense, infrastructure, a system of justice, money and credit, some research, and public education. Beyond these basic tasks that the private sector cannot provide, government should stand aside and let markets and entrepreneurs provide for economic growth. While this approach has yielded some gains, the human cost has been high indeed, as noted in our discussion below of international debt.

Broad-Based Sustainable Development

After the rise and fall of these varied development strategies, the 1990s have witnessed the emergence of a "consensus among development professionals . . . that the goal of development today is broad-based sustainable development (BBSD)."[5] BBSD evolved out of the perceived failure of previous approaches and is comprised of four components.

First comes economic development, defined as maximum growth of real per capita income accompanied by structural transformation of developing economies so as to remove the myriad restrictions and regulations that throttle private enterprise and encourage illegal economic activity in developing nations.[6]

Second is human development, measured typically by life expectancy and literacy rates—two indices that reflect the development of a society's ability to provide health and education to the population.

The third element of BBSD is political development. This is perhaps the component of the contemporary development model that has generated the most controversy. Most observers maintain that freedom and democracy are key elements of human progress, and must therefore be included in the definition of human development. Others emphasize the relationship between political development and economic development, and focus on efficient governance rather than the insurance of basic liberties and freedoms as the key political requirement of BBSD.

Fourth, BBSD demands that development be sustainable, defined in the report of the UN Commission on Environment and Development as: "Development that meets the needs of the present without compromising the ability of future generations to meet their own needs."

The BBSD model explicitly rejects the dominant assumption of prior development theory that there are no limits to global growth. Instead, BBSD assumes that industrial output, consumption, and pollution must be curbed if development is not to create more problems than it solves. While in the past, economic growth has been associated with environmental degradation, BBSD emphasizes recent research indicating that more environmentally sensitive programs can deliver economic development without fatally compromising global and local resources.

Debate swirls in the development community, not only about the details of broad-based sustainable development, but about the overall feasibility of the model as well. Can the paradigm be implemented in the rough-and-tumble context of national politics? Can remote but essential environmental needs be preserved in the face of pressing need today? Can the South fairly be expected to hew to this modest and forward-looking model while the North has already achieved development in a frenzy of consumption and growth? The prospects for economic development and a sustainable global tomorrow hinge on the just and effective resolution of these questions.

International Debt

The global debt crisis of the 1980s provides a glimpse of the tragic results when the hard questions of Broad-Based Sustainable Development are not tackled. The crisis involved issues in global trade, politics, and development and demonstrates how the failure of long-term vision, combined with unequal positions of players from the North and South, can effectively derail development and promote poverty. We explore the debt crisis as a case study in what can go wrong in global development.

Even at its height in the mid-1980s, the crisis that made the headlines was never a development crisis, was never about global poverty, or hunger, or slashed AIDS education and high bread prices, was never, in fact, about the South—the debtors—at all. Indeed, this "crisis"—the media-genic Western problem of a potential collapse of international banking—was essentially over by the beginning of 1990, when the major private lenders stopped lending to the Third World and at the same time increased their reserve holdings to cover potential losses. It is roughly since that time that debt per se has diminished as a news item of much interest here in the West. Of course, how much, and under what terms, banks would collect the outstanding arrears owed by Third World nations remains an important question for shareholders and executives. But for one-half of the debt equation—for the lenders, for the international banking community—the "debt crisis" is finished, and has been for some time.

For the other half—for the borrowers, the governments, and above all the people of the South—the crisis grinds on undiminished, perhaps abated only in the macabre sense that punishment so remorseless and long-lasting can scarcely be characterized as crisis at all. Within the community of the borrowers, it is possible, and indeed increasingly necessary, to draw important distinctions. While the debt crisis from the lending perspective was concentrated in Latin America—for it was here that major commercial banks faced the greatest exposure—the most generalized quarter of borrowers' suffering is in Africa. And while the "debt crisis" of the 1980s involved commercial loans made for profit by private banks, much of the lending underlying the continuing African crisis is in the form of bilateral nation-to-nation credits due to governments and international institutions.

So, while massive capital infusions have eased the burden in Latin America, and U.S. banks are returned to profitability, Africa remains in crisis, driven largely though not exclusively by debt. It is a crisis measurable in undelivered social services, rotting infrastructure, endemic food shortages and malnutrition, eviscerated AIDS prevention and treatment programs—measurable, in short, by reference to any of the basic indices of human misery.

Origins of the Debt Crisis

The standard explanation is that the debt crisis of the past ten years was the unfortunate outcome of the chance conjuncture of unforeseeable events. This explanation holds that the crisis was in large part just bad luck, and it has the cardinal virtue of exculpating most of the major players. The scenario runs something like this: Higher oil prices in the mid-1970s meant recession in the industrialized West, and left banks flooded with massive deposits from oil-rich nations. Finding their habitual customers unready to borrow, bankers turned to the global South. There, they found an eager market, as developing economies, flush from the successful development decade of the 1960s, were receptive to the infusion of capital to offset rising energy prices. When interest rates turned sharply higher in 1980–1982, and commodity export prices tumbled at the same time, these same countries found themselves saddled with much higher debt costs and diminished resources with which to pay. Compounding this conjunctural problem was widespread and egregious economic mismanagement by debtor nations and an increasingly bearish sentiment in credit markets. Slowly at first, then more swiftly, sources of new capital dried up and debt service exceeded revenues; meanwhile, profligate and bloated governments continued spending and borrowing, as if nothing had changed. When the government of Mexico announced in 1982 that it could no longer make interest or principal payments on its foreign debt, the crisis was on. Nation after debtor nation declared their incapacity to meet their financial obligations, creating fear for the solvency of the international banking system in the West and eliminating sources of capital for development and survival in the South.

In time, not only did new capital inflows end, but rising interest payments yielded the grotesque spectacle of net capital transfers out, *from* Southern countries *to* Western banks—and multilateral development institutions. By 1987, even the International Monetary Fund (IMF) was receiving some $8.6 billion more in loan repayments and interest charges than it lent out. It is difficult to overestimate the social and economic damage wrought in debtor nations in the mid to late 1980s: "As for the debtor countries, many have fallen into the deepest economic crises in their histories," said economist Jeffrey Sachs, not overstating the case. The vicious cycle of poverty accelerated throughout the decade; money that might have been used to build maternity clinics or schools went instead to Western banks and multinational institutions. To raise foreign exchange, developing countries dumped more of their resources at reduced rates, thereby depleting non-renewable resources and further depressing prices. Capital that could have created jobs was siphoned abroad, so that un- and underemployment only worsened. For many countries there was only one way out: cooperation with the rigorous policies of reform demanded by the World Bank and IMF for renewed access to international capital.

Most African countries, some quickly, some more reluctantly, have come to the lending table. Much of Africa, with the aid of a little arm-twisting from the World Bank and the IMF, have been introducing the most radical economic and social adjustments since independence. Part of the movement involves "democratization," part the abandonment of social and/or socialist policies. But the heart of reform is "structural adjustment," a cluster of liberal, free-market values: Governments should spend within their means, keep their exchange rates competitive, let markets determine prices, withdraw from regulation and subsidy, and sell off state enterprises. The reforms have been wrenching, as we have already seen. But is it worth it? Are they working?

The answer depends on who you ask. It is in fact a propitious moment to revisit this question, a question fundamental to the future of the debt crisis and its possible resolution. The World Bank's 1994 report reached the unsurprising conclusion that those countries that have implemented the prescribed austerity measures and economic reforms showed marked improvement in economic growth, while those that did not continued to deteriorate. Six of the 29 sub-Saharan African countries studied have effectively instituted macroeconomic reform: Ghana, Tanzania, Gambia, Burkina Faso, Nigeria, and Zimbabwe. These six experienced a median increase of almost 2 percent in the amount of goods and services produced per person, bringing median growth levels up from a negative level to an average of 1.1 percent a year during 1987–1991. Reducing the deadweight of regulation has allowed farmers to plant more, yielding food surpluses in Tanzania and Nigeria, while salutary government belt-tightening has eliminated swaths of subsidized social programs along with thousands of bogus names from civil service payrolls. The bank touted all of this as a "success story" ("World Bank's Plans Pay Off," read the *New York Times'* giddy headline), although the report grimly acknowledges that "current growth rates among the best African performers are still too low to reduce poverty much" and the best it can conclude is that "the majority of the poor are probably better off and almost certainly no worse off."

And indeed, there is much to be said for the more pessimistic view that judges adjustment in the negative, that contends that structural adjustment causes more problems than it solves. An excellent opportunity to evaluate this view was provided by the 1994 devaluation of the African franc in 14 West African nations, which sent the currency into free fall—a step taken at the insistence of the IMF and World Bank. The result was an overnight halving of the buying power of millions: an instant doubling of the price of bread and health care. And while the bank characterized devaluation as "the easy part of the reform process," bitter rioting, violent strikes, and widespread layoffs have been a predictable corollary.

When countries resist such reforms, they face alternative pressures, no less fearsome. Citing the country's arrears and noncompliance with the strictures of structural adjustment, the World Bank abruptly terminated its entire Zairian program in January 1994 and transferred its staff. Along with its programs, the bank took away the resources fundamental to a variety of key social service programs, notably Project SIDA, once the continent's largest and most effective AIDS research and education program. Now lacking even the means to test or screen blood, medical workers can only guess at infection rates that are already high and threaten to rise meteorically.

Such then are the costs of the debt crisis, and its human face: untreated and untreatable diseases, unschooled children, and unfilled bellies. And a less tangible but equally destructive cost may be the long-term loss of confidence in the possibility of genuine North-South partnership in global development. Bullying and bossing governments and nations already prickly about sovereignty may succeed when Western financial support is so desperately needed, but it would not seem to bode well for the future of global partnership. Perhaps a street-level articulation of growing frustration, suspicion, and anger toward the West and its "help" can be found in the Zimbabwean argot for the AIDS acronym: "American-Invented Disease to Stop Sex," in a country thought to have one of Africa's highest rates of HIV infection.

None of which is to say that external debt is the cause of all the problems in the developing world. Far from it: Debt is at once symptom and cause of countless mistakes made on both sides of the development equation, powerful as a contributing explanation and as a metaphor for the development debacle of the 1980s. Nor do we argue that some elements of structural adjustment do not and will not pay handsome dividends. Quite the contrary: There is no doubt that many of Africa's woes can be blamed on the policies of its leaders, which smothered national economies with complex regulatory regimes of permits and licenses designed chiefly to throttle farmers and entrepreneurs while lining the pockets of the bureaucrats who distribute these authorizations. The issue, then, isn't if reform is needed, but in what measure, under what circumstances, with what protections; the problem, in short, is to ensure that the medicine isn't more painful than the disease.

Justice, Debt, and Dueness

Much discussion of the debt crisis has revolved around a reflexive notion of justice in the free market, "market justice." Subject to deeper scrutiny, the debt crisis forces critical reevaluation of notions of marketplace ethics and offers a window to the broader comparison of market and distributive justice. While it is true that debtor governments freely contracted the loans, so did the banks, lending to borrowers hitherto deemed uncreditworthy. It is important to point out that the banks in this crisis deviated in an exaggerated fashion from standard procedure. Rather than settling for the difference between interest paid and interest earned, banks cast about for lucrative opportunities to invest their "petro-dollars," and, along with borrowing governments, bet speculatively on continued high commodity prices and general prosperity in the South. Bankers invited their vulnerability, stood to make windfall profits from these loans, and there is no standard, even the standard of market justice, that justifies immunity from ensuing loss, notwithstanding the truculent 1990 declaration of a consortium of U.S. banks that "any government effort to enforce debt forgiveness would be contested in the courts as an unconstitutional taking of property."

The reflexive principle of dueness is further weakened by the reality that it is the mass of people, and above all the poorest, that will endure the greatest suffering for debt that they did not approve and that was not assumed in their interest. That people are not responsible for contracts made by their unjust governors is as ancient a foundation of justice as can be found, dating at least as far back as Aristotle's *Politics*. And if Western banks chose to collaborate with unresponsive, unaccountable Southern governors, there is no sound argument in logic or precedent for imposing the full burden of these losses on populations excluded from the entire affair.

Violence, Militarism, and Debt

The debt crisis from the outset has been perceived as a financial affair first and a development issue second. Two reflections on the violent dimension of the crisis and the West's preferred solution of structural adjustment merit mention in these pages.

First, the sharp decline in living standards in debtor nations, as well as the clear reversal of the trend toward economic development, have resulted in increased potential for political violence across the global South. Dozens, perhaps hundreds, of violent protests, with thousands of mortalities, have occurred specifically in response to IMF/World Bank austerity measures since 1982. In addition to these "IMF riots," an incalculable amount of political violence could be related to the climate engendered by adjustment.

Moreover, such violence cannot be dismissed as a mere policing problem; rather, its significance spills over into national and international security issues. The whole gamut of "interdependent" security problems (e.g., terrorism, refugeeism, drug trafficking) is related to the betrayal of the development promise in the 1980s. While these tangled ties defy precise disaggregation, there should be no doubt that the impact of the crisis ranges well beyond balance sheets and macroeconomic policies. On the contrary, debt has played a role in recent, tragic events in the Americas, Asia, and Africa.

A second observation is that structural adjustment has the peculiar by-product of enhancing the military proportion of affected economies, as cutbacks in the military are excluded from the ravages of adjustment by the broad protection of activities related to national sovereignty. The irony that educating children and healing the sick are excluded from this protection while all manner of violence is safeguarded scarcely needs highlighting, but we should recognize that the debt crisis and structural adjustment have solidified, even accelerated, the egregious predominance of the military in many of the world's poorest economies. And at the same time, the crisis has hardened the realist worldview that so often favors the destructive over the constructive.

Just as the debt provided a splendid metaphor for the lost development decade of the 1980s (unbridled capital of the North meets reckless governance in the South, with the world's poorest left to pay the price), the recent disposition of the crisis in the 1990s effectively symbolizes the West's mounting solipsism in global affairs (the debt crisis is over, declares the media, while the human costs of the crisis accelerate).

For in Africa, at least, the debt crisis lives and grows. The continent's foreign debt reached an estimated $183.4 billion in 1992, roughly 110 percent of Africa's total Gross National Product; per capita income fell during the past decade, and the region suffers from a lack of new capital and the flight of much indigenous wealth. The resolution of the debt problem, and restructuring of the international financial system more generally, are probably necessary preconditions for sustained economic development in Africa.

The pillars of international finance—the so-called Bretton Woods institutions—turned 50 years old in 1994, an event that we can hope will spark fruitful reevaluation. The World Bank marked its half-century with a "vision paper" that contained some encouraging news: The bank acknowledged its historical failures to link economic development and sound environmental stewardship and promised to restrain its enthusiasm for absurd, enormous projects like dams and power plants. Not a bad start, but hardly more than that. With the gap between the world's rich and poor increasing, with the destruction of the Earth's natural environment accelerating, and with violent conflict within and between states at epidemic proportions, we will need far more from our international financial system than marginal efficiency improvements. What's needed is a forum for global development and investment, where risks are shared and where the allocation of wealth and resources can be effectively facilitated for the good of a genuinely interdependent world.

Global Development, Global Hunger

One of the tragic consequences of the debt crisis was a significant surge in the incidence of global hunger in the world's poorer countries. While it is important to recognize that hunger and development are different problems, any survey of development must address the hunger issue. Hunger is the most extreme and devastating outcome of the systemic poverty that accompanies underdevelopment, and the eradication of hunger must rank high among the priorities of all development organizations. Hunger, a problem of politics, policy, and poverty, can only be confronted in the context of the broader perspective of economic development.

No one can say for sure how many hungry people there are in the world. One reason for this is that there is no universally accepted definition of hunger. Recent scholarship has offered the concepts of food shortage, food poverty, and food deprivation to organize the disparate data on hunger and its prevention and to bridge the differing perceptions of hunger's cause held by those who emphasize the distribution of food and hunger and those who focus on the symptoms of undernutrition.

Food Shortage

The clearest picture of hunger is found in food-short countries: absolute shortages where there is simply not enough food to sustain the population within a given region. Most often, natural disaster, war, or societal disruption lies at the heart of food shortage. Recent data prepared by the UN shows that in the late 1980s, 1,570 million people, or 31 percent of the world's population, lived in 49 countries where the total dietary supply was less than that required for health, growth, and productive work. Of these 49 countries, 31 were located in sub-Saharan Africa, 6 in South Asia, and 6 in the Western Hemisphere.

Such measurements adequately reflect the cruel prevalence of hunger in today's world, but do not show the depth of nutritional deprivation. To see the most poignant faces of hunger, we must consider the faces of famine. These are the widespread, persistent, and often near-complete food shortages that attract the attention of the media and that for many in the Western world are synonymous with world hunger. In 1988, at least 5 countries with a combined population of 204 million people—4 percent of the world's population—suffered famine within their national territory. In many cases, the victims of war are inseparable from the victims of famine, as the famines most resistant to relief are those created or aggravated by violent conflict. Indeed, combatants in many contemporary wars have intentionally disrupted the flow of food, using food as a weapon in acts of inconceivable cruelty. Again drawing on data from the end of the previous decade, we see that wars were fought in 23 countries, 17 of which experienced significant disruptions of the food supply. The continuing armed conflict in the Sudan in 1988–1989 provides a stark example: An estimated 260,000 people died of starvation while relief and development agencies were forced by military menace to suspend operations.

It is important to note, however, that although famine provides the most familiar image of hunger, famine accounts for only 10 percent of hunger-related deaths. Other forms of chronic, persistent hunger, less graphic and, sadly, less compelling, are largely unnoticed by international consciousness. This is the hunger of underdevelopment, and it is just as deadly as famine.

Food Poverty

An equally important element in the overall hunger equation is the concept of food poverty: The food-poor hungry live in households that are unable to pay for food or that lack access to the resources needed to feed themselves even when food is generally available within their region. Their poverty can issue from a wide variety of factors: insufficient land, low wages, unemployment, low prices for produce or manufacture, and a score of others. Amartya Sen, the foremost contemporary philosopher and economist working on hunger issues, identifies these factors as failures of "entitlement": Whether through direct cultivation, participation in an exchange economy, or protection by social insurance, individuals of all societies possess some means of access or entitlement to food. In many societies, however, this entitlement is insecure and is liable to failure in periods of economic or social turbulence. It is this condition that allows the unconscionable spectacle of occasional or even widespread hunger in areas enjoying general food availability.

The best available research indicates that in 1988, just over 1 billion people in developing countries lived in households too poor to obtain the caloric intake necessary for work, and 500 million lived in households too poor to obtain the caloric intake necessary for minimal activity among adults and healthy growth in children.

Food Deprivation

All hungry people are food deprived. This category includes, of course, those who live in regions of scarcity or reside in food-poor households. But more difficult to identify are individuals deprived of nutrition available within the household. This deprivation may result from ignorance, abuse, or neglect, and often falls most brutally on the most vulnerable.

Above all, deprivation indicators show the toll hunger exacts from children. Twenty-one million infants—16 percent of the world's total—are born underweight, while 168 million children, or 29 percent of the world total, are underweight for their age. Women, characteristically disempowered within the family unit, are often the last to be fed even though they are major contributors to family food supplies, as will be demonstrated in the following subsection; they too suffer disproportionately from food deprivation. Taken together, these three perspectives on food scarcity provide a coherent profile of global hunger. Though the numbers are different according to each definition and measurement, the overarching message is the same: Well more than 1 billion people are hungry today.

Food Supply and Population

Hunger, of course, is not a static and quantifiable commodity, but rather articulates a relationship of people to food. The grim litany of statistics presented above suggests an obvious question: Is there enough food to feed the world's population?

For the great bulk of history, the answer to this question would have been an unequivocal "no." Population grows geometrically while food supply, for centuries, could only grow arithmetically. These elementary facts gave rise to the apocalyptic theories of Malthus, who reasoned in his famous "Essay on Population" (1798) that only through periodic calamities such as famine and war, which abruptly reduce population, could food supply and population remain in equilibrium.

In a superb historical irony, however, Malthus published his theories just as they were becoming obsolete. Since the late eighteenth century, humanity has developed techniques to draw more food from the land and to distribute it more efficiently, allowing for a hitherto unimaginable increase in food supply *and* population. In the roughly two centuries since Malthus, the population of the world has increased from about 1 billion to 5.5 billion; by 2000, the global population will reach 6 billion. But the production of food in the same period, and especially in the most recent generations, has accelerated even more dramatically.

Indeed, the planet's food supply—often called our "carrying capacity"—appears now to be sufficient to feed every living woman, child, and man. Recent research suggests that the world's current food output could sustain 6 billion people—more than 100 percent of the world's population—on a basic, predominantly vegetarian diet. However, if we improve the diet slightly to include more animal products, we exceed our carrying capacity, for at that standard, there is only food enough to feed about 4 billion people, or some 80 percent of the population. And if we suppose a richer diet incorporating a wider variety of foods, there is only sufficient food to feed about 2.5 billion people, or less than 50 percent of the world's population. Remember, though, that if more people had the ability to buy food, it is certain that the incentive of market demand would spur the production of more food for sale. That is, although current supplies are adequate to feed the global population, more and richer food could be produced if social, ethical, or economic development so demanded.

Hunger, Poverty, and Development

Hunger, then, is not a function of overall global food shortage, nor even of local food scarcity. Instead, recent research indicates that hunger is a function of poverty, disempowerment, and underdevelopment. The hungry lack entitlement to food, the economic opportunity to access the market, and are in some cases unable to command food due to prejudices within the family structure. The emergence of food surplus has been accompanied by increasingly complex and stratified societies with correspondingly greater opportunities for entitlement failure. More than ever, it is the daily inadequacy of food *entitlement*—not the failure of *nature*—that lies at the root of hunger. At bottom, hunger is a problem of politics and development policy.

One need only review the habits and condition of the world's poorest to confirm this assertion. According to recent World Bank statistics, the poor spend at least half of their annual income on food; this figure is often as high as 70 to 80 percent. And of this disproportionate food budget, more than half again goes to the local food staples (rice, corn, etc.), indicating the inadequacy of the diet of the poor. Poverty is usually the fundamental cause of malnutrition, and the greatest burden is often borne by women and children as the distribution of consumption within poor households tends to favor males and income-earning adults. The poor suffer from a broad range of debilitating disadvantages that underlie the hunger problem—they have less access to publicly provided goods and government relief; they tend to receive less and poorer education; and they are often set apart by cultural and/or racial barriers. As characteristics of structural poverty that the development enterprise endeavors to eradicate, these unfortunate realities closely tie the ongoing problem of hunger with the broader goals of global development.

The Role of Women in Development

Development will only make inroads against hunger and poverty when the central role of women in development informs policy and programs. Our discussion of hunger demonstrates that women often suffer disproportionately from underdevelopment. A corresponding reality is that women play a pivotal role in economic development, both within and beyond the home. For as producers of food, managers of community resources, and transmitters of culture and values, women play a determinate role in the success and sustainability of development. Yet Third World women have been frequently disregarded or affected adversely by development policies and, in their daily struggle to ensure family survival, have been dealt the most severe and immediate blows of recent food, energy, and debt crises.

Indeed, the postcolonial portrait of the Third World drawn by Western social scientists and policymakers looked something like *American Gothic* with only a man and a pitchfork. While the UN Decade for Women (1975–1985) did much to redress the global invisibility of women and to construct a more balanced picture of international development, women still remain out of focus in the overall development picture.

This does not mean that Third World women should be singled out for exclusive examination: "Add-women-and-stir" solutions have been proven inadequate in policy making, scholarship, and education. The objective is to locate women in the web of economy, polity, and culture which determines development processes—to see not only the varied impact of development on women, but the critical role of women in shaping development.

In the 1970s, social scientists began to correct what was perceived to be a three-tiered male bias in analyses of Third World societies: the androcentrism of investigators, of Western culture, and of indigenous cultures. Rayna Reiter, in a seminal work outlining the new "anthropology of women," summed up the emergent feminist critique: "Too often women and their roles are glossed over, underanalysed, or absent from all but the edges of the description." What women do is perceived as "household work" and what they talk about is called "gossip," while men's work is viewed as the economic base of society and their conversation is seen as important social communication. Reacting against the traditional presentation of men's information as "a group's reality, rather than as only part of a cultural whole," the task of women-in-development scholarship in the 1970s was to piece together what women actually do, rather than what men say they do. This initial analysis of the role of women in developing societies was essentially an attempt to fill in the gaps, reconstructing women's social, political, and economic lives as a corrective to traditional disregard and misrepresentation.

At the core of the question of women in development is a cluster of women divided by class, culture, and ethnicity. They are awkwardly yet inevitably unified by a position of inferiority, which has been historically determined by the material and ideological structures of gendered subordination.

The "women question" in development lies between the twin perils of multiculturalist romanticism and neoethnocentrism. While we must try to represent fairly the different cultures, the oppression of women cannot be dismissed as an acceptable manifestation of an alternative belief system. Conversely, we must guard against the myopic assumption that the goals of Western feminists are necessarily relevant to or shared by Third World women.

Women's Work

Women's productive work in and out of the home is economically undervalued and statistically underestimated. The invisibility of women's work is a function of a historically determined sexual division of labor and the concomitant development of cultural lexicons that define "work" as that labor—usually masculine—which has perceived social worth. Valuations of skill, for example, are often only tenuously related to training or ability; valuation is determined instead by the status of the people—men and women—who typically perform a particular task. The relationship between women's status and the sexual division of labor is a pressing contemporary issue with critical policy implications ranges from conflicts over development strategy in the Third World to debates concerning comparative worth and the feminization of poverty in the United States.

To explain women's roles in the formal and informal economies of the Third World, we need to survey the connections between women's work and industrialization, agrarian commercialization, migratory patterns, family structure, and domestic power relations. The important ties between global economies and indigenous labor structures can be illuminated in a debate concerning the liberating or constricting impact of capitalist penetration: Has development provided new opportunities for women, or instead undercut their economic autonomy? Discussions of economic opportunity could include the educational and legal structures that determine access to labor markets, the cultural values that define the appropriate behavior of women, and the demographic imperatives that influence women's family roles and obligations.

The staggering variety of women's work reflects the creativity of female survival. Those who consider the characteristics of domestic labor are not aware that "housework" in the Third World may include, among other things, the bearing and raising of children, the supervision of ritual and education, the cleaning and maintenance of dwellings, the collection of fuel and firewood, the preparation of food, the production of petty commodities, and the provision of community services.

The female contribution is particularly noteworthy—and especially neglected—in the agrarian domain. Women account for 40 to 80 percent of all agriculture production in the South, depending on the country. But because such labor is perceived as a component of women's household responsibilities, the work remains undervalued, underappreciated, and scarcely recognized as work at all.

Women and the Development Equation

The conviction that the experiences and problems of women in the Third World are not just instructive but singular underlies the increasing visibility of women's issues in development. While this proposition may be axiomatic to development scholars and professionals, it is important to recognize that the significance of women in development may not appear self-evident. The need to illuminate the fundamental moral and ethical issues at stake in the study of women in development is therefore of primary importance. An excellent introduction to the moral dimension of women in development can be found in Amartya Sen's assertion that "More Than 100 Million Women Are Missing."[7]

Sen's analysis begins by debunking the widely held belief that women outnumber men worldwide; this notion is revealed as an inaccurate projection of the experiences of the Western world. Sen demonstrates that women should outnumber men but do not, except in the developed world and in small pockets of the global South. There is, he concludes, a deficit of 100 million women worldwide—missing women who have vanished, victims of various and not fully understood social, economic, and political structures. The balance of this discussion on gender explores possible explanations and in the process feeds directly into some key issues of women in development (WID) research: women and education, women and the economy and the marketplace, and the empowerment of women.

The analysis is sobering in its simplicity and provides a powerful ethical basis for an examination of WID. In the context of a deficit of 100 million persons, it is impossible to see WID as an exclusively Southern or feminist concern; the problem is revealed instead as a life-and-death issue. For those not focusing on women in development, Sen suggests the dimensions of the subject and offers broader lessons on interrelatedness and the peril of ethnocentrism. And for those who do focus on WID, the article shows with eloquence and urgency why the problem demands our attention.

The survival of women in the Third World is, of course, a central development issue. It depends, in large part, on the ways in which gender has historically shaped consciousness, culture, and power. In the Southern crucible, gender and development have not forged a successful bond. Women appear to be fighting a losing battle for survival. To outline their struggle we need to examine the ways in which the role and status of women determine and are determined by global structures of production, reproduction, politics, and ecology.

Determining compatibility of economic growth, sustainable resource use, and poverty-induced survival strategies demands attention to women's role in development. The viability of production practices in rural communities depends on the technical and social organization of work. Women cultivate crops and care for livestock, collect fuel and wild produce, and manage water resources. They are often the primary bearers and transmitters of indigenous ecological knowledge. Male outmigration, spurred by opportunities for cash-cropping or urban employment, increasingly leaves women as conservators of traditional agrarian practices, though they may lack the time or labor power necessary to implement these ecologically sound techniques.

Those hoping for the creation of a sustainable future ought to consider the complicated ways that human societies reproduce themselves in interaction with the environment. "While discussions of the environment may conjure up undisturbed wilderness for inhabitants of the industrialized nations," warns one observer, "it is important to remember that Third World families experience environmental problems predominantly as livelihood crisis. Women who manage rural households experience soil erosion, deforestation, and contaminated water supplies directly, because these events impinge on their ability to provide for their families."[8] Consequent survival strategies of the poor, such as farming marginal land or decreasing fallow to boost short-term income, chip away at the ecosystem upon which production depends, exacerbating the unsustainable cycle of human poverty and ecological degradation.

The Politics of Patriarchy and Protest

The state mediates women's lives through its policies regarding the provision of child and health care, the structure of educational and employment opportunity, and the regulation of wages and taxation. It is an arbiter of gender ideologies in its relations with the media, schools, political parties, and religious organizations. Its institutional manifestations, however, influence citizens differently according to the gender, race, and class of the individual and the socioeconomic organization of the polity.

To explore women's response to state ideology and hegemonic culture, we should consider female participation in revolutionary movements, political organizations, and economic self-help groups. Women's attempts to alter state policy or gain access to state resources do not always take familiar forms, such as party activism or union strikes. To express discontent and effect change, a popular culture of feminist resistance often employs techniques foreign to Americans: foot dragging, machine breaking, arson, gossip, boycotts, theft, spirit possession, and other forms of disenfranchised rebellion.

Such resistance has a goal and should be read as part of a protest against national and international orders often hostile to women's interests. But we must not assume that the protests of Third World women are directed at the same targets as those of Western liberalism and feminism. Women around the world are struggling for emancipation, but gender remains just one mode of analysis, however important. Alongside gender, issues such as culture, race, and class represent important variables in the overall development equation.[9]

Development and Population Growth

The world can be divided roughly into two segments: countries that have completed the "demographic transition" to slow or zero population growth and enjoy improving living standards and countries where population growth remains rapid and living standards are threatened.

As of 1986, 2.3 billion people lived in slow-growth areas of Western Europe, North America, Eastern Europe, Australia, New Zealand, and East Asia. The collective population growth rate of these regions is 0.8 percent per year. Here, rising living standards and low fertility rates are mutually reinforcing.

In the rest of the world, home to 2.6 billion people, the population continues to soar, growing more than three times as fast as in the slow-growth sector. The results of this division are best dramatized in long-term population projections. Whereas the U.S. population is expected to level off at about 290 million, a 20 percent increase over 1986, and western Germany's population is expected to stabilize at 52 million—some 15 percent below present levels—the populations of Kenya and Nigeria are expected to more than *quintuple* before finally leveling off sometime in the middle of the twenty-first century. To put the issue into concrete terms, if the Nigerian projection proves accurate, the population of that one country in 2050 will be almost as great as the population of the entire African continent today.

The issue of population growth is inextricably linked to problems of development and hunger. The dominant school of thought in the 1960s and 1970s—which remains influential today—held that explosive population growth makes the provision of decent conditions for all nearly impossible and hampers efforts to adequately house, educate, and employ the population, as an ever-increasing demand for social and economic opportunities swamps efforts to boost supply. As one Dutch observer noted, "A development policy without a population policy is like mopping the floor during a flood."

The significance of population rate reduction in development thinking persuaded many development organizations to sponsor large-scale family planning programs, especially in the 1960s and 1970s. Unfortunately, many such programs involved invasive techniques, up to and including sterilization; unsurprisingly, these efforts proved extremely unpopular. Additionally, many voices within the development community and from the global South argued that the emphasis on population control skirted the central problem of economic opportunity, and amounted to little more than blaming the victims of underdevelopment for their suffering. This viewpoint maintains that rapid population growth is a symptom of underdevelopment, and not a cause, in that child labor represents an important contribution to the economic security of the poorest households and provides poor parents the only available safety net for old age. On this view, improvements in living standards—and above all in the status and empowerment of women—would bring down birthrates as a matter of course. More recently, observers from both North and South have embraced the more balanced view that development is the best form of population control: The hallmarks of underdevelopment, such as illiteracy, economic insecurity, and inadequate social services, are also obstacles to reduced fertility. An international consensus now understands population control and development to be interrelated objectives: Success with respect to one requires improvements in the other.

Moreover, many of the development-related threats to our environment discussed in the next subsection are directly attributable to soaring population. The soil, water, and forests of the Earth are undermined by attempts of ever greater numbers of people to wrest sustenance from ever more marginal resources. And the intense migrations caused by growing populations are at the root of much internal and external dislocation. Urban populations are the fastest growing: By the year 2000, some 49 percent of humanity will be city dwellers. The perception of opportunities for higher wages continues to attract rural residents to urban areas, which overtaxes the employment capabilities, social services, and physical environment of the cities. Many rural communities, meanwhile, suffer from heavy outmigration and experience a reduction in productive capacity due to insufficient labor at harvest time. As development is the process by which society attempts to provide for an increasing population, environment is the physical and cultural context which delimits and defines the contours of development. It is to this subject that we now turn.

Development and the Environment

Perhaps nowhere is the interdependence of North and South, developed world and developing world, better illustrated than by our global environment. While human beings have exploited the Earth's natural resources since time out of mind, recent decades have witnessed a growing awareness that the riches of our planet are not limitless. Concerns for the depletion of nonrenewable resources, scarcity, and various types of degradation have sustained a generation of "green" activism in the West, spanning from the first Earth Day in 1970 through the much-heralded Earth Summit in Rio de Janeiro in 1992.

One lesson of the ongoing dialogue on environmental issues is that while North and South share a common environmental future, their interests and prescriptions have often been at cross-purposes. As a historical matter, the environmental movement emerged in the 1960s and 1970s among middle-class action groups in Europe and the United States largely concerned with preserving their own lifestyles and health. Predictably, this movement found little support in the developing South, where the exploitation of finite natural resources was regarded as the means to economic growth. Indeed, the new-found Northern concern for the environment was sometimes seen as an attempt to limit the development potential of the Third World and freeze the industrial advantage of the North. Environmental damage had proved to be an unfortunate but tolerable by-product of industrialization and economic development in the North, and would likewise be the acceptable cost of economic security in the South.

However, by the late 1970s new research and evidence forced policymakers of both the North and South to regard environment and development as fully interdependent concerns. Environmental problems, we realized, spring not only from economic growth, but from activities induced by the *lack* of development as well. And the "pollution of poverty"—the ecological degradation associated with underdevelopment—was itself identified as a barrier to economic security. By the late 1980s, the international consensus that environmentally sound development was necessary in both developed and developing nations was captured by Gro Harlem Brundtland, former prime minister of Norway, who wrote in her introduction to *Our Common Future*, the report of the United Nations World Commission on Environment and Development: "'Environment' is where we all live, and 'development' is what we all do in attempting to improve our lot within that abode. The two are inseparable."[10] But however well intentioned, the emerging international consensus faces a menacing array of environmental problems that jeopardize, above all, the disenfranchised of the Third World in their ongoing struggle for food and economic security. This subsection explores the key environmental challenges implicated in development or the lack thereof.

Desertification

On every continent of the Earth, land is degraded and is losing its productive capacity due to soil erosion, salinization, alkalinization, and chemical degradation. Where this degradation is sustained in arid and semi-arid areas, the result is desertification—formerly productive lands are transformed into barren desert.

For a variety of reasons, this phenomenon is particularly dangerous in the developing world. In food-insecure regions, farmers are pushed by necessity to cultivate ever more marginal lands with relentless intensity. The result is that vulnerable lands are constantly overworked and increasingly at risk. Ancient but time-consuming techniques for preserving fertility, such as terracing and intercropping, have been ignored as farmers respond to mounting competition for scarce cropland. Even where direct cultivation is not a threat to soil fertility, overgrazing often is. Throughout the developing South, increasing population pressure and accelerated desertification go hand in hand.[11] It is estimated that some 60,000 square kilometers are affected annually, with some of the poorest regions of the world—including Bangladesh and sub-Saharan Africa—suffering the worst losses.[12] Some 4.5 billion hectares around the world—35 percent of the Earth's land surface—are afflicted with desertification.[13] Thus, the struggle to meet near-term development needs is undercutting the environment's capacity to provide long-term sustainable development.

Deforestation

The search for additional agricultural land and wood for shelter and fuel has resulted in the reduction of the world's forests by more than one-third. Here again, the developing countries, with their abundant tropical forests, have been particularly affected. Throughout the 1980s and 1990s, the rate of forest depletion has radically increased in the Third World, and it is estimated that by 2020, virtually all the accessible forests in developing countries will have been cut.[14]

The direct effect of this trend is that those who depend on wood for their fuel will find new sources in increasingly short supply. While the problem is perhaps most acute in Africa, where nearly 75 percent of total energy needs are met by wood, wood scarcity and its consequences are exacting their price in Latin America and Asia as well. Estimates vary, but it is safe to conclude that of the 2.5 billion people who depend on wood fuel, nearly half already live in areas experiencing severe wood deficits. Forecasts suggest that this number could double by 2005.

Deforestation is largely perceived as a rural problem, and certainly the bulk of the wood-dependent population is rural. But a large percentage of the world's urban poor also rely on wood fuel, which they must buy at costs that increasingly burden their already meager budgets. In such countries as Ethiopia, Guatemala, Burkina Faso, Niger, and Haiti, fuelwood costs can absorb up to half a household's income. Under the circumstances, the poor can hardly be reproached for harvesting protected forests, thereby only worsening their dire situation over the long term. Each year, according to an estimate by the U.S. Environmental Protection Agency, the area of woodlands cleared in the tropics is equivalent to the area of Tennessee, and worldwide estimates are even more alarming.

Further, the costs of deforestation are not limited to biomass depletion and economic inflation. Where trees are cut down faster than they are replenished, the ecosystem suffers severe shock. Throughout northern and sub-Saharan Africa the wood-fuel energy crisis compounds the problem of desertification, discussed above: The annihilation of trees leads to erosion and soil depletion, turning hitherto productive agricultural land into desert unfit for cultivation or even grazing. In addition, when wood-fuel shortages force people to burn dung and crop residues, the soil is further deprived of the valuable nutrients of these organic fertilizers.

On a less localized level, deforestation's most frightening impact on the environment may be its contribution to the problem of global warming. The Greenhouse Effect, which is causing the global climate to grow hotter at an unprecedented rate, is largely attributed to an increase in carbon dioxide in the atmosphere. Trees are the chief natural agents that absorb carbon dioxide and lead the fight against the Greenhouse Effect. Dead trees, however, release carbon dioxide, as does the burning of fossil fuels such as coal and oil. If the number of trees dying exceeds the number of new trees, the balance of carbon dioxide in the atmosphere increases and combines with such pollutants as fluorocarbons to speed global warming.[15]

An additional indirect effect of deforestation is the drastic destruction of habitat for *terrestrial biota*—that is, the diversity of life forms, animal and plant, that flourish in tropical forests. This diversity is under sustained and deadly attack. Reliable estimates suggest that, at a minimum, 50,000 invertebrate species per year—roughly 140 per day—become extinct by the destruction of their tropical rainforest habitat. And while most of these species are rather small, at least one species of bird, mammal, or plant is condemned daily to annihilation by the process of deforestation.[16]

For many, aesthetic and ethical considerations provide all the justification necessary to engage the problem of eliminating countless life forms. But self-interest may offer a more compelling reason to husband biological diversity. The genetic material found in plants and animals in the global South help support agriculture, medicine, and industry in countries far removed from the Third World. Creatures believed useless, even harmful, have been repeatedly found to play crucial roles in natural systems or in advanced technological applications. Third World germ plasm (a fundamental hereditary material) has proved indispensable in U.S. agricultural growth and is the key ingredient in drugs that treat cancer and other illnesses. Much of the future potential of our medical and industrial sciences may reside in the biodiversity of the destroyed forests. But for the moment, we have not even catalogued the species we are killing off, much less evaluated their benefits or potential. The losses are irretrievable and potentially vast.

Numerous other environmental concerns inform the overall development equation. Accelerated urbanization, a by-product of rapid population growth, has created massive marginal settlements on the periphery of Southern metropolises. These communities suffer from a lack of clean water and basic sanitation, conditions which in turn nourish the development and spread of infectious diseases. Water and air pollution represent another unhappy by-product of uneven development and urbanization.[17] Finally, the increased marginality of human settlement in the South—whether in cities, at the edge of freshly cut forests, or on the arid perimeters of desertified regions—leaves populations ever more vulnerable to natural disasters such as floods, earthquakes, and landslides. Where the promise of development has been broken, the environmental consequences for us all have been grave. Our common environmental future requires a shared engagement for just and measured global development.

Development, Refugees, and Migration

Just as development is inextricably linked to environmental issues of unprecedented gravity, so too is it implicated in a migratory movement that presents an equally formidable humanitarian challenge: the world refugee crisis. More people are on the move today than ever before in human history, and while the causes of displacement are varied, the relationship of refugeeism to underdevelopment is direct and undisputed.

Forced migration has been with us since the beginning of international relations, dating at least as far back as the biblical story of the exodus from Egypt. In the twentieth century, however, massive human displacements became one of the harrowing, commonplace by-products of total war, associated not only with the world wars, but also with narrower national conflicts such as the Spanish Civil War. The contemporary refugee system emerged in the wake of World War II, as the memory of the rejection of Jewish emigrés from Germany that condemned them to death in the Holocaust coupled with the spectacle of millions of homeless in Europe created the political climate for a global commitment to resettlement. Hence, the United Nations High Commission for Refugees (UNHCR) was created, and international conventions for identifying refugees and granting asylum were ratified.[18]

International law distinguishes between refugee migration and migration in general. The UNHCR defines a refugee as "a person who has left his or her home country, and who has a well-founded fear of persecution upon returning to it on account of race, religion, nationality, membership in a particular social group, or political opinion." Following this definition, the best current estimates place the world refugee population at 16.25 million persons.[19] Over 95 percent of these 16 million are from Third World nations; some 75 percent are women and children. Sources estimate that roughly 6 million live in refugee camps, where the average stay is more than five years. And while a lucky few refugees have resettled in the West or achieved self-sufficiency in their country of first asylum, the overwhelming majority are condemned to open-ended sentences in overcrowded Third World shelters. Most refugees have been forced from their countries by violent political upheaval; others are the victims of sustained campaigns of racism or religious or ethnic discrimination.

This grim litany of statistics tells a story at odds with perceptions popular in the West. Refugeeism does not reflect economic upward mobility but is rather the tragic consequence of political collapse and unchecked discrimination. Moreover, the wealthier industrialized countries, far from bearing the brunt of the crisis, are largely shielded from it. Europe and North America, with some 22 percent of the world's population—and, of course, an overwhelming greater proportion of the world's wealth and resources—offer refuge to only 17 percent of its official refugees. Nevertheless, Western governments have almost universally acted to restrict asylum policy in the past decade, as the humanitarian demands of those forced out of their homelands have been drowned out in the United States and Europe by broad and controversial debate about immigration policy in times of economic recession.

The relevance of these issues for development is plain. First, a grossly disproportionate share of the burden of hosting refugees has fallen upon the world's poorest nations. The already overtaxed economies of these countries strain still further to meet the demands of migratory populations. Second, the design and implementation of development projects have been substantially influenced by refugee flows. Since at least the 1960s, development practitioners have acknowledged the necessity of providing longer-term development aid to the displaced rather than mere emergency aid, and to synthesize such programs with the more expansive development agendas for host countries.[20] That is, because refugees often spend years, even lifetimes, in camps outside their homelands, development projects are increasingly tailored to account for the needs of migrants. Additionally, the tragic images of suffering in refugee camps, the seeming intractability of the refugee crisis as one conflict after another multiplies its dimensions, and the inadequacy of the supply of relief relative to demand for it have all contributed to a sense of "compassion fatigue" in richer nations. Public sentiment in the United States and Europe has hardened to a problem that at times seems beyond solution, reflected in more parsimonious official asylum and assistance policies and reduced voluntary giving.

As troubling as the refugee story may be, it captures only a part of the broader migration problem. Refugee analysis, as indicated by the UNHCR definition above, is concerned only with those persons who have crossed borders to escape persecution. In the early 1990s, however, as international support for the asylum-seekers flagged, the international community has reoriented its refugee policy to keep would-be refugees at home. In numerous global hot spots, we witness "the phenomenon of persons who clearly wanted and needed to flee their countries—that is, to become refugees—being prevented from doing so."[21] So long as the persecuted and displaced remain in their country of origin, they are denied refugee status and can become in no sense the charge of the international community. Such individuals share many characteristics of refugees, but they are considered even more vulnerable because they lack international protection and access to relief. Ironically, then, the persecution of these persons resides in being forced to stay, rather than forced to leave, constituting the cruel flip side of the refugee crisis. Accurate statistics for internally displaced civilians are difficult to compile, but any credible reckoning would place their numbers at no less than 25 million people. Like their refugee counterparts, the internally displaced have acute need for relief assistance and require the attention of development programs, both to enhance their lives as migrants and to facilitate their return home to lives of normalcy and self-sufficiency.

Moreover, refugee statistics are confined to those who flee their home countries to escape political or ethnic persecution. Economic refugees—persons who leave home to escape intolerable poverty, hunger, or famine—are not counted in the international tables and do not benefit from international protections. Indeed, it is these uprooted people who inspire the greatest fear and reservation among Northern populations; their quest for a viable standard of life is often seen as a direct threat to the jobs and social entitlements of citizens in advanced industrial economies. The porous borders that separate Europe from the Middle East and North Africa, and the U.S./Mexico frontier, witness much economic migration, although considerable South-South cross-border movement is similarly motivated. The lack of reliable statistics renders detailed analysis of such migration difficult, but the undisputed prevalence of the practice speaks volumes about the state of global development. Economic migration is a graphic, tragic yardstick of global economic stability and economic justice; people forced to move to find a subsistence standard of life are irrefutable proof of economic failure in a world of plenty. Until the promise of global development approaches realization, cross-border migration to escape poverty (which has proved so potent and polarizing an issue in U.S. politics) will remain a blight on the international political landscape.

It is worth noting that development itself is also the cause of large-scale forced migration. Recent estimates suggest that some 10 million people are uprooted annually as a result of infrastructure projects in Southern countries, with World Bank projects alone accounting for 2 million yearly displacements. That development efforts somtimes occasion involuntary resettlement does not mean that the development program should necessarily be abandoned, because real opportunities to improve living standards sustainably might be lost with such an approach. But, whether by avoiding the necessity of displacement, or by budgeting sufficient resources to ensure quality resettlement for those adversely effected, development projects must anticipate this unintended consequence of even the best-intentioned efforts. Resettlement can become an arm of development policy, where provisions are made for the constructive reintegration of the displaced into the economy. The alternative is that the harmful byproducts of development efforts may outweigh the benefits, as resettlement typically leaves already poor people poorer still.[22]

"Development refugees" are not the only large and growing category of refugee overlooked by the standard definition. As broad swaths of earth become unfit for human habitation due to the environmental degradation, more and more people flee their homes to escape environmental decline and danger.[23] Because neither governments nor international law accord official status to environmental refugees, data on their numbers and plight are difficult to obtain, but estimates of a global population of more than 10 million and growing seem safe. Desertification remains the single largest cause of environmental migration, as refugee populations move from "region to region, cultivating one plot of marginal land after another, exacerbating the problem when the land no longer produces enough to meet basic needs."[24] Rising sea levels, caused by global warming, are expected to rival desertification as an agent of displacement, with chunks of densely populated land—disproportionately affecting communities in the low-lying delta lands of Africa and South Asia—facing permanent inundation. When truly natural catastrophes such as earthquakes, and, conversely, fully human disasters like toxic or nuclear contamination are figured into the equation, the awesome threat of environmental displacement becomes evident.[25]

While many of these concerns remain for the moment potential, it is important to recognize that environmentally motivated migration has already exacted a deadly toll in many parts of the world. Deforestation has robbed nature of dense stands of trees, its greatest defense against mudslides and landslides. Result: hitherto harmless storms in Latin America unleash tumbling mounds of earth and rocks over defenseless valley hamlets, killing and injuring indiscriminately. In South Asia, meanwhile, deforestation and overcultivation have diminished the soil's ability to absorb water, so that rainwater and atmospheric moisture run directly to rivers rather than passing through the process of soil absorption and plant transpiration. Result: downstream in the deltas of Bangladesh, massive, deadly floods that once struck twice a century now afflict the country every two or three years. Moreover, the migrations engendered by environmental overload aggravate the toll of such calamities, as people exploit ever more precarious and vulnerable lands in search of agricultural viability. The "natural" disasters that appear with numbing regularity on Western news broadcasts are in fact less natural than they appear. They are in large measure the consequence of environmental degradation and the migration it causes.

Indeed, the phenomenon of environmental refugees vividly demonstrates the risks where environmental and development crises intersect. Underdevelopment leads to unsustainable, environmentally unsound agricultural patterns, which in turn spur outmigration when land turns barren. The people on the move find ever more marginal terrain from which to eke out a harvest or two, upon which the vicious cycle swiftly begins anew. As by-products of the process, nature's own defenses against disaster are eroded, and the Southern cities grow exponentially, creating unsafe, marginally habitable urban environments. Crises thus occur more frequently and wreak greater carnage—so that still more people migrate, and the problem takes the shape of an endless, destructive loop. The solution lies only with broad-based sustainable development, and in this way our analysis, too, comes full circle.

International Aid

The role of Northern governments, private organizations, and multilateral institutions in facilitating durable development leads us to the question of international aid. Since 1960, about $1.4 trillion has been transferred in various forms of aid from rich countries to poorer ones. But the mandate for continuing foreign aid is under attack everywhere in the North, and nowhere more so than in the United States. The development community is facing hard questions about the success of aid projects, and hard challenges in an era where domestic concerns dominate the political agendas of Northern societies. As of this writing, the outcome of these challenges is uncertain; the following review of the major players in development assistance, the scope of aid, critiques of aid, and a brief balance sheet is designed to foster more clear-eyed consideration of this foundational question of contemporary international relations.

There are three major categories of international aid: official, governmental development assistance, channeled through government agencies such as the United States Agency for International Development (USAID) and the Canadian International Development Agency (CIDA); aid from multilateral donors such as the United Nations and the World Bank; and private assistance provided by voluntary organizations, typically funded by the donations of concerned citizens. While much of this aid is directly administered by the donor agency, via missions in Southern countries, the majority of direct government assistance is still received and implemented by Southern governments. Voluntary organizations active at relief and development sites in the Third World constitute a third, and increasingly important, implementer of Northern assistance.

Direct government assistance to the South is provided by 21 wealthy, industrialized countries (plus the European Commission which disburses aid on behalf of the European Union) that comprise the Development Assistance Committee (DAC) of the Organization for Economic Cooperation and Development (OECD).

The Scandinavian nations of Norway, Sweden, and Denmark are the most generous donors, with aid levels between and 1 and 1.2 percent of gross domestic product (GDP). Meanwhile, although the United States is the world's largest donor in real terms with annual development assistance of some $8 billion, the United States devotes only 0.15 percent of its GDP to foreign aid, less than all other industrial countries. Put otherwise, roughly $44 of the annual taxes paid by an average U.S. family goes to foreign aid, while in Denmark, the equivalent figure is $900. The average OECD member donates about 0 percent of GDP, and the United Nations has fixed 0.7 percent of GDP as a target figure for DAC countries.

Aid programs are motivated by various, sometimes competing, motivations, of which poverty reduction is but one. National security is a powerful alternative motivator. One-quarter of the United States' $21 billion foreign aid budget consists of military assistance. Areas considered strategically important, such as the Middle East, Eastern Europe, and the former Soviet Union, have benefited from U.S. aid disproportionate to their development needs. Observers must therefore distinguish between all foreign aid, which includes military assistance, and aid earmarked specifically for development. Moreover, even development aid serves many policy masters. USAID, for example, has been burdened with as many as 33 official goals, most directly tied to national security concerns; and while a recent reevaluation at the agency boiled the mandate down to 4 goals, none directly address poverty reduction. The aid programs of other nations serve their self-interest in more subtle ways. Roughly 25 percent of all Northern aid is tied to the purchase of the donor nation's goods and services, so that the wealth sent abroad is guaranteed to pay dividends back at home; and some $12 billion annually is given for "technical assistance"—advice, training, and development project design—of which 90 percent is spent on Northern consultants. Seen in its most skeptical light, these Northern aid programs might be seen as a elaborate subsidies for the domestic development industry. Still other donor nations—most aggressively Japan—direct development assistance primarily to countries that are potential markets for domestic exports.

Even where the impulse behind assistance is humanitarian, results on the ground have been erratic. The standard canard—that aid is no more than "poor people in rich countries helping rich people in poor countries"—has a measure of truth in it. Recent studies of the U.S. assistance program show that over $250 per recipient of U.S. aid was sent to relatively high-income countries, but less than $1 per person was earmarked for the poorest countries. The ten countries that contain two-thirds of the world's poorest people receive but one-third of world assistance. Still worse, within donor countries, aid-supported services seldom reach the neediest. Analysts attribute these spending patterns to the priorities of recipient governments, which often labor under political pressure to satisfy urban populations over their poorer rural counterparts, and may favor showy capital improvement projects like dams or hospitals over less glamorous poverty reduction in the countryside. Donor governments, however, must bear responsibility for the fact that developing nations with large military budgets receive more aid than their pacific counterparts, as national security interests justify the underwriting of large military establishments.

Perhaps in response to the perceived failure of official aid to meet its humanitarian mission, perhaps more in response to competing pressures on domestic agendas, and partly because the end of the cold war has reduced the West's interest in subsidizing military regimes throughout the South, the political commitment to global aid is on the wane in the North. Throughout the 1980s, the official development assistance disbursed by industrialized countries increased by some 25 percent in real terms, but growth slowed sharply in the early 1990s; and by 1993, the net flow of assistance to developing countries fell to $56 billion, down from $61 billion the year before. U.S. development engagement abroad has followed the international trend: American assistance to sub-Saharan Africa fell by almost half a billion dollars between 1985 and 1992. Budget cuts in 1994 hit the poorest parts of the U.S. development portfolio hardest, as USAID closed 8 of its 35 African missions. And, in response to strong domestic pressure to cut assistance, the United States announced plans in April 1995 to cut by nearly half the nation's annual pledge of overseas food aid, which had remained unchanged for two decades.

Reduced aid exacts a profound human toll overseas. Due to the structural adjustment policies that accompany World Bank loans, reviewed in the discussion of international debt above, many poorer countries must give budget priority to debt service, giving enhanced importance to assistance revenues. Numerous African countries report that current foreign debt is greater than GDP, and up to 60 percent or more of government revenues are absorbed by debt obligations. In the near term, international assistance allows nations to make up the subsequent shortfall and meet other social demands of developing countries. "If we didn't have aid, we could not pay salaries," reports Mali's minister of finance, describing a characteristic sub-Saharan dilemma. "If we can't pay salaries, that means social disturbances, that means no scholarships for students, that means we give up on preparing for the future."[26] Other Southern politicians observe that Western financial support for nascent democracies in Africa and around the Third World might be critical in sustaining freedom: By contributing to prosperity under democracy on the one hand, and signaling to would-be despots that freedom pays in the post–cold war world on the other, aid represents an important and timely investment in global democracy. But few expect substantial infusions of new aid given the current inward-looking climate in the West, and even efforts to achieve meaningful debt forgiveness—which would yield many of the same benefits as direct aid—have failed to reach fruition, as noted in our foregoing discussion of debt.

But the portrait of international assistance in the mid-1990s is not all bleak. First, even as the U.S. government moves to slash overseas funding, polls strongly suggest that the American public remains more generous than their representatives and that current hostility to assistance springs from misconception rather than indifference. According to polls taken in 1993 and 1994, Americans believe that the government devotes 20 percent or more of its spending to foreign assistance; the real figure is about 1 percent, only half of which again is development aid administered by USAID. Asked to estimate the appropriate U.S. investment in international aid, respondents said about 5 percent—or five times current outlays. Thus, a reservoir of humanitarian support remains untapped in the United States, with the potential to undergird a new North-South partnership for development.

Second, in response to criticism that too little aid reaches the poorest, many governments are increasingly delivering aid through private and voluntary organizations such as charities and church groups, known in the trade as nongovernmental organizations (NGOs).[27] Such organizations have always played a key role in development, but they have proliferated rapidly in recent years in both North and South. NGOs are better than governments at implementing small projects and delivering assistance to those who need it most; furthermore, NGO-administered funding is more likely to be used for purely humanitarian and developmental purposes, rather than military or security reasons. Less funding is lost to wasteful overhead and corruption as well. Local participation, decentralization, and familiarity at the grass-roots level provide NGOs with a competitive edge over government organs, and NGOs are estimated to be more than twice as effective at reaching the poorest of the poor with meaningful development aid.

The growing perception that private aid groups are better able to identify needs and deliver help has persuaded the U.S. government to increase the proportion of aid delivered through NGOs from 17 percent in 1992 to 30 percent in 1995 and to a projected 40 percent in 1996.[28] Nor has the attractiveness of NGOs been lost on private organizations and individuals, who continue to generously support voluntary development work. The OECD counted over 2,500 NGOs in Northern countries in 1990 (up from 1,603 in 1980) and countless counterparts in Southern localities.[29] The rising nongovernmental tide is best reflected by the NGO presence at large UN conferences such as the 1992 Earth Summit in Rio de Janeiro and the 1995 Social Summit in Copenhagen, where voluntary organizations played a role as prominent as governments', giving voice to the grass-roots interests they represent—and earned the ear of national policymakers and the international media. While nongovernmental efforts are not a panacea, they offer an efficient and people-centered development alternative to large government and multilateral projects, and constitute a direct channel for constructive aid and communication between concerned individuals of the North and South.

Moreover, it is important that the considerable accomplishments of two generations of development be fairly evaluated. Televised images in the first half of the 1990s have left too many Northerners with the perception that the countries of the developing world are hopelessly poverty-stricken and conflict-ridden. From Main Street, USA, to the floor of the Senate, the shibboleth that aid is invariably squandered and that our programs are no more than "money down a rat hole," has been invoked to undermine support for assistance. But the record of foreign assistance and development discloses important successes: In little more than a generation, average real incomes in the Third World have more than doubled; child death rates have been reduced by more than half; malnutrition rates have tumbled by over 30 percent; life expectancy has increased by about a third; and the percentage of rural families with access to safe water has risen from less than 10 percent to more than 60 percent.[30] Literacy rates are up 33 percent in the last 25 years, and primary school enrollment has tripled in that period. Indeed, virtually every index of human development reproduced in chapter 5 of this volume discloses dramatic gains for human well-being across the Third World.

International aid has figured heavily in these successes. Limiting our survey to official U.S. aid, we find that more than 3 million lives are saved annually through USAID immunization programs; that in the 28 countries with the largest USAID-sponsored family planning programs, the average number of children per family has dropped from 6.1 in the mid-1960s to 4.2 today; and that over 850,000 people have been reached with HIV/AIDS prevention education. Other AID programs, the work of USAID's counterparts from other nations, and the contribution of NGOs, magnify these successes many times. Need remains great and much work remains to be done. But development assistance has already reaped substantial rewards for North and South alike.

However, aid programs, and especially government agencies, continue to labor under institutional shortcomings that limit their effectiveness in the field. The discourse of development aid—including the catalogue of success stories above—too often suggests that development is something that is imposed upon the poor. In fact, it is the people of the South, and not the development institutions of the North, that are the true repositories of development expertise; the success stories are theirs, not ours. Better evaluation, coordination, and above all, greater appreciation for the dynamics and issues of local experience are necessary preconditions for more effective development. An insightful critique of international aid has noticed that such changes will require

> a fundamental change in the posture of the aid community as a whole toward the poor, which must be reflected in a responsive approach to their organized initiatives. Implicit in this approach is not only a genuine respect for the capacity of the poor to manage their own development, but, perhaps more importantly, an appreciation for their understanding of their own circumstances, their knowledge of external constraints and internal capabilities, their creativity and their ability to define appropriate development paths for their immediate and wider communities.[31]

Development assistance, and even crisis relief, cannot succeed without the participation of national and community-based indigenous organizations and individuals. With their help, important efficiencies are discovered and costly mistakes are avoided. This central insight—that effective development assistance demands popular, community involvement—lies behind the increased role for NGOs in the overall development equation and justifies optimism that the next generation of global aid will yield still better results than those just past.

Development as Reconciliation

To conclude, we pause briefly on one final, crucial piece of the development puzzle: conflict and reconciliation. The great tragedies that have required large-scale assistance in recent years—in Bosnia, in Rwanda, in Ethiopia, in Sudan—are all attributable to brutal civil conflict that undermined economic security as well as political stability. More broadly, low-intensity conflict has persisted in many of the world's poorest nations for better than 30 years. From the Horn of Africa, where Eritrean and Tigrean nationalists engaged in more than three decades of struggle with Ethiopia, to the now-infamous combat between Hutus and Tutsis that has riven Burundi as well as Rwanda, to South Africa, where black populations combated against apartheid for a generation, conflict has consumed the African continent. The costs have been staggering. The toll in human lives is compounded by the sterile economic investment in weapons and warfare, and the corresponding impoverishment of social and economic development. The environment is another victim, as war scars the earth with bombing and shelling, while refugees fleeing conflict raze forests for firewood and shelter. Insecurity has stunted long-term economic planning, and international aid has been squandered on soldiers and the military establishment. Countless opportunities for sustainable development have been passed over in pursuit of strategic advantage.

The tragedy of conflict is not limited to Africa. Many nations of Latin America and Asia have likewise witnessed unremitting military action and violence, sometimes in the form of border skirmishes between countries, sometimes in the guise of nationalist or insurrectionary groups pressing varied claims. In the context of global development, it is futile to linger long on the merits of the many disputes. What is important to recognize is that civil conflict represents a deadly drag on development. A nation at arms is an unlikely candidate for sustained and secure growth, and for too long, too many nations of the South have suffered from endemic conflict. Reconciliation has emerged as a necessary precondition for effective, sustained development.

Moreover, development itself is increasingly understood as a potential source of conflict. Where development projects advance the interests of some groups to the disadvantage of others, they may serve to exacerbate social inequality. The least empowered groups—too often the urban poor, landless agricultural workers, or indigenous peoples—sometimes find that the price of economic growth for wealthier segments of the population comes at their expense. In the Amazon region, for example, logging and ranching development has jeopardized the livelihood of indigenous groups; and in Nigeria, the wealth generated by oil production has failed to reach the poorest indigenous groups.[32] The tension resulting from such inequitable development can erupt—and in these instances has erupted—into sustained or sporadic armed conflict, setting back the cause of broad-based development even farther.

This realization has contributed to the heightened role for NGOs, indigenous and Northern, in the global development enterprise. Reconciliation can best be facilitated by the moral or religious leadership that comes from community groups working in partnership with like-minded groups at home and abroad. Equitable development planning is likewise liable to emerge from the grass roots, while projects imposed from above or abroad offer the greatest potential for unforeseen victims and unforeseen conflict. Neither local political leadership, and still less external forces, have the standing in Southern communities to bring people together and resolve local differences. The reconciliation most likely to achieve lasting results brings individuals together, "person by person, family by family, community by community, to help people over the hurdles placed in their way by political leaders or others seeking to keep the sides apart."[33]

Conflict resolution, then, merits full consideration along with the other components of global development. The pages that follow offer details on the statistics, the organizations, and the individuals who have shaped the contemporary development debate. The message throughout, beyond the data and the description, reinforces the notion that reconciliation lies at the heart of global development: humankind's reconciliation with the environment and with cultural diversity; reconciliation with within nations and across borders; reconciliation of competing demands of self-interest and humanitarian engagement; reconciliation of ourselves with our brothers and sisters. Development, then, really is the new word for peace. Like making peace, doing development is no small labor, but is within our reach and well worth the effort.

Notes

1. The role of government and nonprofit organizations in the overall international development equation is treated in chapter 5, Organizations.

2. A detailed discussion of the theoretical paradigms of economic development is beyond the scope of the current volume. For a concise and accessible survey of the paradigms of development, see Weaver, "Are There Still Competing Paradigms of Development?" in Savitt, ed., *Teaching Global Development*, Notre Dame, 1994. For a brief overview of development economics and further detail on these issues, see Kusterer, Rock, and Weaver, *Capitalism with a Human Face: Broad Based Sustainable Development* (forthcoming).

3. Export-led growth has also been tried in Brazil, Malaysia, and the Ivory Coast, among others. As many commentators have noted, the successes of East Asia may be attributed to effective land reform and general education programs to create human capital—that is, effective and productive labor forces which allow labor-rich countries to thrive even without natural resources.

4. What's more, the wave of external borrowing created the underlying financial conditions that led to the debt crisis of the 1980s, discussed below.

5. Weaver, "Are There Still Competing Paradigms of Development," 43.

6. In many developing countries, the "informal economy"—i.e., economic activity that operates outside the system of taxation and regulation and is thus at least nominally illegally—provides the only real dynamism in the economy. Allowing the entire economy to profit from such liberty, and to free informal economies from the costs and fears of the regulatory apparatus is thus a key development goal. For the importance of informal economies, see Hernando de Soto, *The Other Path: The Invisible Revolution in the Third World* (1989).

7. *New York Review of Books*, 20 December 1990.

8. Jane Collins, "Women and the Environment: Social Reproduction and Sustainable Development." In *The Women and International Development Annual*, vol. 2.

9. Those interested in further resources on women in development are referred to two helpful organizations. The first is International Women's Rights Action Watch (IWRAW), a "global network of activists and scholars that monitors changes in law and policy in accordance with the principles of the 'Convention on the Elimination of All Forms of Discrimination against Women.'" IWRAW materials provide a potent and accessible resource which effectively introduces scholars to the immediacy of women's struggle in developing countries—the stark and ongoing problem of oppression and the international policy options for its elimination.

The second institution is the Upper Midwest Women's History Center (UMWHC). The Women's History and Culture Collection of the UMWHC provides a variety of resources that are designed to ensure an approach to global issues that is "both multicultural and fair." The Women in Development material "presents current perspectives of contemporary Third World women and concentrates on common themes of women and the family, work, and empowerment."

10. *Our Common Future* (1987), xi. This volume, comprising the whole of the World Commission on Environment and Development report, is a fine introduction to the study of sustainable development. Its issuance galvanized international attention on the environmental implications of the development issue.

11. See generally, "Conserving Soils," in Lester Brown et al., *State of the World 1984* (1984). The *State of the World* reports, issued annually, are perhaps the best overall source of current and reliable information about environment and development information.

12. Peter Bartelmus, *Environment and Development* (1989).

13. United Nations Environmental Programme, *General Assessment of Progress in the Implementation of the Plan of Action to Combat Desertification* (1984).

14. Ibid., 25. Readers desiring further detail on deforestation and rainforests are directed to another volume in ABC-CLIO's Contemporary World Issues series, *Rainforests of the World* by Kathlyn Gay (1993).

15. See David E. Newton, *Global Warming* (1993) in the ABC-CLIO Contemporary World Issues series, for a solid introduction to the topic.

16. John C. Ryan, "Conserving Biological Diversity," in *State of the World 1990* (1990). The essay provides a superb introduction to broader issues in biodiversity and its destruction. See also John Maxwell Hamilton, *Entangling Alliances* (1990), for an able demonstration of the interdependent nature of global environmental issues, especially biodiversity.

17. The urban explosion throughout the global South presents a vast development challenge, implicating problems such as water supply, sani-

tation, and disease control, among many others. The urban population in the developing world quadrupled to 1.15 billion in the 35 years following 1950, and by the year 2000, eight of the world's ten largest cities will be in the South, compared with three in 1960. For further details on this important issue, readers are referred to chapter 5 of the United Nations *Human Development Report 1990*, "Urbanisation and Human Development: A Special Focus."

18. The literature on refugees is well developed. In addition to the *World Refugee Survey*, cited below, readers seeking a consise introduction to the topic are referred to "Refugees in the Post–Cold War Era: Does Anybody Care Anymore?" in *Global Perspectives*, Fall 1993, and "Refugees: The Rising Flood," in *World Watch*, May/June 1994. Also see the bibliographic entries on refugees, in chapter 6, Selected Print Resources, below.

19. See the 1994 *World Refugee Survey*, prepared by the U.S. Committee for Refugees, Table 1. The *Survey* provides a superb introduction and overview to the global refugee issue, and includes a detailed statistical analysis of the problem. Readers seeking a solid book-length overview are referred to Gil Loescher and Ann Dull Loescher, *The Global Refugee Crisis* (1994), another volume in the ABC-CLIO Contemporary World Issues series.

20. See Richard Black and Vaughan Robinson, *Geography and Refugees: Patterns and Processes of Change*, especially chapter 1.

21. Bill Frelick, "The Year in Review," in *1994 World Refugee Survey*, 3.

22. See "Moving People," *The Economist*, 23 April 1994, 48.

23. Jodi L. Jacobson's *Environmental Refugees: A Yardstick of Habitability* (Worldwatch Paper 86, 1988) provides a superb, concise introduction to the topic.

24. Ibid., 38.

25. Jacobson estimates that the number of environmental refugees will increase sixfold in the next 50 years, ultimately dwarfing traditional categories of refugees.

26. Quoted in Howard W. French, "African Democracies Worry Aid Will Dry Up," *New York Times*, 12 March 1995, A12.

27. Many leading NGOs are profiled in chapter 5 below.

28. Barbara Crossette, "Gore Says U.S. Will Shift More Foreign Aid to Private Groups," *New York Times*, 13 March 1995, A8.

29. For example, one expert counts some 25,000 NGOs in a single Indian state. See *The Economist*, 7 May 1994, 20.

30. See Jonathan Power, "Our View of the Third World Is Warped," *Los Angeles Times*, 7 November 1993, M8.

31. Stephen Hellenger et al., *Aid for Just Development: Report on the Future of Foreign Assistance* (1988). Readers interested in more detail on the aid issue are urged to consult this excellent volume.

32. For these examples and further information on the relationship of conflict and development, see the superb publication "Conflict and Development," No. 5 in the series "From Information to Education," published in 1994 by the Panos Institute of Washington, D.C.

33. Kenneth Hackett, Executive Director, Catholic Relief Services. Speech entitled "A Practitioner's View," delivered at the Conference on Planning and Conducting Large Scale Emergency Operations: U.S. Army, Europe, Heidelberg, Germany, 13–15 June 1995.

Chronology 2

Global development in the modern era can be only imperfectly represented in a chronology. Much of the progress that development has wrought has been earned only slowly, over time; unlike some other important historical phenomena, the great events in development are seldom apparent until long after they take place. Still more problematically, many of the chronological moments in contemporary development are tragedies—natural disasters, mass exoduses of displaced persons, outbreaks of famine and disease. Indeed, because the worst calamities of development are discrete crises while the achievements mount almost imperceptibly over the course of years, the perception of development offered by the mass media often amounts to an unending string of disappointments, setbacks, and problems.

In the chronology that follows, we endeavor to avoid this effect by noting the success stories as well as the setbacks. Moments such as the founding of an organization or the date of national independence serve as the date-to-note achievements that might otherwise be reflected only in time-series data. Readers will thus find references to community and collaborative enterprises that have changed and promoted development, but whose accomplishments cannot conveniently be located on a timeline. On the other hand, we do not avoid notice of the many obstacles that have slowed the path of contemporary global development. Tragically, they comprise an important part of today's development story.

The chronology is organized by decade and sketches a generation of uninterrupted growth and increasing enthusiasm following World War II. The 1970s bring warning signs and the 1980s a sharp reversal of fortune. But beyond these broader strokes, we emphasize the importance of North-South relations and the reality of mutual interdependence, along with the central and courageous part that Southern communities, institutions, and individuals have played in improving our world. Notwithstanding the many disasters that appear in the pages that follow, this is a hopeful chronology that tells a story of progress and engagement and includes the promise of a better global tomorrow.

The 1940s   The end of World War II signaled the beginning of the contemporary world order and brought into existence many of the institutions that continue to define today's development enterprise. The great events in global development in the 1940s centered on the close of hostilities and the preparations for reconstruction in Europe and around the world. Most significantly, the great institutions that still define the development debate were born in the years just after 1945. Some of today's leading Northern NGOs commenced operations in the wake of the dislocations of World War I, but many more were created to respond to the destruction and desolation in post-1945 Europe. Along with the nongovernmental community response came the official reaction of governments and coalitions. Even prior to war's end, an international conference was convened at Bretton Woods, New Hampshire, where Western leaders laid the groundwork for the World Bank and International Monetary Fund (IMF), in the conviction that orderly rebuilding was a necessary precondition for a durable peace. The U.S. government, too, engaged postwar reconstruction in an unprecedented way by launching

the Marshall Plan in 1948. Perhaps most importantly, the birth of the United Nations gave the
world an international forum where international
grievances—and ultimately the case for development—could be made on a peaceful, ongoing basis.

1944   The International Monetary Fund (IMF), the International Bank for Reconstruction and Development
(commonly known as the World Bank), and the
General Agreement on Tariffs and Trade (GATT)
are created at the UN Monetary and Financial Conference held at Bretton Woods, New Hampshire.
Each of the new institutions responded to a major
goal of the conference—the GATT was designed to
liberalize trade by reducing tariffs; the IMF was
created to stabilize and regulate international
monetary exchange; and the World Bank's mission
was to provide an international credit institution
that would facilitate postwar economic development. While GATT has been superseded by the
World Trade Organization pursuant to the conclusion of the Uruguay Round in 1994 (see below), the
IMF and the World Bank continue to play a major
role in contemporary development. Critics of the
Bretton Woods Agreement note that developing
countries had not yet attained independence at the
time of the conference, and so had no say in the
design of the international economic order.

1945   World War II ends in Europe in April, and in the
Pacific in August following the atomic bombing of
Hiroshima and Nagasaki. As was the case after
World War I, the ending of hostilities leaves Europe
replete with homelessness; some persons have been
forced to cross borders and acquire the status of
refugees, while others stand in need of relief at
home. European communities from London to
Moscow are devastated; starvation and disease are
endemic. The carnage and suffering of the war
spurs the creation of many voluntary relief and development efforts in the United States.

1945 (*cont.*) With the end of the World War comes the beginning of the cold war. The Western bloc is led by the United States, while the Eastern bloc is led by the Soviet Union. Military superiority and influence in the emerging nations of Africa and Asia become the cornerstones of competition between the ideological rivals. Often the two forms of competition merge in "proxy wars" in the South, where rival factions supported by the two blocs engage in civil war for local political control. The legacy of high military expenditure and recurrent civil conflict is a substantial drag on development.

The United Nations Charter is signed on 26 June at San Francisco, California. According to Article One of the Charter, the UN's purpose is to maintain international peace and security; to develop friendly relations among nations; to cooperate in solving international economic, social, cultural and humanitarian problems, and in promoting respect for human rights. Through the subsequent establishment of subsidiary agencies such as the UN Development Programme, the UN Environmental Programme, and UNICEF, the UN will take a direct and substantial role in Southern development. And as a political forum where all nations convene on the basis of equality, irrespective of military or economic might, the UN offers an important global platform for nations of the developing world.

Lutheran World Relief (LWR) is founded as a response by American Lutherans to the suffering of their co-religionists in Europe. The organization soon extends its scope beyond Europe and to persons of all faiths, to become one of the most influential and innovative Northern relief and development organizations.

CARE is founded by 22 U.S. voluntary agencies as the Cooperative for American Remittances to Europe. The organization's first mission is to purchase millions of Army surplus ration kits and send them to the needy of Europe as "Care Packages." The agency has since expanded its activities and scope of operations and changed its name to Cooperative for Assistance and Relief Everywhere.

1946   The United Nations International Children's Emergency Fund (UNICEF) is created in October by the UN General Assembly. The Fund was initially intended to provide relief to poor, young victims of World War II. But in 1953, the General Assembly extended the UNICEF's mandate indefinitely, and UNICEF had already begun to focus its attention on the widespread malnutrition, disease, and social ills that plagued millions of children throughout the developing world.

Church World Service (CWS) is founded by the Federal Council of Churches, the Foreign Missions Conference, and the American Committee of the World Council of Churches. CWS is the unit of the National Council of Churches of Christ in the U.S.A. responsible for overseas development and relief assistance. CWS works substantially with partner NGOs in the South.

1948   The Marshall Plan to facilitate economic recovery in war-torn Europe begins. Although officially known as the European Recovery Program, the plan is almost universally remembered by the name of Secretary of State John Marshall, and dispensed over $13 billion between 1948 and 1952. The plan is widely hailed as a key factor in Europe's rapid return to economic security and comes to stand for the potential of bold foreign assistance. The success of the program secured a permanent place for international aid in the postwar economic system, and provided a paradigm for assistance to the Third World. Indeed, substantial U.S. humanitarian initiatives almost invariably invoke the plan's success as proof that bold and decisive assistance can pay dramatic near-term dividends. However, the Marshall Plan's success must be seen in the context of the

1948 (*cont.*) special circumstances of the postwar era and the reconstruction of already developed economies that it undertook. The expectation that similar programs in the global South would yield similarly swift results, although widespread among some policymakers, was never realistic and was not realized.

The World Health Organization (WHO) is created on 7 April. The Organization exists to facilitate the attainment of the highest possible level of health for all peoples. WHO was a catalyst in the world's successful fight against smallpox, which WHO declared eradicated in 1980, and is now a leading advocate for large-scale immunization the world over.

The Joint Commission for Rural Reconstruction in China begins work to assist peasant farmers in the Szechuan province by providing funding and technical assistance. The program, a joint U.S.-Chinese project undertaken pursuant to the U.S. China Aid Act of 1948, is remarkably successful and demonstrates the potential of grassroots, local-empowerment development strategies. The substantial achievements of the program end with the Communist takeover of Szechuan and the rest of the Chinese mainland in 1949.

1949 Raul Prebisch, one of the founders of the dependency school of development economics, publishes *The Economic Development of Latin America and Its Principal Problems.* In this and in subsequent writings over the following decade, Prebisch argues that the orthodox theory of world trade that had brought rapid growth to European countries in the nineteenth century would not work for developing nations of the post–World War II era. The strength and diversity of the U.S. economy freed America from the need to import from poorer countries, so that these nations would not be able to accumulate the capital to expand. Because the economic superiority of the United States and other wealthier countries resulted from their monopoly of manufacturing, Prebisch and others argued for the industrialization of the Third World, or what became known as "import substitution industrialization."

The Chinese Revolution culminates with victory for the Communists. The Communist regime combined an elaborate totalitarian apparatus with disciplined action for economic development.

The 1950s From the perspective of global development, the 1950s were marked by equal measures of continuity and change. In many ways, the contours of contemporary development were taking shape. As the postwar reconstruction of Europe was consolidated, global policymakers, development planners, and NGOs increasingly focused on the global South. Citizens and nations of the South, meanwhile, began to articulate their concerns and claims in the global arena with more force. The first sense of a collective, unified Southern consciousness emerged at the Bandung conference in 1955, from which would evolve a cluster of nations self-consciously distinct from both East and West, defined by their own "non-alignment" in the bipolar cold war world.

Moreover, the exceptional economic growth and human development characteristic of the post-1945 era was already well under way during the 1950s. Although the 1960s are better known for Southern growth, the 1950s, too, registered substantial gains. The modern development enterprise, complete with foreign missions, multilateral agencies, and permanent nongovernmental activity, became a feature on the international scene during these years.

Still, for all the change, much remained the same in North-South relations. It was not until the end of the decade that the first African colony earned its independence, and the great wave of decolonization would not strike until the early 1960s. Notwithstanding early assertions by Southerners, the key

The 1950s (*cont.*)	roles on the world stage and the leading ideologies that animated international affairs were largely defined by the North. Here too, the first stirrings of Southern ideology began to challenge the established order. But the 1950s were transitional years—a decade of prologue to more far-reaching changes that the 1960s would bear.
1950	The first World Bank mission to a developing country—to Colombia—is established. The mission's objectives are to fulfill the "basic human needs" of Colombians.
	World Vision, a Christian humanitarian organization, is founded. The organization initially focused on relief and child care, but now is involved in community development work around the world.
1951	The UN General Assembly appoints the United Nations High Commission for Refugees (UNHCR). This institution was the successor to the International Refugee Organization (in existence from 1946 to 1952) which had settled more than 1 million displaced persons in the aftermath of World War II. The UNHCR Office has two main functions: First, UNHCR seeks to promote the international endorsement of standards for the treatment and definition of refugees; and second, to seek permanent solutions to the problems of refugees. More than 125 nations now belong to UNHCR, which has won two Nobel Prizes for its humanitarian efforts.
	The Ford Foundation is founded. The Foundation now has 15 field offices in its International Division and is the largest private foundation in the world dedicated to development and its discrete subfields. The Foundation supports a variety of development programs and often explores alternative development solutions.
1952	President Harry S Truman announces the Four Point Plan, which he labels a "bold new program"

designed to abolish humanity's "ancient ene-
mies—hunger, misery and despair." Introducing
the program on 20 January, Truman articulates a
humanitarian and internationalist vision, asserting
that "only by helping the least fortunate of its members to help themselves can the human family
achieve the decent satisfying life that is the right of
all people." Other rich countries soon join the
United States in an international aid program, and
the contemporary commitment to international aid
was soon established.

Alfred Sauvy coins the term *Third World*, to corre-
spond to the Third Estate of the French Revolution,
which comprised most of the people and productivity of France but enjoyed none of the benefits. In
1956, Parisian journal *Tiers Monde* embraced the
term as its title. Within ten years, Third World becomes the common term to designate the states of
Asia, Africa, and Latin America.

Economic Development and Cultural Change, the first
journal devoted to global development, begins
publication.

The government of India promulgates its first Five
Year Plan for economic growth, the first such plan
in any developing country. The plan aims at "maximum production, full employment, the attainment
of economic equality and social justice." Mid-term
economic plans—typically five years—become the
standard tool of Southern government Planning
Commissions.

1954   The Agricultural Trade Development and Assistance Act—better known as PL 480 or the Food for
Peace Act—is enacted by the U.S. government. The
law provides food aid to selected countries as relief
or at reduced cost. Billions of dollars of food aid
have been shipped under the act, which has
achieved important humanitarian ends, but which
has also been widely criticized for its negative

1954 (*cont.*)   economic effects on donor nations and local food producers. Many have complained that the low-cost arrival of surplus U.S. grain on local markets depresses prices and renders local production of food unprofitable. In this way, PL 480 may have acted to discourage food self-sufficiency.

1955   The Asia-Africa Conference is held in Bandung, Indonesia. This meeting brings together leaders of recently decolonized and soon-to-be decolonized nations to find common political ground, and is often cited as the beginning of the "non-aligned movement." The conference thus marked the entry to international politics of a new group of emerging countries defined by their refusal to formally ally with either of the global superpowers.

1957   Ghana becomes the first sub-Saharan African country to attain independence from colonial rule. The next five years witness a rapid and unanticipated surge toward African independence, as the great majority of today's African states emerge.

The 1960s   In the developing world as in the developed world, the 1960s was a decade of dizzying change and enormous promise. In the first years of the decade, national liberation passed from aspiration to reality, as nations achieved independence by the dozen. With just a few exceptions, decolonization was complete by mid-decade, as the modern political map took shape. Greater assertiveness accompanied independence, and the Group of 77 consolidates the spirit of the Bandung conference, giving voice to Southern issues on the global political stage.

Meanwhile, economic change matched, perhaps exceeded, political change as the driving force in development. The UN declared the 1960s the "First Development Decade" and set goals for annual economic growth at 5 percent in the developing world. Although many experts considered these goals unrealistic when they were announced, they were in fact easily exceeded, as Southern development outpaced the most optimistic models and, indeed, all historical experience.

Underlying much of this growth, and the broader sense of optimism in the development communities, were technological innovations such as the Green Revolution. In a matter of years, the development and cultivation of high-yielding grain varieties transformed nations of perpetual food shortage into self-sufficient food exporters. Politics, economics, and technology changed together and brought a new sense of possibility to the developing world. For the first time, the end of famine, and the realization of development's promises, seemed close at hand.

1960   In recognition of the growing gap between the rich countries of the North and the poor of the South, the UN declares the 1960s to be the First Development Decade. The General Assembly stresses general goals, such as promoting self-sustaining economic growth, and member nations are reminded of their global responsibility to break the cycle of poverty. The UN identifies international trade as "the primary instrument for economic development" and sets a target goal for member nations to achieve a minimum rate of growth of aggregate national income of 5 percent by the end of the decade.

UN General Assembly issues Declaration on Decolonialization, formally recognizing "the legitimacy of the struggle of the colonial peoples to exercise their right to self-determination by all the necessary means at their disposal."

Seventeen newly independent states, 16 of them African, join the United Nations.

The Stages of Economic Growth by W. W. Rostow is published, stimulating debate throughout the world about the conditions supposedly needed in order for development to occur. (See chapter 3,

1960 (*cont.*) Biographical Sketches and chapter 6, Selected Print Resources, for more information.)

The World Food Programme is established by the UN General Assembly and the Food and Agriculture Organization to stimulate and advance economic and social development by providing food aid.

The International Development Association (IDA) is established to provide loans on more generous terms than those provided by the World Bank. While legally and financially distinct from the bank, the IDA is the bank's concessionary lending affiliate and is administered by the same officers and staff. IDA's assistance concentrates on the poorest countries of the Third World.

1961 In September, the Organization for Economic Cooperation and Development (OECD) is established in Paris by 24 market economy nations, including Japan, the United States, and Canada. The OECD is designed to coordinate and promote policies that enhance economic growth, financial stability, and trade among members. It is governed by a council of representatives from all member states.

The OECD forms over one hundred specialized committees, one of which is the Development Assistance Committee (DAC), which is created to provide a forum for principal aid donors to discuss all aspects of assistance policy, aid programs, and the amount and nature of contributions. The original members of the DAC are Belgium, Canada, France, the Federal Republic of Germany, Italy, the United Kingdom, the United States, the Netherlands, and Japan, with Denmark joining in 1963 and Sweden and Austria the following year. One of the goals of the DAC, in addition to promoting the growth of aid, is to promote equitable sharing among donor nations of the aid burden. This goal has far from been achieved; in 1994 Scandinavian countries contributed seven times more than the United States as a percentage of gross national product (GNP).

The U.S. Agency for International Development (USAID) is created as a result of the Foreign Assistance Act, replacing the International Cooperation Agency and the Development Loan Fund. The objectives of the agency include safekeeping national security, providing humanitarian assistance, and protecting U.S. commercial interests. The four program areas of USAID are Development Assistance, Economic Support Fund, Food for Peace, and Disaster Assistance.

President John F. Kennedy launches the Peace Corps on 21 September with the objectives of helping developing countries meet basic manpower needs, enhancing cultural understanding of developing countries and improving U.S. understanding of developing nations.

1963   On 25 May the Organization of African Unity (OAU) is formed in Addis Ababa, Ethiopia. The goal of the OAU is to allow Africans to "speak with one voice" to the international community and to facilitate cooperation within the continent. The charter is signed by 32 member governments. The OAU is an observer in UN General Assembly sessions and has been instrumental in persuading the UN to recognize liberation movements.

1964   UN Conference on Trade and Development (UNCTAD) is established as an executing agency of the UN and meets for the first time in Geneva, with Raul Prebisch serving as secretary-general. The purpose of UNCTAD is to promote international trade to accelerate economic development, to formulate principles and policies on international trade, and to initiate action for the adoption of multilateral trade agreements. Serving as a center for harmonizing trade and development, UNCTAD quickly becomes closely affiliated with its members from

1964 *(cont.)* developing countries who take this opportunity to voice their concerns and needs. As a result, the agency has been labeled as a pressure group for the South, and occasionally has encountered opposition to its continued funding in the General Assembly. At the first meeting, members agree to a scheme for supplementing financial measures, and an aid target of 1 percent of national income is set.

The Group of 77, the 77 developing countries present at the first meeting of UNCTAD, is established. At the UNCTAD meeting in Geneva the Group of 77 sets the agenda for what emerged a decade later as the call for a New International Economic Order (NIEO). The Group of 77 now consists of over 120 members and refers to the caucus of all developing nations in the United Nations.

1965 The United Nations Development Programme (UNDP) is established by the merger of the UN Special Fund of the Economic and Social Council, and the Expanded Programme of Technical Assistance. The UNDP offers grants for training, resources, and needs assessments and is the largest grant assistance program in the UN system. Since its inception, the UNDP has been among the most important international voices in the global development arena.

UNICEF wins the Nobel Peace Prize in recognition of its extensive efforts on behalf of the world's children and the way in which this work has helped to promote peace throughout the world.

1966 The Green Revolution is launched with the development of a high-yielding variety (HYV) of rice by the International Rice Research Institute in the Philippines. Norman Borlaug then goes on to develop a high-yielding, short-stemmed strain of wheat, launching the Green Revolution in Mexico. According to the World Bank, within less than a decade half of the developing world's wheat acreage and one-third of its paddy fields were converted to these high-yielding, semi-dwarf varieties. While HYV have the capacity to yield up to six times more than traditional varieties, they also require costly maintenance, including an abundant water supply, fertilizers, and pesticides, which lead critics to argue that the Green Revolution favors wealthier farmers, widening the gap between rich and poor. India and Mexico are held up as the Green Revolution's success stories, both becoming self-sufficient in grain production in a relatively short period and in time producing surpluses for export. This signified a switch from subsistence farming to cash crops, which decreased the food security of countries' poorest even as it increased their potential cash earnings.

1967   Julius Nyerere, the President of Tanzania, writes *The Arusha Declaration,* a blueprint for development in Tanzania. He argues that development depends on the self-reliance of the Tanzanian people combined with the efficient use of the nation's resources. When Tanzania's economic conditions worsen by the end of the decade, Nyerere faces pressure from the IMF to abandon the principles laid out in his declaration and implement a structural adjustment program. Related to Nyerere's vision as laid out in the declaration is the establishment of "ujamaa" villages, which seek to consolidate the scattered agricultural communities of Tanzania into more compact units, so as to provide educational, health, and agricultural services in an efficient manner. While the ujamaa program improves health care and education for rural populations, by the early 1990s farmers have reverted to individual farming practices, and the reputation of the ujamaa program is tarnished by claims of forced resettlement and authoritarian practices.

The Association of South East Asian Nations (ASEAN) is established at a meeting in Bangkok between the foreign ministers of Indonesia, the

1967 (*cont.*)   Philippines, Singapore, Malaysia, and Thailand. The Association's goals focus on the economic, social, and cultural progress of the Southeast Asian region. Two years later, ASEAN holds its first full-scale summit.

Famine in the Biafra region of northern Nigeria is exacerbated by an ongoing war between the Nigerian government and secessionists in Biafra. The government, like most repressive regimes, is hostile to foreign intervention and forbids international relief assistance. By the end of the famine in 1969, 1.5 million have died.

1968   The Canadian International Development Agency (CIDA) is established, replacing the External Affairs Office. The agency is quick to recognize the strength of nongovernmental organizations' work in development and funds Canadian-based organizations in its first year of operation. CIDA also develops an Institutional Cooperation and Development Services Program (ICDS), which encourages Canadian initiatives that contribute to human resource capacities in developing countries.

TechnoServe is founded in the conviction that most development programs to date have been offering paternalistic solutions to the Third World's problems. The agency offers "a working solution to world hunger," and aims to improve the well-being of the poor in developing countries through a process of enterprise development, providing management, technical assistance, and training.

Famine strikes the western Sahel region of Africa. Considered one of the worst catastrophes of the twentieth century in terms of human suffering and death, the famine lasts until 1974. During this time Lake Chad withdraws from its shores, becoming four segregated ponds. The Niger River becomes a stream in many places, receding in 1972 to its lowest point in 30 years. In Mali, 40 percent of the harvest of millet and sorghum, the staple crops, are lost in 1973. The famine also causes widespread ecological damage. By 1974, more than 100,000 have died from starvation or hunger-related diseases.

1969   The Overseas Development Council (ODC) is founded in an effort to foster understanding of "economic and social problems confronting developing countries and of the interests of the U.S. in their development process." The quality of the policy research and analysis issued by the ODC is quickly recognized, and the Council becomes an important resource for legislators, policymakers, and journalists.

The Pearson Commission publishes *Partners in Development*, a review of the First Development Decade. The commission was established in 1967 at the behest of the president of the World Bank, and was chaired by Lester Pearson, the former prime minister of Canada. Representatives from the United Kingdom, Brazil, the United States, Germany, Jamaica, and France comprise the commission, as well as experts in various fields of development. The report reviews the progress made in the 20 years of development assistance to the Third World and finds that progress has been slow and somewhat insignificant, caused in part by the rigidity of multilateral agencies such as the World Bank and USAID. The commission argues for increased aid to developing countries and helps to shape the agenda for the Second UN Development Decade.

The Bellagio Conference on agricultural development is held in Bellagio, Italy. This series of meetings and consultations ultimately leads to the creation of the Consultative Group on International Agricultural Research (CGIAR) in 1971, a group mandated to increase, coordinate, and improve the efficiency of financial and technical assistance in agricultural production.

The 1970s   Along with the world economy in general, the path of global development wandered indecisively in the 1970s. While some of the progress of the previous decade was consolidated or continued, the decade is probably most accurately remembered as the period when Southern aspirations began to collide with global economic and political reality.

For North and South alike, the defining economic event of the decade was the oil price shock of 1973. Oil was, and still is, the lifeblood of industry and development. The fourfold increase in prices signaled the end of uninterrupted economic growth in the West and the beginning of a less generous world order. Because Southern nations were dependent on oil for development, rising prices forced many to borrow heavily to underwrite petroleum purchases. Hence, the oil embargo sowed the seeds for the debt crisis of the 1980s. Meanwhile, many Third World nations found themselves increasingly reliant on the sale of agricultural products, called commodities, on the world market. So long as prices remained stable, so too did Southern economies. But developing nations were left vulnerable to market variations, which struck with a vengeance in the 1980s.

On the political front, the developing nations assumed a greater profile in the United Nations. But here too, the South encountered increasing resistance. The call of the Group of 77 for a new international economic order made little headway, and political turmoil in individual Southern nations, while often serving to overturn oppressive regimes, seldom paved the way to sustainable democracy or sustainable development.

1970   The Second UN Development Decade is announced on 24 October, the twenty-fifth anniversary of the United Nations. The General Assembly adopts an international development strategy for the decade, declaring that the "ultimate objective" is to bring about sustained improvement in the well-being of the individual and "bestow benefits to all." For the first time an official link is made between the environment and development, as the strategy affirms a commitment "to safeguard the environment." Emphasis is placed on the provision of aid; economically advanced countries are asked to contribute a minimum of 1 percent of GNP in financial transfers to developing countries by 1972, the majority of which should be in the form of overseas development assistance.

Earth Day is celebrated for first time on 22 April. Twenty million Americans take part in teach-ins and demonstrations for stronger laws to protect the environment.

Ester Boserup's *Women's Role in Economic Development* is published, bringing the issue of women in development into an international context. The publication of this book stimulates study and debate about women's economic and social roles around the world for the first time. Boserup exposes the human dimension of economic development and concentrates her study on the gender roles applied to various sectors, especially agricultural production. She argues that modernization has brought negative consequences for women because new technologies have devalued women's work.

1971   Bangladesh declares independence from Pakistan in March. Prior to this, Bangladesh had been one of five Pakistani provinces, known as East Pakistan. Tensions between the central government and East Pakistan had been ongoing and heightens in March when independence is declared. The Pakistani army immediately takes over the eastern province, and 9 million refugees from the new Bangladesh flee to India. The international community immediately recognizes Bangladesh as independent and its 1972 constitution is hailed as exemplary. However, it is not until 1974 that Pakistan surrenders and recognizes Bangladeshi independence. By the end of the war, 1 million people have lost their lives.

1971 (*cont.*) AFRICARE is founded by African and American leaders in response to the drought and famine sweeping West Africa.

Medicins Sans Frontièrs (MSF), or Doctors without Borders, is established in France as the world's largest medical emergency organization. Working on programs in nutrition, immunization, sanitation, and public health, MSF quickly establishes a sound reputation for providing effective and fast relief to emergency situations.

1972 United Nations Conference on the Human Environment, held in Stockholm, Sweden, in June, officially launches the international environmental movement. The rapid deterioration of the environment by air and water pollution, soil erosion, waste, noise, and other agents is the focus of attention at the conference. Representatives of 112 nations attend, with the goal of bringing to the attention of people and governments the evidence of man's damage to the natural environment, and to encourage and provide guidelines for action by governments and international organizations. The outcome of the conference is the Declaration on the Human Environment, the first acknowledgment by the community of nations that new principles of behavior and responsibility must govern relations with the environment. The conference also produces an Action Plan, consisting of over 100 recommendations calling on governments, UN agencies, and international organizations to cooperate in specific measures to deal with the wide range of environmental problems. Perhaps most significant of the conference's outcomes is the establishment of the United Nations Environment Programme (UNEP).

UNEP is created as a coordinating body to lead and direct environmental initiatives at the international level, tackling environmental issues that face both the developed and the developing world. It is also responsible for promoting environmental law, education, and training for the management of the environment. The UNEP's program encompasses the following areas: human settlements; human and environmental health; ecosystems; oceans and environmental development; natural disasters; energy; and other support activities. UNEP's Governing Council is composed of representatives from 58 countries and its headquarters are in Nairobi.

Limits to Growth is published, commissioned by the Club of Rome, an international association of scientists, educators, and leaders. The study focuses on the global trends in population, resource consumption, industrial output, and pollution. The international community reacts strongly to the report and it is recognized as an important warning of the dangers of unchecked growth in population, resource consumption, and levels of pollution.

The Bangladesh Rural Advancement Committee (BRAC) is founded by Fazle Abed to assist refugees of the war of liberation. BRAC goes on to embrace broader programs for development, including credit and rural development programs and health and education programs, and is now one of the most well-known Southern NGOs.

The Self Employed Women's Association (SEWA) is created in Ahmedabad, India, out of the Textile Labor Union. SEWA becomes the registered trade union of self-employed women workers, representing women who were not unionized under the Textile Labor Union, such as used-garment workers, handcart pullers, and street vendors with no economic security and no access to credit. SEWA addresses the multiple needs of these women by providing a variety of basic functions from legal aid to the establishment of a cooperative credit and savings facility.

1973   The Organization of Petroleum Exporting Countries (OPEC) sharply limits production and raises

1973 (*cont.*) oil prices fourfold. Developing and developed countries feel the pinch, and many Third World nations are forced to borrow money on international capital markets to buy oil so that development efforts can continue. The price shock thus sows the seeds for the debt crisis of the 1980s. Meanwhile, higher prices cause recession in the West, depressing international trade and aid, and more specifically, dampening demand for Southern exports. The uninterrupted upward trajectory of the post–World War II economy is thus abruptly altered.

Masses of village women embrace their trees to protect them from lumber contractors as the Chipko movement begins organizing against deforestation in the Uttarakhand region of the Indian Himalayas. Chipko, which literally means "hugging," is an environmental grassroots movement to foster preservation and conservation of India's forests. The movement's demands include replacement of the contract system of forest exploitation with forest-labor cooperatives, the provision of raw materials at concessionary rates to local forest-based industries, and a ban on the felling of trees in sensitive areas.

The World Bank announces a new "basic needs" approach to development that sets poverty, rather than economic growth, as its target. Studies by the development community show that increases in GNP do not necessarily lead to an improvement in living conditions; the poorest populations in countries with increasing GNP are still suffering from hunger, poverty, and neglect. World Bank president Robert McNamara described basic needs strategy as "provid[ing] better access for the absolute poor in their societies to essential public services, particularly basic education, primary health care, and clean water. These fundamental services . . . are the key to the poor's being able to meet their own basic needs." World Bank loans to support basic needs programs rise from 5 percent in 1968 to 30 percent in 1980.

The military government of General Augusto Pinochet comes to power in Chile, overthrowing Salvador Allende. The new regime reverses land reforms instituted during Allende's presidency, restoring enormous holdings to the country's wealthy. Pinochet introduces economic polices that are a radical departure from the development approaches of previous leaders, concentrating on privatization and foreign investment. Chile's economy experiences steady growth, with the exception of the recession of the early 1980s, and becomes known as the "Chilean miracle." Not surprisingly this miracle increases the gap between rich and poor; between 1968 and 1985 the share in GNP of the richest 205 Chileans increases from 47 percent to 60 percent. Pinochet remains in power until December 1989, when the first elections since 1973 are held and Patricio Aylwyn is elected.

1974   The Group of 77 sponsors the Declaration and Programme of Action on the Establishment of the New International Economic Order (NIEO) which the General Assembly readily adopts. The NIEO is based "on equity, sovereign equality, interdependence, common interest and cooperation among all States" and its main objective is to "correct inequalities and redress existing injustices." Among the goals of this program are to facilitate the development efforts of poor nations by changing unfair or inadequate rules in regard to trade and monetary affairs, and to promote more equal patterns of trade, technology flow, and communication. According to the Group of 77, the ultimate goal, to "eliminate the widening gap between developed and developing countries, will require the renegotiation of debt, improved terms of trade and more access to Northern technology." Many OPEC countries do not agree with this view and dismiss the NIEO as a Third World wish list. The UN, however, follows up in December with the adoption of the Charter of Economic Rights and Duties of States which reemphasizes the need for international

1974 (*cont.*) relations based on equity and sovereign equality. The NIEO, if nothing else, serves as a symbol of unity for the Group of 77 and as a widely heard articulation of their goals and frustrations.

The World Population Conference is held in Bucharest, Romania, in August and concentrates almost exclusively on the question of whether population growth is a contributing cause of underdevelopment. The conference, attended by representatives from 136 countries, adopts a World Population Plan of Action featuring policy recommendations and the findings of preconference symposia on population and development; population and the family; population, resources, and the environment; and population and human rights. The American delegation's recommendation for setting national goals for reduction in population is rejected and is accused of espousing "neo-Malthusian rhetoric." The correlation between women's increased education and participation in the labor force and declines in birthrates finally receives international recognition, and consensus is reached on the importance of improving the status of women.

Reaction to the extreme food shortages and shrinkage of global food stocks is voiced in November at the World Food Conference in Rome. Attended by representatives from 133 states, the conference leads to the creation of the World Food Council and International Fund for Agricultural Development (IFAD). The conference also adopts the Universal Declaration on the Eradication of Hunger and Malnutrition which identifies the "bold objective . . . that within a decade no child will go to bed hungry." The need for technological and financial aid to the Third World is articulated and all nations are called upon to take steps to stabilize world food markets, promote fair prices, and improve access to markets. Recommendations on food production objectives, the role of women in development, and agricultural and rural development priorities are also offered. The conference calls for the expansion of agricultural production by a minimum of 4 percent annually in developing countries, for at least 10 million tons of grain to be provided as food aid, and for world trade in food products to be expanded and liberalized.

International Fund for Agricultural Development (IFAD) is established following its proposal at the World Food Council, though it will not receive its first donor pledges and become operational until 1977. Composed of 143 country members, 21 of which are OECD countries, 12 of which are OPEC countries, and 110 of which are developing countries, IFAD is mandated to fund rural development programs specifically aimed at the poorest of the world's people. It is the only UN agency that focuses exclusively on the needs of small farmers and the rural poor. Since its inception, IFAD has played a catalytic role in the effort to tackle poverty alleviation from the grassroots level upwards. IFAD continuously explores new ways of mobilizing the poor and enlisting their participation, skills, and traditions in the struggle to attain food security.

The Worldwatch Institute is founded by Lester Brown to conduct research on a range of issues including population trends, renewable energy, and food and agriculture, with the goal of fostering public understanding of global environment threats. In 1984, the Worldwatch Institute publishes its first *State of the World* report, a global assessment of the earth's sustainability.

The Percy Amendment (named after Senator Charles Percy) is added to the 1961 Foreign Assistance Act and mandates a shift in development assistance policies to give particular attention to those programs, projects, and activities which "tend to integrate women into the national economies of foreign countries, thus improving their status and assisting the total development effort." As a result of

1974 (*cont.*)   this amendment, USAID creates an office of Women in Development.

1975   International Women's Year is inaugurated at the World Conference for Women in Mexico City. The conference focuses on "Equality, Development and Peace," and proposes recommendations for the upcoming 10 years, which is declared the International Decade for Women. The conference succeeds in demonstrating that women are prepared to speak out on their own behalf.

The Lome Convention is signed in Togo, between the European Economic Community and 59 developing countries in Africa, the Caribbean, and the Pacific. The goal of the Convention is to help stabilize earnings from commodities exported to the European Community and to protect developing economies from vacillating world market prices. There have been two additional conventions since 1975, one in 1979 and another in 1985.

1976   The Grameen Bank is started in Bangladesh by Muhammed Yunus, a professor of economics, who experiments with providing credit to the landless poor. Yunus begins the bank by lending his own money to anyone with an income-earning venture to see whether the loans would be repaid. The bank offers small start-up loans with low interest rates which foster the entrepreneurial spirit in the establishment of such activities as paddy husking and dairying. Repayment rates are over 95 percent, and the bank expands rapidly. Borrowers, who are largely illiterate and mostly women, are organized into small groups and repay their loans on a weekly basis. By 1979, the Grameen Bank receives capital from the national Bank of Bangladesh, and in 1983 IFAD offers $3.4 million at 3 percent interest to assist the bank in its expansion from 83 branches to a targeted 17,000 in 1995. IFAD also persuades the Norwegian Agency for Development, the Ford

Foundation, and Swedish International Development Agency to allocate an additional $15 million.

"Club du Sahel" is created in Dakar by a number of member countries of OECD to channel assistance to countries of the Sahel region repeatedly plagued by famine-causing droughts. The aim is to administer and organize aid programs more effectively than is possible through bilateral country agreements.

UN Conference on Human Settlements is held in Vancouver, Canada, in June to review the state of the world's human settlements. As a result of the conference, the UN Centre for Human Settlements (also known as Habitat) is set up in Nairobi, and also includes the Centre for Housing and Building. The Habitat International Council, made up of NGOs and community-based organizations from around the world, is also set up this same year.

1977   The Green Belt Movement is started by the National Council of Women of Kenya, under the leadership of Dr. Wangari Maathai. The primary goal of the movement is to establish "green belts" in each community, with at least 1,000 trees planted on open spaces, in school grounds, and along roads. This grassroots organization quickly establishes itself as an influential environmental movement that concentrates on the planting of indigenous trees. Tree planting becomes a national passion shared by the news media, political leaders, schools, and Kenya's 6,000 women's groups.

UN Conference on Desertification, sponsored by the UNEP, meets in Nairobi and warns of an increase in arid land. This conference is considered one of the best the UN has organized in terms of scientific data and explanation of an issue. Desertification is described as the conversion of productive land into wasteland by human mismanagement. The important point is made that desertification is a symptom, not a cause, of poor

1977 (*cont.*) agricultural development and declining yields. A Plan for Action to Combat Desertification is adopted by the representatives of 95 nations, 50 UN bodies, and 65 non-governmental bodies.

UN Water Conference is held in Mar Del Plata, Argentina, in recognition that one-fifth of the world's urban population and four-fifths of the rural population lack adequate clean drinking water. The World Health Organization estimates that 80 percent of all sickness and disease in the world is attributable to inadequate access to water or sanitation, and UNICEF argues that the infant mortality rate could be halved if there was accessible safe water and sanitation worldwide. The Water Conference announces 1981 to 1990 to be the International Drinking Water Supply and Sanitation Decade with the goal of "clean drinking water and adequate sanitation for all by 1990." During this decade, water will become the focal point of many integrated rural development projects. The Decade Action Guide is produced to urge governments to use the appropriate technologies in management of water supplies.

The Independent Commission on International Development Issues is formed with former West German chancellor, Willy Brandt, serving as chairperson. Twenty diplomats from five continents set out to "suggest ways of promoting adequate solutions to the problems involved in development and in attacking absolute poverty." In 1980, the commission issues *North-South: A Program for Survival* calling for cooperation in trade, investment, and monetary relations in a package similar to that proposed in the New International Economic Order. This influential report summarizes the crisis facing the South and confirms that the structures in the international economic system work against the South and reproduce relationships of inequality. The commission recommends an action program of emergency and long-term measures, including a re-vamped system of food security to avert famine. Brandt and his colleagues also suggest the development of a Common Fund for stabilizing the prices of commodities, industrial adjustment policies with a view of removing projectionist barriers, and an international code of conduct for sharing technology. The thrust of the report's argument is that the South needs to have more participation in decision making, and it is in the North's interests to help rectify the existing inequalities and contribute to the development of the South.

1978   In Nicaragua, opposition against the dictator, Anastasio Somoza, is mounting following the assassination of the editor of *La Prensa*, the opposition newspaper. While neither the government nor the National Guard is believed to be guilty of the killing, the assassination strengthens the support of the Sandinista National Liberation Front (FSLN). A national strike shuts down 80 percent of the stores and factories in major towns in its first week. Demands for Somoza's immediate resignation come from a variety of sources, including the Catholic Church, business leaders, rural populations, and, of course the FSLN. In August, the Sandinistas seize the National Palace, holding members of the Congress hostage until their demands are met. Among their demands are the release of prisoners, publication of a series of FSLN communiqués, and $10 million in cash. The siege ends almost 48 hours after it began as thousands of people line the streets to cheer the rebels as they drive out of the city to catch planes to Panama, Venezuela, and Cuba. Less than a year later, Somoza agrees to resign in exchange for asylum in the United States, and a *junta* government replaces the regime that had controlled Nicaragua for over 40 years. The number of people who died in the insurrection from September 1978 to July 1979 is estimated, by the Red Cross, to be over 10,000, 90 percent of whom were civilians.

1979   World Conference on Agrarian Reform and Rural Development (WCARRD) is held in July at FAO headquarters in Rome. The conference marks a turning point in development planning by encouraging developing countries to examine their individual conditions, identify target groups, and formulate plans tailored to their own needs rather than replicating Western policies and recommendations. Governments of developed and developing countries are urged to take steps to ensure more equitable access of farmers to land, rural services, and inputs, and to refrain from new trade barriers. Program recommendations include land reform, increased participation, fairer prices, and increased employment in rural areas. "Growth with equity and participation" is the goal of the conference and the WCARRD Programme of Action emphasizes the need to expand and improve basic services that have a direct bearing on agricultural production. This meeting also represents the first time an intergovernmental conference gives serious consideration to the special needs of rural women and calls for their integration in development.

In El Salvador, the military stages a coup in October that overthrows General Humberto Romero, curbing, at least temporarily, the power of the economic elite. In 1979, six Salvadoran families held more land than 133,000 small farmers.[1] The civilian-military junta institutes a series of redistributive measures, such as a land reform program and the nationalization of the banks and coffee marketing system. Meanwhile, rebel groups begin to mobilize as the Farabundo Marti Front for National Liberation (FMLN) coalition and by January 1981 will launch a guerrilla war. The guerrillas' principal demand is a fundamental redressing of the inequalities of the economic and political systems. The government perceives the growing tendency of rural peasants to organize into unions and cooperatives as a threat, and intimidation and violence become widespread. A 1984 USAID study found that one-third of the applicants in the first phase of the agrarian reform program were not farming the land because they had been threatened, evicted, or "disappeared." The civil war will last for the next six years and will claim approximately 75,000 lives and force an estimated 1 million people to flee the country.

After six years of fierce oppression by the Khmer Rouge of Kampuchea (Cambodia), famine strikes the region. The civil war of 1970–1975, followed by the brutal rule of the Khmer Rouge, had already cost approximately 1.5 million lives. By October the Indochina Refugee Action Center is reporting that 80 percent of the children are suffering from the severest form of malnutrition and only approximately 5 percent of the rice paddies are in cultivation. In November, President Carter issues a proclamation designating each Saturday and Sunday until Thanksgiving as days for Americans to donate money to the Cambodian relief cause in their places of worship.

The UN General Assembly adopts the Convention on the Elimination of All Forms of Discrimination against Women, the result of the work of the Commission on the Status of Women. By 1991 the convention is signed by over 100 countries. The convention addresses and protects the natural rights of women, as well as their social and cultural rights. Governments are obligated to modify social and cultural patterns that are based on the idea of "inferiority or superiority of either of the sexes or on stereotyped roles for men and women."

The 1980s   The tragic decade in the history of contemporary global development, the 1980s have rightly earned the appellation of development's lost decade. The debt crisis that exploded on the world stage in 1982 heralded the sharp reversal of Southern fortunes. Within a matter of years, developing countries were sending more wealth to the North in the form of

The 1980s
(*cont.*) interest payments than they were receiving in continuing investment and assistance. Meanwhile, tumbling commodity prices meant that Third World revenues dropped precipitously. The collective impact was that governments and agencies had fewer resources to invest in human development. Education and health programs were slashed or eliminated everywhere in the South, along with food security measures and poverty reduction efforts.

Tragedies of human and natural origin exacerbated the fiscal crisis. Drought coincided with civil conflict to loose a devastating famine upon Ethiopia; two years of hunger and starvation finally shocked the world's conscience and spurred a massive humanitarian response in 1985. Floods in Bangladesh and earthquakes in Latin America were among the most destructive in a remorseless series of natural disasters. The AIDS virus struck Africa with punishing force, further eroding the human capital of the continent.

The collapse of the Berlin Wall at decade's end seemed to signal a turning of fortune for growth and Southern development. But even the potential "peace dividend" expected at the end of the cold war represented an ambiguous benefit for the developing world; as the global competition of the superpowers waned, so too did the West's strategic interest in nourishing developing nations. A "lost decade," indeed—while international interest and aid receded, living standards fell, incomes stagnated, and the signs of misery increased all across the South.

1980 Another International Development Strategy is drawn up for the Third United Nations Development Decade. In this plan, the General Assembly demands that specific targets be reached on a number of international issues including trade, monetary reform, and aid. According to the General Assembly, developed countries should aim to contribute 0.7 percent of their GNP by 1985, and developing countries should set a target for annual growth in gross domestic product of 7 percent. These goals would prove to be wildly unrealistic in coming years of recession and debt. This decade does, however, witness environmental issues becoming embedded in many development policies.

In February, the World Bank, Inter-American Development Bank, Asian Development Bank, African Development Fund, and six other multinational development agencies sign the Declaration of Environmental Policies and Procedures Relating to Economic Development. The banks pledge to institute assessment and evaluation measures to the projects they fund to protect and enhance environmental resources. Unfortunately these environmental assessments will prove to be little more than window dressing for most projects, and guidelines are, for the most part, ignored.

Zimbabwe gains independence and ushers in a government committed to aggressive social and economic change. Neighboring South Africa, threatened by the positive example being set by the Zimbabwean government, engages in direct sabotage of Zimbabwe's equipment and infrastructure. The postindependence government, however, succeeds in making a smooth transition to black majority rule. The government honors its promise of no expropriation of white farms, reassuring the white community that it is welcome to work within the new democratic framework. While there is no redistribution of land, the government places priority on social spending for the communal lands that are home to most of the black community. Between 1982 and 1988, the government dramatically expands primary health care programs in rural areas and improves its supportive price policy to the benefit of smallholders in communal lands.

The Lagos Plan of Action is announced by the UN Economic Commission for Africa and the

1980 (*cont.*)   Organization for African Unity. This plan for African development seeks to overcome the current situation through a combination of domestic self-reliance and external support. A principal objective of the plan is the progressive integration within Africa, leading to the creation of an African Economic Community by the end of the century. The OAU is responsible for the Plan's implementation and assists in setting a goal for the continent to reach 1 percent of world industrial output by 1985 and 2 percent by 2000. In 1988, the figure remained less than .5 percent and the OAU dropped the Plan at its 1985 conference stating that the Plan had failed "not because of [its] objectives or general strategy, but because Africa was unable to mobilize the means for their achievement."[2]

The Refugee Act is passed in the United States, bringing its laws and regulations into compliance with international refugee standards. The act endorses the international definition of a refugee as someone with a "well-founded fear of persecution." The act abolishes parts of previous law that accorded potential refugees preferences on geographical or ideological grounds.

Mid-Decade for Women Conference is held in July in Copenhagen to discuss progress made thus far in the UN Decade for Women. Equality is defined as not just a legal issue, but also as equality of participation in development, as beneficiaries and as agents. Governments are urged to support women's groups, to establish commissions to assess women's rights, and to increase the number of women in public office.

The Southern Africa Development Coordination Conference is held in Zambia and attended by heads of state from Angola, Botswana, Lesotho, Malawi, Mozambique, Swaziland, Tanzania, Zimbabwe, and Zambia. The aim of the conference is to lessen economic dependence on South Africa and encourage self-reliance.

1981   World Food Day (WFD) is created by the member nations of the FAO with the purpose of focusing attention on all food and farm problems. It is sponsored jointly by the FAO, national governments, and the NGO community. A small observance of World Food Day is held on 16 October, the anniversary of the FAO's founding, at the headquarters of the U.S. Department of Agriculture in Washington. By 1988, WFD is observed in 150 nations and in the U.S. it has the support of over 400 sponsoring organizations.

UNHCR wins its second Nobel Peace Prize for its work with Asian refugees.

Poverty and Famines by Amartya Sen is published, shedding new light on the study of famines. Sen argues that it is lack of "entitlement to food," and not food shortages, that causes famines. Sen identifies factors such as insufficient land, low wages, unemployment, or low prices for produce as failures of "entitlement." Sen exposes the role of economic and political roots of famine, pointing to periods of food shortages in which famine was averted because access to food, however limited the supply, was maintained.

The World Bank issues its *Berg Commission Report* (officially entitled *Accelerated Development in Sub-Saharan Africa: An Agenda for Action*), which addresses the severe economic and developmental problems in Africa. Standing in sharp contrast to the Lagos Plan's self-reliance model, the Berg Report offers recommendations that emphasize an export-led growth strategy for Africa. The report is sharply critical of African governments for their failures to design policies for economic growth, attributing Africa's problems to failed domestic policies, such as overvalued exchange rates,

1981 (*cont.*) inappropriate pricing policies, and excessive state intervention. The report proposes greater emphasis on production for export; cutting wages; and charging fees for state services such as education, health care, water, and electricity. Many Africans respond negatively to the report's down-playing of the role of external factors in the crisis. During the 1980s, the bank will condition new loans to developing countries on their implementing Structural Adjustment Programs along the lines suggested in the *Berg Report*.

1982 The Mexican government announces that it can no longer make interest or principal payments on its foreign debt, heralding the emergence of the broader international debt crisis. Nation after Southern nation, saddled with heavy debt and suffering from low prices on global commodity markets, follows Mexico's lead. The solvency of international banks is threatened, and traditional sources of capital for the South dry up. The nations of Latin America hold the greatest debt and are the first affected; but within a few years, many African nations find themselves unable to meet their debt obligations and suffering from lack of capital. The crisis dominates the decade, and while banks write off substantial amounts, Southern nations will pay millions of dollars to Northern banks and multilateral agencies.

The Working Group on Indigenous Populations is set up as part of the UN Commission for Human Rights in Geneva with the mandate to review governments' policies toward indigenous populations and to prepare a draft of a Universal Declaration of the Rights of Indigenous People. Within two years the General Assembly establishes a Voluntary Fund for Indigenous Populations, which allows indigenous representatives from all over the world to travel to Geneva to report, testify, and debate the issues involved.

In the face of mounting debt and strict adjustment policies demanded by the IMF, developing countries are spending less than ever on health services. As a result, malnutrition, low birthrates, and child deaths are on the rise among the poor. In response, UNICEF launches its maternal and child health care program with the aim of cutting in half the death rate in children under five and women of child-bearing age by the next decade. Among the basic elements of the program are growth monitoring, breast feeding, oral rehydration therapy (ORT), and immunization. ORT and immunization are the lowest-cost public health weapons ever designed and are capable of overcoming a group of illnesses which are responsible for more than half of all child deaths. Egypt is one of the first countries to put the oral rehydration therapy into action on a nation-wide scale.

In Ethiopia, crops fail in the northern provinces of Eritrea and Tigray due to lack of adequate rains. Development practitioners recognize the growing possibility of an impending famine but the Ethiopian government, Western governments, and the media ignore the warning signs. As the famine intensifies in the coming months the Ethiopian government argues that it is caused by drought and soil degradation. However, research has indicated that the most significant causes of famine in Ethiopia were official government policies. The organization Cultural Survival undertakes the largest and most systematic research on the causes of the famine and finds that government taxes had stripped peasant producers of any food security they might have had, and the artificially low price for food crops set by the government had led many farmers to leave their crops in the field. Even the natural causes of the famine, such as the drought which lasts through 1985, were exacerbated by government policies.[3]

1983   The World Commission on Environment and Development is established by the UNEP and headed

1983 (*cont.*) by Gro Harlem Brundtland, prime minister of Norway. The Brundtland Commission is asked to formulate a "global agenda for change" that will reexamine the critical environmental and development issues and formulate realistic proposals to solve them. During its five years of working on its report, the commission, composed of representatives from 21 nations, holds public hearings on each continent and comes to focus on the central theme of how development can serve next century's world of twice as many people relying on the same environmental resources. The report, entitled *Our Common Future,* is published in April 1987.

U.S. President Ronald Reagan launches the Caribbean Basin Initiative to promote free trade and free enterprise with the goal of enhancing economic development in the Caribbean region. The Initiative is also introduced for security reasons, motivated by U.S. fears of the emergence of Nicaragua as a Marxist country. Under the terms of the Initiative, the 22 participating nations of the Caribbean are granted duty-free access to U.S. markets. However, from 1984 to 1987 exports to the United States decline. In 1987, the Gibbons-Pickle Bill extends the agreement to 2007 and increases sugar quotas.

Drought returns to the Sahel region of Africa. Over the next two years the numbers of "drought affected" regions continue to multiply as famine sweeps the continent once again. Chad, Mali, and Niger experience the worst droughts in their histories. However, policymakers from multilateral and nongovernmental organizations are beginning to argue that drought need not lead to famine; World Bank senior vice president Ernest Stern states "famine is not only the result of inadequate rainfall. The effects of drought . . . are the results of long-term trends."[4]

The second UN International Conference on Population is held in Mexico City in August. Among the issues discussed are social and economic policy, health care, abortion, and family planning. The U.S. delegate to the conference (Senator James Buckley) announces that U.S. population policy will place primacy on sound economic policies based on free markets. The United States pledges to continue to fund family planning programs as a "small part" of its total development assistance. The U.S. position is reflective of President Reagan's position on abortion; the position paper reads: "The U.S. does not consider abortion an acceptable element of family planning programs and will no longer contribute to those of which it is a part."[5] As a result of this position, the U.S. government prohibits USAID from funding the two largest international family planning organizations: International Planned Parenthood Federation and the United Nations Population Fund. Other delegations emphasize the significance of the "women in development" problem in population; female delegates from such countries as Zimbabwe and Australia note the connections between high fertility rates and the lack of education, health care, and employment opportunities for women.

1984   The American Council for Voluntary International Action (InterAction) is established as a broadly based membership association of over 100 organizations working in international development, humanitarian and emergency relief, and development education.

The Ethiopian famine finally receives international attention in October when footage showing residents of a refugee camp in northern Ethiopia is aired in the United States and Europe. Overnight, Ethiopia becomes a major news story and the international symbol of suffering and starvation. From October to January, more money is raised, publicly and privately, than during any emergency humanitarian effort in history. The UN opens its Office of Emergency Operations in Ethiopia (UNEOE) to

1984 (*cont.*)   facilitate the collaboration of all UN agencies, African governments, and nongovernmental organizations. The UNEOE immediately dispatches field monitors to try to locate food shipments and correct abuses. NGOs expand operations dramatically as their national governments channel as much aid as possible through them to avoid a bilateral arrangement that would enable the Ethiopian government to use aid as a weapon of war. Despite well-known tensions between the Ethiopian and U.S. governments, by April 1985, the United States is the largest single donor in the worldwide effort, with its position summarized by USAID director: "A starving child knows no politics."

On 1 October USAID launches a congressionally mandated child survival program mirrored on UNICEF's Child Survival Campaign. Congress also creates the Child Survival Fund, designating additional primary health resources for poor mothers and children in developing countries. Congressional earmarks for child survival programs grow from $0 in 1984 to $275 million in 1993.

DAWN (Development Alternatives with Women for a New Era), a network of Southern women activists, scholars, and policymakers, is established to offer strategies of development, free from all forms of discrimination. With the Decade for Women drawing to a close, DAWN argues that the approach of merely integrating women into existing economic and social structures has failed. DAWN's platform document, entitled *Development, Crises and Alternative Visions: Third World Women's Perspectives*, is published in time to have a profound effect at the Nairobi Conference marking the end of the Decade for Women, the following year.

A group of Ireland's and the UK's most well known pop stars organize under the name Band Aid and record the song "Do They Know It's Christmas/Feed the World" to raise money for victims of the Ethiopian famine. The record sells more than three million copies in the UK alone, becoming the best-selling record ever. Over $10 million is raised for relief efforts, as well as for long-term development work. Other artists follow Band Aid's example, the most notable being North American artists who form U.S.A. for Africa and record the song "We Are the World" in January 1985. Money raised is allocated for immediate relief in Africa and for the creation of long-term development policies. Ten percent of the funds are allocated for combating hunger and homelessness in the United States. The following summer (1985) the two groups stage a 16-hour international concert, Live Aid, which raises over $100 million from public contributions and $3 billion from pledges from donor governments.

1985   Geneva Conference on the African Emergency is held in March to provide information about the ongoing emergency needs of Africa to the international donor community. Representatives from 125 countries attend.

The World Conference to Review and Appraise the Achievements of the United Nations Decade for Women meets in July in Nairobi, marking the end of the UN Decade for Women. The conference is attended by over 14,000 women and men from around the world. Southern activists argue that the Decade for Women marked a step backward rather than an improvement for women. The decade is credited, however, with heightening awareness of the contributions of women in development, as well as the needs unique to women. A wealth of research and information on women's roles in various development-related sectors was also gathered during this period. Organizations formed during the decade include the International Research and Training Institute for the Advancement of Women (INSTRAW) in 1976 and the International Center for Research on Women (ICRW). These organizations

1985 (*cont.*)   serve as catalysts to promote the full participation of women, as well as to improve the quality of information on women in development. Perhaps the most valuable contribution of the UN Decade for Women is the opportunity it provided women to gather together, network, and mobilize for change.

The UN Development Fund for Women (UNIFEM) becomes an autonomous body within the UN to provide technical and financial aid to women's initiatives in developing countries. Originally set up in 1976 as the Voluntary Fund for the UN Decade for Women, UNIFEM is dedicated to empowerment of women in their struggle for equality, development, and peace.

"Days of tranquillity" silence the guns in El Salvador for three days as government troops and guerrillas allow teams from the Ministry of Health and the International Red Cross to vaccinate nearly a quarter of a million children. The two sides agree to another brief cease-fire the following year, and 140,000 children and 77,000 women are vaccinated. This initiative spurs the idea that child health could be a "bridge to peace" in the troubled region of Central America.

1986   The International Fund for Agricultural Development (IFAD) launches a $300 million Special Programme for Sub-Saharan African Countries Affected by Drought and Desertification. The program is designated to assist those countries struck by drought and famine in 1983–1985. Short-term interventions assist in the rehabilitation of smallholders' agricultural production while long-term initiatives focus on the environment and institutional components.

Fears that the multilateral trading system was seen to be weakening are exacerbated by a period of stagnation in world trade. In an attempt to strengthen the system, the so-called Uruguay

Round negotiations begin in the Uruguayan city of Punta del Este in September. The Uruguay Round aims to bring about further liberalization and expansion of world trade by improving access to markets through reducing or eliminating tariff and nontariff barriers. These multilateral trade negotiations are the most ambitious to date and include the participation of 117 countries, with extensive involvement of developing countries. After continuous negotiations that span 8 years, the Uruguay Round finally comes into effect in January 1995 with implementation (such as the establishment of the World Trade Organization, which will replace GATT) spread over the next 10 years. While overall global trade should be enhanced, the treaty's benefits for the global South are much less certain.

The Institute for Natural Resources in Africa is founded to strengthen national institutions in Africa, to help attract African scientists who studied abroad back to their native countries, and in general, to help provide the African scientists with the necessary framework to allow for high quality research.

The UN Program of Action for Africa is announced. This four-year program involves the mutual commitments by African countries, which promise to undertake economic reforms, and donor nations who commit to provide sustained assistance including balance of payment support.

1987   World Bank creates a Women in Development division to address the needs of women and to incorporate them into development programs. The bank places a coordinator for women in development in each of its four regional complexes and engages in such efforts as the launching of research on women's agricultural productivity in Africa (financed by the UNDP); an international initiative to provide "safe motherhood"; and increasing the number of projects that include actions specifically

1987 (*cont.*) addressed to women. By 1989, the share of women's participation and involvement in World Bank agricultural projects has increases from 9 percent in the years previous to 1987, to 30 percent.

In August, the seven Central American presidents sign the Esquipulas II Agreement, or the "Arias Peace Plan," in Guatemala City. The peace plan provides a comprehensive settlement of Central America's conflicts and includes provisions for the repatriation of refugee populations. Each government agrees to declare a cease-fire, open negotiations with unarmed opposition groups, restore civil rights, and hold free elections. The plan also encourages Central American governments to work together on regional economic development and trade, reinforced through ongoing meetings of the region's economic ministers. The following year a UN General Assembly resolution establishes the Special Plan of Economic Cooperation for Central America. Costa Rican president, Oscar Arias, who was instrumental in bringing about the peace agreement, wins the 1987 Nobel Peace Prize.

The South Commission, a group of representatives from developing countries who examine strategies for political cooperation among Third World nations, holds its inaugural meeting in Geneva in October, chaired by Julius Nyerere, former president of Tanzania. The group emphasizes self-reliance and the collective responsibility of the South for its own development. In 1990, the commission publishes *The Challenge to the South*, a comprehensive report that looks at development from a Southern perspective.

UNICEF publishes *Adjustment with a Human Face*, which examines structural adjustment policies from the point of view of their effect on the poor. Its overall conclusion is that standards of health and education have declined in many countries where adjustment policies have been in effect. Instead of current policies that usually include cuts in government expenditure, currency devaluation, and privatization of state-owned assets, UNICEF proposes "adjustment with a human face." Alternatives are available, the report argues, as long as governments and the international community make the commitment to protect the poorest while working to restore economic growth. The resounding message of the report that "no adjustment policy is acceptable which allows children to be sacrificed for the sake of financial stability" gains wide support among scholars, policymakers, and other UN agencies.

1988   A major flood in Bangladesh causes the deaths of several thousand people from water-borne diseases and starvation. Mounting evidence points to environmental damage in neighboring Nepal and India as exacerbating the problem. Food reserves are destroyed and farmers are forced to mortgage land as collateral against loans from private moneylenders. The government's response proves to be much more efficient in handling the crisis than it was with the floods of 1973. Bangladesh now has a food grain monitoring system and the government takes a more active role in stabilizing grain prices.

1989   The UN Economic Commission for Africa (ECA) introduces its report, *African Alternative Framework to Structural Adjustment Programmes,* where it proposes "structural transformation" in place of structural adjustment. This alternative approach relies on a human-centered strategy of economic recovery involving an end to subsidies, except for social programs and key industries. The ECA, headed by Dr. Adebayo Adedeji, urges African nations to shift their emphasis away from export-led development, reduce military spending, guarantee minimum prices for food crops, and implement land reform. Emphasis is placed on the need to keep human development at the forefront of development.

1989 (*cont.*)   In response to the ECA's report, the World Bank publishes *From Crisis to Sustainable Growth*, a thorough analysis of the African economic situation. This report, written with significant input from African economists, evaluates the past ten years of structural adjustment policies (SAPs) and acknowledges their limited success. The bank argues that SAPs should continue, but with "broadened and deepened special measures . . . to alleviate poverty and protect the vulnerable."[6] The report calls for many of the same "transformations" urged by the ECA's report, such as human-centered development, agriculture as the primary foundation for growth, enhanced intra-African trade, and involvement of the populace in the planning and implementation of development programs. The common priorities articulated by these two reports is a hopeful sign for a consensus of views on African development.

The Brady Plan is announced in March by U.S. Treasury Secretary Nicholas Brady as a possible solution to the international debt crisis. The plan proposes the introduction of official collateral from the IMF, the World Bank, the Inter-American Development Bank, and the Japanese government in exchange for a reduction in bank claims. In this way, banks can keep the same expected value of repayment by accepting greater security in exchange for lower claims. Debtor countries are asked to follow sound economic policies and encourage the return of flight capital, aided by creditor governments reducing regulatory impediments to debt relief. Creditor banks are called on to work with debtor countries to provide "a broader range of alternatives for financial support." Restoration of confidence, evidenced by resuming flows of private capital, is a central goal of the plan. The plan's primary objective is to avoid an international financial crisis through the restoration of the debtor countries' access to voluntary capital markets and the achievement of reasonable growth in debtor countries. In the case of Mexico, the Brady Plan includes an agreement that restructures Mexico's debt; in essence, the banks agree to write off 35 percent of Mexico's debt in return for assurances that the remaining 65 percent would be honored.

The UN negotiates an agreement between the warring factions of Sudan's civil war, who for years had been using food aid as a weapon for war by obstructing food production. The agreement, called Operation Lifeline Sudan, allows for the delivery of humanitarian supplies to both factions of the war. Both the government and the armed opposition—the Sudan People's Liberation Movement—permit the passage of food and other humanitarian assistance through "corridors of tranquility." For six months, Operation Lifeline facilities the flow of aid and distributes over 100,000 tons of food aid to displaced persons. This effort marks one of the first times humanitarian assistance is delivered to the needy in the midst of a civil war, regardless of where they were located or by whom they were governed.

In September, after an 11-year occupation, Vietnamese troops withdraw from Cambodia, leaving the Hanoi-installed Heng Samrin regime in power. Despite the withdrawal, the Khmer Rouge continues to carry out a "holy war" against the Vietnamese, accusing Vietnam of keeping more than one million disguised soldiers and civilian settlers in Cambodia. The Khmer Rouge, based in refugee camps along the border in Thailand, begin to take control of territory in northern Cambodia.

After ten years of consultations involving governments, UN agencies, and 50 NGOs, the Convention on the Rights of Children is brought before the UN General Assembly for adoption. The convention aims to set universal standards for the defense of

1989 (*cont.*)   children against neglect, exploitation, and abuse, and applies to three main areas of children's rights: survival, development, and protection. The document brings together in one comprehensive code the legal benefits and stipulations concerning children. Today, the convention has been signed by 178 countries and is the most widely ratified human rights treaty in history.

Advocates, planners, and scientists from 14 countries meet in Bellagio, Italy, in November to discuss the effects of the end of the cold war on the struggle against hunger and poverty. The group concludes that it is possible to end half the world's hunger by the year 2000. The Bellagio Declaration, a set of achievable goals accompanied by the means of achievement, is drawn up as a result of this meeting. World leaders are urged to strive toward four main objectives: to end deaths from famine, to end hunger in half of the poorest households, to cut malnutrition in half for mothers and small children, and to eradicate iodine and vitamin A deficiencies. These are identified as realistic goals that "can end half of world hunger in the 1990s."

The 1990s   At mid-decade, there is still reason to hope that the 1990s will bring the return of sustained and sustainable development to the global South. Recent years have brought a number of highly visibile calamities to the developing world, most notably in Somalia in 1993 and Rwanda in 1994. But the development community, in North and South alike, seems to be learning important lessons about the role of conflict in derailing development, about the role of nongovernmental organizations in resolving conflict and facilitating reconciliation, and about the necessity of a truly global partnership to resolve development problems that ultimately menace people everywhere.

However, the mid-1990s have witnessed a rising tide of nationalism and introspection in many Western nations, with concomitant reductions in international aid and restrictions in immigration and asylum policies. As our chronology reaches the present, it shows development at a crossroads on the eve of the next millennium. The goals articulated as World War II closed remain as compelling now as then, and a half-century's experience leaves us better prepared to engage effectively our collective problems. The challenge of development figures prominently in the agenda of the global tomorrow.

1990   Fourth UN Development Decade is declared the decade of Human Development. The UN Committee for Development announces that people should be placed firmly in the center of development, adding that "the process of economic development is coming increasingly to be understood as a process of expanding the capabilities of people." The reduction of absolute poverty, protecting the environment, and economic growth continue to be the strategic priorities for this decade.

In April, the Sudanese government allows a large new UN relief effort to begin operations in the drought-stricken northwest region. Known as the Special United Nations 1991 Drought Operation, or SUNDOS, it links relief with development. The $15 million program is unlike previous relief efforts in that it is not simply a provision of free food. Instead, it is engaged in such activities as digging wells, installing latrines, rehabilitating schools and hospitals, and training in basic health and hygiene techniques, such as the use of oral rehydration salts (ORS).

On 2 August, Iraq invades Kuwait, leading to the Persian Gulf War, which has been called the "most destructive war" since 1945.[7] The war, which officially begins with the U.S.-led Operation Desert Storm in January 1991, results in one of the largest movements of civilians in the shortest periods of time and leads to unprecedented environmental de-

1990 (*cont.*)   struction. Roughly 600 Kuwaiti oil wells are set on fire during the conflict, blazing for up to nine months. The burning oil emits a 15,000-square-kilometer cloud of smoke, soot, and toxic carcinogenic chemicals. The war lasts only 43 days though its physical, social, and environmental consequences continue to be felt for years.

UNICEF holds the World Summit for Children at UN headquarters in New York in September. Leaders from 71 nations set out their agenda for the next 10 years: reducing the main childhood diseases; halving the number of severely malnourished children; reducing by one-third the number of deaths in children under five; educating at least 80 percent of children; halving of maternal mortality rates; increasing immunization coverage for 90 percent of the world's children; providing access to safe water and sanitation for all families; and providing basic education for all children. In total, 27 specific goals are agreed upon and eventually endorsed by over 150 heads of state.

UNDP issues its first annual *Human Development Report*, placing people, not figures, at the center of development. The report sparks lively debates and influences planning in countries that introduce human development concepts into their national plans and budgets.

1991   On 30 September the Haitian army overthrows Haiti's first freely elected president, Jean Bertrand Aristide, in a military coup. The army sets out to repress the once vibrant civil society by targeting all forms of independent association. Popular organizations, the independent media, the church, and anyone else who brings together previously powerless people are a target for the army's brutality and violence. In December, member nations of the Organization of American States (OAS), including the United States, impose an embargo on Haiti, resulting in the loss of approximately 140,000 Haitian jobs. By December 1993, 42,576 Haitians have fled by boat and are interdicted by the U.S. Coast Guard, while thousands of others have fled overland to the Dominican Republic.

In October, the UN Peace Plan for Cambodia is signed in Paris by 19 nations and the 4 Cambodian factions, including the Khmer Rouge. The plan calls for disarmament, democratic elections, and the repatriation of the nearly 370,000 refugees living in Thailand.

In Somalia, the ongoing conflict takes a dramatic turn when at least 30,000 people are killed in fighting between factions of the ruling party, beginning in November. By mid-1992, the UN estimates that 2,000 to 5,000 Somalis are dying each day from war and hunger-related diseases. Most humanitarian organizations refuse to operate in the country until it is safe.

1992   In January, the warring factions of El Salvador's 12-year civil war sign a peace accord, reached under the auspices of the UN. The leftist guerrillas of the FMLN disarm their 8,000 fighters and become a legal party. In return, the right-wing Arena government, led by President Alfredo Cristiani, halves the strength of the armed forces. The UN monitors the implementation of the peace accords, including the cease-fire and the creation of a new civilian police force. In November, thousands of secret American documents are released in Washington relating to El Salvador's death squads, going back more than a decade, which implicate men in the current Arena government, as well as indicate that Presidents Bush and Reagan knew much more about the death squads' activities than they told Congress.

UN Conference on Environment and Development (the Earth Summit) is held in Rio de Janeiro, Brazil, and over 100 countries are represented, making it

1992 (*cont.*)   the largest intergovernmental gathering in history. The conference reaffirms the Declaration of the UN Conference on the Human Environment adopted at Stockholm in 1972, and establishes new goals. Twenty-seven principles guide the conference, affirming such ideals as "development must be fulfilled so as to equitably meet the developmental and environmental needs of present and future generations." The conference results in the drafting of an action plan to lead environmental development into the twenty-first century. The plan, called Agenda-21, focuses on program areas relevant to development including indigenous peoples, human settlements, children, desertification (an issue not even mentioned at Stockholm), health, and women. Governments agree to work toward the establishment of an international environment that promotes sustainable development through trade liberalization, the provision of adequate resources to developing countries, encouraging macro-economic policies that are conducive to sustainable development, and making trade and the environment mutually supportive. The Earth Summit succeeds in making the international community aware that despite progress since 1972, the health of the planet continues to be a priority.

The *Wapenhans Report* is published, shedding a critical light on the World Bank. Written by former bank vice president, Willi Wapenhans, the report argues that the World Bank routinely fails to live up to its own criteria for success.

Bosnia-Herzegovina declares independence from Yugoslavia and nationalist Bosnian Serbs respond by attacking towns in northern and eastern Bosnia, systematically killing or driving out the non-Serb populations. The nationalist Serbs quickly take control over two-thirds of Bosnia's territory and continue their campaign, called "ethnic cleansing." The majority of those killed or driven from their homes are Muslims. Although the nationalist Serb forces are committing the greatest number of atrocities, other forces such as government forces and the Croats in western Herzegovina, also ignore the rules of war and attack Serb civilians. In August, the UN passes Security Council Resolution 770 which calls on states to take "all measures necessary" to facilitate the delivery of relief supplies to civilians. By year's end, an estimated 740,000 people are internally displaced, food reserves are running low, and starvation begins among the 4.3 million Bosnians at risk. The international response is to provide humanitarian assistance for those subjected to human rights abuses, but for the most part, to ignore the abuses directly.

A peace agreement is signed in October between the Mozambican Liberation Front (Frelimo), a force controlled by the country's Marxist-Leninist government, and the rebel army Renamo (Mozambican Resistance Movement), in Rome. The rebels earned notoriety as the "the Khmer Rouge of Africa" for their wanton brutality against the civilian population. As many as 1 million Mozambicans are estimated to have died in the 16-year civil war or as a result of war-induced famine. Approximately 5.7 million Mozambicans were forced from their homes, and refugees are spread over 6 neighboring countries. The UNHCR undertakes its largest repatriation effort ever, which is expected to take 3 years and repatriate as many as 1.7 million refugees. The effort, which is estimated to cost $209 million, is slowed by the 2 million landmines which lie strewn across the country. However, hopes for a lasting peace are high; the fact that Mozambique, unlike many war-torn societies, did not fight its civil war along clear ethnic lines is a positive sign.

In December, after nearly two years of increasing civil conflict in Somalia, the United States leads a multinational armed intervention to secure and protect the provision of humanitarian aid. Extreme looting and extortion have obstructed the efforts of

1992 *(cont.)*   relief workers for months, and the situation is compounded by the total absence of a functioning government and the destruction of Somalia's physical infrastructure. Clan-based factional armies and gangs of heavily armed bandits in the capital, Mogadishu, block relief food and steal supplies with impunity. Between 300,000 and 500,000 have died since 1991, according to UN estimates. The UN Security Council passes Resolution 794 in response to U.S. pressure, and by early 1993 nearly 35,000 troops from 24 countries are participating in the effort, known as Operation Restore Hope, to secure relief distribution access. The presence of international troops enables relief food and other needed assistance to reach beneficiaries, but the warring factions remain heavily armed and dangerous. The U.S. diplomatic effort focuses on agreements between major warlords, ignoring, at least at the outset, the participation of civil society. Minimal disarmament occurs and no government is formed. The U.S. and UN peacekeeping troops gradually become targets of General Mohammed Farah Aideed, the strongest clan military leader. In October 1993, President Clinton announces the U.S. troops' withdrawal, which is to be completed by March 1994. Other nations quickly follow suit, resulting in a resurgence of warfare between the tribal factions with relief workers once again coming under bandit attack.

1993   International Year of the Rights of Indigenous People is launched by the UN following a decade of work with indigenous peoples that focused primarily on violations of their human rights. The Worldwatch Institute identifies indigenous people as "the keepers of human variety"—native people who have resisted assimilation and extermination and struggled to maintain the integrity of their cultures and ways of life. The Year of the Rights of Indigenous People helps to raise awareness about indigenous peoples' skills and their relationship with nature and the environment, demonstrating that modern development has much to learn from these often-marginalized populations. Two summit meetings are held during the year, enabling the indigenous peoples themselves to carry out a number of their own activities and initiatives and bring together their demands and resolutions before the international community. In 1992, Rigoberta Menchu, a Quiche Indian woman from Guatemala, won the Nobel Peace Prize, bringing broader international attention to the struggle for justice common to all indigenous people.

The collective return of Guatemalan refugees living in Mexico begins in January after the Guatemalan government accedes to the Permanent Commissions of Guatemalan Refugee's (CCCP) demands. Over 2,000 refugees return, met by a huge delegation of well-wishers including Rigoberta Menchu. Guatemala remains the only country in Central America still formally at war, although peace negotiations have been in effect, albeit with few results, since 1990. Negotiations between the Guatemalan government and insurgent Guatemalan National Revolutionary Unity (URNG) intensify during the summer when an attempted coup is turned around by strong pressure from democratic and civilian sectors. On 1 June, President Jorge Serrano Elias is ousted by the military and the Guatemalan Congress elects Ramiro de Leon Carpio as president. Although Carpio has a sound reputation as a defender of human rights, the human rights situation fails to improve significantly. In December, Carpio asks President Clinton to authorize Temporary Protected Status for Guatemalans in the United States; Guatemalans are the single largest nationalist group with asylum pending in the United States at year's end.

The U.S. Committee for Refugees releases a new study of the civil war in Sudan, claiming that the

1993 (*cont.*)   death toll of 1.3 million in southern Sudan is twice as high as previous estimates. The report, *Quantifying Genocide in the Southern Sudan: 1983–1993*, concludes that 300,000 persons have died during 1992 and the first five months of 1993, making it one of the deadliest periods in the country's civil war. The violence of war, war-related famine and disease, and government policies that spread conflict, all have contributed to the death toll. Despite the fact that more people have died in Sudan than in Bosnia and Somalia combined, the media's coverage of the crisis is scant.

The World Conference on Human Rights is held in Austria on 14–25 June. The conference adopts the Vienna Declaration and Programme of Action, which proposes a common plan for the strengthening of human rights around the world. One goal is the universal ratification of the Convention on the Rights of the Child by the end of 1995.

Eritrea is admitted as a member state of the UN and the OAU in September, marking the end of a 30-year war for independence. In April, 98 percent of the population voted by referendum in favor of independence, and on 24 May the country celebrates the second anniversary of its victory over Ethiopia. Issaias Afwerki, leader of the Eritrean People's Liberation Front (EPLF), is elected president of Africa's fifty-second nation. The joy of independence is tempered by the grim costs of the war: Some 100,000 are believed to have died in the struggle while 450,000 Eritrean refugees remain in Sudan. In June, the UN Department of Humanitarian Affairs and the Eritrean government publish a joint appeal for $262 million to fund a Program for Refugee Reintegration and Rehabilitation of Resettlement Areas in Eritrea (PROFERI). This three-and-a-half-year program calls for the repatriation of up to 150,000 Eritreans in the first two years. By the end of the year, international donors contribute only $11 million of the requested monies.

Dominated by General Sani Abacha, a military regime seizes power in Nigeria. The regime is said to
be one of the most oppressive in Nigerian history.
Political opponents are arbitrarily jailed, and the
Ogoni minority is the target of brutal oppression.
Abacha's complicity with drug traffickers allows
Nigeria to become a key transshipment point for
Asian heroin and Latin American cocaine, and leads
the Clinton administration to declare Nigeria in-
eligible for foreign aid in 1994. Nigeria has been
ruled by soldiers for 25 of its 35 years as an independent country.

1994 The North American Free Trade Agreement
(NAFTA) between the governments of Canada, the
United States, and Mexico goes into effect on 1 January, immediately eliminating tariffs on about half of
U.S. exports to Mexico and 75 percent of U.S. imports from Mexico. Among the objectives behind
the agreement, as stated in its preamble, are to
strengthen bonds of friendship and cooperation between the three countries; to contribute to the har-
monious expansion of world trade and provide a
catalyst for broader international cooperation; to
create new employment opportunities; and to promote sustainable development. Proponents of the
agreement argue that free trade will promote economic growth in all three countries, and that each
country will be able to specialize in goods and services suited to their respective economic structures
and natural resources. Critics charge that NAFTA
will make Mexico more dependent on the United
States and increase environmental degradation in
Mexico and the United States.

In southern Mexico, groups of armed indigenous
and mestizo peoples from the state of Chiapas stage
a revolt to coincide with the passage of NAFTA.
Calling themselves the EZLN, the Zapatista
Liberation Army, the rebels occupy four towns in
Chiapas, taking over municipal offices and liberating prisoners in jail. Their fight, they declare, is

1994 (*cont.*) against the Mexican government to protest the widespread abuses by wealthy landowners and the government. The government's initial reaction is to try to crush the insurgency militarily but a vast civil movement emerges to pressure both sides to negotiate. Fifty-six people are killed in two days of fighting. The rebels offer to open negotiations with three moderators, including Nobel Laureate Rigoberta Menchu, and among their demands is that the government reinstate Article 27 of the Constitution, which was repealed in preparation for NAFTA. Article 27 prevents the privatization of community-held land. The fact that the government chose negotiation over repression is unprecedented and encouraging.

A new majority in the United States House of Representatives eliminates the Select Committee on Hunger. The committee, created in 1984 at the height of famine in Ethiopia, is a casualty of budget-cutting and a political climate increasingly hostile to international assistance. Although foreign aid constitutes only 1 percent of the U.S. federal budget, and humanitarian aid only half of that total, some legislators call for sharp reductions notwithstanding continuing need. Polls demonstrate, however, that the U.S. public supports continuing overseas assistance.

On 6 April, a suspicious plane crash kills Rwandan president, Juvenal Habyarimana, and the president of Burundi, both of whom were Hutus. Political rivalry between Hutu and Tutsi ethnic groups intensifies, and extremist Hutus slaughter approximately 200,000 Tutsis in five weeks. The violence stems from a power struggle between political factions that has been exploited and exacerbated by traditional ethnic rivalries. Hundreds of thousands of Tutsis flee to Tanzania (250,000 refugees in one month alone), Zaire, and other countries. On 31 May, UN secretary-general, Boutros Boutros-Ghali, reports that the killing in Rwanda "constitutes genocide." The Rwandan Patriotic Front (RPF), primarily made up of Tutsis, tries to seize power. A cease-fire is announced in June, and France dispatches troops later that month. Within three weeks of French arrival, the final Hutu-dominated government forces flee and the RPF declares victory. Meanwhile, the plight of the refugees has worsened, exacerbated by outbreaks of cholera, bubonic plague, and measles in the camps. By the end of the year, stability seems to be returning, with a civilian president in place and the ex-commander of rebel army, Paul Kagame, serving as vice president. However, real stability remains questionable with more than one million Rwandans still in exile.

On 11 May, Nelson Mandela is sworn in as the first black president of South Africa, bringing an end to apartheid. In the first election to include participation of the black majority, the African National Congress wins more than 62 percent of the vote. Just four years earlier, Mandela had been serving a life sentence for trying to overthrow the government.

The International Conference on Population and Development is held in September in Cairo, Egypt. While passionate arguments about abortion and sex education receive the focus of the media, the delegates at the conference reach consensus that the population issue revolves around women having greater control of their own bodies and lives. The Cairo Conference, after 20 years of study, argues that the principal forces behind falling fertility are rising education levels, lower child death rates, increased economic security, and progress toward gender equality. There is also widespread agreement of the need to reduce the levels of abortion and maternal mortality, to extend reproductive health services to women in all communities, and to raise the level of female education. The 184 governments represented at the conference reach an unprecedented consensus in drafting a 20-year Programme of Action that aims to achieve a balance between

1994 (*cont.*) population and the world's resources. This action
plan is unique in that it proposes policies that
address the linkages between consumption and
production patterns, economic development, population growth and structure, and environmental
degradation. The Programme of Action calls for the
global economy to place greater emphasis on social
development and to protect the most vulnerable
members of society, including women, who represent the majority of the world's poor. The Programme of Action also represents the first time that
reproductive and sexual health and reproductive
rights of women become central to an international
agreement on population. Among the goals of the
Programme of Action is universal availability of
family planning by the year 2015.

1995 The World Summit for Social Development is held
in Copenhagen in March. Delegates from 187 member states, as well as representatives from hundreds
of nongovernmental organizations, meet to discuss
the principal themes: poverty, unemployment, and
social disintegration. The Programme of Action
drafted at the conference goes beyond addressing
the fulfillment of basic needs and encompasses empowerment and opportunity, cultural development, and spiritual growth. Among the proposals
approved at the Summit is the "20:20 compact," a
strategy based on shared responsibility. Donors
agree to direct 20 percent of their foreign aid at basic
social programs, and in return, recipient nations
agree to direct at least 20 percent of their national
budget to such programs. The 20:20 compact is approved as a bilateral option, making it optional
rather than an international requirement. Also recommended is a "Global Demilitarization Fund"
proposed by Nobel Laureate Oscar Arias. Arias
suggests that developing countries' efforts toward
disarmament be rewarded; if developed nations
would agree to a 3 percent per year reduction in
military spending, one-fifth of these savings could
be earmarked toward a demilitarization fund that

would reward those countries that work toward disarming their armed forces, reintegrating military personnel into society, and encouraging civic education. The Clinton administration announces a new 10-year program to help keep girls in school in Africa, Asia, and Latin America. The program, to be administered by USAID, will seek to increase either the literacy rate or the percentage of girls who complete primary education by 20 percent.

Rwandan government troops kill an estimated 2,000 civilians in April. The government has been forcibly moving people out of refugee camps for months; nearly all remaining refugees (numbering about 2 million) are Hutu. This act of violence suspends the $611 million that Rwanda was pledged to receive in January, which would have been the first major infusion of foreign aid since the new government came to power. This comes on the heels of accusations from international development agencies, such as Doctors Without Borders, that Hutu leaders in the camps are holding refugees hostage and organizing them into groups as part of a plot to counterattack the new government in Rwanda. Refugees who voice dissent are kidnapped or killed, and international aid is being manipulated by the militias to reorganize, stockpile food, and recruit new members. As a result of these actions, Doctors Without Borders announces its withdrawal from all camps in Zaire and Tanzania in February.

The Fourth World Conference on Women, entitled Action for Equality, Development and Peace, is scheduled to be held in Beijing, China, in September. Areas of concern to be addressed at the conference include: poverty; access to education; power sharing; commitment to women's rights; health and employment; effects of armed conflict; economic participation; and violence against women.

Notes

1. Bread for the World, *Hunger 1992*, 77.

2. Julius Nyaang'oro and Timothy Shaw, eds., *Beyond Structural Adjustment in Africa*, 37.

3. Jason Clay, in *The Moral Nation*, edited by Bruce Nichols and Gil Loescher, 248.

4. Lloyd Timberlake, *Africa in Crisis*, 19.

5. Ruth Dixon-Mueller, *Population Policy & Women's Role*, 73.

6. Bread for the World, *Hunger 1992*, 69; original quote from *African Alternative Framework*, 4.

7. Bread for the World, *Hunger 1992*, 143.

Biographical Sketches 3

This chapter profiles the leading figures in the field of development. Collectively considered, these individuals reflect the broad and constantly changing definition of development. Each of these men and women have dedicated their lives to the process of development and, in the diversity and variety of their undertakings, they reflect the complexity of the issue. We profile individuals who have made a difference across the development spectrum in areas such as debt, environmental degradation, foreign policy, international aid, and grass-roots organization. Development "leaders" are theorists and activists, community leaders, and policy-makers; each plays a significant role in defining development and shaping our future. However, for every public face of development, there are hundreds of unseen faces and unrecognized names, people who are perhaps the real leaders of development.

Adebayo Adedeji

Born in Nigeria in 1930, Adebayo Adedeji is a leading African economist who served as head of the UN Economic Commission for Africa (ECA) until 1991. As UN Economic Commissioner for Africa, Adedeji became a sharp critic of the World Bank and the International Monetary Fund's structural adjustment programs. In 1989, he published *African Alternative Framework to Structural Adjustment Programmes,* which argued that structural adjustment demands accelerated change for weak economies and ignores long-term development needs and all alternatives. His program promoted multiple exchange rates, differential interest rates, and selective price policies to ensure food self-sufficiency. Adedeji's report was based on the research of over 100 international economists and was widely accepted by the Organization of African Unity. In 1991, he stepped down from this post at ECA and was honored with a special "vote of appreciation and thanks . . . in honor of this great servant"—the first time that a UN functionary had been so recognized. Before retiring, Adedeji organized a conference on the "People's Participation in Economic Development" at Arusha, Tanzania. Adedeji's commitment to economic reform continued into his retirement; he ran for the presidency of Nigeria, but failed to win the nomination of the Social Democratic Party.

Peggy Antrobus

Born in Grenada and educated in St. Vincent and St. Lucia, Peggy Antrobus has worked in various Caribbean countries with both governments and nongovernmental organizations. In 1974, Antrobus was appointed by the government of Jamaica to establish their Women's Bureau, and since that time her work has focused on programs aimed at enhancing women's roles in development. In 1978, she established the Women and Development Unit within the School of Continuing Studies at the University of the West Indies. Antrobus is a founding member and coordinator of the network of Third World feminists promoting Development Alternatives with Women for a New Era (DAWN). DAWN was launched on the eve of the Nairobi Conference in 1984, marking the end of the Decade for Women, and their publication, *Development, Crises and Alternative Visions,* revolutionized development thinking, bringing the concerns of women into the development discourse.

Ahangamage Tudor Ariyarante

Ahangamage Ariyarante is the founder of the Sarvodaya Shramadana Movement in Sri Lanka. The movement began in 1958 when Ariyarante was a young science teacher at a prestigious Buddhist high school. There he organized a two-week "holiday work camp" for students interested in experiencing the realities of the poor. The movement quickly expanded beyond the school system and grew into a village self-help movement with a focus on development. Ariyarante went to India to learn from the Gandhian experience, bringing back the teachings of nonviolence and self-reliance. In 1968, he initiated the Hundred Villages Development Scheme, and in 1987 he was recognized for his work with the Sarvodaya Shramadan Movement by being awarded the first Alan Shawn Feinstein World Hunger Award. Ariyarante also serves as chairperson of the board of trustees of the Asian Institute of Rural Development in Bangalore, and as vice-president of the Liaison Committee for Food Corps International.

J. Brian Atwood

The current administrator of the United States Agency for International Development (USAID), J. Brian Atwood was born in 1942 in Wareham, Massachusetts. Before his appointment with USAID in June 1993, Atwood served for eight years as the president of the National Democratic Institute for International Affairs, an organization which promotes democracy in transitional societies around the world, achieving notable successes in Nicaragua, Chile, Namibia, Panama, and Eastern Europe. Atwood entered the Foreign Service in 1966 and served in the Ivory Coast and Spain. In 1972, he was a legislative assistant for foreign policy and defense for Senator Thomas Eagleton (D-Mo.). He also worked under Secretaries of State Cyrus Vance and Edmund Muskie as assistant secretary. In 1981, Atwood became dean of professional studies and academic affairs at the Foreign Service Institute. Since his appointment as administrator of USAID, Atwood has been responsible for reorganizing and reinventing the agency. Twenty-three missions have been closed, staff reduced, and new goals have been established, focusing on broad-based economic growth, protecting the environment, building democracy, stabilizing population growth, and providing humanitarian assistance. In the face of Congress's threats of dissolving USAID and cutting foreign aid, Atwood has spearheaded the campaign to educate about and preserve foreign aid.

Peter Bauer

Born in Budapest in 1915, Peter Bauer is considered a pioneer of development theory. A conservative economist, Bauer argues for the free-market approach to economic development. He taught economics at the London School of Economics from 1960 to 1983, and has written extensively on the field of economic development, including the role of trading activity and the significance of the informal sector in developing countries emphasizing the adverse effects of government intervention. A "classical" economist, Bauer argues that enterprise, trade, and the enlargement of markets are the engines of development, and he opposes barriers to trade and investment. He has also written somewhat controversial arguments on the limitations of aid as a tool of development, arguing that foreign aid should be left to charitable organizations. He rejects the notion of "Western guilt" for its exploitation of the Third World, and counters the dependency theorists' argument that the West played a significant role in causing underdevelopment with the contention that the West has been the "principal agent of material progress" in the global South. Bauer is also known for his challenges of widely held views on the legacy of colonialism and the West's role in the Third World. His publications include: *The Economics of Under-Developed Countries* (1957); *Dissent on Development* (1971); and *Reality and Rhetoric* (1984).

David Beckmann

President of Bread for the World (BFW), a Christian citizens' movement against hunger, David Beckmann is also president of Bread for the World Institute, the research and education branch of BFW. Prior to his appointment at BFW, Beckmann, who is also a Lutheran pastor, was an economist at the World Bank for 15 years. At the World Bank he was responsible for helping to shift the bank's focus toward greater collaboration with private voluntary organizations and toward greater poverty reduction programs. Beckmann earned degrees from Yale University, Christ Seminary, and the London School of Economics. At his ordination he was commissioned to be a missionary-economist, and went on to work in Bangladesh for a church-related relief and development agency. He is the author of many books and articles on Christian faith and economics, most recently co-authoring *Transforming the Politics of Hunger* (1994).

Robert Berg

Robert Berg is the president of the International Development Conference (IDC), a coalition of leaders of 135 national associations and organizations concerned with U.S.–Third World development policies. The IDC is the oldest and largest forum on development in the United States. Its activities include a campaign to encourage nongovernmental organizations (NGOs) to increase their advocacy and public education activities. Berg's consulting assignments have included serving as senior consultant to the World Summit for Children in 1990 and senior consultant to a consortium of 12 institutions for the largest study ever done on U.S.–Third World economic cooperation policies. From 1982 to 1987 Berg was the senior fellow of the Overseas Development Council (ODC), a Washington, D.C., think tank. At ODC he co-directed the Committee on African Development Strategies, a group whose work has continuing influence on U.S. legislation. From 1977 to 1982 Berg was the founding director of evaluation for the USAID and from 1980 to 1982 he also served as founding chairman of evaluation for OECD's Development Assistance Committee in Paris. His publications include *Cooperation for International Development: The United States and the Third World in the 1990s* (editor). He was also co-editor of *Strategies for African Development*, which won the 1986 World Hunger Media Award.

Chandi Prasadd Bhatt

Chandi Bhatt is a leader of the Chipko Movement of Northern India, which has become an international symbol of the ability of a relatively small local community to battle successfully against the forces of state and private capital. In 1964, Bhatt and his coworkers founded a worker's cooperative, the Dasholi Gram Swarajya Mandal (DGSM), which organized unskilled and semi-skilled construction workers. The cooperative started a new enterprise involving the collection of roots and herbs from the forest which employed over 1,000 people between 1969 and 1972. In 1971, the cooperative opened a small manufacturing plant that produced turpentine and resin from pine sap. However, the Indian Forestry Department would not allot adequate supplies of pine sap so the plant was forced to close down—one of many government obstacles facing the cooperative's efforts. At the same time, the government allotted 300 ash trees to the Simon Company, a sporting goods manufacturer. When the agents from Simon Company arrived to supervise the cutting of the trees, Bhatt helped to organize the villagers; they marched, beating drums and singing traditional songs, and the Simon Company left without felling a single tree. When the Forestry Department announced the auction of almost 2,500 trees in Reni Forest, Bhatt warned the villagers of the landslides and floods this deforestation could cause, and suggested they hug the trees as a tactic to save them. It was the women who listened to Bhatt's warning, and thus the Chipko Movement was born—and with it the symbolic sight of masses of village women embracing their trees to save them. The Chipko Movement spread through the leadership of women and is connected horizontally through "runners," such as C. P. Bhatt, who carry messages of Chipko happenings from village to village.

Ester Boserup

A Danish researcher, Ester Boserup is most well known for her pioneering work in the field of women in development. Boserup began her career as an economist for the Danish government, and then went on to work for ten years for the UN Economic Committee for Europe. Boserup lived in Senegal and India for ten years where she worked as a development consultant and free-lance writer. From 1971 to 1980 she served as a member of the UN Committee of Development Planning. In 1979, she joined the staff of the UN International Research and Training Institute for the Advancement of Women (INSTRAW). Boserup is the author of the path-breaking book *Women's Role in Economic Development* (1970), which stimulated much of the study and debate during the UN Decade for Women (1975–1978). In her book, Boserup presents the innovative argument that modern technologies require an increase of labor input, thus altering the work assignments of men and women, and ultimately increasing, rather than decreasing, the work burden for women. A well known women-in-development (WID) expert, Irene Tinker, summarized Boserup's contribution to the field, saying: "Boserup's theory legitimized efforts to influence development policy with a combined argument for justice and efficiency."

Lester Brown

Lester Brown co-founded the Worldwatch Institute, a global environmental research institute that analyzes interdisciplinary environmental data from around the world, in 1974, and continues to serve as its president and senior researcher. Born in 1934 in New Jersey, Brown was educated at Rutgers University and Harvard

University. He began his career at the U.S. Department of Agriculture (USDA), where he published his first major analysis of the environmental impact of growing affluence, *Man, Land, and Food,* in 1963. In 1965, he won the USDA Superior Service Award. Brown left the USDA to become senior fellow at the Overseas Development Council (ODC), where he is still a board member. In 1974, with the support of former Secretary of Agriculture Orville Freeman, Brown founded the Worldwatch Institute. Today, in addition to being president and researcher, Brown also serves as co-author of *State of the World,* the flagship annual publication of the Worldwatch Institute, and as editor of *World Watch,* the bimonthly publication. Brown was the recipient of the UN Environment Prize in 1989 and is the author of many books including *By Bread Alone* (1974); *The Twenty-Nine Days* (1978); and *Building a Sustainable Society* (1981).

Gro Harlem Brundtland

The former prime minister of Norway and the current chairperson of the World Committee on Environment and Development (WCED), Gro Brundtland was born in 1939 and educated in the fields of medicine and public health. In 1974, she was named Norway's environment minister and has been the leader of the Labour Party since 1981. It was Brundtland's background and her struggles as environment minister that led the secretary-general of the United Nations to appoint her to establish and chair an independent commission to address the major environmental challenges to the world community. The WCED is more commonly known today as the Brundtland Commission. In 1983, the Brundtland Commission published their proceedings, *Our Common Future,* which examines current development problems and formulates realistic proposals to solve them. The commission has been successful in bringing international attention to the relations between environment and development and raising the issue of global responsibility.

Sukhomoy Chakravarty

Economist Sukhomoy Chakravarty was born in India in 1934 into an intellectually eminent family. After attending Presidency College in Calcutta, he went on to earn his Ph.D. at the Netherlands School of Economics. From 1959 to 1961 he was assistant professor of economics at the Massachusetts Institute of Technology. Chakravarty served as chairperson of the Delhi School of Economics in 1964, then joined the India Planning Commission from 1971 to 1977. From 1983 to 1985 he chaired a committee to review the monetary system of India. Throughout his career Chakravarty played a central role in planning and public policy in India. He served under three different prime ministers as chairman of the Economic Advisory Council, a position he held until his death in 1990. Additionally, he served as chairman of the Indian Council of Social Science Research, a public institution that supports research in the social sciences, from 1987 to 1990. He was the author of a number of books, including his most well known and influential, *Capital and Development Planning*, which he wrote in 1969, and was lauded for offering a substantial contribution to development planning. Chakravarty was one of only two people ever to receive the Mahalanobis Memorial Gold Medal, in 1974. Chakravarty served as vice-president of the International Economic Association from 1983 to 1986, and in 1986 was named Honorary President of the Association.

Bernard Chidzero

Bernard Chidzero has been a significant figure in the recent history of the United Nations, as well as of his native Zimbabwe, for almost 30 years. Born in Zimbabwe in 1927, Chidzero joined the UN as a social affairs officer of the UN Economic Commission for Africa and as a representative of the UN Technical Assistance board from 1960 to 1963. From 1977 to 1980 he served as deputy secretary-general of the UN Conference of Trade and Development (UNCTAD) and director of the Special Fund Program. Additionally, Chidzero served as a commissioner on the Brundtland Commission in 1983 and assisted in drafting the report presented to the General Assembly in 1987. He returned to Zimbabwe in the 1980s. Because of his education and work abroad he was one of the few potential leaders of Zimbabwe who remained neutral during the liberation struggle. Shortly after his return, Chidzero was named minister of economic planning and development, and in 1985 was elected a member of Parliament from Harare. Chidzero played an important role in directing his nation's economic growth during the 1980s, a period of economic recession. In 1988, he was named senior minister in charge of all economics ministries. Chidzero was candidate for secretary-general of the UN in 1990, but lost to Boutros Boutros-Ghali.

Domitila Barrios de la Chungara

Domitila Chungara was born in the mining encampment at Siglo XX, in the central highlands of Bolivia, in 1937 and grew up in abject poverty. Siglo XX is known for its long struggle against the military regimes of the Bolivian government; Chungara herself lived through two massacres in 1965 and 1967. Like many women of her community, Domitila Chungara's activism grew out of the desire to survive and protect those she loved. She married a miner and has seven children. In 1963, she became active in the House-wives Committee of Siglo XX, an organization developed in re-sponse to the repression of the government; women whose husbands had been imprisoned went on a hunger strike until the release of their husbands. At first the Housewives Committee was ignored and ridiculed by the Miners' Union, despite its crucial role in freeing the union leaders. Chungara was jailed and tortured for protesting the massacre in 1967 and her husband was blacklisted by the Ministry of the Interior and barred from employment. After years of facing recrimination and torture for speaking out, in 1975 Chungara was invited by the United Nations to speak at the Tribunal at the International Women's Conference in Mexico. The Tribunal was set up for speakers and representatives of nongov-ernmental organizations, and Chungara was the only Bolivian woman invited. In 1977, she wrote a book about her life entitled *Let Me Speak.* Chungara ran as a candidate for vice-president for the Party of the Revolutionary Left in the 1978 elections. Chungara has been living in exile since the latest of Bolivia's military regimes came to power in 1980.

Jason Clay

Jason Clay is the founder and director of Rights and Resources, a nonprofit environmental and human rights organization that ad-dresses global issues of economic and social justice through inter-national trade. The organization's mission is to assist local communities with small-scale enterprise development, land and resource rights, and sustainable management of natural resources through programs that are socially acceptable, economically sound, and environmentally sustainable. Clay edited the journal *Cultural Survival Quarterly* for ten years, and in 1989 founded Cultural Survival Enterprises, the trading division of Cultural Survival, Inc., a human rights organization working with indigenous peoples throughout the world. Clay received his Ph.D. in anthropology from Cornell University, and his publications include 7 books and nearly 200 articles.

Monsignor Robert J. Coll

Monsignor Robert J. Coll served as executive director of Interfaith Hunger Appeal, a partnership of four faith-based international relief and development organizations (Catholic Relief Services, Church World Service, Lutheran World Relief, and the American Jewish Joint Distribution Committee) from 1985 to 1994. In 1974, Monsignor Coll, in conjunction with Protestant and Jewish clergymen, designed a Third World assistance program called Operation Rice Bowl. This is a Lenten ecumenical community action program which today is sponsored by Catholic Relief Services (CRS) and has raised over $50 million for domestic and international food assistance and development programs. In 1980, Monsignor Coll joined the staff of Catholic Relief Services as assistant to the executive director. He was appointed European director of CRS in 1983, administering the Food Program in Poland. The following year he became coordinator of Church Drought Action Africa for the Ethiopian famine. In that capacity he organized an international food appeal which brought over 30,000 metric tons of food to the famine-ridden people of Ethiopia.

Hernando de Soto

A Peruvian entrepreneur, Hernando de Soto is the author of the best-selling and influential book, *The Other Path.* Son of a diplomat, de Soto studied in Switzerland, the United States, and Canada, earning his master's degree in international economics and law from the University of Geneva. In *The Other Path,* which combines political analysis of Peru with analysis of its informal economy, de Soto argues that the poor have always found ways to employ themselves. De Soto claims that the informal sector provides 60 percent of Peru's work hours, 70 percent of its housing, and 95 percent of its mass transportation. Despite the recent growth in the Peruvian government, de Soto proposes the formalization of the informal sector by providing basic economic rights. De Soto is the director of the Instituto Libertad y Democracia (ILD) and a member of the UN Commission for Development Planning. In 1990, the ILD helped streamline the process for setting up a formal business by designing and running the Unified Business Registry, which became law in 1991. Since then, more than a quarter of a million businesses that would not otherwise have formalized have registered. Additionally, the ILD developed a pilot program called PROFORM, which is the result of a ten-year study on the issue of land ownership funded in part by USAID and the United Nations Development Programme (UNDP). PROFORM offers a comprehensive approach to granting land titles.

Rene Dumont

Rene Dumont has been influential in the field of development for over half a century. Born in 1904 in Cambrai, France, Dumont is one of the world's most well-known agronomists. His fieldwork began in Southeast Asia in 1929, and he then went on to work in Cuba and Bangladesh. He served as an advisor to several governments on the economic planning of agricultural development. Dumont was one of the first to argue that European solutions are not the answer to Africa's problems. Among the 20 additional books he has written are: *False Start in Africa* (1966); *The Growth of Hunger* (1980); and *Stranglehold on Africa* (1983). In addition to his writings on agricultural development and the African peasantry, Dumont is also well known as an accurate (yet often ignored) forecaster of environmental trends: He warned against desertification in Africa 15 years before the UN began to focus on it. Dumont taught at the Institute of Political Science in Paris, and also served as director of research at the Institut National Agronomique. He ran for the French presidency in 1974 and won a slim 1.3 percent of the vote, yet he did succeed in popularizing ecological concern in France. In recognition of his pioneering contributions to agronomy, Dumont was made Chevalier of the Legion of Honor.

Juan M. Flavier

Working on behalf of the rural poor for more than 25 years, Juan Flavier was born in Baguio City, Philippines, and completed his medical studies at the University of the Philippines and Johns Hopkins University. In 1978, Flavier was appointed president of the International Institute of Rural Reconstruction. He also served as secretary of Health in the Philippines and as past president of the Family Planning Organization of the Philippines. He is a pioneer in family planning for developing countries and has published 3 books (including *Doctor to the Barrios,* which has been translated into 8 different languages) and over 30 articles. Flavier is on the World Bank/NGO Committee and in 1986 he won the Ramon Magsaysay Award for International Understanding.

Andre Gunder Frank

Born in Berlin in 1929, Andre Gunder Frank has made a significant contribution to the field of development theory, specifically the dependency school. Frank's argument, in direct opposition to Bauer's (see above), is that colonialism is the cause of underdevelopment, and that colonialism continues to exist today in the guises of international trade, foreign investment, and even development assistance. Frank's influential article, "The Development of Underdevelopment," published in 1966, argued that these modern forms of colonialism—trade and foreign investment—were responsible for the removal of economic surplus and resources from the Third World. Frank moved to Brazil in 1962 and much of his analysis is based on his experience and research in Latin America. Critics cite his reductionist tendencies and his focus on Latin America as shortcomings, yet many of his arguments continue to be relevant and powerful contributions to the development debate.

Paulo Freire

Paulo Freire was born in Recife, Brazil, in 1921 into a middle-class family. When the economic crisis of 1929 reached Brazil, Freire's family was plunged into poverty—an experience which shaped the rest of his life. Freire has dedicated his life to working with the poor, using education as his tool. Observing a "culture of silence" that engulfs the lower classes, Freire saw education as the means of lifting this cloak of silence and sparking empowerment. He developed a method for teaching the illiterate, which not only taught them to read using materials that had a practical effect on their lives, but also involved reflection and action against the oppressive elements of society or government. Freire began his career working as the coordinator of the National Commission of

Popular Culture and at the National Plan of Literacy Training. He was jailed during the military coup of 1964 for 70 days because his teaching methodology was considered a threat to the old order. After his release from prison, Freire went into exile for 16 years. He first moved to Chile, where he lived for 5 years, working with the UN Education, Science, and Cultural Organization (UNESCO) and the Chilean Institute for Agrarian Reform in their adult education programs. In 1969 , he came to the United States to work at Harvard University's Center for Studies in Development and Social Change. The following year Freire moved to Geneva, where he was employed by the World Council of Churches (WCC). At the WCC Freire worked on literacy projects for Tanzania and Guinea-Bissau that focused on the re-Africanization of their countries. He went on to establish the Institute of Cultural Action in Geneva in 1971. In 1980, Freire at last returned home to Brazil to teach at Pontificia Universidade Catolica de São Paulo and at the Universidade de Campinas in São Paulo, where he still teaches today. Freire was named secretary of education of São Paulo from 1989 to 1991, and is the author of such well-known books as: *Pedagogy of the Oppressed; Education for Critical Consciousness; The Politics of Education;* and most recently, *Pedagogy of Hope.*

Susan George

Active with the Transnational Institute (TNI) since it was founded in Holland in 1973, Susan George is currently the institute's associate director. The Transnational Institute, the international wing of the Washington-based Institute for Policy Studies, was instrumental in founding and leading the Debt Crisis Network. George has made a significant contribution to the discussion of the world food system and the impact of agribusiness and multinational corporations on it. George has played an important role in the presentation of TNI's analysis of the food crisis at the 1974 World Food Conference. She has also written extensively on the repercussions of the debt crisis in the North and South. While not an economist herself, she believes the debt crisis is "too serious to be left to financiers and economists." George's first book, *How the Other Half Dies: The Real Reasons for World Hunger,* published in 1977, received widespread attention for being an innovative exposé of the food trade and agribusiness. George has written four additional books including *A Fate Worse Than Debt* (1990), a study of the human costs of the world financial crises.

Father Nzamujo Godfrey

A Nigerian-born priest, Father Nzamujo Godfrey established the Songhai Project, a program to foster agricultural autonomy in Benin. Godfrey was teaching and studying in the United States when the 1984 famine hit Africa. He returned to his home continent to establish a farm which would serve as a research and training center for representatives of rural communities. The Songhai Project focuses on crop production, aquaculture, and livestock production, and calls for African farmers to use their own resources. The production system of the farm is based on the comparative advantages that Africa has: its heat, biological life, culture, and heritage. In 1993, Father Godfrey was awarded the Africa Prize for Leadership in recognition of this work with the Songhai Project.

James P. Grant

James P. Grant served as the Executive Director of the United Nations International Children's Emergency Fund (UNICEF) for 15 years and was known throughout the world as one of the most dedicated public servants of his generation. Grant was born in China of missionary parents and was educated at the University of California at Berkeley. In 1951, he earned a doctorate in jurisprudence from Harvard University and then moved to South Asia to work on U.S. aid programs. He was the director for USAID's programs in Sri Lanka from 1956 to 1958. Grant returned to Washington, D.C., from 1962 to 1964 to serve as deputy assistant secretary of state for Near East and South Asian Affairs. Following a 3-year term as assistant administrator for USAID, Grant left the agency to help found the Overseas Development Council, where he served as president for 11 years, from 1969 to 1980. In 1980, Grant was appointed executive director of UNICEF. Among the highlights of Grant's career at UNICEF was the 1982 launching of the Child Survival Campaign, which advocated the use of GOBI, a series of low-cost interventions involving growth monitoring, oral rehydration with a simple preparation, breast feeding and birth spacing, and immunization for the reduction of preventable deaths. As executive director of UNICEF, Grant has been credited with saving millions of young lives by promoting simple, low-cost methods to prevent the spread of disease. He was the principal author of *The State of the World's Children*, a series of policy-oriented reports published by UNICEF. In 1988, Grant was awarded the Alan Shawn Feinstein Award for the Prevention and Reduction of World Hunger. President Clinton awarded Grant the highest civilian honor, the Presidential Medal of Freedom, in 1994 for his "compassion and courage in his crusade for the world's children." Grant died in January 1995.

Kenneth Hackett

Kenneth Hackett is the Executive Director of Catholic Relief Services (CRS), one the United States' largest and most effective non-governmental organizations (NGOs). Hackett also serves as vice president of Caritas Internationalis, the international network of Catholic relief agencies, and as president of Interfaith Hunger Appeal. Hackett began his career with a Peace Corps assignment in Ghana, where he served as an advisor to an agricultural cooperative movement and later worked on a United Nations development project on Lake Volta. Following the Peace Corps, Hackett joined CRS as program director in Sierre Leone—the youngest person ever appointed to this position in the history of CRS. After three years in Africa, Hackett returned to the agency's headquarters in New York to serve in the Africa Region Office as a development assistant. In 1978, he was appointed director of the region, and in this capacity oversaw the relief operation in Ethiopia—the largest relief operation undertaken in the history of CRS. Before his appointment as executive director, Hackett also served as the CRS director of external affairs, country representative in the Philippines, and regional director for East Africa.

John Maxwell Hamilton

A journalist who currently works at the World Bank, John Maxwell Hamilton has reported from Latin America, Asia, and Africa for the *Christian Science Monitor*, ABC Radio, and other news organizations. During the Carter administration he worked at USAID, specializing in Asian development issues. Hamilton, who earned his Ph.D. in American civilization from George Washington University, also served on the House Foreign Affairs Committee. However, Hamilton is most known for his innovative exploration of the issue of interdependence; he is responsible for helping to shape public opinion about the complexity of U.S.–Third World relations. His book, *Main Street*

America and the Third World, published in 1986, traced the way that Third World countries influence the lives of Americans every day. Four years later he continued this theme with his book, *Entangling Alliances,* where he argued that interdependence is an exorable phenomenon demanding new approaches for U.S. policymakers and citizens.

Margaret Wambui Kenyatta

Born in 1928, Margaret Wambui Kenyatta is the daughter of Jomo Kenyatta, a leading figure of the Kenyan independence movement and the first president of Kenya. Kenyatta grew up in exile in England, returning to Kenya as an adult. Upon her return, she contributed to the nationalist movement by training teachers for the independent Kikuyu schools. Kenyatta became a public figure during her father's imprisonment, when her image of fidelity for her father won her the respect and endearment of her fellow citizens. She entered into politics in 1960 with the formation of the Kenyan African National Union. Kenyatta served as president of the Council of Kenyan Women for three terms. From 1970 to 1976 Kenyatta was elected mayor of Nairobi, during which time she concentrated on public health issues. In 1978, she was named the permanent representative to the UN Environment Programme, a position of special importance as Nairobi is the headquarters for these programs. Kenyatta has now retired from public life, but before her retirement she was very active in the UN Year of Women (1975) and was a strong presence at the 1985 Conference on Women in Nairobi.

David Korten

David Korten is the president and founder of the People-Centered Development Forum, an international voluntary organization dedicated to strenghthening the role of voluntary action in the realization of a people-centered development vision. Korten is also a visiting professor at the Asian Institute of Management in the Philippines. Prior to this position, Korten was a faculty member of Harvard University's graduate schools of management and public health. Korten has more than 30 years of field experience in Asia, Africa, and Latin America where he was employed by such agencies as USAID and the Ford Foundation as a writer, teacher, and consultant on development management. He is the author of a number of influential books, among them, *Getting to the 21st Century: Voluntary Action and the Global Agenda*, a damning critique of the development policies of the past three decades. Korten is known for his powerful challenges to conventional development wisdom and management practice.

Michael Lipton

Currently professor of development economics at the University of Sussex, England, Michael Lipton began his fieldwork experience in India in 1965, and since then has lived and conducted research in ten countries in Asia and Africa. He has directed a number of major research project teams, such as a grain storage project in India, which analyzed the size and distribution of costs and benefits from alternative grain storage systems. Lipton has served as consultant on numerous World Bank projects, including the Poverty Alleviation Workshop in Kuala Lumpur in 1991. Lipton is the co-author (with Sukhomoy Chakravarty) of *Planning Crisis Theory*, an influential book which sparked numerous debates as to whether there is an urban bias in the process of economic development that marginalizes the rural poor. Lipton also contributed to the analysis of measuring extreme poverty, arguing that the best measurement is food consumption. Among Lipton's numerous publications are *Why People Stay Poor* and *New Seeds and New People*.

Wangari Muta Maathai

A well-known environmentalist and activist, Wangari Muta Maathai is the founder of the world-famous Green Belt Movement, a Kenyan grass-roots environmental effort involving rural women's commitment to reforestation and the restoration of their natural habitat. The major activity of the Green Belt Movement is the planting of indigenous trees that were destroyed during the colonial period. The movement has resulted in the planting of thousands of trees and the establishment of over 65 tree nurseries to reduce the effects of deforestation. Additionally, it provides women with leadership opportunities and trains women to plant and cultivate seedlings. Maathai is also noted for being the first Kenyan woman to earn a doctorate, to be appointed to a professorship, and to chair a department. She was a featured speaker at the 1992 Rio Earth Summit, and has won ten international awards, including the 1991 Africa Leadership Prize from the Hunger Project. Since the founding of the Green Belt Movement in 1977, Maathai has been a very visible and public figure. She recently came under attack by the Kenyan Parliament for her attempts to halt the government's plans to build a 60-story building on Nairobi's Uhuru Park, the major park within the capital city. The government threatened to ban the Green Belt Movement, and Maathai disappeared into hiding. While plans for the building on Uhuru Park have been canceled due to an international outcry against the project, Maathai and the Green Belt Movement continue to conflict with the government.

Robert McNamara

Robert McNamara served as president of the World Bank from 1968 to 1980. Under McNamara's stewardship, the World Bank became the world's largest source of international development assistance: In 1968, it was lending about $1 billion per year; by 1980 this figure rose to $12 billion a year; funding increased from 62 new projects funded in 1968 to 266 projects in 1981. His tenure at the bank was characterized not only by vast expansion in financial investment in developing countries, but also by a significant reorientation in the kinds of projects funded. During this period, the World Bank turned its focus on developing countries, including more research on poverty alleviation, more lending for agricultural sectors (especially in rural development), and a new focus on reaching the poorest of the poor and meeting their basic needs. During McNamara's presidency the bank hired more staff from developing countries and more women (bringing the percentage up to a paltry 12 percent in 1980, from 6.3 percent in 1968). McNamara's interest and commitment to rural development was also evidenced in the creation of new units such as Agriculture and Rural Development; Urban Projects Development; and the Population, Health, and Nutrition Department. Before McNamara's leadership, the World Bank had a tendency to equate development solely with economic growth; McNamara's influence helped to shift this view to include an evaluation of basic needs and investment in human resource development.

McNamara's years as secretary of defense during the Vietnam War, as well as his years at the World Bank, have left him with no shortfall of critics. Many argue that McNamara was responsible for turning the World Bank into a huge bureaucracy where creativity and initiative were stifled. Without doubt, McNamara was enormously powerful, but equally clear was that he sought to transform the World Bank into an institution that embraced a broader definition of development that included millions who were previously invisible to the establishment. Whether those millions have fared better or worse for being "noticed," of course, remains open for debate.

Rigoberta Menchu

The 1992 Nobel Peace Prize laureate, Rigoberta Menchu is a Quiche Maya Indian woman from Guatemala who has become a leader in the stuggle of the Guatemalan Indians. Her best-selling autobiography, *I, Rigoberta Menchu*, was published in 1983 to great acclaim and tells the story of her life of hardship, which mirrors the stories common to many indigenous communities in Latin America. After the coming to power of the Lucas Garcia regime in 1978, Menchu's brother, father, and mother were all killed in separate incidents by the army. Her father, Vincente Menchu, was a leader in the Indian resistance and was burned to death when he and a group occupied the Spanish embassy in Guatemala City. Menchu learned Spanish, the language of her oppressors, in order to share her experiences with the world. In addition to speaking out against the injustices commited against her community, Menchu also tells of the tremendous spiritual richness that is an integral part of the Quiche lifestyle. Menchu's life is still constantly in danger; she has lived in exile but refuses to adandon her country and people. When she was awarded the Nobel Peace Prize, Menchu was commended for standing out "as a vivid symbol of peace and reconciliation across ethnic, cultural, and social dividing lines, in her own country, on the American continent, and in the world."

Jamil Nishtar

When appointed head of the Agricultural Development Bank of Pakistan (ADBP), which is part of the national banking system, in 1978, Jamil Nishtar immediately set out to reform the entire system of rural banking. He opened new services for farmers in small rural villages through a system of Mobile Credit Officers (MCOs), commonly known as "bankers on bikes" who act as advisors to the farmers, as well as officers of the bank. Nishtar saw credit as an instrument of development. He sought to combine credit with education and services, and even some advocacy with local authorities on behalf of the farmers. Nishtar was successful in securing backing from international banks (the International Fund for Agricultural Development [IFAD], the World Bank, and the Asian Development Bank), and the ADBP managed to give 55 billion rupees in loans in 1979. By 1982, Nishtar's corps of MCOs reached 18,000 villages, lending 1,370 rupees. ADBP lending to farmers reached an all-time high in the mid-1980s. Nishtar, who died in 1987, contributed greatly to the livelihood of thousands of small Pakistani farmers and his program has been rewarded with repayment rates of 90 percent, versus 45 percent in 1978. Loans now comprise over half of the agricultural budget, when in 1978 they consisted of just 10 percent.

Julius Nyerere

The ex-president of Tanzania, Julius Nyerere is regarded today as one of the most beloved leaders of Africa. Nyerere was already a leader long before Tanzanian independence in 1961. In 1954 , the Tanganyika African National Union, one of the most united African nationalist movements, was formed with Nyerere as president, and when independence arrived Nyerere was already serving as chief minister. A month later he resigned from the premiership to concentrate on reorganizing and redirecting the party to meet the needs of the newly independent nation. Nyerere returned to power as president in 1962 and after a presidency of 25 years, he became one of the first African leaders to step down voluntarily. While his economic policy, which endeavored to create a unique brand of African socialism, was not successful, Nyerere succeeded in creating a positive moral and social climate and good educational standards. In 1967, he wrote the *Arusha Declaration,* that introduced a new approach to the problem of development, placing priority on a state-centric strategy that included provision of basic health services, universal primary education, collectivized agriculture, and the creation of state-run institutions. Nyerere also introduced a philosophy of self-help, called *ujamaa,* meaning "familyhood" or sharing on a family basis. This philosophy complemented his idea of African socialism, whereby people came together in villages to cooperate in production and self-improvement. This idealistic notion did not translate well into reality; the villagization program was guided by a disciplinarian and exploitive attitude toward the peasantry, which even Nyerere's charisma could not soften. The 1980s proved to be the decade of economic deterioration, and after public disputes with the IMF over structural adjustment policies, Nyerere decided not to run again in 1985. Since his retirement, Nyerere has continued to work toward building a strong, more self-reliant global South. From 1987 to 1990 he chaired the South Commission, a group of representatives from developing countries who examine the problems of the global South and suggest strategies for its future. The commission published *The Challenge to the South*, a "seminal document for the future of South-South cooperation," in 1992.

Bernard Ledea Ouedraogo

Founder of the Naam movement, Africa's largest grass-roots movement, Bernard Ledea Ouedraogo was born in Upper Volta (now Burkina Faso) and educated by French colonialists. Determined to continue his education, he went on to study at the Sorbonne in Paris. He returned to Burkina Faso to work for the economic and social development of his tribe, the Mossi. After years of working as a teacher and school director, Ouedraogo founded the Naam movement, which is based on traditional associations in Mossi society formed for collective work. He discovered that the Naam group—the traditional village body composed of young people that undertakes various activities—had highly developed cooperative characteristics. Using this as the defining structure, Ouedraogo helped to form Naams to dig wells, build dams, and install mills, among other development activities. There are now over 4,000 Naam associations throughout Burkina Faso, Mali, and Senegal. Ouedraogo was successful in showing farmers that the traditional functions of the Naams could be transformed into functions adapted to modern development. Ouedraogo is a highly effective grass-roots communicator, with responsibilities ranging from consciousness-raising to educating groups on technical issues. He also works with such international organizations as UNICEF, moving back and forth between his village world and the international development industry, seeking help abroad while trying to inspire his people at home to work together. Naams have achieved success in "developing without harming," an expression dear to Ouedraogo. His method is to respect and build upon the existent social structure of the Mossi. Ouedraogo also serves as the general secretary and co-founder of the International 6-S Association, a nongovernmental aid and training network that encompasses nine countries in West Africa.

Raul Prebisch

Considered a "pioneer" of development economics, Raul Prebisch laid the foundation for the dependency school. Born in Tucuman, Argentina, Prebisch served as undersecretary of finance for Argentina from 1930 to 1932 and executive secretary to the UN Commission for Latin America from 1948 to 1962. However, Prebisch is most known for his role in the creation of the UN Conference on Trade and Development, of which he was the first secretary-general from 1964 to 1969. Prebisch also served as advisor to the secretary-general of the UN on development problems. His writings, and specifically his policy proposals on development, have been very influential, especially in relation to the New International Economic Order (NIEO). The NIEO is a set of proposals made by developing countries in 1974 for structural changes designed to redress the imbalances in the world economic system. Prebisch's arguments stress the need for synthesis of economic and political liberalism, and focus on the development of countries on the world economic periphery. In 1949, Prebisch published *The Economic Development of Latin America*, which argued that the orthodox theory of world trade could not be applied to the developing countries of the post–World War II era. Instead, Prebisch argued, the nations of the South should concentrate on the domestic production of goods that were currently being imported, or in other words, engage in import-substitution policies. His recent book *Capitalismo Periferico* argues for the need to combine the best features of socialism and political economic liberalism. Prebisch was awarded the Jawaharlal Nehru award for International Understanding in 1974. In 1977, he was the recipient of the Dag Hammarskjold honorary medal of the German UN Association, and in 1981 he won the Third World Prize from the Third World Foundation.

W. W. Rostow

A ranking official in the Kennedy and Johnson administrations, W. W. Rostow authored the *The Stages of Economic Growth* (1960). In this book, Rostow presents a widely adopted stage theory of development. Using the metaphor of an airplane, he identified five stages: airplane at rest (prescientific culture); preconditions for take-off (traditional society is challenged/upset—opportunity for fundamental change); take-off (political power tied to economic growth, modern technology); drive to maturity (two generations, marked by steady growth of the economy and the development of internal markets); and high mass consumption. While still considered today to be one of the most important theories of development, Rostow's stages have been criticized for denying political choice and flexible development paths. Rostow has dedicated his life's work to the problems of economic and social development of Latin America, Africa, the Middle East, and Asia. In 1951, he set up the Center for International Studies at MIT, which first directed a study on Soviet society. He was then commissioned to do similar studies on China for President John Kennedy. Rostow's work for U.S. foreign affairs is extensive; he served as chairman of the Policy Planning Council at the State Department from 1961 to 1966 and director of the National Security Council from 1966 to 1969.

Michael Schneider

Michael Schneider has been the executive vice president of the American Jewish Joint Distribution Committee (JDC) since 1987. JDC works to meet Jewish needs around the globe, sponsoring programs of relief, rescue, reconstruction, and education. Before his appointment as executive vice president, Schneider was director of JDC-Israel. When JDC was invited to return to Hungary in 1979, he was the first returning director for JDC-Hungary programs during the cold war. He was also the first returning director to Czechoslovakia and represented JDC in Yugoslavia. Schneider played a critical role in coordinating the American response to the rescue of Ethiopian Jewry, and continues to play a leadership role in the rescue of Jews from other areas of distress, as well as directing JDC's relief and Jewish cultural activities in over 40 countries.

Amartya Sen

One of the most influential scholars in the field of development economics, Amartya Sen was born in India and was educated at Presidency College in Calcutta, as well as Trinity College and

Cambridge University in England, where he received a Ph.D. in 1959. Sen is currently the Lamont University Professor at Harvard University and a member of the departments of economics and philosophy. Before teaching at Harvard, Sen was a professor of economics at Oxford University. He is the author of a number of important books, such as: *On Economic Inequality* (1973), *Poverty and Famines: An Essay on Entitlement and Deprivation* (1981), and *On Ethics and Economics* (1987). Sen's work focuses on the ethical issues of economics, as he offers alternative explanations for the existence of famines, poverty, and inequality. He argues that famines are not simply caused by shortages of food supply, but rather occur when there is a collapse for particular groups in their "entitlement" to food. Sen's work has been pathbreaking in revealing the links between economics and ethics. He has presented methods for measuring poverty and inequality, as well as theories on the causes of famine and poverty, and methods of cost-benefit analysis. Sen was awarded the Feinstein Hunger Award in 1990 for his dedication to the study of the ethical issues of economics.

Gita Sen

An internationally recognized development economist, Gita Sen has made a significant contribution to the field of development with her research on gender and development, including gender dimensions of population policies and the linkages between population and the environment. Sen's work on the issue of population challenges the conventional view that defines growth in numbers as the problem and birth control as the answer. She sees population as being intertwined with issues of women's health, health care in general, and women's rights. Sen earned her B.A. at the University of Poona, her M.A. at Delhi School of Economics, and completed her Ph.D. at Stanford College. From 1989 to 1992, Sen was on the staff of the Centre for Development Studies (CDS) in Thiruvananthapuram, Kerala, in southern India, where she coordinated a UN Population Fund program which provided training in population and development for mid-career people from developing countries for a ten-month period. Sen is a founding member of Development Alternatives with Women for a New Era (DAWN) and is the editor of *Development, Crises and Alternative Visions: Third World Women Perspectives* and the co-editor of *Population Reconsidered: Empowerment, Health and Human Rights*, supported by the Swedish International Development Agency. Dr.

Sen recently spent two years as a visiting professor at the Harvard Center for Population and Development Studies in Boston. She is currently professor of economics at the Indian Institute of Management in Bangalore.

Arthur Simon

In 1973, Arthur Simon founded Bread for the World, a citizens lobby on hunger that has influenced numerous U.S. policies related to overcoming hunger at home and abroad. Simon served as Bread for the World's president for almost two decades. Currently Simon is the director of the Washington office of Christian Children's Fund. His book, *Bread for the World,* won the national Religious Book Award, and was described by the late Nobel Prize economist Gunnar Myrdal as a "clear and convincing" analysis of world hunger. In 1973, he and his brother, Senator Paul Simon, wrote *Politics of World Hunger,* which now has over 300,000 copies in print. Simon has received a number of awards and honorary degrees, including the 1990 Presidential End Hunger Award for Lifetime Achievement.

Kathleen Staudt

Having written extensively on the subject of women in development (WID), and specifically on the gender dimensions of state-society relations, Kathleen Staudt's most recent book, *Managing Development,* was published in 1991. Staudt began her fieldwork experience as a Peace Crops volunteer in the Philippines in the mid-1960s. In 1979, after earning her Ph.D. in political science, she served as an analyst/program officer for USAID in their Women in Development Office. Staudt's experience at USAID was the basis for her book, *Women, Foreign Assistance and Advocacy Administration,* which analyzes the efforts of an advocacy office to press for implementation of WID policy and to institutionalize this policy in the core of USAID's procedures. Staudt's research work on nongovernmental organizations has taken her to northern Mexico and the Caribbean, and to Kenya where she studied the delivery of agricultural extension services to men and women farmers. Staudt is currently a professor of political science at the University of Texas at El Paso.

Irene Tinker

Another key figure in the field of women in development, Irene Tinker was born in 1927 in Wisconsin. Tinker was educated at Radcliffe College and went on to earn her Ph.D. at the London School of Economics. She was the founder of the Equity Policy Center (EPOC) and served as its president from 1978 to 1989. She has also served as the president of International Center for Research on Women (which she also founded) and the U.S. Council for the UN International Research and Training Institute for the Advancement of Women (INSTRAW). She was appointed by President Jimmy Carter as director of the ACTION office of Policy and Planning and was the U.S. delegate to the UN Commission on the Status of Women. Her field research is based mostly in India and Indonesia. She has authored and edited numerous publications, including *Persistent Inequalities,* published in 1990. Tinker received an award for Outstanding Leadership in Women in Development from the Association for Women in Development in 1989.

Lawrence Turnipseed

The executive director of Church World Service and Witness, Lawrence Turnipseed is a longtime specialist in southern Asian affairs. Turnipseed began his career as a United Methodist missionary in Hong Kong from 1958 to 1973. He has served as associate general secretary in the United Methodist Church's General Commission on Christian Unity and Interreligious Concerns since 1973. In 1981, Turnipseed was appointed director of the Southern Asia Office for the National Council of Churches. Throughout his career, Turnipseed has worked with church groups and service agencies in 13 countries in South and Southeast Asia, coordinating development efforts in such areas as Cambodia. In 1982, Turnipseed assisted in bringing the first groups of Amerasian children to the United States from Vietnam. Turnipseed recently chaired the U.S. Committee to End Child Prostitution in Asian Tourism, and also chaired task forces in Muslim-Christian and Jewish-Christian relations.

Sima Wali

An Afghani refugee who was forced to flee her home country when her family came under attack during the Communist coup,

Sima Wali fled first to Frankfurt and then to New York. In New York, Wali found employment with the Secretariat for Women in Development at the New TransCentury Foundation. As the status of Afghani refugees had not yet been decided by the U.S. government, her first few months in the United States were marked with anxiety and fear, made worse by the fact that she had no knowledge of her parents' whereabouts. Wali advanced rapidly in her career, becoming the executive director of Refugee Women in Development, an organization she founded. Wali avoids direct political activity as she does not desire to use her organization as a political entree. Through Refugee Women in Development, Wali hopes to create a forum for women through which they can explore and reevaluate their positions in a foreign land.

Barbara Ward

Described as "one of the most widely read and influential writers on economic and international affairs," Barbara Ward served as the economic advisor to India and Pakistan during the 1940s and chaired the Society of International Development. She was also a writer for *The Economist,* covering the Marshall Plan for Europe and becoming foreign editor in 1940. In 1970, she organized a conference at Columbia University to discuss the role of foreign aid; the UN Development Programme director, the director of the International Monetary Fund, and the president of the World Bank (then Robert McNamara) were among those who attended. In 1974 Ward led the Rome Forum on World Food Problems. She wrote 20 very influential and widely read books and thousands of articles, including *Only One Earth,* which was the basic text and inspiration to the UN Conference on the Human Environment. In 1979 she wrote *Progress for a Small Planet,* wherein she discussed the interrelations between energy provision, food supply, and the process of urbanization. Throughout her life, Ward infused a strong moral sense to her arguments and she was a continuous proponent for foreign aid.

Kathryn Wolford

Kathryn Wolford has been the executive director of Lutheran World Relief (LWR), the well-regarded relief and development agency, since 1993. Prior to her appointment as executive director, Wolford served as LWR's program director for Latin America. She began her career with the National Council of Churches/Church World Service (CWS) working in the Office on Development Policy and the Office on Global Education. Wolford was the first Caribbean regional representative for CWS, based in the Dominican Republic. She also worked as an electoral observer on behalf of the National Council of Churches in Nicaragua and Haiti. Wolford received a B.A. from Gettysburg College and M.A.s in public policy studies and in religious studies. In 1994, Gettysburg College awarded her with the honorary degree of Doctor of Public Service.

Muhammad Yunus

Founder of the Grameen Bank, known today as a real "success story of development," Muhammad Yunus began the bank as an action-research project in 1976 in the village of Jobra in Bangladesh. The aim of the project was to provide banking facilities to the landless poor, who were required to organize themselves into groups of five, with an elected chairman and weekly meetings. Yunus saw group borrowing as protection for the bank, and demanded that loans be repaid in weekly installments within one year. By 1982 the membership had grown to 28,000, 11,000 of whom were women. The success of the bank astounded those who questioned the feasibility of providing credit to landless clients; less than 1 percent defaulted on their loans. In 1983, the project was converted into an independent bank, with Yunus as the chief executive. He is adamant about "wearing the hat of the banker" (not the social reformer) and stresses that the bank is a good business, not a humanitarian effort. Funding for expansion came from the International Fund for Agricultural Development (IFAD) and by 1987 the Grameen Bank was reaching 6,000 villages in 6 of Bangladesh's 64 districts. Today over 75 percent of the loans go to women and Yunus's model of rural credit has been adapted in Africa and even North America.

Facts and Statistics 4

The information in this chapter is organized into seven sections: Human Development, Economic Development, Demographics of Development, Health Services, Gender, Environmental Degradation, and Refugees—all of which echo and reinforce the major concerns for global development discussed in chapter 1.

Human Development: Definitions and Indicators

As much of the foregoing should make clear, there is no single definition of development that adequately embraces all facets of the enterprise and responds to the emphases of the many communities that collectively participate in development.

However, notwithstanding considerable diversity, most definitions share substantial common ground. There is broad agreement, for example, that human development brings together the production and distribution of commodities and the expansion and use of human capabilities. It focuses on choices—on what people should have and do to be able to ensure their own livelihood.

Human development is concerned not only with basic need satisfaction, but also with individual development as a participatory and dynamic process.

Similarly, there are three basic measurements that are almost universally accepted for assessing human development. The first indicator is longevity—life expectancy at birth. Longevity is accepted as a foundational criterion due to a broad consensus that a long life is valuable in itself and that various indirect benefits (such as adequate nutrition and good health) are closely associated with higher life expectancy. To reach an accurate idea of the state of worldwide mortality, one must examine the diversity between different social groups, age groups, and nationalities (Table 1).

The second generally accepted indicator is knowledge, most often evaluated in terms of literacy. Literacy provides a crude reflection of the access to education, which is an important element of productive life in modern society, as well as a means to personal fulfillment. Literacy provides the first step in learning, offering the ability to expand and improve one's position in life. Data from four generations of development work indicate that there have been important advances in literacy throughout the Third World. However, there are also significant disparities, notably the wide variations in male and female literacy. The disproportionate suffering of women from the component problems of development, including hunger, refugeeism, and work discrimination, is a central theme in modern development studies.

The third broadly accepted indicator is personal command over the resources necessary for a decent living. Accurate measurement of this indicator entails data on land, credit, income, and other resources. Due to the scarcity and complexity of such data we must make the best use of an income indicator. Per capita income can be used as a starting point. However the presence of nontradable goods and services and the distortions from exchange rate anomalies, tariffs, and taxes undermines per capita income data in nominal prices as a measurement. This information is enhanced by using purchasing power–adjusted real gross national product (GNP) per capita (Table 2). This measure provides a better approximation of relative purchasing power and ability to command resources for a decent living standard. It must be kept in mind, however, that this indicator fails to expose the uneven distribution of wealth within nations and societies.

Table 1: Global Demographic Indicators

Developing Countries
Africa (sub-Saharan)

	Population (millions) 1994	Population (millions) 2010	Population annual growth rate 1990-92 (%)	Total Fertility rate 1992	Percent Age <15 1994	Percent Age 65+ 1994	Percent of population urbanized 1994	Life expectancy at birth (years)	Infant mortality rate (under 1) per 1,000 live births 1994	Under 5 mortality rate per 1,000 live births 1960	Under 5 mortality rate per 1,000 live births 1992	Maternal mortality rate per 100,000 live births 1980-91
Total	570.0	901.0	..	6.5	46	3	27	52	..	..	..	..
Angola	11.2	17.6	2.9	7.2	45	3	28	46	170	345	292	..
Benin	5.3	8.4	2.9	7.1	47	3	38	46	88	310	147	160
Botswana	1.4	2.1	3.1	5.2	48	3	26	62	45	170	58	250
Burkina Faso	10.1	15.5	2.6	6.5	48	4	21	48	101	318	150	810
Burundi	6.0	9.1	2.9	6.8	46	4	6	48	108	255	179	..
Cameroon	13.1	21.2	2.9	5.8	45	3	41	56	74	264	117	430
Cape Verde	0.4	0.6	..	4.4	44	5	44	68	40	164	61	..
Central African Republic	3.1	3.9	2.6	6.2	43	3	47	44	105	294	179	600
Chad	6.5	9.8	2.2	5.9	41	3	32	48	123	325	209	960
Comoros	0.5	0.9	..	7.1	48	3	28	56	..	..	..	..
Congo	2.4	3.2	2.9	6.3	44	3	41	49	82	220	110	900
Côte d'Ivoire	13.9	23.7	3.8	7.4	47	2	39	52	91	300	124	..
Djibouti	0.6	0.9	..	6.6	41	2	77	49	..	..	..	..
Equatorial Guinea	0.4	0.6	..	5.9	43	4	37	51	..	..	..	..
Eritrea	3.5	5.4	..	..	..	..	..	..	123	294	208	..

Table 1: Global Demographic Indicators continued

	Population (millions) 1994	Population (millions) 2010	Population annual growth rate 1990-92 (%)	Total Fertility rate 1992	Percent Age <15 1994	Percent Age 65+ 1994	Percent of population urbanized 1994	Life expectancy at birth (years)	Infant mortality rate (under 1) per 1,000 live births 1994	Under 5 mortality rate per 1,000 live births 1960	Under 5 mortality rate per 1,000 live births 1992	Maternal mortality rate per 100,000 live births 1980-91
Ethiopia	55.2	89.0	2.6	7.0	49	3	15	52	123	294	208	560x
Gabon	1.1	1.4	3.6	5.2	33	6	46	54	95	287	158	190
Gambia	1.1	1.5	..	6.2	45	2	26	45	95	..	158	190
Ghana	16.9	26.6	3.3	6.1	45	3	34	56	103	215	170	1,000
Guinea	6.4	9.3	2.6	7.0	44	3	26	43	135	337	230	800
Guinea-Bissau	1.1	1.5	2.0	5.8	43	3	20	44	141	336	239	700x
Kenya	27.0	44.4	3.5	6.4	49	2	25	59	51	202	74	170x
Lesotho	1.9	2.8	2.6	4.8	41	4	19	61	108	204	156	..
Liberia	2.9	4.8	3.2	6.8	45	4	43	55	146	288	217	..
Madagascar	13.7	22.4	3.2	6.6	45	3	22	56	110	364	168	570
Malawi	9.5	14.7	4.3	7.6	48	3	17	44	143	365	226	400
Mali	9.1	15.0	3.0	7.1	46	4	22	45	122	400	220	2,000
Mauritania	2.3	3.5	2.7	6.5	44	4	39	48	118	321	206	..
Mauritius	1.1	1.3	1.1	2.0	30	5	39	69	20	84	24	99
Mozambique	15.8	25.4	1.7	6.5	44	3	27	47	167	331	287	300
Namibia	1.6	2.6	3.0	6.0	45	3	33	59	62	206	79	370x

	Population (millions) 1994	Population (millions) 2010	Population annual growth rate 1990-92 (%)	Total Fertility rate 1992	Percent Age <15 1994	Percent Age 65+ 1994	Percent of population urbanized 1994	Life expectancy at birth (years)	Infant mortality rate (under 1) per 1,000 live births 1994	Under 5 mortality rate per 1,000 live births 1960	Under 5 mortality rate per 1,000 live births 1992	Maternal mortality rate per 100,000 live births 1980-91
Niger	8.8	14.3	3.3	7.1	49	3	15	47	191	320	320	700
Nigeria	98.1	162.0	3.2	6.6	45	3	16	54	114	204	191	800
Rwanda	7.7	10.4	3.1	8.5	48	3	5	46	131	191	222	210
Senegal	8.2	12.4	2.8	6.2	47	3	39	49	90	303	145	600
Sierra Leone	4.6	6.9	2.5	6.5	45	3	32	43	144	385	249	450
Somalia	9.8	15.9	2.6	7.0	47	4	24	47	125	294	211	1,100
South Africa	41.2	58.4	2.5	4.2	39	2	57	65	53	126	70	84x
Sudan	28.2	43.0	3.0	6.2	46	3	23	53	100	292	166	550
Swaziland	0.8	1.3	..	5.0	47	3	23	56	..	..	..	..
Tanzania	29.8	48.4	3.4	6.8	47	2	21	51	111	249	176	340x
Togo	4.3	7.4	3.0	6.6	49	3	29	56	86	264	137	420
Uganda	19.8	30.7	2.9	7.3	47	3	11	42	111	218	185	300
Zaire	42.5	68.6	3.3	6.7	45	3	40	52	121	286	188	800
Zambia	9.1	13.9	3.4	6.5	48	2	49	44	113	220	202	150
Zimbabwe	11.2	16.8	3.3	5.5	48	3	27	56	60	181	86	..

Table 1: Global Demographic Indicators   *continued*

	Population (millions) 1994	Population (millions) 2010	Population annual growth rate 1990-92 (%)	Total Fertility rate 1992	Percent Age <15 1994	Percent Age 65+ 1994	Percent of population urbanized 1994	Life expectancy at birth (years)	Infant mortality rate (under 1) per 1,000 live births 1994	Under 5 mortality rate per 1,000 live births 1960	Under 5 mortality rate per 1,000 live births 1992	Maternal mortality rate per 100,000 live births 1980-91
South Asia												
Afghanistan	17.8	34.7	1.4	6.9	46	4	18	42	165	360	257	640
Bangladesh	116.6	164.8	2.5	4.8	44	3	14	53	97	247	127	600
Bhutan	0.8	1.1	2.2	5.9	39	4	13	49	131	324	201	1,310
India	911.6	1,163.3	2.0	4.0	36	4	26	57	83	236	124	460
Nepal	22.1	32.3	2.7	5.6	44	3	8	51	90	279	128	830
Pakistan	126.4	191.1	3.2	6.3	44	3	28	60	95	221	137	500
Sri Lanka	17.9	21.0	1.5	2.5	35	4	22	73	15	130	19	80
East Asia and the Pacific												
Burma (Myanmar)	45.4	59.2	2.1	4.3	36	4	25	59	83	237	113	460
Cambodia	10.3	15.7	2.5	4.5	44	3	13	49	117	217	184	500
China	1,192.0	1,376.1	1.5	2.3	28	6	28	70	35	209	43	95
Fiji	0.8	0.9	..	3.0	38	3	39	64	..	..	..	..
Hong Kong	5.8	6.3	1.2	1.4	21	9	..	78	6	52	7	6
Indonesia	199.7	250.3	2.0	3.2	37	4	31	60	71	216	111	450
Korea, N.	23.1	28.5	1.8	2.4	29	4	60	69	25	120	33	41

	Population (millions) 1994	Population (millions) 2010	Population annual growth rate 1990-92 (%)	Total Fertility rate 1992	Percent Age <15 1994	Percent Age 65+ 1994	Percent of population urbanized 1994	Life expectancy at birth (years)	Infant mortality rate (under 1) per 1,000 live births 1994	Under 5 mortality rate per 1,000 live births 1960	Under 5 mortality rate per 1,000 live births 1992	Maternal mortality rate per 100,000 live births 1980-91
Korea, S.	44.5	49.7	1.2	1.7	24	5	74	71	8	124	9	26
Laos	4.7	7.2	2.8	6.7	45	4	19	51	98	233	145	300
Malaysia	19.5	26.6	2.6	3.7	36	4	51	71	14	105	19	59
Mongolia	2.4	3.5	2.7	4.7	44	4	57	65	61	185	80	140
Papua New Guinea	4.0	5.7	2.3	5.0	40	4	13	55	54	248	77	900
Philippines	68.7	89.3	2.4	4.0	39	4	44	64	46	102	60	100
Singapore	2.9	3.3	1.1	1.7	23	6	100	74	6	40	7	10
Solomon Islands	0.4	0.6	..	5.5	47	3	13	61	..	..	..	..
Thailand	59.4	68.8	1.5	2.3	29	5	19	69	27	146	33	50
Vietnam	73.1	91.7	2.2	4.0	39	5	21	65	37	219	49	120
Latin America and the Caribbean												
Total	470.0	584.0	..	..	36	5	71	68	22	..	..	..
Argentina	33.9	39.9	1.3	2.8	30	9	86	71	22	68	24	140
Bolivia	8.2	11.4	2.5	4.7	42	4	58	61	80	252	118	600
Brazil	155.3	179.7	2.0	2.9	35	5	76	67	54	181	65	200
Chile	14.0	17.4	1.7	2.7	31	6	85	72	15	138	18	67

Table 1: Global Demographic Indicators *continued*

	Population (millions) 1994	Population (millions) 2010	Population annual growth rate 1990-92 (%)	Total Fertility rate 1992	Percent Age <15 1994	Percent Age 65+ 1994	Percent of population urbanized 1994	Life expectancy at birth (years)	Infant mortality rate (under 1) per 1,000 live births 1994	Under 5 mortality rate per 1,000 live births 1960	Under 5 mortality rate per 1,000 live births 1992	Maternal mortality rate per 100,000 live births 1980-91
Colombia	35.6	44.5	1.9	2.7	34	4	68	71	17	132	20	200
Costa Rica	3.2	4.4	2.8	3.2	36	5	44	76	14	112	16	36
Cuba	11.1	12.3	0.9	1.9	23	9	73	77	10	50	11	39
Dominican Republic	7.8	9.9	2.3	3.5	38	3	60	68	42	152	50	..
Ecuador	10.6	14.0	2.6	3.8	39	4	57	69	47	180	59	170
El Salvador	5.2	7.3	1.5	4.2	44	4	45	66	47	210	63	..
Guatemala	10.3	15.8	2.9	5.5	45	3	38	65	55	205	76	200
Guyana	0.8	1.0	1.1*	2.6	33	4	33	65	48	126	69	..
Haiti	7.0	9.8	1.9	4.9	40	4	31	46	87	270	133	340
Honduras	5.3	7.6	3.3	5.1	47	4	44	66	45	203	58	220
Jamaica	2.5	3.0	1.2	2.5	33	8	52	74	12	76	14	120
Mexico	91.8	118.5	2.3	3.3	38	4	71	70	28	141	33	110
Nicaragua	4.3	6.7	2.9	5.2	46	3	62	63	54	209	76	..
Panama	2.5	3.3	2.1	3.0	35	5	49	72	18	104	20	60
Paraguay	4.8	7.1	3.0	4.4	40	4	51	67	28	90	34	300
Peru	22.9	29.5	2.2	3.7	38	4	71	65	46	236	65	300

	Population (millions) 1994	Population (millions) 2010	Population annual growth rate 1990-92 (%)	Total Fertility rate 1992	Percent Age <15 1994	Percent Age 65+ 1994	Percent of population urbanized 1994	Life expectancy at birth (years)	Infant mortality rate (under 1) per 1,000 live births 1994	Under 5 mortality rate per 1,000 live births 1960	Under 5 mortality rate per 1,000 live births 1992	Maternal mortality rate per 100,000 live births 1980-91
Suriname	0.4	0.5	..	2.8	41	4	70	69	..	..	..	..
Trinidad & Tobago	1.3	1.5	1.3	2.8	32	6	69	71	19	73	22	110
Uruguay	3.2	3.6	0.6	2.4	26	12	89	73	20	47	22	36
Venezuela	21.3	28.4	2.5	3.2	38	4	84	70	20	70	24	..
Middle East and North Africa												
Algeria	27.9	38.2	2.8	5.0	44	4	50	67	60	243	72	140x
Bahrain	0.6	0.8	..	3.8	32	2	81	71	..	..	..	..
Cyprus	0.7	0.8	..	2.3	26	10	62	76	..	..	..	..
Egypt	58.9	80.7	2.5	4.2	40	4	45	62	43	258	55	270
Iran	61.2	100.4	3.8	6.1	47	4	57	65	44	233	58	120
Iraq	19.9	34.5	3.3	5.8	48	3	70	64	64	171	80	120
Jordan	4.2	6.6	3.2	5.8	41	3	70	67	25	149	30	48x
Kuwait	1.3	2.3	3.0	3.8	43	2	..	76	14	128	17	6
Lebanon	3.6	5.0	0.5	3.2	33	5	86	75	35	91	44	..
Libya	5.1	8.9	3.9	6.5	47	3	76	63	70	269	104	70x
Morocco	28.6	38.1	2.6	4.5	40	4	47	67	50	215	61	300x

Table 1: Global Demographic Indicators   continued

	Population (millions) 1994	Population (millions) 2010	Population annual growth rate 1990-92 (%)	Total Fertility rate 1992	Percent Age <15 1994	Percent Age 65+ 1994	Percent of population urbanized 1994	Life expectancy at birth (years)	Infant mortality rate (under 1) per 1,000 live births 1994	Under 5 mortality rate per 1,000 live births 1960	Under 5 mortality rate per 1,000 live births 1992	Maternal mortality rate per 100,000 live births 1980-91
Oman	1.9	3.4	4.2	6.8	36	3	12	71	24	300	31	..
Qatar	0.5	0.6	..	4.5	23	1	91	73	26	..	..	..
Saudi Arabia	18.0	30.5	4.4	6.5	43	2	79	70	35	292	40	41
Syria	14.0	24.2	3.5	6.3	48	3	51	66	34	201	40	140
Tunisia	8.7	11.3	2.3	3.6	37	5	59	68	32	244	38	70
Turkey	61.8	81.3	2.3	3.6	35	4	61	67	70	217	87	150
United Arab Emirates	1.7	2.9	4.2	4.6	32	1	83	72	18	240	22	..
Yemen	12.9	22.1	3.5	7.3	51	4	31	54	107	378	177	..

Industrial Countries

	Population (millions) 1994	Population (millions) 2010	Population annual growth rate 1990-92 (%)	Total Fertility rate 1992	Percent Age <15 1994	Percent Age 65+ 1994	Percent of population urbanized 1994	Life expectancy at birth (years)	Infant mortality rate (under 1) per 1,000 live births 1994	Under 5 mortality rate per 1,000 live births 1960	Under 5 mortality rate per 1,000 live births 1992	Maternal mortality rate per 100,000 live births 1980-91
Albania	3.4	4.0	1.8	2.8	33	5	36	72	28	151	34	..
Australia	17.8	20.9	1.5	1.9	22	12	85	77	7	24	9	3
Austria	8.0	8.2	0.3	1.5	18	15	54	76	7	43	9	8
Belgium	10.0	10.1	0.1	1.6	18	15	97	76	9	35	11	3
Bulgaria	8.4	8.4	0.1	1.9	20	14	67	72	16	70	20	9
Canada	29.1	33.4	1.1	1.8	21	12	77	77	7	33	8	5
Czech Republic	10.3	10.9	..	2.0	21	13	..	72	11	..	12	..

	Population (millions) 1994	Population (millions) 2010	Population annual growth rate 1990-92 (%)	Total Fertility rate 1992	Percent Age <15 1994	Percent Age 65+ 1994	Percent of population urbanized 1994	Life expectancy at birth (years)	Infant mortality rate (under 1) per 1,000 live births 1994	Under 5 mortality rate per 1,000 live births 1960	Under 5 mortality rate per 1,000 live births 1992	Maternal mortality rate per 100,000 live births 1980-91
Denmark	5.2	5.3	0.1	1.7	17	16	85	75	7	25	8	3
Finland	5.1	5.2	0.4	1.8	19	14	80	75	6	28	7	11
Former Soviet Union												
Armenia	3.7	4.0	:	2.6	31	6	68	70	29	:	34	:
Azerbaijan	7.4	8.6	:	2.8	33	5	54	71	37	:	53	:
Belarus	10.3	10.7	:	2.0	23	11	67	71	20	:	23	:
Estonia	1.5	1.6	0.6	2.1	22	12	71	70	20	:	24	:
Georgia	5.5	6.1	:	2.3	25	9	56	73	25	:	29	:
Kazakhstan	17.1	18.6	:	3.0	31	6	58	69	43	:	50	:
Kyrgyzstan	4.5	5.6	:	4.0	38	5	37	69	49	:	60	:
Latvia	2.5	2.8	0.5	2.0	21	12	70	69	22	:	27	:
Lithuania	3.7	4.2	0.8	2.0	22	11	69	71	17	:	20	:
Moldova	4.4	4.6	:	2.6	28	8	48	69	31	:	36	:
Russian Federation	147.8	145.2	:	2.1	22	11	73	68	28	:	32	:
Tajikistan	5.9	8.7	:	5.4	43	3	31	69	65	:	85	:
Turkmenistan	4.1	5.3	:	4.6	40	4	45	66	72	:	91	:
Ukraine	51.5	49.7	:	2.0	21	12	68	69	21	:	25	:

Table 1: Global Demographic Indicators *continued*

	Population (millions) 1994	Population (millions) 2010	Population annual growth rate 1990-92 (%)	Total Fertility rate 1992	Percent Age <15 1994	Percent Age 65+ 1994	Percent of population urbanized 1994	Life expectancy at birth (years)	Infant mortality rate (under 1) per 1,000 live births 1994	Under 5 mortality rate per 1,000 live births 1960	Under 5 mortality rate per 1,000 live births 1992	Maternal mortality rate per 100,000 live births 1980-91
Uzbekistan	22.1	29.9	..	4.4	41	4	40	69	56	..	68	..
France	58.0	58.8	0.5	1.8	20	15	74	77	7	34	9	9
Germany	81.2	78.2	0.2	1.5	16	15	85	76	7	40	8	5
Greece	10.4	10.9	0.5	1.5	19	14	58	77	8	64	9	5
Hungary	10.3	9.9	-0.2	1.8	19	14	63	69	15	57	16	15
Ireland	3.6	3.9	0.2	2.2	27	11	56	74	5	36	6	2
Israel	5.4	6.9	2.3	2.9	31	9	90	76	9	39	11	3
Italy	57.2	58.1	0.2	1.3	16	15	68	77	8	50	10	4
Japan	125.0	130.4	0.5	1.7	17	14	77	79	4	40	6	11
Netherlands	15.4	16.7	0.6	1.7	18	13	89	77	6	22	7	10
New Zealand	3.5	4.1	0.9	2.1	23	11	85	75	8	26	10	13
Norway	4.3	4.5	0.4	1.9	19	16	72	77	6	23	8	3
Poland	38.6	41.3	0.6	2.1	25	10	62	71	14	70	16	11
Portugal	9.9	10.3	0.1	1.5	20	13	34	74	11	112	13	10
Romania	22.7	23.0	0.4	2.2	22	11	54	70	23	82	28	72
Slovakia	5.3	5.9	..	..	25	10	57	71	12	..	14	..

	Population (millions) 1994	Population (millions) 2010	Population annual growth rate 1990-92 (%)	Total Fertility rate 1992	Percent Age <15 1994	Percent Age 65+ 1994	Percent of population urbanized 1994	Life expectancy at birth (years)	Infant mortality rate (under 1) per 1,000 live births 1994	Under 5 mortality rate per 1,000 live births 1960	Under 5 mortality rate per 1,000 live births 1992	Maternal mortality rate per 100,000 live births 1980-91
Spain	39.2	40.7	0.3	1.4	19	14	78	77	8	57	9	5
Sweden	8.8	9.2	0.3	2.0	18	18	83	78	6	20	7	5
Switzerland	7.0	7.5	0.6	1.6	16	15	68	78	7	27	9	5
USA	260.8	300.4	1.0	2.0	22	13	75	76	9	30	10	8
United Kingdom	58.4	61.0	0.2	1.9	19	16	92	76	7	27	9	8
Yugoslavia (former)	10.5	11.6	0.6	1.9	23	10	47	72	19	113	22	27
World	5,607	7,022	..	3.4	33	6	43	65	..	..	..	..

Notes

* Growth rate for 1980-91.

X Indicates data that refer to years or periods other than those specified in the column heading, differ from the standard definition, or refer to only part of a country.

Source: *Causes of Hunger*. Silver Spring, MD: Bread for the World Institute, 1994. Reprinted by permission of the publisher.

Table 2: Gross National Product per Capita

SUB-SAHARAN AFRICA	1984	1985	1986	1987	1988	1989	1990	1991	1992	1993
	530	520	500	500	500	490	480	470	450	440
Benin	390	410	390	360	380	340	350	360	350	360
Botswana	..	..	1,520	1,220	1,810	1,910	..	..	..	..
Burkina Faso	220	240	240	240	250	250	250	250	250	240
Burundi	200	220	230	220	230	220	220	220	220	210
Cameroon	1,110	1,230	1,210	1,100	940	910	790	750	710	610
Cape Verde	490	520	540	560	590	610	550	560	620	620
Central African Republic	410	410	420	380	380	380	370	360	350	310
Chad	160	180	170	160	190	190	180	190	190	190
Comoros	340	330	430	490	500	450	510	480	520	460
Congo	1,670	1,390	970	1,000	890	980	950	830	800	590
Côte d'Ivoire	850	920	900	890	820	710	620	580	570	530
Equatorial Guinea	..	..	..	..	..	..	..	..	..	..
Ethiopia	..	..	..	..	..	..	..	..	..	..
Gabon	6,480	6,040	4,350	3,430	3,830	3,950	4,190	4,160	3,820	3,740
Gambia, The	270	270	270	270	270	260	270	300	450	450
Ghana	350	360	360	360	370	360	360	370	370	360
Guinea	..	..	360	360	340	350	360	360	360	360
Guinea-Bissau	170	180	170	180	190	190	210	200	220	220
Kenya	350	340	360	360	370	370	370	370	360	360
Lesotho	510	470	440	430	430	470	510	460	440	460
Madagascar	230	230	220	210	210	210	210	180	180	180
Malawi	170	160	140	140	130	130	140	150	120	130
Mali	210	210	220	230	220	240	240	220	230	220
Mauritania	440	450	460	450	450	480	450	480	480	450
Mauritius	1,220	1,280	1,520	1,730	1,780	1,810	1,970	2,030	2,150	2,190

	1984	1985	1986	1987	1988	1989	1990	1991	1992	1993
Mozambique	90	80	80	80	90	90	100	100	90	110
Namibia	1,320	1,380	1,410	1,340	1,400	1,440	1,410	1,420	1,420	1,460
Niger	300	310	320	310	310	280	290	280	260	250
Nigeria	370	380	270	280	280	310	340	330	330	320
Rwanda	360	360	370	340	350	330	300	310	310	280
Senegal	610	620	640	650	650	650	660	640	650	620
Seychelles	..	3,980	3,410	3,510	3,640	3,570	3,820	3,690	5,240	4,890
Sierra Leone	150	140	140	140	140	140	140	140	130	130
Somalia	110	110	110	120	110	110	..	..	..	..
South Africa	2,200	2,160	2,180	2,280	2,300	2,200	2,050	2,010	1,890	1,890
Sudan	..	..	..	..	..	..	..	..	..	..
Swaziland	860	890	840	840	..	830	860	840	820	..
Tanzania	..	..	..	..	..	..	..	..	..	..
Togo	380	390	390	370	390	390	400	380	320	260
Uganda	450	430	410	400	420	440	450	460	460	480
Zaire	200	190	200	210	200	190	190	190	..	..
Zambia	230	200	190	240	260	200	220	..	190	200
Zimbabwe	600	630	610	580	620	630	640	640	570	560
SOUTH ASIA	*280*	*290*	*300*	*310*	*330*	*340*	*350*	*340*	*350*	*350*
Bangladesh	160	170	170	170	170	170	180	180	190	190
Bhutan	..	..	..	..	..	..	..	..	..	..

Table 2: Gross National Product per Capita   continued

1984	1985	1986	1987	1988	1989	1990	1991	1992	1993	
300	310	310	320	350	360	370	360	370	370	India
..	..	..	..	..	..	..	..	..	..	Nepal
320	330	330	340	350	350	360	350	370	370	Pakistan
400	390	390	400	400	400	420	430	440	470	Sri Lanka
..	..	..	..	..	..	..	..	..	..	*EAST ASIA AND PACIFIC*
..	..	..	..	..	..	..	..	..	..	China
..	..	..	..	..	..	..	..	..	..	Fiji
410	420	410	430	430	460	480	500	520	550	Indonesia
2,410	2,530	2,860	3,210	3,610	3,890	4,200	4,540	4,720	4,960	Korea, Rep.
290	290	300	280	270	300	310	310	320	330	Lao PDR
1,960	1,840	1,670	1,810	1,960	2,080	2,260	2,390	2,570	2,760	Malaysia
1,550	1,600	1,680	1,660	1,750	1,780	1,690	1,540	1,340	1,290	Mongolia
..	..	..	..	..	..	..	..	..	..	Myanmar
830	820	820	830	870	780	720	780	800	890	Papua New Guinea
570	540	550	570	620	630	630	620	620	610	Philippines
850	830	870	950	1,070	1,170	1,270	1,350	1,450	1,540	Solomon Islands
1,030	1,020	880	820	860	890	920	..	..	..	Thailand
..	..	..	..	..	..	..	..	..	..	Vanuatu
..	..	..	..	..	..	..	..	..	..	Western Samoa
1,750	*1,750*	*1,770*	*1,810*	*1,780*	*1,760*	*1,740*	*1,770*	*1,790*	*1,820*	*LATIN AMERICA AND CARIBBEAN*
..	..	..	..	..	..	..	..	..	..	Antigua and Barbuda

	1984	1985	1986	1987	1988	1989	1990	1991	1992	1993
Argentina	3,490	3,140	3,330	3,340	3,280	2,900	2,960	3,240	3,530	3,700
Barbados	..	..	..	..	..	..	..	..	..	..
Belize	1,430	1,280	1,350	1,540	1,660	1,750	1,880	1,800	1,870	1,760
Bolivia	730	690	650	650	650	660	680	690	690	700
Brazil	1,740	1,830	1,990	2,020	1,990	2,010	1,880	1,860	1,820	1,880
Chile	1,270	1,300	1,370	1,510	1,680	1,830	1,810	1,910	2,100	2,150
Colombia	1,030	1,020	1,090	1,100	1,120	1,120	1,110	1,110	1,140	1,150
Costa Rica	1,440	1,430	1,570	1,520	1,510	1,530	1,560	1,590	1,670	1,740
Dominican Republic	680	660	700	720	790	760	660	650	680	710
Ecuador	1,180	1,190	1,080	1,030	1,050	1,040	1,070	1,090	1,120	1,080
El Salvador	860	890	920	880	890	880	850	860	870	900
Guatemala	870	830	820	820	830	840	840	870	890	900
Guyana	290	310	400	330	310	200	190	300	320	340
Haiti	370	360	360	350	340	340	330	320	..	..
Honduras	870	880	880	890	930	930	900	890	880	900
Jamaica	1,280	1,220	1,000	1,150	1,260	1,290	1,320	1,210	1,460	1,450
Mexico	1,860	1,860	1,640	1,690	1,670	1,720	1,800	1,830	1,840	1,780
Nicaragua	1,120	1,060	1,030	1,060	830	710	710	610	560	550
Panama	1,930	2,360	2,410	2,360	1,790	1,770	1,800	1,980	2,130	2,250
Paraguay	1,040	970	920	930	940	970	1,100	1,010	1,000	1,060
Peru	1,120	1,120	1,210	1,300	1,120	980	960	920	880	980
St. Lucia	..	..	..	..	..	..	..	..	..	..
Suriname	..	..	..	..	..	..	..	..	..	..
Trinidad and Tobago	4,710	4,690	4,200	3,800	3,440	3,360	4,360	4,260	4,070	3,880
Uruguay	1,820	1,810	2,080	2,320	2,310	2,300	2,230	2,420	2,630	2,680
Venezuela	2,910	2,770	2,480	2,590	2,590	2,410	2,570	2,660	2,740	2,600

Table 2: Gross National Product per Capita   continued

	1984	1985	1986	1987	1988	1989	1990	1991	1992	1993
MIDDLE EAST AND NORTH AFRICA	..	..	..	..	..	..	..	..	..	..
Algeria	3,120	3,260	2,780	2,740	2,540	2,660	2,480	2,390	2,330	2,210
Egypt, Arab Rep.	680	690	660	640	710	700	700	710	700	700
Iran, Islamic Rep.	3,330	3,220	2,740	2,610	2,340	2,340	2,500	2,690	2,780	2,730
Jordan	720	740	820	790	830	820	840	880	840	800
Morocco	..	..	..	..	..	..	..	..	..	..
Oman	..	..	..	..	..	..	..	..	..	..
Saudi Arabia	..	..	..	..	..	..	..	..	..	..
Syrian Arab Republic	1,120	1,170	1,030	980	1,070	960	1,060	990	..	..
Tunisia	1,260	1,260	1,160	1,220	1,190	1,190	1,250	1,260	1,320	1,320
Yemen, Rep.	..	..	..	..	..	..	..	..	..	..
EUROPE AND CENTRAL ASIA	..	..	..	..	..	..	..	..	..	..
Armenia	..	..	..	..	..	..	..	..	..	..
Azerbaijan	..	..	..	..	..	..	..	..	..	..
Belarus	..	..	..	..	..	..	..	..	..	..
Bulgaria	2,870	2,900	2,930	3,130	3,490	3,340	2,840	2,420	2,430	2,310
Estonia	..	..	..	..	..	..	..	..	..	..
Georgia	..	..	..	..	..	..	..	..	..	..
Greece	4,430	4,500	4,530	4,560	4,760	4,890	4,870	5,010	5,050	5,040
Hungary	2,270	2,280	2,250	2,390	2,420	2,510	2,430	2,390	2,240	2,190
Kazakhstan	..	..	..	..	..	..	..	..	..	..
Kyrgyz Republic	..	..	..	..	..	..	..	..	..	..
Latvia	..	..	..	..	..	..	..	..	..	..

	1984	1985	1986	1987	1988	1989	1990	1991	1992	1993
Lithuania	..	..	..	..	..	..	..	..	..	..
Moldova	..	..	..	..	..	..	..	..	..	..
Poland	1,450	1,540	1,600	1,620	1,680	1,740	1,500	1,450	1,460	1,540
Portugal	3,410	3,560	3,890	4,130	4,370	4,690	4,910	5,070	5,200	5,140
Romania	1,930	1,670	1,680	1,680	1,910	1,640	..	..	1,390	1,440
Russian Federation	..	..	..	..	..	..	..	..	..	..
Tajikistan	..	..	..	..	..	..	..	..	..	..
Turkey	1,380	1,460	1,520	1,620	1,510	1,550	1,640	1,570	1,660	1,760
Turkmenistan	..	..	..	..	..	..	..	..	..	..
Ukraine	..	..	..	..	..	..	..	..	..	..
Uzbekistan	..	..	..	..	..	..	..	..	..	..
Low- and middle-income economies	..	..	..	..	..	..	..	..	..	..
Low-income economies	..	..	..	..	..	..	..	..	..	..
China and India	..	..	..	..	..	..	..	..	..	..
Middle-income economies	..	..	..	..	..	..	..	..	..	..
High-income economies	**14,420**	**14,810**	**15,250**	**15,680**	**16,300**	**16,740**	**16,970**	**17,060**	**17,230**	**17,400**
OECD members	14,790	15,200	15,660	16,090	16,720	17,170	17,410	17,480	17,630	17,790
Japan	17,470	18,250	19,100	19,880	21,030	21,870	22,680	23,680	23,980	24,030
United States	17,590	17,940	18,230	18,560	19,130	19,510	19,560	19,270	19,500	19,940
WORLD	**3,060**	**3,110**	**3,160**	**3,220**	**3,310**	**3,370**	**3,380**	**3,380**	**3,400**	**3,420**

Source: *World Tables 1995*. Baltimore, MD: The Johns Hopkins University Press, 1995. Reprinted by permission of The International Bank for Reconstruction and Development/The World Bank.

These components are the starting point for a review of the data on human development and the formation of human capabilities. The United Nations Development Program has synthesized this information into a Human Development Index (HDI) as a measure of the relative socioeconomic progress of nations. The HDI enables people and their governments to evaluate progress over time and to determine priorities for policy intervention. It also permits instructive comparisons of the experiences in different countries. As such, it perhaps constitutes the best overall indicator of development currently available, and it is presented here as Table 3. The literacy index column refers to the percentage of the population that is literate; the schooling index column refers to the percentage of the population that completes the standard curriculum; the adjusted gross domestic product (GDP) column is an attempt to account for statistical variations among national data to allow effective cross-national comparisons of GDP; the human development index column is an aggregate figure of the basic development data reflected in the other columns, designed to provide an overall assessment of human development in comparative context; and the last column endeavors to show the relationship between a nation's raw wealth and its performance in providing human development—in a sense, it shows how well any given nation invests its wealth from the point of view of development.

However, for a fuller understanding of the complex development enterprise of today, we must look behind these initial measurements and examine major contributing factors: economic growth, trade, debt, and foreign aid; food production and access to food; the provision of health services; gender differences in the development equation; environmental degradation and the challenges posed therein; and the issue of refugees. Alongside this discussion we will look at the various attempts to solve and relieve the plight of those in the developing world.

Poverty

Reducing poverty is perhaps the basic objective of development, for all the components of human development—education, health, and welfare—move in close direct proportion with poverty rates. When we succeed in attacking the poverty problem, we will succeed in lifting literacy rates, raising life expectancy, reducing child mortality, and ensuring food security. Environmental stability and

Table 3: Human Development Index

HDI rank	Life expectancy at birth (years) 1992	Adult literacy rate (%) 1992	Mean years of schooling 1992	Literacy index	Schooling index	Educational attainment 1992	Real GDP per capita (PPP$) 1991	Adjusted real GDP per capita	Human development index 1992	GNP per capita rank minus HDI rank[a]
High human development	74.1	97.3	9.8				14,000		0.886	
1 Canada	77.2	99.0	12.2	0.99	0.82	2.80	19,320	5,347	0.932	10
2 Switzerland	77.8	99.0	11.6	0.99	0.77	2.75	21,780	5,370	0.931	-1
3 Japan	78.6	99.0	10.8	0.99	0.72	2.70	19,390	5,347	0.929	0
4 Sweden	77.7	99.0	11.4	0.99	0.76	2.74	17,490	5,342	0.928	0
5 Norway	76.9	99.0	12.1	0.99	0.80	2.78	17,170	5,341	0.928	0
6 France	76.6	99.0	12.0	0.99	0.80	2.78	18,430	5,345	0.927	7
7 Australia	76.7	99.0	12.0	0.99	0.80	2.78	16,680	5,339	0.926	11
8 USA	75.6	99.0	12.4	0.99	0.83	2.81	22,130	5,371	0.925	1
9 Netherlands	77.2	99.0	11.1	0.99	0.74	2.72	16,820	5,340	0.923	7
10 United Kingdom	75.8	99.0	11.7	0.99	0.78	2.76	16,340	5,337	0.919	9
11 Germany	75.6	99.0	11.6	0.99	0.77	2.75	19,770	5,347	0.918	1
12 Austria	75.7	99.0	11.4	0.99	0.76	2.74	17,690	5,343	0.917	2
13 Belgium	75.7	99.0	11.2	0.99	0.75	2.73	17,510	5,342	0.916	2
14 Iceland	78.1	99.0	9.2	0.99	0.61	2.59	17,480	5,342	0.914	-6
15 Denmark	75.3	99.0	11.0	0.99	0.73	2.71	17,880	5,343	0.912	-8
16 Finland	75.4	99.0	10.9	0.99	0.72	2.70	16,130	5,336	0.911	-10
17 Luxembourg	75.2	99.0	10.5	0.99	0.70	2.68	20,800	5,364	0.908	-15
18 New Zealand	75.3	99.0	10.7	0.99	0.71	2.69	13,970	5,310	0.907	6
19 Israel	76.2	95.0	10.2	0.95	0.68	2.58	13,460	5,307	0.900	6
20 Barbados	75.3	99.0	9.4	0.99	0.63	2.61	9,667	5,255	0.894	14
21 Ireland	75.0	99.0	8.9	0.99	0.60	2.58	11,430	5,295	0.892	6
22 Italy	76.9	97.4	7.5	0.97	0.50	2.45	17,040	5,340	0.891	-5
23 Spain	77.4	98.0	6.9	0.98	0.46	2.42	12,670	5,303	0.888	0
24 Hong Kong	77.4	90.0	7.2	0.90	0.48	2.28	18,520	5,345	0.875	-2
25 Greece	77.3	93.8	7.0	0.94	0.46	2.34	7,680	5,221	0.874	10

Table 3: Human Development Index continued

HDI rank	Life expectancy at birth (years) 1992	Adult literacy rate (%) 1992	Mean years of schooling 1992	Literacy index	Schooling index	Educational attainment 1992	Real GDP per capita (PPP$) 1991	Adjusted real GDP per capita	Human development index 1992	GNP per capita rank minus HDI rank[a]
26 Cyprus	76.7	94.0	7.0	0.94	0.47	2.35	9,844	5,257	0.873	4
27 Czechoslovakia	72.1	99.0	9.2	0.99	0.62	2.60	6,570	5,196	0.872	29
28 Lithuania	72.6	98.4	9.0	0.98	0.60	2.57	5,410	5,154	0.868	35
29 Estonia	71.2	99.0	9.0	0.99	0.60	2.58	8,090	5,229	0.867	15
30 Latvia	71.0	99.0	9.0	0.99	0.60	2.58	7,540	5,218	0.865	15
31 Hungary	70.1	99.0	9.8	0.99	0.65	2.63	6,080	5,182	0.863	23
32 Korea, Rep. of	70.4	96.8	9.3	0.97	0.62	2.55	8,320	5,233	0.859	4
33 Uruguay	72.4	96.5	8.1	0.97	0.54	2.47	6,670	5,199	0.859	20
34 Russian Federation	70.0	98.7	9.0	0.99	0.60	2.57	6,930	5,205	0.858	15
35 Trinidad and Tobago	70.9	96.0	8.4	0.96	0.56	2.48	8,380	5,234	0.855	11
36 Bahamas	71.9	99.0	6.2	0.99	0.41	2.39	12,000	5,299	0.854	-10
37 Argentina	71.1	95.5	9.2	0.96	0.62	2.53	5,120	5,120	0.853	6
38 Chile	71.9	93.8	7.8	0.94	0.52	2.39	7,060	5,208	0.848	28
39 Costa Rica	76.0	93.2	5.7	0.93	0.38	2.24	5,100	5,100	0.848	36
40 Belarus	71.0	97.9	7.0	0.98	0.47	2.42	6,850	5,203	0.847	10
41 Malta	75.7	87.0	6.1	0.87	0.41	2.15	7,575	5,219	0.843	-9
42 Portugal	74.4	86.2	6.4	0.86	0.43	2.15	9,450	5,252	0.838	-5
43 Singapore	74.2	92.0	4.0	0.92	0.27	2.11	14,734	5,313	0.836	-22
44 Brunei Darussalam	74.0	86.0	5.0	0.86	0.33	2.05	14,000	5,310	0.829	-15
45 Ukraine	70.0	95.0	6.0	0.95	0.40	2.30	5,180	5,135	0.823	23
46 Venezuela	70.1	89.0	6.5	0.89	0.43	2.21	8,120	5,230	0.820	9
47 Panama	72.5	89.6	6.8	0.90	0.45	2.25	4,910	4,910	0.816	23
48 Bulgaria	71.9	94.0	7.0	0.93	0.47	2.33	4,813	4,813	0.815	28
49 Poland	71.5	99.0	8.2	0.99	0.54	2.52	4,500	4,500	0.815	30
50 Colombia	69.0	87.4	7.5	0.87	0.50	2.25	5,460	5,157	0.813	41
51 Kuwait	74.6	73.9	5.5	0.74	0.37	1.85	13,126	5,306	0.809	-23
52 Mexico	69.9	88.6	4.9	0.89	0.32	2.10	7,170	5,211	0.804	-1
53 Armenia	72.0	98.8	5.0	0.99	0.33	2.31	4,610	4,610	0.801	20

HDI rank	Life expectancy at birth (years) 1992	Adult literacy rate (%) 1992	Mean years of schooling 1992	Literacy index	Schooling index	Educational attainment 1992	Real GDP per capita (PPP$) 1991	Adjusted real GDP per capita	Human development index 1992	GNP per capita rank minus HDI rank [a]
Medium human development	68.0	80.4	4.8				3,420		0.649	
54 Thailand	68.7	93.8	3.9	0.94	0.26	2.14	5,270	5,144	0.798	28
55 Antigua and Barbuda	74.0	96.0	4.6	0.96	0.31	2.23	4,500	4,500	0.796	-15
56 Qatar	69.6	79.0	5.8	0.79	0.39	1.97	14,000	5,310	0.795	-36
57 Malaysia	70.4	80.0	5.6	0.80	0.37	1.97	7,400	5,215	0.794	4
58 Bahrain	71.0	79.0	4.3	0.79	0.29	1.87	11,536	5,296	0.791	-25
59 Fiji	71.1	87.0	5.1	0.87	0.34	2.08	4,858	4,858	0.787	15
60 Mauritius	69.6	79.9	4.1	0.80	0.28	1.87	7,178	5,211	0.778	5
61 Kazakhstan	69.0	97.5	5.0	0.98	0.33	2.28	4,490	4,490	0.774	10
62 United Arab Emirates	70.8	65.0	5.6	0.65	0.37	1.67	17,000	5,340	0.771	-52
63 Brazil	65.8	82.1	4.0	0.82	0.27	1.91	5,240	5,142	0.756	-11
64 Dominica	72.0	97.0	4.7	0.97	0.31	2.25	3,900	3,900	0.749	-2
65 Jamaica	73.3	98.5	5.3	0.99	0.35	2.32	3,670	3,670	0.749	22
66 Georgia	73.0	99.0	5.0	0.99	0.33	2.31	3,670	3,670	0.747	14
67 Saudi Arabia	68.7	64.1	3.9	0.64	0.26	1.54	10,850	5,289	0.742	-36
68 Turkey	66.7	81.9	3.6	0.82	0.24	1.88	4,840	4,840	0.739	10
69 Saint Vincent	71.0	98.0	4.6	0.98	0.31	2.27	3,700	3,700	0.732	8
70 Saint Kitts and Nevis	70.0	99.0	6.0	0.99	0.40	2.38	3,550	3,550	0.730	-23
71 Azerbaijan	71.0	96.3	5.0	0.96	0.33	2.26	3,670	3,670	0.730	21
72 Romania	69.9	96.9	7.1	0.97	0.47	2.41	3,500	3,500	0.729	17
73 Syrian Arab Rep.	66.4	66.6	4.2	0.67	0.28	1.61	5,220	5,140	0.727	21
74 Ecuador	66.2	87.4	5.6	0.87	0.37	2.12	4,140	4,140	0.718	28
75 Moldova, Rep. of	69.0	96.0	6.0	0.96	0.40	2.32	3,500	3,500	0.714	6
76 Albania	73.0	85.0	6.2	0.85	0.41	2.11	3,500	3,500	0.714	10
77 Saint Lucia	72.0	93.0	3.9	0.93	0.26	2.12	3,500	3,500	0.709	-20
78 Grenada	70.0	98.0	4.7	0.98	0.31	2.27	3,374	3,374	0.707	-11

162 Facts and Statistics

Table 3: Human Development Index continued

HDI rank		Life expectancy at birth (years) 1992	Adult literacy rate (%) 1992	Mean years of schooling 1992	Literacy index	Schooling index	Educational attainment 1992	Real GDP per capita (PPP$) 1991	Adjusted real GDP per capita	Human development index 1992	GNP per capita rank minus HDI rank[a]
79	Libyan Arab Jamahiriya	62.4	66.5	3.5	0.66	0.24	1.57	7,000	5,207	0.703	-38
80	Turkmenistan	66.0	97.7	5.0	0.98	0.33	2.29	3,540	3,540	0.697	8
81	Tunisia	67.1	68.1	2.1	0.68	0.14	1.50	4,690	4,690	0.690	4
82	Kyrgyzstan	68.0	97.0	5.0	0.97	0.33	2.27	3,280	3,280	0.689	13
83	Seychelles	71.0	77.0	4.6	0.77	0.31	1.85	3,683	3,683	0.685	-44
84	Paraguay	67.2	90.8	4.9	0.91	0.33	2.14	3,420	3,420	0.679	6
85	Suriname	69.9	95.6	4.2	0.96	0.28	2.19	3,072	3,072	0.677	-37
86	Iran, Islamic Rep. of	66.6	56.0	3.9	0.56	0.26	1.38	4,670	4,670	0.672	-22
87	Botswana	60.3	75.0	2.5	0.75	0.17	1.67	4,690	4,690	0.670	-29
88	Belize	68.0	96.0	4.6	0.96	0.31	2.23	3,000	3,000	0.666	-19
89	Cuba	75.6	94.5	8.0	0.95	0.53	2.42	2,000	2,000	0.666	21
90	Sri Lanka	71.2	89.1	7.2	0.89	0.48	2.26	2,650	2,650	0.665	38
91	Uzbekistan	69.0	97.2	5.0	0.97	0.33	2.28	2,790	2,790	0.664	13
92	Oman	69.1	35.0	0.9	0.35	0.06	0.76	9,230	5,248	0.654	-54
93	South Africa	62.2	80.0	3.9	0.80	0.26	1.86	3,885	3,885	0.650	-33
94	China	70.5	80.0	5.0	0.80	0.33	1.93	2,946	2,946	0.644	49
95	Peru	63.6	86.2	6.5	0.86	0.44	2.16	3,110	3,110	0.642	3
96	Dominican Rep.	67.0	84.3	4.3	0.84	0.29	1.97	3,080	3,080	0.638	11
97	Tajikistan	70.0	96.7	5.0	0.97	0.33	2.27	2,180	2,180	0.629	19
98	Jordan	67.3	82.1	5.0	0.82	0.33	1.98	2,895	2,895	0.628	1
99	Philippines	64.6	90.4	7.6	0.90	0.51	2.31	2,440	2,440	0.621	14
100	Iraq	65.7	62.5	5.0	0.62	0.33	1.58	3,500	3,500	0.614	-41
101	Korea, Dem. Rep. of	70.7	95.0	6.0	0.95	0.40	2.30	1,750	1,750	0.609	8
102	Mongolia	63.0	95.0	7.2	0.95	0.48	2.38	2,250	2,250	0.607	1
103	Lebanon	68.1	81.3	4.4	0.81	0.29	1.92	2,500	2,500	0.600	-20

HDI rank	Life expectancy at birth (years) 1992	Adult literacy rate (%) 1992	Mean years of schooling 1992	Literacy index	Schooling index	Educational attainment 1992	Real GDP per capita (PPP$) 1991	Adjusted real GDP per capita	Human development index 1992	GNP per capita rank minus HDI rank[a]
104 Samoa	66.0	98.0	5.8	0.98	0.39	2.35	1,869	1,869	0.596	1
105 Indonesia	62.0	84.4	4.1	0.84	0.27	1.96	2,730	2,730	0.586	16
106 Nicaragua	65.4	78.0	4.5	0.78	0.30	1.86	2,550	2,550	0.583	33
107 Guyana	64.6	96.8	5.1	0.97	0.34	2.28	1,862	1,862	0.580	44
108 Guatemala	64.0	56.4	4.1	0.56	0.27	1.40	3,180	3,180	0.564	-2
109 Algeria	65.6	60.6	2.8	0.61	0.19	1.40	2,870	2,870	0.553	-37
110 Egypt	60.9	50.0	3.0	0.50	0.20	1.20	3,600	3,600	0.551	12
111 Morocco	62.5	52.5	3.0	0.52	0.20	1.25	3,340	3,340	0.549	-10
112 El Salvador	65.2	74.6	4.2	0.75	0.28	1.77	2,110	2,110	0.543	-15
113 Bolivia	60.5	79.3	4.0	0.79	0.27	1.85	2,170	2,170	0.530	6
114 Gabon	52.9	62.5	2.6	0.63	0.17	1.42	3,498	3,498	0.525	-72
115 Honduras	65.2	74.9	4.0	0.75	0.27	1.77	1,820	1,820	0.524	8
116 Viet Nam	63.4	88.6	4.9	0.89	0.33	2.10	1,250	1,250	0.514	34
117 Swaziland	57.3	71.0	3.8	0.71	0.25	1.67	2,506	2,506	0.513	-21
118 Maldives	62.6	92.0	4.5	0.92	0.30	2.14	1,200	1,200	0.511	14
Low human development	55.8	47.4	2.0				1,170		0.355	
119 Vanuatu	65.0	65.0	3.7	0.65	0.25	1.55	1,679	1,679	0.489	-26
120 Lesotho	59.8	78.0	3.5	0.78	0.23	1.79	1,500	1,500	0.476	4
121 Zimbabwe	56.1	68.6	3.1	0.69	0.21	1.58	2,160	2,160	0.474	-3
122 Cape Verde	67.3	66.5	2.2	0.67	0.15	1.48	1,360	1,360	0.474	-10
123 Congo	51.7	58.5	2.1	0.59	0.14	1.31	2,800	2,800	0.461	-23
124 Cameroon	55.3	56.5	1.6	0.57	0.11	1.24	2,400	2,400	0.447	-13
125 Kenya	58.6	70.5	2.3	0.71	0.15	1.56	1,350	1,350	0.434	21
126 Solomon Islands	70.0	24.0	1.0	0.24	0.07	0.55	2,113	2,113	0.434	-11
127 Namibia	58.0	40.0	1.7	0.40	0.11	0.91	2,381	2,381	0.425	-43
128 São Tomé and Principe	67.0	60.0	2.3	0.60	0.15	1.35	600	600	0.409	10

Table 3: Human Development Index continued

HDI rank		Life expectancy at birth (years) 1992	Adult literacy rate (%) 1992	Mean years of schooling 1992	Literacy index	Schooling index	Educational attainment 1992	Real GDP per capita (PPP$) 1991	Adjusted real GDP per capita	Human development index 1992	GNP per capita rank minus HDI rank[a]
129	Papua New Guinea	55.3	65.3	1.0	0.65	0.07	1.37	1,550	1,550	0.408	-21
130	Myanmar	56.9	81.5	2.5	0.82	0.17	1.80	650	650	0.406	19
131	Madagascar	54.9	81.4	2.2	0.81	0.14	1.77	710	710	0.396	31
132	Pakistan	58.3	36.4	1.9	0.36	0.12	0.85	1,970	1,970	0.393	8
133	Lao People's Dem. Rep.	50.3	55.0	2.9	0.55	0.20	1.30	1,760	1,760	0.385	24
134	Ghana	55.4	63.1	3.5	0.63	0.24	1.50	930	930	0.382	-1
135	India	59.7	49.8	2.4	0.50	0.16	1.16	1,150	1,150	0.382	12
136	Côte d'Ivoire	51.6	55.8	1.9	0.56	0.13	1.24	1,510	1,510	0.370	-19
137	Haiti	56.0	55.0	1.7	0.55	0.11	1.21	925	925	0.354	4
138	Zambia	45.5	74.8	2.7	0.75	0.18	1.68	1,010	1,010	0.352	-4
139	Nigeria	51.9	52.0	1.2	0.52	0.08	1.12	1,360	1,360	0.348	6
140	Zaire	51.6	74.0	1.6	0.74	0.11	1.59	469	469	0.341	20
141	Comoros	55.4	55.0	1.0	0.55	0.07	1.17	700	700	0.331	-10
142	Yemen	51.9	41.1	0.9	0.41	0.06	0.88	1,374	1,374	0.323	-16
143	Senegal	48.7	40.0	0.9	0.40	0.06	0.86	1,680	1,680	0.322	-29
144	Liberia	54.7	42.5	2.1	0.42	0.14	0.99	850	850	0.317	-14
145	Togo	54.4	45.5	1.6	0.45	0.11	1.02	738	738	0.311	-9
146	Bangladesh	52.2	36.6	2.0	0.37	0.13	0.87	1,160	1,160	0.309	13
147	Cambodia	50.4	37.8	2.0	0.38	0.13	0.89	1,250	1,250	0.307	17
148	Tanzania, U. Rep. of	51.2	55.0	2.0	0.55	0.14	1.24	570	570	0.306	22
149	Nepal	52.7	27.0	2.1	0.27	0.14	0.68	1,130	1,130	0.289	17
150	Equatorial Guinea	47.3	51.5	0.8	0.52	0.05	1.08	700	700	0.276	4
151	Sudan	51.2	28.2	0.8	0.28	0.05	0.62	1,162	1,162	0.276	-14
152	Burundi	48.2	52.0	0.4	0.52	0.03	1.07	640	640	0.276	6
153	Rwanda	46.5	52.1	1.1	0.52	0.07	1.11	680	680	0.274	-1
154	Uganda	42.6	50.5	1.1	0.51	0.07	1.08	1,036	1,036	0.272	14
155	Angola	45.6	42.5	1.5	0.43	0.10	0.95	1,000	1,000	0.271	-35

HDI rank	Life expectancy at birth (years) 1992	Adult literacy rate (%) 1992	Mean years of schooling 1992	Literacy index	Schooling index	Educational attainment 1992	Real GDP per capita (PPP$) 1991	Adjusted real GDP per capita	Human development index 1992	GNP per capita rank minus HDI rank[a]
156 Benin	46.1	25.0	0.7	0.25	0.05	0.55	1,500	1,500	0.261	-14
157 Malawi	44.6	45.0	1.7	0.45	0.12	1.02	800	800	0.260	-1
158 Mauritania	47.4	35.0	0.4	0.35	0.03	0.73	962	962	0.254	-31
159 Mozambique	46.5	33.5	1.6	0.34	0.11	0.78	921	921	0.252	14
160 Central African Rep.	47.2	40.2	1.1	0.40	0.07	0.88	641	641	0.249	-25
161 Ethiopia	46.4	50.0	1.1	0.50	0.07	1.07	370	370	0.249	10
162 Bhutan	47.8	40.9	0.3	0.41	0.02	0.84	620	620	0.247	3
163 Djibouti	48.3	19.0	0.4	0.19	0.03	0.41	1,000	*1,000*	0.226	-38
164 Guinea-Bissau	42.9	39.0	0.4	0.39	0.03	0.81	747	747	0.224	3
165 Somalia	46.4	27.0	0.3	0.27	0.02	0.56	759	*759*	0.217	7
166 Gambia	44.4	30.0	0.6	0.30	0.04	0.64	763	*763*	0.215	-22
167 Mali	45.4	35.9	0.4	0.36	0.03	0.74	480	480	0.214	-12
168 Chad	46.9	32.5	0.3	0.33	0.02	0.67	447	447	0.212	-7
169 Niger	45.9	31.2	0.2	0.31	0.01	0.64	542	542	0.209	-21
170 Sierra Leone	42.4	23.7	0.9	0.24	0.06	0.53	1,020	*1,020*	0.209	-7
171 Afghanistan	42.9	31.6	0.9	0.32	0.06	0.69	700	*700*	0.208	-2
172 Burkina Faso	47.9	19.9	0.2	0.20	0.01	0.41	666	*666*	0.203	-19
173 Guinea	43.9	26.9	0.9	0.27	0.06	0.60	500	*500*	0.191	-44

a. A positive figure shows that the HDI rank is better than the GNP per capita rank, a negative the opposite.

Note: Figures in italics are UNDP estimates.

Source: *Human Development Report 1994.* Copyright © 1994 by the United Nations Development Programme. Reprinted by permission of Oxford University Press, Inc.

population control are likewise positive by-products that should accompany poverty reduction. Because poverty is at the root of so many of development's constituent problems, much of the following discussion, indeed much of the subject of global development, comes back to focus on poverty issues. Substantial progress has been made in confronting poverty, but it remains a problem of staggering dimensions, and it continues to grow rapidly in sub-Saharan Africa. As we head into the next century, no task should figure higher on the agenda of global development than the reduction of poverty.

Economic Development

Statistics on Developing the World's Economy

The economic capacity of a nation plays a critical role in its ability to develop toward sustainable self-sufficiency. Considered over the long term, the data on economic growth produce an encouraging portrait of contemporary global development: In the years between 1950 and 1990, the annual output of the world's economy expanded almost fivefold from nearly $4 trillion to $19 trillion, an annual gain of 4.2 percent. Moreover, this economic growth corresponds to many overall successes in development since World War II. However, the most recent data are far less positive, and nowhere so much so as in these raw economic data are the faltering rates of recent growth and the consequences of the lost development decade of the 1980s made clear.

Unsurprisingly, the means of quantifying economic growth and distribution and income are controversial; many traditional economic indicators fail to reflect problems such as the unequal distribution of income or the depletion of resources, and so project a rosier view of economic development than is sometimes warranted. Despite their flaws, however, general indicators such as gross national product (GNP) and gross domestic product (GDP) provide a general view of the economic welfare of individual countries; and recent statistics measure for "purchasing-power parity," which reflects what life necessities relative amounts of money buy in various countries, allowing more meaningful cross-national comparisons.

There is an enormous disparity between those living in industrialized countries and those of developing countries. Based on purchasing-power parity, the average 1991 GDP per capita is $18,988 for countries in the Organization for Economic Cooperation and Development (OECD), compared with just $2,377 per capita for developing countries. The United States and India provide a graphic example of this disparity: In 1991, the average American enjoyed purchasing power equivalent to $22,130, while his or her Indian counterpart commanded purchasing power of only $1,150. Even though many developing countries have been growing more rapidly (in percentage terms) than industrial economies in recent decades, the absolute size of the gap between rich and poor considered in terms of per capita GNP continues to widen. Such disparities in income and in access to resources and technology cannot be ignored. During the past five decades, the world income increased sevenfold (real GDP) and income per person more then tripled (per capita GDP), but this is spread unevenly. Between 1960 and 1991, the share of world income for the richest 20 percent of the global population rose from 70 percent to 85 percent. Over the same period, all but the richest fifth saw their share of world income fall—the meager share for the poorest 20 percent declined from 2.3 to 1.4 percent. Thus, one-fifth of humankind, mostly in the industrial countries, has well over four-fifths of the global income and other development opportunities.

Economic security requires an assured basic income derived from wages or at least some public social welfare provisions. Only about a quarter of the world's population may at present be economically secure in any sense. In the past two decades, the number of jobs in industrial nations has increased at half the rate of GDP growth and has failed to keep in line with population growth. In 1993, more than 35 million people were seeking work, a high proportion of whom were women. The problems are greatest in developing countries, where open registered unemployment is commonly above 10 percent and total unemployment probably way beyond that. It is the young who are hit hardest by this problem; in Africa the open unemployment rate for youths was 20 percent in the 1980s. Unemployment figures do not fully reflect the severity of the situation, which is compounded by a lack of public social welfare, leaving people with little or no income.

Table 4 demonstrates how so many of these problems have been aggravated since 1980. Throughout Africa and Latin America, many developing countries actually experienced *negative*

Table 4: Basic Indicators

		Population (millions) mid-1993	Area (thousands of sq. km)	GNP per capita[a] Dollars 1993	GNP per capita[a] Avg. ann. growth (%), 1980–93	Avg. annual rate of inflation (%) 1970–80	Avg. annual rate of inflation (%) 1980–93	Life expect. at birth (years) 1993	Adult illiteracy (%) Female 1990	Adult illiteracy (%) Total 1990
	Low-income economies	3,092.7 t	39,093 t	380 w	3.7 w	7.3 w	14.1 w	62 w	53 w	41 w
	Excluding China & India	1,016.1 t	26,244 t	300 w	0.1 w	13.4 w	27.1 w	56 w	61 w	49 w
1	Mozambique	15.1	802	90	–1.5	..	42.3	46	79	67
2	Tanzania[b]	28.0	945	90	0.1	14.1	24.3	52	..	..
3	Ethiopia	51.9	1,097	100	..	..	..	48	..	..
4	Sierra Leone	4.5	72	150	–1.5	12.5	61.6	39	89	79
5	Viet Nam	71.3	332	170	..	..	..	66	16	12
6	Burundi	6.0	28	180	0.9	11.8	4.6	50	60	50
7	Uganda	18.0	236	180	..	..	..	45	65	52
8	Nepal	20.8	141	190	2.0	8.5	11.5	54	87	74
9	Malawi	10.5	118	200	–1.2	8.8	15.5	45	..	..
10	Chad	6.0	1,284	210	3.2	7.7	0.7	48	82	70
11	Rwanda	7.6	26	210	–1.2	14.3	3.4	..	63	50
12	Bangladesh	115.2	144	220	2.1	20.8	8.6	56	78	65
13	Madagascar	13.9	587	220	–2.6	9.9	16.1	57	27	20
14	Guinea-Bissau	1.0	36	240	2.8	5.7	58.7	44	76	64
15	Kenya	25.3	580	270	0.3	10.1	9.9	58	42	31
16	Mali	10.1	1,240	270	–1.0	9.9	4.4	46	76	68
17	Niger	8.6	1,267	270	–4.1	10.9	1.3	47	83	72
18	Lao PDR	4.6	237	280	..	..	..	52	..	..
19	Burkina Faso	9.8	274	300	0.8	8.6	3.3	47	91	82
20	India	898.2	3,288	300	3.0	8.4	8.7	61	66	52
21	Nigeria	105.3	924	300	–0.1	15.2	20.6	51	61	49
22	Albania	3.4	29	340	–3.2	..	5.6	72	..	..
23	Nicaragua	4.1	130	340	–5.7	12.6	664.6	67	..	..
24	Togo	3.9	57	340	–2.1	8.9	3.7	55	69	57
25	Gambia, The	1.0	11	350	–0.2	10.6	16.2	45	84	73
26	Zambia	8.9	753	380	–3.1	7.6	58.9	48	35	27
27	Mongolia	2.3	1,567	390	0.2	..	13.8	64	..	..
28	Central African Republic	3.2	623	400	–1.6	12.1	4.2	50	75	62
29	Benin	5.1	113	430	–0.4	10.3	1.4	48	84	77
30	Ghana	16.4	239	430	0.1	35.2	37.0	56	49	40
31	Pakistan	122.8	796	430	3.1	13.4	7.4	62	79	65
32	Tajikistan[c]	5.8	143	470	–3.6	1.4	26.0	70	..	2
33	China	1,178.4	9,561	490 [d]	8.2	0.6	7.0	69	38	27
34	Guinea	6.3	246	500	..	..	..	45	87	76
35	Mauritania	2.2	1,026	500	–0.8	9.9	8.2	52	79	66
36	Zimbabwe	10.7	391	520	–0.3	9.4	14.4	53	40	33
37	Georgia[c]	5.4	70	580	–6.6	..	40.7	73	..	1
38	Honduras	5.3	112	600	–0.3	8.1	8.2	68	29	27
39	Sri Lanka	17.9	66	600	2.7	12.3	11.1	72	17	12
40	Côte d'Ivoire	13.3	322	630	–4.6	13.0	1.5	51	60	46
41	Lesotho	1.9	30	650	–0.5	9.7	13.8	61	..	..
42	Armenia[c]	3.7	30	660	–4.2	0.7	26.9	73	..	1
43	Egypt, Arab Rep.	56.4	1,001	660	2.8	9.6	13.6	64	66	52
44	Myanmar	44.6	677	..	..	11.4	16.5	58	28	19
45	Yemen, Rep.	13.2	528	..	..	..	..	51	74	62
	Middle-income economies	1,596.3 t	62,452 t	2,480 w	0.2 w	22.1 w	90.1 w	68 w	..	17 w
	Lower-middle-income	1,095.8 t	40,604 t	1,590 w	–0.5 w	8.3 w	35.2 w	67 w	..	19 w
46	Azerbaijan	7.4	87	730	–3.5	1.7	28.2	71	..	3
47	Indonesia	187.2	1,905	740	4.2	21.5	8.5	63	32	23
48	Senegal	7.9	197	750	0.0	8.5	4.9	50	75	62
49	Bolivia	7.1	1,099	760	–0.7	21.0	187.1	60	29	23
50	Cameroon	12.5	475	820	–2.2	9.0	4.0	57	57	46
51	Macedonia, FYR	2.1	26	820	..	..	..	72	..	..
52	Kyrgyz Republic[c]	4.6	199	850	0.1	0.8	28.6	69	..	3
53	Philippines	64.8	300	850	–0.6	13.3	13.6	67	11	10
54	Congo	2.4	342	950	–0.3	8.4	–0.6	51	56	43
55	Uzbekistan[c]	21.9	447	970	–0.2	1.0	24.5	69	..	3
56	Morocco	25.9	447	1,040	1.2	8.3	6.6	64	62	51
57	Moldova[c]	4.4	34	1,060	–2.0	0.9	32.4	68	..	4
58	Guatemala	10.0	109	1,100	–1.2	10.5	16.8	65	53	45
59	Papua New Guinea	4.1	463	1,130	0.6	9.1	4.8	56	62	48
60	Bulgaria	8.9	111	1,140	0.5	..	15.9	71	..	..
61	Romania	22.8	238	1,140	–2.4	..	22.4	70	..	..
62	Jordan[e]	4.1	89	1,190	..	..	..	70	30	20
63	Ecuador	11.0	284	1,200	0.0	13.8	40.4	69	16	14
64	Dominican Republic	7.5	49	1,230	0.7	9.1	25.0	70	18	17
65	El Salvador	5.5	21	1,320	0.2	10.7	17.0	67	30	27
66	Lithuania[c]	3.7	65	1,320	–2.8	..	35.2	70	..	..
67	Colombia	35.7	1,139	1,400	1.5	22.3	24.9	70	14	13
68	Jamaica	2.4	11	1,440	–0.3	17.0	22.4	74	1	2
69	Peru	22.9	1,285	1,490	–2.7	30.1	316.1	66	21	15
70	Paraguay	4.7	407	1,510	–0.7	12.7	25.0	70	12	10
71	Kazakhstan[c]	17.0	2,717	1,560	–1.6	0.7	35.2	70	..	3
72	Tunisia	8.7	164	1,720	1.2	8.7	7.1	68	44	35

Note: For other economies see Table 1a. For data comparability and coverage, see the technical notes. Figures in italics are for years other than those specified.

		Population (millions) mid-1993	Area (thousands of sq. km)	GNP per capita[a]		Avg. annual rate of inflation (%)		Life expect. at birth (years) 1993	Adult illiteracy (%)	
				Dollars 1993	Avg. ann. growth (%), 1980–93	1970–80	1980–93		Female 1990	Total 1990
73	Algeria	26.7	2,382	1,780	–0.8	14.5	13.2	67	55	43
74	Namibia	1.5	824	1,820	0.7	..	11.9	59	..	..
75	Slovak Republic	5.3	49	1,950	..	..	..	71	..	..
76	Latvia[c]	2.6	65	2,010	–0.6	..	23.8	69	..	..
77	Thailand	58.1	513	2,110	6.4	9.2	4.3	69	10	7
78	Costa Rica	3.3	51	2,150	1.1	15.3	22.1	76	7	7
79	Ukraine[c]	51.6	604	2,210	0.2	0.1	37.2	69	..	2
80	Poland	38.3	313	2,260	0.4	..	69.3	71	..	..
81	Russian Federation[c]	148.7	17,075	2,340	–1.0	–0.1	35.4	65	..	2
82	Panama	2.5	76	2,600	–0.7	7.7	2.1	73	12	12
83	Czech Republic	10.3	79	2,710	..	..	..	71	..	..
84	Botswana	1.4	582	2,790[f]	6.2	11.6	12.3	65	35	26
85	Turkey	59.6	779	2,970[f]	2.4	29.6	53.5	67	29	19
86	*Iran, Islamic Rep.*	64.2	1,648	..	..	..	17.1	68	57	46
Upper-middle-income		**500.5 t**	**21,848 t**	**4,370 w**	**0.9 w**	**36.3 w**	**158.7 w**	**69 w**	**17 w**	**14 w**
87	Venezuela	20.9	912	2,840	–0.7	14.0	23.9	72	17	8
88	Belarus[c]	10.2	208	2,870	2.4	0.0	30.9	70	..	2
89	Brazil	156.5	8,512	2,930	0.3	38.6	423.4	67	20	19
90	South Africa	39.7	1,221	2,980	–0.2	13.0	14.7	63	..	..
91	Mauritius	1.1	2	3,030	5.5	15.3	8.8	70	..	..
92	Estonia[c]	1.6	45	3,080	–2.2	..	29.8	69	..	..
93	Malaysia	19.0	330	3,140	3.5	7.3	2.2	71	30	22
94	Chile	13.8	757	3,170	3.6	186.2	20.1	74	7	7
95	Hungary	10.2	93	3,350	1.2	3.4	12.8	69	..	..
96	Mexico	90.0	1,958	3,610	–0.5	18.1	57.9	71	15	13
97	Trinidad and Tobago	1.3	5	3,830	–2.8	18.5	4.8	72	..	..
98	Uruguay	3.1	177	3,830	–0.1	63.7	66.7	73	4	4
99	Oman	2.0	212	4,850	3.4	28.0	–2.3	70	..	..
100	Gabon	1.0	268	4,960	–1.6	17.5	1.5	54	52	39
101	Slovenia	1.9	20	6,490	..	..	..	73	..	..
102	Puerto Rico	3.6	9	7,000	1.0	6.5	3.2	75	..	..
103	Argentina	33.8	2,767	7,220	–0.5	134.2	374.3	72	5	5
104	Greece	10.4	132	7,390	0.9	14.3	17.3	78	11	7
105	Korea, Rep.	44.1	99	7,660	8.2	19.5	6.3	71	7	g
106	Portugal	9.8	92	9,130[f]	3.3	16.9	16.4	75	19	15
107	*Saudi Arabia*	17.4	2,150	..	–3.6	24.5	–2.1	70	52	38
108	*Turkmenistan*[c]	3.9	488	..	..	2.4	16.5	65	..	2
Low- and middle-income		**4,689.0 t**	**101,544 t**	**1,090 w**	**0.9 w**	**18.5 w**	**72.8 w**	**64 w**	**..**	**33 w**
Sub-Saharan Africa		559.0 t	24,274 t	520 w	–0.8 w	13.8 w	16.1 w	52 w	62 w	50 w
East Asia & Pacific		1,713.9 t	16,369 t	820 w	6.4 w	9.7 w	7.1 w	68 w	34 w	24 w
South Asia		1,194.4 t	5,133 t	310 w	3.0 w	9.7 w	8.6 w	60 w	69 w	54 w
Europe and Central Asia		494.6 t	24,242 t	2,450 w	–0.3 w	4.6 w	35.3 w	69 w	..	5 w
Middle East & N. Africa		262.5 t	11,015 t	..	–2.4 w	16.9 w	10.7 w	66 w	57 w	..
Latin America & Caribbean		466.3 t	20,507 t	2,950 w	–0.1 w	46.7 w	245.0 w	69 w	18 w	15 w
Severely indebted		**385.8 t**	**17,968 t**	**2,640 w**	**–1.1 w**	**52.4 w**	**302.7 w**	**67 w**	**27 w**	**23 w**
High-income economies		**812.4 t**	**32,145 t**	**23,090 w**	**2.2 w**	**9.5 w**	**4.3 w**	**77 w**	**..**	**..**
109	New Zealand	3.5	271	12,600	0.7	12.5	8.5	76	g	g
110	Ireland	3.5	70	13,000	3.6	14.2	4.8	75	g	g
111	Spain	39.5	505	13,590	2.7	16.1	8.4	78	7	5
112	†Israel	5.2	21	13,920	2.0	39.6	70.4	77	..	..
113	Australia	17.6	7,713	17,500	1.6	11.8	6.1	78	g	g
114	†Hong Kong	5.8	1	18,060[h]	5.4[h]	9.2	7.9	79	..	..
115	United Kingdom	57.9	245	18,060	2.3	14.5	5.6	76	g	g
116	Finland	5.1	338	19,300	1.5	12.3	5.8	76	g	g
117	†Kuwait	1.8	18	19,360	–4.3	21.9	..	75	33	27
118	Italy	57.1	301	19,840	2.1	15.6	8.8	78	g	g
119	†Singapore	2.8	1	19,850	6.1	5.9	2.5	75	g	g
120	Canada	28.8	9,976	19,970	1.4	8.7	3.9	78	g	g
121	Netherlands	15.3	37	20,950	1.7	7.9	1.7	78	g	g
122	†United Arab Emirates	1.8	84	21,430	–4.4	..	..	74	..	..
123	Belgium	10.0	31	21,650	1.9	7.8	4.0	77	g	g
124	France	57.5	552	22,490	1.6	10.2	5.1	77	g	g
125	Austria	7.9	84	23,510	2.0	6.5	3.6	76	g	g
126	Germany	80.7	357	23,560	2.1[i]	5.1[i]	2.8[i]	76	g	g
127	Sweden	8.7	450	24,740	1.3	10.0	6.9	78	g	g
128	United States	257.8	9,809	24,740	1.7	7.5	3.8	76	g	g
129	Norway	4.3	324	25,970	2.2	8.4	4.6	77	g	g
130	Denmark	5.2	43	26,730	2.0	10.1	4.6	75	g	g
131	Japan	124.5	378	31,490	3.4	8.5	1.5	80	g	g
132	Switzerland	7.1	41	35,760	1.1	5.0	3.8	78	g	g
World		**5,501.5 t**	**133,690 t**	**4,420 w**	**1.2 w**	**11.4 w**	**19.6 w**	**66 w**	**..**	**33 w**

† Economies classified by the United Nations or otherwise regarded by their authorities as developing. a. See the technical notes. b. In all tables GDP and GNP data cover mainland Tanzania only. c. Estimates for economies of the former Soviet Union are preliminary, and their classification will be kept under review. Note that in all tables, Turkmenistan should be classified as lower-middle-income. d. Preliminary estimate, see the technical note to Table 1, paragraph 8. e. In all tables, data for Jordan cover the East Bank only. f. Reflect recent revision of 1993 GNP per capita from $2,590 to $2,790 for Botswana; from $2,120 to $2,970 for Turkey; and from $7,890 to $9,130 for Portugal. g. According to UNESCO, illiteracy is less than 5 percent. h. Data refer to GDP. i. Data refer to the Federal Republic of Germany before unification.

Source: *World Development Report 1995: Workers in an Integrating World.* Copyright © 1995 by The International Bank for Reconstruction and Development/The World Bank. Reprinted by permission of Oxford University Press.

growth, measured in GNP per capita, in the period 1980 to 1991—a trend unthinkable in the first decades of international development. Considered collectively, the World Bank's group of low-income countries barely eked out 1 percent growth over this period, while lower middle-income nations saw annual growth fall by an average .01 percent per year. The high-income nations of the OECD, however, enjoyed 2.3 percent annual growth over the same period: The rich get richer, and the poor, relatively at least, get poorer.

Furthermore, nominal wages have remained stagnant, or have risen slowly, while inflation has sharply eroded their real value. In the 1980s some of the countries hit hardest by inflation were Nicaragua with 584 percent, Argentina with 417 percent, Brazil with 328 percent, and Uganda with 107 percent. Inflation has caused the real value of wages to fall worldwide. In Latin America real wages fell by 20 percent in the 1980s. In many African countries the value of minimum wage fell sharply in the same period: by 20 percent in Togo, 40 percent in Kenya, and 80 percent in Sierra Leone. Women are the worst affected as they typically receive wages 30–40 percent lower than men. Income insecurity has hit the industrial countries as well. It is worth noting that the traditional global South is not the only region struggling under these global economic forces: In the 1990s, Ukraine experienced 1,445 percent inflation, the Russian Federation had 1,353 percent, and Lithuania had 1,194 percent inflation, while in the European Union, 44 million people (approximately 28 percent of the work force) receive less than half the average of their country.

These conditions are still more acute for particularly vulnerable segments of the population. In 1994, about 65 million disabled people needed training and job placement to attain economic security. Only 1 percent will receive meaningful services. The disabled are, for the most part, found among the poorest quarter of the population. Unemployment rates for these groups are as high as 84 percent in Mauritius and 46 percent in China. In such an environment people look to the government for support, but often to no avail. Social welfare programs in developing nations provide assistance unevenly and fail to reach many needy citizens, while budgetary problems and ensuing cutbacks—typically required as one consequence of the international debt crisis—have reduced social security payments. Homelessness is the severest effect of economic insecurity. In

Calcutta, Dhaka, and Mexico City, more than 25 percent of the people are homeless.

External Debt

A major contributor to the development debacle of the 1980s was the international debt crisis. The year 1982 marked the beginning of the crisis, when Mexico became unable to meet its obligations to international commercial banks. The causes and implications of the crisis are spelled out in more detail above, in chapter 1, but in short, many developing nations, for a variety of reasons, had borrowed heavily in the 1970s and found themselves unable to meet their obligations when world commodity prices plummeted in the early 1980s. The crisis threatened the solvency of major Western commercial banks to whom debt was owed, and programs of "structural adjustment" imposed by the World Bank as a condition for assistance in loan repayment demanded drastic cuts in social services throughout the South. Over the past ten years developing countries have struggled to try to curtail their debts and to initiate programs to encourage growth and expansion. Although progress has been made the problem remains acute.

As of 1991, the total external debt of developing countries stood at approximately $1.5 trillion, which is owed to commercial banks and governmental and multilateral lending institutions. As a ratio to GNP, Africa's debt is the highest among major developing regions, although the proportion of export earnings needed for debt servicing—that is, the sum of repayments of principal and interest payments made on external debt—is less for Latin America and the Caribbean. The burden of international debt has been shifting to the world's poorest regions, where it takes a greater human toll. Indeed, for many developing countries, external debt comprises a significant proportion of GNP, and debt service, which must be earned in hard currency in international trade, absorbs a significant portion of total foreign exchange generated from the export of goods and services, thereby limiting the potential for domestic investment or consumption. Throughout the low-income sector, exclusive of China and India, outstanding debt obligations stand at 85.7 percent of GNP, up almost threefold from 1980. More disturbing still, debt constitutes some 307.7 percent of exported goods and services, and service of the debt alone absorbs more than a quarter of the export earnings of the world's poorest nations. So while the threat to international banks may have passed, continuing debt obligations continue to exert a numbing drag on fragile economies, with high human costs such as reduced educational and health expenditures.

International Trade

Issues of international trade also figure prominently in the overall development equation. The general rule is that most developing countries are net exporters of primary (or agricultural or commodity) products and most industrialized countries import primary goods and export secondary (or manufactured) goods. In most developing countries, the value of total trade or imports to GNP is very high, and sustained economic development is everywhere linked to the ability of nations to profitably trade with one another. Moreover, export growth contributes directly to economic growth, and, more importantly, permits more imports and a more rapid modernization of production. The ideal result of increased international trade is efficient Third World industry that meets the market test of international competition.

Unfortunately, trends since the beginning of the 1980s in international trade have tended to aggravate rather than alleviate Third World poverty. The global economy of the past 15 years has been characterized first by sharp recession, then by steady growth in the developed world, high real interest rates, declining commodity prices, and the collapse of lending to the less developed world in the face of a mounting debt crisis.

The recession of 1982 hurt world trade overall, but developing-country trade fell proportionately more than elsewhere and created the baseline for the continuing difficulties of poorer nations in the global trade arena. Two factors accounting for the slump in export earning by the Third World—the lasting decline in the world market demand for the commodity products of the developing world and the steep drop in raw materials prices from the end of 1980—are illustrative of the trade predicament of developing countries.

Weak demand for Third World exports has been especially damaging. The recession faced by industrialized countries translated into less cash available there for the purchase of imports. In the early 1980s, some Third World countries compensated for this demand drop by increased trade among themselves; during this period, South-South trade was the most dynamic segment of trade for developing countries, but the burden of debt payments and high-priced oil soon squelched this trade opportunity. Demand was further dampened by the upswing in protectionist measures in the advanced countries which had previously provided much of the Third World's exports.

Slackening demand has been accompanied by falling prices. As developing countries produce more for export and compete with each other for increasingly scarce outlets, prices naturally tumbled throughout the 1980s and early 1990s; economic slow-down in the industrialized world and the emergence of synthetics to replace primary goods have merely intensified the problem. The net effect has been a sharp check on the export revenue of less developed countries—and this as spiraling debt payments and high-priced oil increased their need for cash earnings.

Attempts by Southern governments to resolve this apparent conundrum have often proved ruinous to the poor. In order to earn the needed foreign exchange, developing countries concentrate their agricultural sectors on cash crops for export (products not for home consumption, but to be sold abroad for hard currency [e.g., coffee, cotton, jute]), often inviting foreign investment by multinational agribusiness firms to produce them.

The land used by developing countries to grow major export crops increased by more than 15 percent from 1974 to 1994, meaning less land is given over to farming food for the domestic poor. Since much of this is high-quality, fertile, peasant land, peasant farmers have been forced onto fragile, marginal soils that are quickly exhausted—a process that has also contributed to soil erosion, desertification, and other environmental woes discussed elsewhere in this volume.

Recent data offer some cause for optimism. The volume of world trade has increased in recent years, and developing countries have shared in this upswing. Raw data on trade demonstrate that many Southern nations are doing a brisk international business. Commodity prices in many sectors have recovered substantially since the early 1990s, easing some of the pressure on governments to raise foreign exchange. Finally, the recently concluded Uruguay Round of the General Agreement on Tariffs and Trade (GATT) will usher in a new, liberalized regime in global trade. If the developing world joins in trade liberalization, nations of the South stand to participate in the significant projected benefits. But the bottom line remains troubling: The poorest 20 percent of world population had less than 1 percent of world trade (Figure 1), and no existing international

Figure 1:
Global Economic Disparities

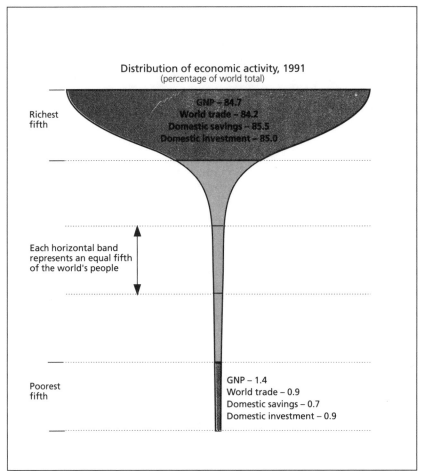

Distribution of economic activity, 1991
(percentage of world total)

Richest
fifth

GNP – 84.7
World trade – 84.2
Domestic savings – 85.5
Domestic investment – 85.0

Each horizontal band
represents an equal fifth
of the world's people

Poorest
fifth

GNP – 1.4
World trade – 0.9
Domestic savings – 0.7
Domestic investment – 0.9

Source: *Human Development Report 1994.* Copyright © 1994 by the United Nations Development Programme. Reprinted by permission of Oxford University Press, Inc.

institutions possess the means or the will to redress this punishing imbalance.

International Aid and Financial Transfers

International development assistance has played a meaningful role in the development process over the past 40 years. Aid has often been resented by donor and recipient nations alike, the former due to the harsh conditions sometimes attached to needed aid, the latter due to the exaggerated notion that development aid has not yielded durable benefits. But notwithstanding the considerable discord on both sides of the equation, there is little doubt that transfers of technology, financial resources, and equipment have contributed to many successes of Southern development in the contemporary era.

Throughout the North, and especially in the United States, the illusion persists that foreign aid constitutes a major drain on domestic resources. In reality, industrial countries allocate only 0.3 percent of their combined GDP to overseas development assistance today. Among industrial nations, the United States is the most parsimonious donor, giving less than 0.2 percent of GDP on a per capita basis—giving that, contrary to popular belief, amounts to less than 1 percent of the total U.S. budget.

What assistance is available often fails to reach the neediest of the South. Ten countries with 65.9 percent of the world's poor receive only 31.7 percent of official development assistance and 43.9 percent of World Bank aid (Table 5). Moreover, countries with perceived strategic value, or high military spending, often benefit from greater receipts. Finally, even within recipient nations, the poorest of the poor are frequently the hardest to reach and lack political clout, and so benefit the least from international aid. Development programs that cooperate with grass-roots, indigenous nongovernmental organizations are increasingly favored for their ability to respond to these deficiencies.

Official assistance is the most visible form of North-South cooperation for development, but it represents only a small element of the relationship. Private capital flows—that is, investment by firms in Southern countries, generally in search of profit—trade flows (discussed above), and debt payments constitute important avenues of financial exchange. Indeed, the crushing burden of debt service in the 1980s created the perverse spectacle of net resource flows from the developing world to the

Table 5: Official Development Assistance to the Poorest

Ten developing countries with highest number of poor people	Percentage of population in poverty 1980–90	Number of poor (millions) 1992	Poor as % of total world poor 1992	ODA per poor person (US$) 1992	ODA as % of total ODA 1992
India	40	350.0	26.9	7	5.2
China	9	105.0	8.1	28	6.5
Bangladesh	78	93.2	7.2	19	3.8
Brazil	47	72.4	5.6	3	0.5
Indonesia	25	47.8	3.7	44	4.6
Nigeria	40	46.4	3.6	7	0.5
Viet Nam	54	37.6	2.9	16	1.3
Philippines	54	35.2	2.7	49	3.8
Pakistan	28	35.0	2.7	33	2.6
Ethiopia	60	31.9	2.5	41	2.9
Total	29	854.5	65.9	17	31.7

Source: *Human Development Report 1994.* Copyright © 1994 by the United Nations Development Programme. Reprinted by permission of Oxford University Press, Inc.

rich industrialized world. The year 1991 witnessed the return of positive net flows to the South, thanks to easing debt burdens coupled with substantial increases in private investment.

The World Bank and Economic Development

In 1944, the World Bank and the International Monetary Fund (IMF) were formed to help ensure that international cooperation paved the way for improved living standards and economic stability. As noted in the discussion in chapter 5, Organizations, the focus of these so-called Bretton Woods institutions has varied considerably in the 50 years since their birth, but in the past decade the emphasis has been on "sustainable development"—that is, development that satisfies current human needs without jeopardizing the resource base on which future generations depend. At the Earth Summit in Rio de Janeiro in 1992, more than 150 governments endorsed the goal of sustainable development and charged international institutions with promoting it, including the World Bank and the IMF. The World Bank's function is not only lending money to underdeveloped nations, but it also provides a "seal of approval" which opens the tap for additional bilateral and multilateral funds, as well as private loans. Projects supported are usually two to three times bigger than the bank's own contribution, with co-financing from other sources making up the difference.

In 1993, the World Bank committed a total of $23.9 billion, making it the world's single largest lender (Table 6). It was created to lend to governments rather than the private sector for development projects and economic plans. Of its total credit, $17 billion was given through the International Bank for Reconstruction and Development. These loans are made to middle-income countries at near market rates with 15- to 20-year payback periods. The remaining $7 billion was in International Development Association (IDA) "credits." These are interest-free, "soft" loans to the world's poorest countries. The World Bank has recently become involved in "adjustment lending," loans designed to relieve balance-of-payments problems while policy reforms are undertaken. In exchange for credit, governments undertake the reorganization of their domestic economies by reducing government spending, reducing subsidies, reducing inflation rates, and lowering trade barriers. Such lending is a response to the 1980s worldwide debt crisis. In 1989, adjustment lending peaked at 29 percent of total lending; however, it declined to $4 billion (17 percent) in 1993.

The Global Environment Facility (GEF) is a partnership between the World Bank, the United Nations Development Program

Table 6: World Bank Lending by Sector, 1993

Sector	Amount (billion dollars)	Share (percent)
Energy	3.6	15
Nonproject	3.6	15
Agricultural and Rural Development	3.3	14
Transport	3.2	13
Education	2.0	9
Urban Development	2.0	8
Population, Health, and Nutrition	1.8	8
Water Supply and Sewerage	1.2	5
Industry	1.1	5
Public-Sector Management	0.6	3
Development Finance Companies	0.6	2
Technical Assistance	0.5	2
Telecommunications	0.4	2
Totals	23.9	101

Source: *The World Bank Annual Report, 1994.* Washington, DC: International Bank of Reconstruction and Development World Bank, 1994.

(UNDP), and the United Nations Environmental Program (UNEP). Created in 1991, the GEF provides governmental grants to cover additional costs of investing in efforts to protect the environment. Though technically distinct from the World Bank, projects accounting for more than 60 percent of GEF funds are implemented by the bank and more than half are attached to larger bank undertakings. Initially, governments committed $12 billion over three years to GEF for projects that would protect biological diversity, combat global warming and ozone depletion, and protect internal waters. In 1992, projects were extended to include land degradation. Though no new funds have been added since the body was founded, governments are considering replenishing the GEF with an additional $2.8–4.2 billion over the next three to four years.

The World Bank's 1992 *World Development Report* concluded that significant policy changes should be made to encourage both environmental protection and economic development. These included removing environmentally harmful subsidies and encouraging the efficient use of resources. In January 1993, a new vice-presidency was established with responsibility for three departments: environment; agriculture and natural resources; and transportation, water, and urban development. Through the introduction of these departments the World Bank hopes to advance development programs in line with the needs of world economies in an effort to encourage economic growth without causing further environmental degradation. Notwithstanding the best efforts of multilateral agencies and NGOs, the early signs of bringing efficient and environmentally sound technologies to the South are not altogether promising. As the computer communications revolution alters yet again the way the world does business, the poorest countries trail far behind. Currently, the South is being left out of the efficiencies created by computers and cyberspace, perhaps auguring another cycle of lagging growth and competitive disadvantage for nations most at need.

Demographics of Development

Population

The nineteenth century marked the beginning of the world's population explosion, which occurred almost simultaneously with the industrial revolution. At the end of the eighteenth century the world's population was less than 1 billion. By 1930, it was 2 billion. World population increased from 2.52 billion in 1950 to 5.57 billion in 1993 and is projected to reach approximately 10 billion by the year 2050 (Table 7). Thus the world had taken almost 150 years to double in population from the 1800s to 1930, but then in less than 60 years it doubled again.

An examination of this dramatic population increase reveals many regional diversities. Africa is experiencing the fastest proportional population increases of all continents (approximately 20 million people per year between 1990 and 1995) and is projected to total 1.58 billion by the year 2025, up from 702 million in 1993. In terms of sheer increase in numbers, Africa does not compare to Asia, which was estimated to gain 58 million people annually between 1990 and 1995. By 2025, the United Nation's Population Division projects the population of Asia will number close to 5 billion, with China and India alone accounting for 60 percent of the Asian population and 35 percent of the global population. Although populations in other world regions are not increasing as rapidly as in Africa, nor as dramatically as in Asia, individual countries will see drastic changes. Many of the poorer countries of Central and South America are expected to experience dramatic increases in population over a 30-year period. Between 1995 and 2025, Nicaragua's population is projected to increase by 105 percent, Bolivia's by 75 percent, and Paraguay's by 88 percent.

Birth, Death, and Fertility Rates

Birthrates, death rates, and total fertility rates fell between 1970 and 1975 and 1990 and 1995, indicating that people are living

Table 7: World's Population Growth

During the Years	Annual Increment (millions)	Annual Growth Rate (percent)
1950–1955	47	1.8
1965–1970	72	2.1
1975–1980	74	1.7
1985–1990	88	1.7
1995–2000	98	1.6
2020–2025	83	1.0

Medium variant projections.
Source: *World Population Monitoring 1991.* New York: United Nations, 1992. 30.

longer and producing fewer offspring than before. Comparisons between developed and developing countries continue to show large differences in these rates. For example, the U.S. estimated birthrate for the period 1990 to 1995 is 15.9 per 1,000, the death rate is 9 per 1,000, total fertility rate is 2.1, and life expectancy is 75.9 years. These figures are in stark contrast to those estimated for Malawi, which has a crude birthrate of 54.5, a crude death rate of 22, a total fertility of 7.6, and a life expectancy of 44.2 years. Countries with large percentages of the population aged 15 years or younger will see the greatest future population growth as these people reach childbearing age. Africa has approximately 45 percent of its population in this category, while industrialized countries, especially Northern European countries, have relatively few young people and long life expectancy, and thus face a growing proportion of pensioners and retirees.

Hunger

Although the world produces more than adequate food supplies for everyone to enjoy a minimally adequate diet (2,350 calories per person per day), hunger and hunger-related deaths claim more lives than any other disaster in human history. It has been estimated that more people died from hunger between 1981 and 1983 than were killed in World War I and World War II combined. Nearly 800 million people (20 percent of the developing world's population) remain undernourished in 1990, the last year for which complete information is available. At least 2 billion faced vitamin and mineral deficiencies that posed serious health threats. UNICEF and the World Health Organization estimate that about 14 million children under the age of five die each year from hunger-related preventable causes. The figures are startling. The child mortality rate ranges as high as 320 per 1,000 in some African nations, and almost 50 countries suffer from over 10 percent child mortality (Table 8).

According to the Food and Agricultural Organization of the United Nations (FAO), the number of chronically undernourished people in the developing world began declining in 1975, from 976 million to 786 million in the 1990s. During the same period, total population in the developing world increased by 1.1 billion. As a result, the proportion of undernourished people dropped from 36 percent in 1970 to 20 percent in 1990. Here again, children provide the best, and most tragic, example of underdevelopment's most

Table 8: Basic Indicators of Child Mortality

	Under-5 mortality rate		Infant mortality rate (under 1)		Total population (millions) 1993	Annual no. of births (thousands) 1993	Annual no. of under-5 deaths (thousands) 1993	GNP per capita (US$) 1992	Life expectancy at birth (years) 1993	Total adult literacy rate 1990	Primary school enrolment ratio (gross) 1986-1992	% share of household income 1980-1991	
	1960	1993	1960	1993								lowest 40%	highest 20%
1 Niger	320	**320**	191	191	8.5	439	140	280	47	28	29	:	:
2 Angola	345	**292**	208	170	10.3	529	154	610x	47	42	91	:	:
3 Sierra Leone	385	**284**	219	164	4.5	217	62	160	43	21	48	:	:
4 Mozambique	331	**282**	190	164	15.3	695	196	60	47	33	60	:	:
5 Afghanistan	360	**257**	215	165	20.6	1086	279	280x	44	29	24	:	:
6 Guinea-Bissau	336	**235**	200	139	1.0	44	10	220	44	37	60	9	59
7 Guinea	337	**226**	203	133	6.3	320	72	510	45	24	37	:	:
8 Malawi	365	**223**	206	141	10.7	580	130	210	44	49x	66	:	:
9 Liberia	288	**217**	192	145	2.9	135	29	450x	56	40	35	:	:
10 Mali	400	**217**	233	120	10.1	515	112	310	46	32	25	:	:
11 Somalia	294	**211**	175	125	9.5	480	101	150x	47	24	11x	:	:
12 Chad	325	**206**	195	121	6.0	264	54	220	48	30	65	:	:
13 Eritrea	294	**204**	175	120	3.4	146	30	110	48			:	:
14 Ethiopia	294	**204**	175	120	51.2	2681	547	110	47	24x	25	21	41
15 Zambia	220	**203**	135	114	8.9	411	83	290	44	73	92	15	50
16 Mauritania	321	**202**	191	116	2.2	102	21	530	48	34	55	14	46
17 Bhutan	324	**197**	203	128	1.7	66	13	180	49	38	25	:	:
18 Nigeria	204	**191**	122	114	119.3	5353	1022	320	53	51	71	:	:
19 Zaire	286	**187**	167	120	41.2	1959	366	230x	52	72	76	:	:
20 Uganda	218	**185**	129	111	19.3	983	182	170	42	48	80	21	42
21 Cambodia	217	**181**	146	115	9.0	351	63	200x	51	35		:	:
22 Burundi	255	**178**	151	107	6.0	276	49	210	48	50	70	:	:
23 Central African Rep.	294	**177**	174	104	3.3	145	26	410	47	38	68	:	:
24 Burkina Faso	318	**175**	183	99	9.8	458	80	300	48	18	37	:	:
25 Ghana	215	**170**	128	103	16.5	683	116	450	56	60	77	18	44

Table 8: Basic Indicators of Child Mortality   continued

		Under-5 mortality rate		Infant mortality rate (under 1)		Total population (millions) 1993	Annual no. of births (thousands) 1993	Annual no. of under-5 deaths (thousands) 1993	GNP per capita (US$) 1992	Life expectancy at birth (years) 1993	Total adult literacy rate 1990	Primary school enrollment ratio (gross) 1986-1992	% share of household income 1980-1991	
		1960	1993	1960	1993								lowest 40%	highest 20%
26	Tanzania, U. Rep. of	249	**167**	147	108	28.8	1387	232	110	51	46x	69	8	63
27	Madagascar	364	**164**	219	100	13.3	604	99	230	56	80	92	:	:
28	Lesotho	204	**156**	138	107	1.9	65	10	590	61		107	9	60
29	Gabon	287	**154**	171	93	1.3	55	8	4450	54	61		:	:
30	Benin	310	**144**	184	87	5.1	249	36	410	46	23	66	:	:
31	Lao Peo. Dem. Rep.	233	**141**	155	96	4.6	209	29	250	51	84x	98	:	:
32	Rwanda	191	**141**	115	81	7.8	407	57	250	46	50	71	23	39
33	Pakistan	221	**137**	137	95	128.1	5162	707	420	59	35	42	21	40
34	Yemen	378	**137**	214	91	13.0	623	85	520	53	39	78	:	:
35	Togo	264	**135**	155	84	3.9	173	23	390	55	43	111	:	:
36	Haiti	270	**130**	182	85	6.9	243	32	370	57	53	56	:	:
37	Sudan	292	**128**	170	77	27.4	1146	147	420x	52	27	50	:	:
38	Nepal	279	**128**	186	90	21.1	782	100	170	54	26	82	22	40
39	Bangladesh	247	**122**	151	94	122.2	4712	575	220	53	35	77	23	39
40	India	236	**122**	144	81	896.6	26063	3167	310	61	48	98	21	41
41	Côte d'Ivoire	300	**120**	165	89	13.4	670	81	670	51	54	69	19	42
42	Senegal	303	**120**	174	63	8.0	340	41	780	49	38	59	11	59
43	Bolivia	252	**114**	152	78	7.7	264	30	680	61	77	85	15	48
44	Cameroon	264	**113**	156	71	12.6	510	58	820	56	54	101	:	:
45	Indonesia	216	**111**	127	71	194.6	5149	572	670	63	82	116	21	42
46	Myanmar	237	**111**	158	81	44.6	1446	160	220x	58	81	97	:	:
47	Congo	220	**109**	143	82	2.4	109	12	1030	51	57		:	:
48	Libyan Arab Jamahiriya	269	**100**	160	67	5.1	211	21	5310x	63	64		:	:
49	Papua New Guinea	248	**95**	165	67	4.2	139	13	950	56	52	71	:	:
50	Kenya	202	**90**	120	61	26.1	1139	103	310	59	69	95	10	62

		Under-5 mortality rate 1960	Under-5 mortality rate 1993	Infant mortality rate (under 1) 1960	Infant mortality rate (under 1) 1993	Total population (millions) 1993	Annual no. of births (thousands) 1993	Annual no. of under-5 deaths (thousands) 1993	GNP per capita (US$) 1992	Life expectancy at birth (years) 1993	Total adult literacy rate 1990	Primary school enrolment ratio (gross) 1986-1992	% share of household income 1980-1991 lowest 40%	% share of household income 1980-1991 highest 20%
51	Turkmenistan	:	**89**	:	71	4.0	131	12	1230	66	98x	:	:	:
52	Turkey	217	**84**	161	67	59.6	1663	139	1980	67	81	113	:	:
53	Zimbabwe	181	**83**	109	58	10.9	441	37	570	56	67	119	10	62
54	Tajikistan	:	**83**	:	64	5.8	222	18	490	69	98x	:	:	:
55	Namibia	206	**79**	129	62	1.6	68	5	1610	59	:	119	:	:
56	Mongolia	185	**78**	128	59	2.4	80	6	780x	64	:	89	:	:
57	Guatemala	205	**73**	137	53	10.0	387	28	980	65	55	79	8	63
58	Nicaragua	209	**72**	140	51	4.1	165	12	340	67	35x	101	:	:
59	Iraq	171	**71**	117	57	19.9	770	55	1500x	66	60	111	:	:
60	South Africa	126	**69**	89	53	40.8	1270	88	2670	63	76x	:	:	:
61	Algeria	243	**68**	148	57	27.1	920	63	1840	66	57	95	18	47
62	Uzbekistan	:	**66**	:	54	22.0	704	46	850	69	97x	:	:	:
63	Brazil	181	**63**	118	52	156.6	3590	226	2770	66	82	106	7	68
64	Peru	236	**62**	143	43	22.9	662	41	950	65	85	126	14	51
65	El Salvador	210	**60**	130	45	5.5	185	11	1170	67	73	76	:	:
66	Egypt	258	**59**	169	46	56.1	1733	102	640	62	48	101	:	:
67	Morocco	215	**59**	133	48	27.0	861	50	1030	64	50	66	17	46
68	Philippines	102	**59**	73	45	66.5	1999	117	770	65	94	110	17	48
69	Kyrgyzstan	:	**58**	:	48	4.6	128	7	820	66	96x	:	:	:
70	Ecuador	180	**57**	115	45	11.3	333	19	1070	67	87	116	:	:
71	Botswana	170	**56**	117	43	1.4	52	3	2790	61	74	119	11	59
72	Honduras	203	**56**	137	43	5.6	207	12	580	66	73	105	9	64
73	Iran, Islamic Rep. of	233	**54**	145	42	63.2	2507	136	2200	67	54	112	:	:
74	Azerbaijan	:	**52**	:	36	7.4	163	8	740	71	97x	:	:	:
75	Kazakhstan	:	**49**	:	42	17.1	308	15	1680	69	97x	:	:	:

Table 8: Basic Indicators of Child Mortality continued

	Under-5 mortality rate 1960	Under-5 mortality rate 1993	Infant mortality rate (under 1) 1960	Infant mortality rate (under 1) 1993	Total population (millions) 1993	Annual no. of births (thousands) 1993	Annual no. of under-5 deaths (thousands) 1993	GNP per capita (US$) 1992	Life expectancy at birth (years) 1993	Total adult literacy rate 1990	Primary school enrolment ratio (gross) 1986-1992	% share of household income 1980-1991 lowest 40%	% share of household income 1980-1991 highest 20%
76 Dominican Rep.	152	**48**	104	40	7.6	213	10	1050	68	83	95	12	56
77 Viet Nam	219	**48**	147	36	70.9	2055	98	240x	64	88	103		
78 China	209	**43**	140	35	1205.2	24903	1071	470	71	78	123	17	42
79 Albania	151	**41**	112	34	3.3	75	3	790x	73		101		
80 Lebanon	85	**40**	65	33	2.9	79	3	2150x	69	80	112		
81 Syrian Arab Rep.	201	**39**	136	33	13.8	583	23	1160	67	64	109		
82 Saudi Arabia	292	**38**	170	33	16.5	590	22	7510	69	62	77		
83 Moldova		**36**		31	4.4	65	2	1300	68	96x			
84 Tunisia	244	**36**	163	30	8.6	231	8	1720	68	65	117	16	46
85 Paraguay	90	**34**	66	28	4.6	153	5	1380	67	90	109		
86 Armenia		**33**		28	3.5	71	2	780	72	99x			
87 Thailand	146	**33**	101	27	56.9	1157	38	1840	69	93	90	16	51
88 Mexico	141	**32**	98	27	90.0	2499	81	3470	70	88	114	12	56
89 Korea, Dem. Peo. Rep.	120	**32**	85	24	23.1	559	18	970x	71		104		
90 Russian Federation		**31**		28	148.3	1779	55	2510	69	99x			
91 Romania	82	**29**	69	23	23.4	365	11	1130	70	97	90		
92 Oman	300	**29**	180	23	1.7	68	2	6480	70		100		
93 Georgia		**28**		24	5.5	83	2	850	73	99x			
94 Jordan	149	**27**	103	23	4.4	176	5	1120	68	80	97	17	48
95 Argentina	68	**27**	57	24	33.5	676	18	6050	71	95	107		
96 Latvia		**26**		22	2.7	36	1	1930	71	99x			
97 Ukraine		**25**		21	51.9	622	16	1820	70	98x			
98 Venezuela	70	**24**	53	20	20.6	533	13	2910	70	88	99	14	50
99 Estonia		**23**		20	1.6	22	1	2760	72	100x			
100 Belarus		**22**		19	10.4	135	3	2930	71	98x			

	Under-5 mortality rate 1960	Under-5 mortality rate 1993	Infant mortality rate (under 1) 1960	Infant mortality rate (under 1) 1993	Total population (millions) 1993	Annual no. of births (thousands) 1993	Annual no. of under-5 deaths (thousands) 1993	GNP per capita (US$) 1992	Life expectancy at birth (years) 1993	Total adult literacy rate 1990	Primary school enrolment ratio (gross) 1986-1992	% share of household income 1980-1991 lowest 40%	% share of household income 1980-1991 highest 20%
101 Mauritius	84	**22**	62	19	1.1	20	0	2700	70	80	106	..	..
102 Yugoslavia (former)	113	**22**	92	19	24.0	337	7	3060x	72	93	94	..	..
103 United Arab Emirates	240	**21**	160	18	1.7	36	1	22020	71	53x	115	..	..
104 Trinidad and Tobago	73	**21**	61	18	1.3	30	1	3940	71	95x	96	..	..
105 Uruguay	47	**21**	41	19	3.2	54	1	3340	72	96	110	..	..
106 Lithuania	..	**20**	..	17	3.8	55	1	1310	73	98x	..	..	..
107 Panama	104	**20**	67	18	2.6	64	1	2420	73	89	106	8	60
108 Bulgaria	70	**19**	49	16	8.9	111	2	1330	72	..	92	24	36
109 Sri Lanka	130	**19**	90	15	17.9	370	7	540	72	88	108	22	39
110 Colombia	132	**19**	82	16	34.0	809	15	1330	69	87	111	11	56
111 Slovakia	..	**18**	..	16	5.4	81	1	1930	72	..	98	11	63
112 Chile	138	**17**	107	15	13.8	309	5	2730	72	93	98	11	63
113 Malaysia	105	**17**	73	13	19.2	543	9	2790	71	78	93	13	54
114 Costa Rica	112	**16**	80	14	3.3	85	1	1960	76	93	103	13	51
115 Poland	70	**15**	62	13	38.5	547	8	1910	72	99x	98	23	36
116 Hungary	57	**15**	51	13	10.5	129	2	2970	70	99x	89	26	34
117 Jamaica	76	**13**	58	11	2.5	55	1	1340	74	98	106	16	48
118 Kuwait	128	**13**	89	11	1.8	53	1	16150x	75	73	55	..	..
119 Portugal	112	**11**	81	9	9.9	114	1	7450	75	85	122	..	..
120 Cuba	50	**10**	39	9	10.9	190	2	1170x	76	94	102	..	..
121 United States	30	**10**	26	9	257.8	4093	42	23240	76	..	104	16	42
122 Czech Rep.	..	**10**	..	9	10.4	146	1	2450	72	..	..	..	..
123 Greece	64	**10**	53	9	10.2	106	1	7290	78	93	97	..	..
124 Belgium	35	**10**	31	8	10.0	122	1	20880	76	..	99	22x	36x
125 Spain	57	**9**	46	8	39.2	426	4	13970	78	95	109	22	37
126 France	34	**9**	29	7	57.4	772	7	22260	77	..	107	17	42
127 Korea, Rep. of	124	**9**	88	8	44.5	731	7	6790	71	96	105	20	42
128 Israel	39	**9**	32	7	5.4	112	1	13220	77	92x	95	18x	40x
129 Italy	50	**9**	44	7	57.8	583	5	20460	77	97	94	19	41
130 New Zealand	26	**9**	22	7	3.5	61	1	12300	76	..	104	16	45

Table 8: Basic Indicators of Child Mortality continued

		Under-5 mortality rate		Infant mortality rate (under 1)		Total population (millions) 1993	Annual no. of births (thousands) 1993	Annual no. of under-5 deaths (thousands) 1993	GNP per capita (US$) 1992	Life expectancy at birth (years) 1993	Total adult literacy rate 1990	Primary school enrolment ratio (gross) 1986-1992	% share of household income 1980-1991	
		1960	1993	1960	1993								lowest 40%	highest 20%
131	Australia	24	8	20	7	17.8	269	2	17260	77	:	107	16	42
132	Canada	33	8	28	7	27.8	394	3	20710	77	97x	107	18	40
133	Switzerland	27	8	22	6	6.9	87	1	36080	78	:	103	17	45
134	United Kingdom	27	8	23	7	57.8	803	6	17790	76	:	104	15	44
135	Austria	43	8	37	7	7.8	91	1	22380	76	:	103	:	:
136	Netherlands	22	8	18	6	15.3	212	2	20480	77	:	102	21	37
137	Norway	23	8	19	6	4.3	64	0	25820	77	:	100	19x	37x
138	Germany	40	7	34	6	80.6	917	7	23030	76	:	105	19	40
139	Ireland	36	7	31	6	3.5	50	0	12210	75	:	103	16	47
140	Hong Kong	52	7	38	6	5.9	75	1	15360	78	77x	108	:	:
141	Denmark	25	7	22	6	5.2	65	0	26000	76	:	96	17	39
142	Japan	40	6	31	5	125.0	1407	9	28190	79	:	102	22x	38x
143	Singapore	40	6	31	5	2.8	44	0	15730	75	83x	108	15	49
144	Sweden	20	6	16	5	8.7	122	1	27010	78	:	100	21	37
145	Finland	28	5	22	4	5.0	65	0	21970	76	:	99	18	38

Source: *The State of the World's Children 1995.* Published for UNICEF by Oxford University Press, Inc.

brutal manifestation. Wasting, stunting, goiter, and chronic malnutrition are unnecessary endemics in many parts of the global South, especially in sub-Saharan Africa (Table 9).

The existence of hunger is unevenly distributed within regions. In sub-Saharan Africa, despite considerable increases in the availability of food in recent years, some 240 million people (about 30 percent of the total) are undernourished. The growth of food output has not kept pace with population growth. Average food availability per person is below minimum requirements, with some 1,500 calories available per person per day. In 1992, drought and crop failure left 23 million South and East Africans dependent on emergency food aid. Though in the Asian Pacific hunger has declined dramatically over the past 20 years, in South Asia 30 percent of all babies are born underweight—the highest ratio for any region in the world. South Asia has the highest proportion of underweight women of childbearing age in the world with 60 percent, and Southeast Asia ranks second with 44 percent. South Asia also has the world's highest incidence of malnutrition among children under five, with the Southeast again ranking second.

In Latin America the situation improved slightly between 1975 and 1990. Malnutrition rates for children under five declined—from 19 percent to 15 percent in Central America and from 16 percent to 8 percent in South America. Between 1970 and 1990, hunger declined dramatically in both relative and absolute terms in the Middle East, from 23 percent of the population (32 million) to 5 percent of the population (12 million).

Food Supply

Notwithstanding rapid population growth in many parts of the Third World, figures reveal that there is enough food produced in the world to feed its population (Table 10). Even in developing countries, per capita food production increased by 18 percent on average in the 1980s. Due to intensive use of resources and increased productivity, there has been an increase in food supplies. The production of major food crops has grown 1.45 percent annually between 1981 and 1991. Between 1990 and 1991, however, production fell from a record 1,971 million metric tons to 1,890 metric tons. Global production of root crops for 1991 remained at the same 1990 level of 574 million tons, while cereal production has nearly doubled since 1970. Over the period 1981–1991, grain

Table 9: Nutrition

| | | % of infants with low birth weight 1990 | % of children (1986-93) who are: | | | % of under-fives (1980-93) suffering from: | | | | | Total goitre rate (6-11 years) (%) 1980-92 | Daily per capita calorie supply as a % of requirements 1988-90 | % share of total household consumption (1980-85) | |
			exclusively breastfed (0-3 months)	breastfed with complementary food (6-9 months)	still breastfeeding (20-23 months)	underweight moderate & severe	underweight severe	wasting moderate & severe	stunting moderate & severe				all food	cereals
1	Niger	15	:	:	53	36	12	16	32	9	95	:	:
2	Angola	19	3	83	41	29	:	9x	35	7	80	:	:
3	Sierra Leone	17	:	94	:	:	:	:	:	7	83	56	22
4	Mozambique	20	:	:	:	:	:	:	:	20	77	:	:
5	Afghanistan	20	:	:	:	:	:	:	:	20	72	:	:
6	Guinea-Bissau	20	:	:	:	23x	:	:	:	19	97	:	:
7	Guinea	21	:	89	:	27	8	:	:	19	97	:	:
8	Malawi	20	3	56	:	20x	:	5	49	13	88	30	9
9	Liberia	:	15	45	26	:	:	3x	37x	6	98	:	:
10	Mali	17	8	:	44	31x	9x	11x	24x	29	96	57	22
11	Somalia	16	:	:	:	:	:	:	:	7	81	:	:
12	Chad	:	:	:	:	:	:	:	:	:	73	:	:
13	Eritrea	:	:	:	:	:	:	:	:	15	:	:	:
14	Ethiopia	16	74	88	35	48x	16x	8x	64x	22	73	49	24
15	Zambia	13	13	:	34	25	6	5	40	51x	87	36	8
16	Mauritania	11	12	39	:	48	:	16	57	25	106	:	:
17	Bhutan	:	:	:	:	38	:	4	56	10	128	:	:
18	Nigeria	16	2	52	43	36	12	9	43	9	93	48	18
19	Zaire	15	:	:	:	28x	:	5x	43x	7	96	:	:
20	Uganda	:	70	67	39	23	5	2	45	:	93	:	:
21	Cambodia	:	:	:	:	:	:	:	:	15	96	:	:
22	Burundi	15	89	66	73	38x	10x	6x	48x	42	84	:	:
23	Central African Rep.	21x	:	:	:	:	:	:	:	63	82	:	:
24	Burkina Faso	17	3	35	:	30	8	13	29	16	94	:	:
25	Ghana	17	2	57	52	27	6	7	31	10	93	50	:

#	Country	% of infants with low birth weight 1990	% of children (1986-93) who are: exclusively breastfed (0-3 months)	breastfed with complementary food (6-9 months)	still breastfeeding (20-23 months)	% of under-fives (1980-93) suffering from: underweight moderate & severe	underweight severe	wasting moderate & severe	stunting moderate & severe	Total goitre rate (6-11 years) (%) 1980-92	Daily per capita calorie supply as a % of requirements 1988-90	% share of total household consumption (1980-85) all food	cereals
26	Tanzania, U. Rep. of	14	32	89	57	29	7	6	47	37	95	64	32
27	Madagascar	10	47	93	45	39	9	5	51	24	95	59	26
28	Lesotho	11	..	..	..	16	2	5	26	16	93	..	..
29	Gabon	..	..	..	..	..	..	..	..	5	104	..	..
30	Benin	..	..	..	..	..	..	..	..	24	104	37	12
31	Lao Peo. Dem. Rep.	18	90	75	..	37	..	11	40	25	111	..	..
32	Rwanda	17	25	29	..	29	6	4	48	49	82	29	10
33	Pakistan	25	15	51	52	40	14	9	50	32	99	37	12
34	Yemen	19	10	86	..	30	4	13	44	32	..	..	..
35	Togo	20	..	..	68	24x	6x	5x	30x	22	99	..	..
36	Haiti	15	..	45	44	37x	3x	9x	40x	4	89	..	..
37	Sudan	15	14	..	..	20	..	14	32	20	87	60	38
38	Nepal	..	..	..	..	70x	5x	14x	69x	44	100	57	36
39	Bangladesh	50	..	..	..	66x	27x	16x	65x	11	88	59	..
40	India	33	..	..	..	69x	27x	..	65x	9	101	52	18
41	Côte d'Ivoire	14x	..	42	95	12	2	9	17	6	111	39	13
42	Senegal	11	9	57	30	20	5	9	22	12	98	49	15
43	Bolivia	12	59	77	35	13x	3x	2x	38x	21	84	33	..
44	Cameroon	13	7	76	62	14	3	3	24	26	95	24	7
45	Indonesia	14	53	..	..	40	..	..	..	28	121	48	21
46	Myanmar	16	..	..	27	32x	9x	..	..	18	114	..	..
47	Congo	16	43	..	..	24	..	5	27	8	103	37	16
48	Libyan Arab Jamahiriya	..	..	..	..	..	..	..	..	6	140	..	..
49	Papua New Guinea	23	..	97	54	35	6	6	..	30	114	..	..
50	Kenya	16	17	..	..	22	..	6	33	7	89	38	16

Table 9: Nutrition *continued*

		% of infants with low birth weight 1990	% of children (1986-93) who are: exclusively breastfed (0-3 months)	breastfed with complementary food (6-9 months)	still breastfeeding (20-23 months)	% of under-fives (1980-93) suffering from: underweight moderate & severe	underweight severe	wasting moderate & severe	stunting moderate & severe	Total goitre rate (6-11 years) (%) 1980-92	Daily per capita calorie supply as a % of requirements 1988-90	% share of total household consumption (1980-85) all food	cereals
51	Turkmenistan	8								20			
52	Turkey	14								36	127	40	9
53	Zimbabwe		11	94	26	12x	2x	1x	29x	42	94	40	9
54	Tajikistan									20			
55	Namibia	12	22	65	23	26	6	9	28	35			
56	Mongolia	10				12x		2x	26x	7	97		
57	Guatemala	14			44	34x	8x	1x	58x	20	103	36	10
58	Nicaragua	15				11	1	1	22	4	99		
59	Iraq	15				12	2	3	22	7	128		
60	South Africa									2	128	34	
61	Algeria	9				9		6	18	9	123		
62	Uzbekistan		4	27						18			
63	Brazil	11	40	62	13	7	1	2	16	14x	114	35	9
64	Peru	11			36	11		1	37	36	87	35	8
65	El Salvador	11				15	2	5	30	25	102	33	12
66	Egypt	10	38	52	18	9	2	3	24	5	132	49	10
67	Morocco	9	48	48	18	9	2	2	23	20	125	38	12
68	Philippines	15	33	61		34	5	6	37	15	104	51	21
69	Kyrgyzstan									20			
70	Ecuador	11	31	31	23	17	0	2	34	10	105	30	
71	Botswana	8	41	82	23	15x			44	8	97	25	
72	Honduras	9				21	4	2	34	9	98	39	
73	Iran, Islamic Rep. of	9								30	125	37	12
74	Azerbaijan									20			
75	Kazakhstan									20			10

		% of infants with low birth weight 1990	% of children (1986-93) who are:			% of under-fives (1980-93) suffering from:						Total goitre rate (6-11 years) (%) 1980-92	Daily per capita calorie supply as a % of requirements 1988-90	% share of total household consumption (1980-85)	
			exclusively breastfed (0-3 months)	breastfed with complementary food (6-9 months)	still breastfeeding (20-23 months)	underweight		wasting		stunting				all food	cereals
						moderate & severe	severe	moderate & severe		moderate & severe					
76	Dominican Rep.	16	10	23	7	10	2	1		19		20	102	46	13
77	Viet Nam	17				52	14	7		60		9	103		
78	China	9				21x	3x	4x		32x		41	112	61	
79	Albania	7										15	107		
80	Lebanon	10											127		
81	Syrian Arab Rep.	11										73	126		
82	Saudi Arabia	7											121		
83	Moldova	8	21	53	25	10x	2x	3x		18x		4	131	37	7
84	Tunisia	8	7	61	8	4	1	0		17		49	116	30	6
85	Paraguay														
86	Armenia	13										10	103	30	7
87	Thailand	12	4	69	34	26x	4x	6x		22x		12	131	35	
88	Mexico		37	36	21	14		6		22		15	121		
89	Korea, Dem. Peo. Rep.														
90	Russian Federation														
91	Romania	7										10	116		
92	Oman	10										20			
93	Georgia					6									
94	Jordan	7	32	48	13		1	3		19		8	110	35	4
95	Argentina	8											131	35	
96	Latvia											10			
97	Ukraine	9				6						11	99	23	
98	Venezuela							2		6					
99	Estonia											22			
100	Belarus														

Table 9: Nutrition continued

#		% of infants with low birth weight 1990	% of children (1986-93) who are:			% of under-fives (1980-93) suffering from:				Total goitre rate (6-11 years) (%) 1980-92	Daily per capita calorie supply as a % of requirements 1988-90	% share of total household consumption (1980-85)	
			exclusively breastfed (0-3 months)	breastfed with complementary food (6-9 months)	still breastfeeding (20-23 months)	underweight moderate & severe	underweight severe	wasting moderate & severe	stunting moderate & severe			all food	cereals
101	Mauritius	9	..	..	..	24	..	16	22	..	128	24	7
102	Yugoslavia (former)	..	..	..	..	..	..	..	..	5	140	27	4
103	United Arab Emirates	6	10	39	26	7x	0x	4x	5x	..	114	19	3
104	Trinidad and Tobago	10	..	..	16	7	2	..	16	..	101	31	7
105	Uruguay	8	..	..	..	..	..	..	..	..	..	..	..
106	Lithuania	10	..	..	..	..	..	..	..	13	..	..	..
107	Panama	6	..	..	..	16	..	6	22	20	98	38	7
108	Bulgaria	..	..	..	..	..	..	..	..	14	148	..	..
109	Sri Lanka	25	14	47	46	29x	2x	18	36	10	101	43	18
110	Colombia	10	17	48	24	10	..	3	17	..	106	29	..
111	Slovakia	..	..	..	..	..	..	..	..	9	102	29	7
112	Chile	7	..	..	..	3x	..	1x	10x	20	120	23	..
113	Malaysia	10	..	..	..	..	..	..	..	3	121	33	8
114	Costa Rica	6	..	..	..	6	..	2	8	..	131	29	4
115	Poland	..	..	..	..	..	..	..	..	10	..	..	..
116	Hungary	9	..	..	..	..	..	..	..	..	137	25	3
117	Jamaica	11	..	..	..	7	1	3	9	..	114	36	14
118	Kuwait	7	..	..	..	6	..	3	12	..	..	..	..
119	Portugal	5	..	..	..	..	..	..	..	15	136	34	8
120	Cuba	8	..	..	..	..	..	1	..	10	135	..	..
121	United States	7	..	..	..	..	..	..	..	..	138	10	2
122	Czech Rep.	..	..	..	..	..	..	..	..	..	..	..	..
123	Greece	6	..	..	..	..	..	..	..	10	151	30	3
124	Belgium	6	..	..	..	..	..	..	..	5	149	15	2
125	Spain	4	..	..	..	..	..	..	..	10	141	24	3

		% of infants with low birth weight 1980	% of children (1986-93) who are:			% of under-fives (1980-93) suffering from:				Total goitre rate (6-11 years) (%) 1980-92	Daily per capita calorie supply as a % of requirements 1988-90	% share of total household consumption (1980-85)	
			exclusively breastfed (0-3 months)	breastfed with complementary food (6-9 months)	still breastfeeding (20-23 months)	underweight moderate & severe	underweight severe	wasting moderate & severe	stunting moderate & severe			all food	cereals
126	France	5	:	:	:	:	:	:	:	5	143	16	2
127	Korea, Rep. of	9	:	:	:	:	:	:	:	:	120	35	14
128	Israel	7	:	:	:	:	:	:	:	:	125	21	:
129	Italy	5	:	:	:	:	:	:	:	20	139	19	2
130	New Zealand	6	:	:	:	:	:	:	:	:	131	12	2
131	Australia	6	:	:	:	:	:	:	:	:	124	13	2
132	Canada	6	:	:	:	:	:	:	:	:	122	11	2
133	Switzerland	5	:	:	:	:	:	:	:	:	130	17	:
134	United Kingdom	7	:	:	:	:	:	:	:	:	130	12	2
135	Austria	6	:	:	:	:	:	:	:	:	133	16	2
136	Netherlands	4	:	:	:	:	:	:	:	3	114	13	2
137	Norway	:	:	:	:	:	:	:	:	10	120	15	2
138	Germany	:	:	:	:	:	:	:	:	:	:	12	2
139	Ireland	4	:	:	:	:	:	:	:	:	157	22	4
140	Hong Kong	8	:	:	:	:	:	:	:	:	125	12	1
141	Denmark	6	:	:	:	:	:	:	:	5	135	13	2
142	Japan	6	:	:	:	:	:	:	:	:	125	17	4
143	Singapore	7	:	:	:	14x	:	4x	11x	:	136	19	:
144	Sweden	5	:	:	:	:	:	:	:	:	111	13	2
145	Finland	4	:	:	:	:	:	:	:	:	113	16	3

Source: *The State of the World's Children 1995*. Published for UNICEF by Oxford University Press, Inc.

Table 10: Indicators of Food Security in Selected Countries

Country	Food Production per Capita Index (1979/81=100) 1991	Food Import Dependency Ratio Index (1969/71=100) 1988/90	Daily per Capita Calorie Supply as a Percentage of Requirements 1988–1990
Ethiopia	86	855	71
Afghanistan	71	193	76
Mozambique	77	300	77
Angola	79	366	80
Rwanda	84	322	80
Somalia	78	134	81
Sudan	80	156	83
Burundi	91	165	85
Haiti	84	364	94

Source: United Nations Development Programme, *Human Development Report*, 1994.

production has increased at an annual rate of 3.34 percent, global stocks increased from 365 million metric tons in 1984 to 464 million metric tons in 1986, and then fell back to the 300–343 million metric ton range.

However, this does not mean that everybody gets to eat. The problems of poor distribution and lack of purchasing power maintain the level of poverty and hunger in developing countries. Disparities in food consumption are revealing—as many as 700 million people do not eat enough to live and work to their full potential. The average African consumes only 87 percent of the calories needed for a healthy and productive life, whereas in rich countries, meat-intense diets have been linked to increased rates of heart disease and cancers.

The need for food relief is recognized throughout the world and efforts have been made to meet its demand; 13.2 million tons of cereal was delivered as aid in 1991, representing .07 percent of the world's total cereal production and approximately 7 percent of stocks in industrialized countries. Regional estimates of food aid flows between 1987 and 1991 fluctuated. Africa and Asia received the largest amount of food aid overall. Sub-Saharan Africa received the largest volume of food aid in 1991 (major recipients being Ethiopia, Sudan, Mozambique, Malawi, Liberia, and Angola). In 1992, the Horn of Africa (i.e., Ethiopia, Somalia, and

Sudan) suffered severe food shortages, the latter two because of civil strife as well as low rainfall. Food aid declined to Latin America, the Caribbean, Eastern Europe, and the former Soviet Union. The Asia-Pacific and North Africa–Middle East regions saw slight increases from 1990 levels. However, while food aid has traditionally constituted an important proportion of total official development assistance, and the United States has traditionally led the world in direct food shipments, there are indications that the historical pattern may be in jeopardy. In April 1995, the Clinton administration indicated that it would cut its promise of yearly food aid by more than 40 percent, from 4.47 million metric tons to 2.5 million metric tons. Overall, donor nation food contributions have been steadily sliding, from 10.2 million tons of grain in 1991 to 9.8 million in 1992, 8 million in 1993, and 6.5 million in 1994.

Though food production worldwide may be keeping pace with population growth, there are doubts as to whether it can maintain this in line with the pressures of projected population increases. Even the most optimistic scenarios would require a near doubling of food production before the middle of the next century if the world is to be fed. Between 1980 and 1990, cropland worldwide only expanded by 2 percent, which means that gains in global harvests came almost entirely from existing croplands. Moreover, as economies of developing countries grow and cities expand to accommodate the increasing populations, land is constantly being taken for housing, transport, and industry. It has been estimated that between 1957 and 1990, China's arable land diminished by at least 35 million hectares. Projections based on China's average agricultural yield and consumption levels indicate that the lost cropland could have supported some 450 million people, about 40 percent of its population. Development based on continuing population pressure and continuing loss of arable lands can only squeeze further the planet's margin of food security.

This pressure may be intensified by exhaustion of another natural resource: the world's marine ecosystems, which support vast numbers of fish that are a vital part of the global food supply. An estimated 1 billion people, mostly in the developed world, depend on fish as their sole source of protein. Yet there are signs that many of the world's marine fisheries are in serious trouble. The annual fish catch from all sources totaled 97 million in 1990, which accounts for 5 percent of the protein that humans consume. However, as a result of intense fishing, using high-tech mechanical fishing equipment, the UN Food and Agricultural Organization (FAO) estimates that all 17 of the world's major fishing areas have either reached or exceeded their natural limits and that 9 are in serious decline.

One of the most demanding challenges facing humanity is finding the means to meet the requirements of our growing population while ensuring that our natural resources are preserved. Technology has greatly enhanced the world's standard of living and increased food production. However, it has also produced many adverse side effects. Irrigation, agricultural chemicals, and high-yield crop varieties boost product yields; but at the same time they are responsible for much of the contamination and depletion of water supplies (see the data on water use in the section on environment below) and the poisoning of wildlife and people. Moreover, technologically oriented production techniques have encouraged intensive, single-crop farming that has reduced agricultural diversity. The emphasis must now be placed on employing the power of technology in a manner that ensures the protection of our land and water resources as well as increasing productivity for the increasing world population. Advances in biotechnology may contribute to solutions: Gabrielle Persley of the World Bank reports that rice varieties bioengineered for virus resistance are likely to be in the near future. The further development of crop varieties with built-in resistance to disease will reduce crop losses to pests.

In sum, the technology and the capacity remains sufficient to meet the world's food demands of today and tommorrow. The challenge is not principally of production, but rather the political and economic challenges of reducing poverty such that all have the purchasing power to acquire food, and the environmental challenge to develop food security sustainably, so that the costs of production do not devastate the world around us.

Health Services

Problems in the Developing World's Health Services

Ready and affordable access to health services is vital for human development. Population growth, insufficient food supply, and poverty naturally induce disease, disabilities, and increased rates of adult and child mortality, and for these reasons, most leading indicators of health and physical well-being in the global South lag far behind their Northern equivalents. Improved health care, then, is a primary challenge of the modern development endeavor.

By some measures, advances in public health provide some of development's best succeess stories. Life expectancy has improved dramatically over the past 40 years in developing countries, rising from 40 years in 1950 to 63 years in 1990. Child mortality, meanwhile, has dropped precipitously in many parts of the world, especially in Asia and Latin America. More accessible vaccinations, greater availability of medical advice, and the provision of basic needs such as safe water and decent sanitation have all played a role in these encouraging trends. Despite these remarkable advances, however, enormous health problems remain. Absolute levels of mortality in developing countries are unacceptably high: Child mortality rates are approximately ten times that of those in established market economies. To a great extent premature mortality, especially among children, is due to preventable deaths resulting from diarrheal and respiratory illness exacerbated by malnutrition.

In developing countries, the major causes of death are infectious and parasitic diseases, which kill 17 million people annually, including 6.5 million from acute respiratory infections, 4.5 million from diarrheal diseases, and 3.5 million from tuberculosis. The malaria parasite's increased resistance to available drugs could lead to a doubling of malaria deaths to nearly 2 million a year within a decade. By the year 2000, the increasing death rate caused by Acquired Immune Deficiency Syndrome (AIDS) in developing countries could rise to more than 1.8 million deaths annually.

A yawning gulf separates the health services provided by rich countries and poor countries. In industrial nations there is a doctor for every 400 people, whereas in developing countries there is 1 doctor for nearly 7,000 persons—in sub-Saharan Africa there is 1 per 36,000. There is also a marked difference in public spending: Whereas health expenditure in established market economies averages $1,860 per person, the corresponding figure for sub-Saharan Africa is only $24, and for Bangladesh a mere $7. That is, the fortunate few in advanced economies benefit from an investment in their physical well-being up to 265 times greater than their counterparts in parts of the South. In too many cases, especially for children, the paucity of investment is the equivalent of a death sentence.

Global expenditure on health care is enormous: In 1990, public outlays for health services was about $1.7 trillion, the equivalent of 8 percent of the total world product. Ninety percent of this was spent by high-income countries. In low-income countries, government hospitals account for the greatest part of their public medical care and these are often inefficient, underfunded, and ill-equipped. Private providers, mainly religious charity organizations, are more technically efficient and give better-quality treatment than public institutions, yet receive no public assistance. The evidence on advances in mortality proves that investment in health care pays real dividends. As with so many elements of the development effort, the key lies in marshalling resources and political will.

Infectious Diseases: AIDS

Recent Western interest in infectious diseases, especially AIDS, and occasionally more exotic (but equally deadly) viruses such as ebola, has trained much-needed attention on issues in African health. The AIDS epidemic has had a devastating effect in Africa and poses a real threat to many countries already in distress. HIV infection rates are thought to range as high as 10 percent of the overall population in countries such as Uganda, and projections indicate that per capita income growth might be slowed by as much as 0.6 percent yearly in the hardest-hit nations of sub-Saharan Africa. The heavy economic impact of AIDS comes partly from the high costs of treatment, which divert much-needed resources from productive investment, and partly from the disproportionate toll the disease takes on skilled adults. Further, the economic impact of the disease ranges well beyond the immediate victim. The death of an adult can force children out of school and into the workplace, albeit without the skills necessary for economic growth. In addition to the tragedy of illness, then, AIDS undermines the delicate economic balance required to break the chain of poverty and progress to sustainable development.

For these reasons, preventing the spread of AIDS constitutes one of the great development challenges of the decade. Projects in Uganda, Thailand, and other Southern nations have demonstrated that early intervention can work to blunt the spread of HIV and AIDS.

Child Malnutrition

Child malnutrition and mortality are the world's most serious nutritional emergencies. Tens of millions of children under the age of five are chronically malnourished. Malnutrition strikes hardest in the last trimester of pregnancy and during the first year of life. Poorly nourished mothers tend to bear underweight babies and a child suffering malnutrition in its first year is likely to suffer below-normal growth even if its nutrition improves thereafter. The implications of malnutrition on a child's health and in the overall development equation are difficult to underestimate. Malnutrition means a child is vulnerable to disease and can never achieve full potential or life expectancy. The costs are emotional, educational, and intellectual, as well as physical; a life begun undernourished is especially likely to perpetuate the chain of poverty and underdevelopment.

The news is not all bad. For instance, the proportion of malnourished children under five in the developing world has declined from 42 percent in 1975 to 34 percent in 1990. However, due to population growth, the number of malnourished children rose from 168 million to 184 million during the same period. Insufficient protein and calories are the main causes of growth deficiencies. Vitamin and mineral deficiencies also have a severe impact; each year the intelligence quotients of 1.2 million children of iodine-deficient mothers are reduced by 10 points. Mild vitamin A deficiency increases the risk of death by 20 percent and causes eye damage that can eventually lead to blindness. As a result, every year 250,000 to 500,000 preschool children go blind while two-thirds die. In 1991, 14 million preschool children were affected.

The problem needs immediate attention. At the World Summit for Children in 1990, the following health plan was drawn up, the demands of which are to be met by the year 2000, allowing for adaptations to meet different countries' needs:

1. The eradication of polio by 2000
2. The elimination of neonatal tetanus by 1995
3. A 90 percent reduction in measels cases and a 95 percent reduction in measles deaths
4. Achievement and maintenance of 90 percent immunization coverage of one-year-old children, plus

universal tetanus immunization for women of
childbearing age
5. Halving the deaths caused by diarrhea and a
one-quarter reduction of the incidence of diarrheal
disease
6. A reduction by one-third in the deaths of children
caused by acute respiratory infections
7. Virtual elimination of vitamin A deficiency and
deficiency disorders
8. A reduction in the incidence of low birth weight to no
more than 10 percent
9. A one-third reduction from 1990 levels in iron
deficiency anemia among women
10. Access for all women to prenatal care, trained
attendants during childbirth, and referral for high-risk
pregnancies and obstetric emergencies

Through the adoption and pursuit of this plan children will
have a better chance to grow up healthy in mind and body.

Gender

The Position of Women

Data concerning the state of human development can be mislead-
ing as it often conceals many disparities. This is especially true
when looking at the position of women in development. Women
constitute half of the world's population, yet they do not have
equal access to land, credit, technology, education, employment,
food, and political power. Women bear a special role in social and
economic reproduction; they are critical to economic security and
have a profound effect on the well-being of their families, communities, and local ecosystems. Moreover, for development to reflect
its underlying spirit of social justice, its benefits in health, education, and welfare must be realized by all. In order to move toward
more egalitarian development, the special role of women, and the
historical discrimination against them in the development process,
must be recognized and reformed.

Statistics covering all types of work demonstrate that in almost every part of the world, women spend more time working
than men. In the formal economic sector, women are increasingly

present and powerful: Recent UN statistics reveal that 59 percent of women in Asia, 60 percent of women in the former Soviet Union, and between 45 and 50 percent of women in Southeast Asia and sub-Saharan Africa are economically active. In Latin America and the Caribbean, between 60 and 70 percent of economically active women are in the service sector. What's more, women frequently work in the informal sector. Self-employment in unregulated industrial industries and small-scale, service-related fields is common. In 1986, women contributed to 53.3 percent of Zambia's informal sector and 43.2 percent of Malaysia's. Women usually incorporate over half the borrowers in nongovernmental organization (NGO) projects targeted at small businesses; and case studies demonstrate that 85 percent of the borrowers in El Salvador's FEDECREDITO program, 60 percent in Indonesia's Badan Kredit Kecamatan program, and 97 percent in Zimbabwe's Federation of Rural Savings Club are women.

Throughout the world the majority of women's work is in the noncash economy, which includes: subsistence agriculture, care for children and family dependents, provision of clothing, primary health care, and household duties. If women's unpaid domestic work was included in the GNP, figures would increase globally. Studies from the early 1980s calculated that female unpaid labor equaled 28 percent of the GNP in Norway (based on equivalent market wages), 23 percent in the United States, 11 percent in the Philippines, and 15 and 22 percent in Chile's and Venezuela's major cities, respectively. Another study suggested that including women's unpaid labor could increase the world's real economy by $4 trillion.

This unpaid labor encompasses a wide range of services and duties. In agriculture women contribute not only to the production of food, but their agricultural work instills in them valuable knowledge concerning local ecosystems. Their experience is vital in crop diversity, harvesting and collection of crops, and health care for small livestock. African women do 95 percent of work related to feeding and caring for their families, which includes food production, while in Asia women provide most of the labor force for the production of rice. Women's participation in agriculture varies between 19 and 35 percent in Latin America, and is 54 percent in the Caribbean. In Africa, women contribute the majority of labor for planting, hoeing, harvesting, transporting, storing, and processing in agricultural enterprises; they dominate as well in marketing. Approximately one-half of the world's food is grown by women and an estimated two-thirds of women workers in developing countries work in the agricultural sector.

Women: Frontline Caretakers in the Home and of the Environment

Throughout the developing world, women are essential in the maintenance and use of forests and their products. In many developing societies, responsibility to collect fuel, fodder, and food from trees and other plants falls to women. In Nepal, women and girls collect 84 percent of the fuel. In Bangladesh it is estimated that women spend an average of three to five hours every day searching for firewood. In Africa, India, and other parts of South Asia, they often spend all day collecting fuel and water, doing domestic work, and farming. In addition to fuel gathering, women spend considerable time in the industry of food collection: searching for fibers, nuts, vegetables, and wild fruit. A 1988–1989 survey in Laos found that all village women in the area in question were involved in some form of forest gathering, and some relied entirely on forest products to support their families during the rainy seasons. Another form of gathering that lies mainly within the sphere of female duties is the collection and subsequent management of the water supply. For the most part women take care of water sanitation, purification, storage, and use in cooking and cleaning.

The World Health Organization (WHO) recognizes women as the foremost practitioners of primary health care across the globe. An estimated 75 percent of health care is known to take place in the home. Women usually make decisions regarding remedies for the ill, what type of treatment should be followed, and when it is necessary to seek outside help. Women everywhere are active in midwifery; 60 to 80 percent of all births in developing countries are midwife assisted.

Barriers to Equality

Due to cultural and religious attitudes, discriminatory laws and practices have resulted in less opportunity for women throughout the world, and, in turn, have prevented them from becoming full and equal partners in their nations' societies and economics. Numerous barriers prohibit women from attaining an equal status. As women are often considered to have less economic value than men, they receive less than boys when a family's resources are limited. Studies in India, Pakistan, Nepal, the Middle East, North Africa, and parts of sub-Saharan Africa show that girls are given less and poorer quality food, stay home from school at an earlier age, engage in harder labor earlier, and receive less medical care than boys.

Poverty presents a major obstacle to the achievement of sustainable development and the acceptance of women's role in society throughout the developing world. The number of poor women continues to grow in absolute terms and in relation to men. According to one estimate, poverty has increased by 47 percent among rural women in comparison to 30 percent among rural men. As women often lack access to resources and much of their labor is unpaid, they have little opportunity to pursue cash-earning occupations. The debt crisis of the 1980s places an even larger burden on the shoulders of the female population. Curtailment of social security and macroeconomics reforms (usually in the form of cutbacks and restraints in fiscal policy) to alleviate national debt and economic stagnation have forced many women to make up for the shortcomings themselves. Thus as the economic picture darkened, women's unpaid labor increased and their opportunity to develop new skills or enter the job market decreased.

Development projects often fail to recognize the division of labor and resources by gender within households, in addition to the division of returns of labor. The implications of this failing have been significant for some projects. For example, in Africa women often farm their own crops on separate plots of land, as well as working on their husbands' plots. The sale of these products often gives them a separate income to fulfill household obligations. Projects which do not take this procedure into account cause women to lose control of their separate crops and often lead to the failure of the project. Projects also suffer when information and training are only given to men. For example, in Thailand the Northeast Rainfed Agricultural Development Project trained men who were only part-time farmers to carry out crops trails, while the female farmers received no training. As a result, the crops were planted incorrectly and did not grow, power tillers provided by the project were not used, and nitrogen-fixing crops intended to fertilize rice did not get planted. Agricultural extension services, based on Western models, have traditionally been staffed by men. In a 1989 global survey, the Food and Agricultural Organization of the United Nations found that only 15 percent of the world's extension service workers were women, ranging from approximately 40 percent in North America to less than 11 percent in Africa and the Middle East. Technical innovations in agriculture, energy, and forestry also often fail to reach women. This is because they are controlled by men or because women cannot afford to buy them. Furthermore, governments and development agencies frequently fail to invest in technologies which cater to the special needs of women. All these factors prohibit the advancement of women and subsequently undermine sustainable development policies.

Wage levels also reflect society's tendency to undervalue female labor. In all countries, women are almost always paid less than men, even for the same work. Furthermore, time-use statistics have shown that women workers throughout the world bear "double day" workloads: that is, they perform unpaid household tasks following a full schedule of paid work. Household demands distract women's ability to compete in the workplace and in the job market.

One major barrier to women's participation in sustainable development is a lack of education. Worldwide, women's literacy rates and levels of education are far below those of men. In 1990, it was estimated that 601.6 million women worldwide (33.6 percent of women), compared to 346.5 million men (19.4 percent of men), were illiterate. Although the literacy gap has narrowed in some regions, it remains considerable in others. In some parts of Africa and Asia the ratio approaches 2 to 1. Furthermore, in many developing countries girls are withdrawn from school in order to get married, fulfill household duties, work on the land, and so on. Since women are perceived to have a lower economic value than men, girls are removed from school as they are of more value at home than in furthering their education. This practice has trapped generation after generation of women in a cycle of poverty and illiteracy. Enrollments in secondary schools, vocational schools, and universities reflect the gap in male-female education levels. Educational and training institutions are dominated by male administrators, and teachers in scientific and technical fields are primarily male. By denying women the opportunity to receive training and education, they are excluded from advances and improvements in development, often in areas in which they play an essential role (i.e., agriculture and food supply).

Women's health is a critical focus of sustainable development. While poor health and nutritional problems exist throughout developing countries, higher rates of malnutrition generally prevail among females than among males of the same age. In many Third World countries, food is distributed in the household according to status rather than nutritional needs. In India and Bangladesh, from birth females receive poorer quantities of food than men. Girls are breast-fed for a shorter time and receive less cereal, fat, sugar, and total calories than boys. Similar discrimination in the allocation of household resources is found in the Middle East, North Africa, sub-Saharan Africa, and South Asia. Malnutrition impairs the physical development of women, in addition to their health and ability to bear healthy children. Data show that in India fewer women survive common diseases than men because they receive less treatment in hospitals and are prescribed less medication. In Africa, AIDS strikes women with greater frequency than men.

Women's poverty, limited education, and constraints in economic opportunity all contribute to high fertility rates. Economic advantages are the main incentives for having large families; offspring provide labor for basic survival and household income, in addition to offering insurance against old age. However, high fertility levels lead to various problems, including strained resources and endangered health for both women and children. Although fertility rates have fallen worldwide, many women lack information and reproductive health services or cannot make use of them because of economic limitations or cultural practices. Reproductive health services are available to approximately 95 percent of women in East Asia, but only 57 percent in Southeast Asia and Latin America, 54 percent in South Asia, 13–25 percent in the Arab states, and 9 percent in sub-Saharan Africa. According to the United Nations Population Fund, if women were able to have the number of children they wanted there would be 27 to 35 percent fewer births in developing countries.

In most developing countries, women lack either ownership or control of land, water, and other resources. Because of their lack of collateral, women are often without any credit or banking services. The Food and Agricultural Organization estimates that women's share in agricultural credit is 10 percent or less. Even as sole breadwinners, women are often denied credit due to biased loan policies. Without credit, they are unable to invest in time-saving equipment and fertilizers to improve agricultural productivity and income. In many developing nations women lack social security and marital rights, and thus have no protection against the loss of a spouse or in cases of abandonment and divorce.

The potential effect of a constructive educational program for women in developing countries would be tremendous. Education integrated with comprehensive training courses, basic health services, expanded economic opportunity, and enforced rights is crucial to sustainable development. As female literacy increases, fertility rates would decrease, and the population as a whole would become better nourished. Women, given the opportunity to expand their economic capabilities, would be inclined to marry later, leading to smaller families. In general, educated women can practice better hygiene, are more knowledgeable about nutrition and basic health care, and are more willing to seek professional help in dealing with serious health matters. Through proper training in agricultural and technical practices women would be able to perform their important economic functions more efficiently and effectively. Without constructively acknowledging women's roles in their individual societies, all attempts to institute sustainable development will be critically undermined.

As in many other segments of development, the empirical data demonstrate that important progress has been made toward eradicating gender inequalities in the development process and harnessing the productive and entrepreneurial capabilities of women. The male-female gap in literacy, schooling, remuneration, and access to economic opportunity and health care, though still unacceptably wide, has been significantly narrowed in recent decades. The task ahead is to ensure that this progress continues and that women remain at the center of the development enterprise.

Environmental Degradation

Natural Resources

Development can only happen in an environmental context—in the physical world where people live. Many previous strategies for obtaining economic security, though productive in the short run, have yielded baleful unforeseen environmental consequences. Environmental hazards due to industrial wastes and other by-products of rapid and scatters hot development are now part of our everyday lexicon: global warming, water and air pollution, deforestation, and soil contamination, just to name a few. The most important lesson in recent development practice is that development can only be successful when it is sustainable—that

is, when the benefits of today do not prejudice the future's opportunity for safe, clean, and healthy development. Though a healthy
physical environment is the essence of human survival, we have
inflicted serious and sometimes irreversible damage on the Earth,
with a blithe disregard for the consequences. In fact, intensive
industrialization and rapid population growth have put the planet
under intolerable strain (Table 11).

Soil Degradation and Desertification

Environmental issues represent a key part of the development
story, because the world around us places limits and conditions
on the kind of economic growth that we can achieve, North and
South. The overuse, and misuse, of land, for example, has led to
topsoil loss and soil degradation in many pockets of the Third
World. Recent estimates indicate that since World War II, 1.2
billion hectares—some 10.5 percent of the world's vegetated land,
or roughly the size of China and India combined—have suffered
at least moderate soil degradation as a result of human activity.
The most widespread desertification, in which formerly arable
land has been rendered into desert, has occurred in Asia where
about 450 million hectares are at least moderately degraded, and
in Africa where moderate or worse desertification affects 320 million hectares. Meanwhile, much of the world's rangeland is already heavily overgrazed and cannot continue to support the
livestock herds and management practices that exist today. The
Global Assessment of Soil Degradation estimates that overgrazing
has depleted approximately 680 million hectares since the 1950s;
projections show that these trends will continue if practices are not
revised or changed. In terms of human development, economic
activity based on previous, unsustainable practices yields increasingly diminished returns. The old model of development by exhaustion is, in short, unsustainable. A new paradigm of renewable
growth is required.

Water and Marine Exhaustion

Analysis elsewhere in the environment generates similar conclusions. Fresh water, which is invaluable for growth and life, is in
increasingly short supply. Water demand rises in exponential
relation to population, as domestic, industrial, agricultural, and
municipal sectors clamor for access to a finite water supply.

Table 11: Human-Induced Land Degradation Worldwide, 1945 to Present

Region	Overgrazing	Deforestation	Agricultural Mismanagement	Other	Total	Degraded Areas (Percent of Total Vegetated Land)
			(Million Hectares)			
Asia	197	298	204	47	746	20
Africa	243	67	121	63	494	22
South America	68	100	64	12	244	14
Europe	50	84	64	22	220	23
North and Central America	38	18	91	11	158	8
Oceania	83	12	8	0	103	13
World	679	579	552	155	1,965	17

Source: Oldeman, L. R., *World Map of the Status of Human-Induced Soil Degradation*, Netherlands, UN Environmental Program and International Soil Reference Centre, 1991.

Twenty-six countries suffer from insufficient renewable water supplies within their own territorial boundaries; today's per capita supply of fresh water is only one-third of the corresponding 1970 figure.

Continuing trends toward urbanization do not bode well for near-term improvement. Consider the vicous water cycle unleashed by the twin demographic processes of chemical-intensive agriculture and rapid migration from country to city: Agricultural and urban wastes flow from the land into the water supply, smoggy clouds pour out contaminants absorbed from industrial smoke, ships flush their sewage tanks indiscriminantly, and cities bulldoze wetlands to extend their land seaward. About three-quarters of the pollution entering the oceans worldwide comes from human activities on land. Most nutrients, sediments, pathogens, persistent toxins, and thermal pollution are drawn from the land. Oil pollution, ordinarily viewed as a result of accidents at sea, actually comes almost as proportionally from the land as from the sea.

All told, the flow of nutrients into the sea has at least doubled since preindustrial times and sediments have nearly tripled as a result of human activity. Pollution degrades estuaries and coastal waters by prompting algae blooms, blocking sunlight, suffocating fish and coastal habitats, and importing pathogens and toxicants. Globally, nutrients and sediments have contributed to the decline of estuaries, coastal wetlands, coral reefs, seagrass beds, and other coastal ecosystems. Another unhappy by-product is the potential exhaustion of the supply of fish and other protein-rich marine food sources. If the current trends of unsustainable development practices persist, the health of the marine environment will continue to deteriorate to the point of fatal degradation. The water needed to spur development in industry and agriculture, as well as to grow the food to feed the hungry, is thus in jeopardy.

Deforestation and Biodiversity Loss

While our oceans suffer at the hand of land dwellers, pressure above sea level also increases worldwide. Increasing population and the failure of traditional cropland due to desertification forces those at the margins to bring increasing areas of new earth under cultivation. One of the most tragic consequences of this process is deforestation. Some 8–10 million acres of forest land are lost each year on areas roughly the size of Austria. Global forest cover is 24 percent less today than in 1700: 3.4 billion hectares compared to 4.5 billion 300 years ago. Between 1980 and 1990 forest area was reduced by approximately 130 million hectares. Over the last decade, 154 million hectares of tropical forests, equivalent to almost three times the land area of France, have been converted into other land uses, with the most severe losses occurring in tropical nations with the most vital rainforest systems. The most reliable projections conclude that if the reduction of 3.7 percent per decade continues, by 2010 the world's forested area will shrink by an additional 7 percent; per capita forest cover will drop by 30 percent (Table 12).

Much is lost along with rainforest cover. Tropical forests are home to as much as 90 percent of the world's plant and animal species. Species diversity provides important agricultural, industrial, and above all medical benefits. Roughly 25 percent of pharmaceuticals dispensed in the United States contain active ingredients derived from plant life, and the ability of emerging technologies to recognize and expand upon the practical potential of diverse life forms is difficult to estimate. The capacity of future generations to sustainably develop may well lie with the diversity of life concentrated in rainforests.

Unfortunately, the destruction of these forests entails the destruction of biodiversity as well. Very conservative estimates of species extinction indicate that, at a minimum, mammal species have perished at a rate 60 times greater than natural over the past 400 years. Other life forms are in similar distress. Habitat loss—largely the destruction of tropical rainforests—constitutes the greatest threat to diversity, and current projections suggest that as much as 10 percent of the world's species will suffer extinction between 1975 and 2015 if current rates of deforestation continue. In addition to the loss of Earth's common biological heritage, species loss has important implications for the developing nations where the phenomenon is most acute. Biodiversity within national frontiers may well offer a valuable natural resource that allows host nations to trade competitively in the international market and attract investment, research, and educational infrastructures. We all lose when biodiversity is undermined, and the global South loses opportunity as well. Projects designed to preserve species thus play an important role in the development context.

Table 12: Population Size and Availability of Renewable Resources, Circa 1990, with Projections for 2010

	Circa 1990	2010	Total Change (Percent)	Per Capita Change
Population	5,290	7,030	+33	—
Fish Catch (tons)	85	102	+20	−10
Irrigated Land (hectares)	237	277	+17	−12
Cropland (hectares)	1,444	1,516	+5	−21
Rangeland and pasture (hectares)	3,402	3,540	+4	−22
Forest (hectares)	3,413	3,165	-7	−30

Source: Reprinted from *State of the World*, 1994, edited by Lester R. Brown, et al., with the permission of W. W. Norton & Company, Inc. Copyright © 1994 by Worldwatch Institute.

Air Pollution

Air pollution is another key environmental issue linked to global development. Pollution in the form of acidic aerosols (acidic aerosols are formed from SO_2 and NO_2 by a chemical that recruits ground-level ozone), nitrogen dioxide (NO_2), ozone, and sulfur dioxide (SO_2) is detrimental to the natural environment. The problem is not unique to the global South—indeed, the deterioration of Europe's forests from air pollution causes losses of $35 billion a year—but air pollution is especially acute in Southern regions. Mexico City produces 5,000 tons of air pollution a year. In Bangkok, more than 40 percent of the city's traffic police reportedly suffer from respiratory problems. Pollution causes numerous diseases, including cancer, neuropsychiatric disease, chronic respiratory problems, and musculoskeletal problems. These consequences tax the already overburdened health care systems of Southern nations and absorb vital productive, human, and monetary energies.

From 1850 to 1990, the consumption of commercial energy (from coal, oil, gas, nuclear power, and hydropower) increased more than a hundredfold, while use of biomass energy (fuel wood, crop waste, and dung) roughly tripled. The combustion of fossil fuels (oil, coal, and gas) emits carbon dioxide (CO_2) into the atmosphere. CO_2 constitutes têf greenhouse gases, which trap infrared radiation that would otherwise escape into the atmosphere. Worldwide consumption of fossil fuel from 1860 to 1949 resulted in the release of an estimated 187 billion metric tons of CO_2. Over the past four decades, fossil fuel use has accelerated, creating an additional 559 billion metric tons of CO_2. Changes in land use, including deforestation for agricultural purposes, are responsible for an additional estimated 220 billion metric tons of CO_2 since 1860. The net effect of these and other air pollutants is the risk of substantial and perhaps menacing climate changes. North and South alike contribute to the the problem of greenhouse gases, and we must likewise solve the problem together. As with the rest of the environment, we share one climate, and changes anywhere threaten sustainable development everywhere.

Refugees

Statistics and Problems

Although migration and flight are long-standing features of international affairs, more people are on the move today than ever before. Those who manage to cross an international boundary and meet the standard criteria of "well-founded fear of prosecution" required by international conventions are called "refugees." Many others, who flee for reasons such as economic displacement, environmental catastrophe, or less universally recognized political reasons, are typically dubbed "illegal migrants." Still more people have fled from violence and persecution but have not crossed an international border: These are the "internally displaced." Collectively, they constitute the world's dispossessed (Table 13).

Determining their exact numbers is an imprecise science. Definitions of what constitutes a refugee vary widely, and governments will jury-rig data on the internally displaced to suit their political ends. Add the difficulty of counting thousands, sometimes millions, of peoples in remote areas without the aid of technical and technological support and the constant shifting of the refugee problem, and the result is that data on refugeeism and migration that must be considered indicative rather than definitive. But for all their uncertainty, the figures are no less grim. Today, their are some 19 million refugees worldwide, up from 2.5 million in 1970. Their numbers increase by an estimated 10,000 *every day*.

Further exacerbating the problem, "official" refugees represent but a fraction of the planet's migratory distress. The internally displaced are more numerous than refugees, and they are more vulnerable as well. For while refugees enjoy some protection under international law and the opportunity for safe haven abroad, the internally displaced lack international protection and assistance mechanisms. In the last decade, the number of internally displaced persons has grown, due mostly to an absence of alternative asylums abroad rather than a desire to remain in their homeland. About 1.3 million persons were estimated to be internally displaced within Bosnia, and 300,000 to be "in hiding" in Haiti. Even these unconscionable figures do not reflect the true situation: The UN High Commission for Refugees and the International Committee for the Red Cross have combined a caseload of more than 2.7 million in Bosnia, virtually the entire population. Official estimates of internally displaced persons put their number at roughly 25 million, but the true figure is undoubtedly much higher.

Changing international attitudes toward refugees in recent years have intensified the crisis of the internally displaced. Political leaders in the industrialized West, confronted with flagging

Table 13: List of Significant Populations of Internally Displaced Civilians, 1993

Country	Estimate	Country	Estimate
Sudan	4,000,000	Sierra Leone	400,000
South Africa	4,000,000	Croatia	350,000
Mozambique	2,000,000	Colombia	300,000–600,000
Angola	2,000,000	Kenya	300,000
Bosnia	1,300,000	Rwanda	300,000
Liberia	1,000,000	Haiti	300,000
Iraq	1,000,000	Cyprus	265,000
Lebanon	700,000	Iran	260,000
Somalia	700,000	Georgia	250,000
Zaire	700,000	India	250,000
Azerbaijan	600,000	Philippines	200,000–1,000,000
Sri Lanka	600,000	Eritrea	200,000
Peru	600,000	Guatemala	200,000
Burma	500,000–1,000,000	Togo	150,000
Burundi	500,000	Djibouti	140,000
Ethiopia	500,000	Cambodia	95,000

Source: *World Refugee Report 1994*, U.S. Committee for Refugees.

economies, have suggested that refugees and illegal immigrants are a cause of sluggish growth. Meanwhile, Southern governments often view the flow of refugees as a threat to their national stability or as an aggravation of already acute economic distress. Thus, international policy in recent years has inclined toward keeping potential refugees at home—that is, privileging the political and economic requirements of potential hosts over the rights and protections due the persecuted.

Contrary to common perception in the United States and elsewhere in the West, it is the poorer parts of the world that bear the greatest refugee burden. Africa has a broader definition of "refugee" than Europeans and Asians, and has shouldered a disproportionate share of the world's refugee flow. In 1993, Ghana, Benin, Guinea, Namibia, Uganda, Tanzania, and Rwanda all played new hosts to refugee flows. Rwanda accepted some 370,000 Burundian refugees in 1993, the same year the United States pushed away fewer than 3,000 Haitians who attempted to flee by boat. Iran has over 4 million refugees, although as of this writing, the process of repatriation to Afghanistan was just beginning. In Malawi, one of every ten people is a refugee. The Western idea that refugees flee their homes to partake of the riches of the North is undermined by reality: Most refugees move from one Southern country to another (Table 14).

Meanwhile, in Western Europe the "institution of asylum" has been seriously undermined. Some governments deny access to their country on the rationale that internal flight alternatives exist within the country of origin. Denmark's Refugee Appeal Board ruled that Tamils could be mandatorily returned to Sri Lanka to live in displaced persons camps outside of the immediate conflict zone, and used this as the reason for the return of Iraqi Kurds to Iraq. Other nations simply deny the existence of refugees at all, using terms like "externally displaced peoples" instead. In 1993, the government of Finland had virtually stopped recognizing anyone as a refugee, accepting only nine refugees in that year, an approval rate of .26 percent. Because European governments refused to apply the standard refugee definition to Bosnians on account of national origin, they were denied the full rights associated with people of refugee status. If allowed to enter a foreign country at all, they found they were only given temporary protection, which could be revoked at any time. Furthermore, in 1993 so many governments imposed visa requirements on Bosnia that few escaped at all.

Table 14: Refugees in Relation to Total Population and Per
Capita GNP of the Asylum Country, 1993

Country	Ratio of Refugee Population to Total Population	Number of Refugees	Total Population (Millions)	GNP Per Capita ($US)
Gaza Strip	1:1	603,000	0.7	N/A
West Bank	1:34	79,000	1.6	N/A
Jordan	1:4	1,073,600	3.8	1,120
Djibouti	1:8	60,000	0.5	N/A
Guinea	1:11	570,000	6.2	450
Lebanon	1:11	329,000	3.6	N/A
Armenia	1:12	290,000	3.6	2,150
Swaziland	1:14	57,000	0.8	1,060
Malawi	1:14	700,000	10.0	230
Croatia	1:16	280,000	4.4	N/A
Rwanda	1:20	370,000	7.4	260
Belize	1:2	28,900	0.2	2,050
Liberia	1:25	110,000	2.8	N/A
Yugoslavia (Serbia/ Montenegro)	1:27	357,000	9.8	N/A
Azerbaijan	1:29	251,000	7.2	1,670
Iran	1:31	1,995,000	62.8	2,320
Syria	1:42	319,000	13.5	11,110
Benin	1:43	120,000	5.1	380
Sudan	1:43	633,000	27.4	400
Mauritania	1:48	46,000	2.2	510
Slovenia	1:53	38,000	2.0	N/A
Burundi	1:53	110,000	5.8	210
Zimbabwe	1:54	200,000	10.7	620
Côte d'Ivoire	1:54	250,000	13.4	690
Zambia	1:54	158,000	8.6	420

Source: *World Refugee Report 1994*, U.S. Committee for Refugees.

This trend toward decertification of refugees has important
implications for development. The same countries that have the
greatest need for economic growth labor are under the greatest
strain of hosting refugees. For the displaced refugees and the host
population alike, precious resources required for growth are
placed under intolerable strain. The increasingly prevalent attitude in the West—that refugees are not victims of a problem but

rather are themselves the problem—suggests that richer nations will increasingly shield themselves from the burdens of cross-border migration, while poorer nations bear a greater share, in both proportional and absolute terms. Such an allocation of responsibility works at cross-purposes with the global development enterprise and offends the principle that all nations must contribute to the resolution of shared global crises.

Military Expenditure

Violent conflict is the primary cause of the international refugee crisis. The fall of the Berlin Wall and the end of the cold war offered promise that global conflict might finally subside and that the tremendous resources devoted to war might be diverted to development. But so far, this hope has proved chimerical. Instead of ending, global conflict seems to be changing—from wars between states to wars within states. The period 1989–1992 witnessed 82 armed conflicts in the world, 79 of which were civil conflicts within the borders of a single nation, driven by ethnic, religious, economic, or political divisions. While this crisis escalates, and while Northern nations move to close access to the dispossessed, governments throughout the world continue to fan the flames of conflict and migration by investing heavily in military equipment and infrastructure.

Developing countries' military expenditures rose three times as fast as those of industrial countries between 1960 and 1987, from $24 billion to $145 billion, an increase of 7.5 percent a year, compared with 2.8 percent for industrial nations. As a result, the developing countries' share of global military expenditure rose from 7 to 15 percent. A significant part of this spending was by countries of the Middle East and North Africa. The remainder of the spending, a staggering $95 billion a year, was by some of the world's poorest countries. For example, in sub-Saharan Africa the proportion of the regional GNP devoted to military spending increased from 0.7 percent in 1960 to 3 percent in 1991.

The development costs of militarism in the global South are high. In addition to the loss of money and resources that might otherwise be devoted to human and infrastructure development, armed conflict, civil or international, exacts a bitter toll on society: It increases costs in health and health services, depresses literacy levels, reduces life expectancy, and increases mortality. Further, as noted above, military conflict causes huge numbers of refugees and internally displaced persons, which places additional strain not only on relief capacities within the country of origin but on those areas which receive the fleeing populations.

As the United Nations Development Programme recently noted, the cold war is not over yet—the job is only half done. The task ahead is to ensure that the peace dividend is not only reaped but sensibly invested. The benefits of peace have been incompletely realized by developing countries. Notwithstanding the end of the cold war, world military spending still equals the income of nearly half the world's people. Humanity's continuing commitment to the weapons of war goes a long way toward explaining why so many people remain vulnerable not only to guns and bullets, but also to drought, disease, and poverty. Breaking the militarism habit, in both North and South alike, remains a key development challenge on the eve of the third millenium.

Organizations 5

This chapter surveys organizations practicing development today. While the most effective development can and often does occur in spontaneous or individual encounters, organizations of diverse origin and mission have been in the front lines of the quest for global development throughout the contemporary era. Organizations have played a leading role in innovation and dissemination of new and better development strategies. Methods of the various organizations working in this field are diverse and even contradictory, ranging from providing multilateral aid to assisting indigenous grass-roots efforts. This chapter surveys the various approaches to development undertaken by four types of organizations: governmental agencies, multilateral institutions, UN agencies, and nongovernmental organizations (NGOs) based in the global North as well as the South.

Governmental Agencies

The first U.S. governmental assistance program was the Marshall Plan, initiated in 1948 in response to the devastation left in the wake of World War II. While a single agency mandated to administer aid had yet to be

219

created at this point, the Marshall Plan symbolizes the first roots of the modern aid program in the United States. The Plan provided grants and loans to Europe and Japan totaling $12.5 billion over four years. At the end of those four years, Europe's overall production was up 37 percent, trade had increased, and inflation was brought under control. The success of this program naturally prompted governments interested in the development of the Southern Hemisphere to replicate this approach there. However, it quickly became apparent that simply infusing capital to Third World governments would not necessarily stimulate industry and agriculture. The infusions of capital and technology may have benefited Third World countries on a macro level, but went unnoticed by, and sometimes even harmed, the majority of the population.

Today, most of the world's foreign aid comes from the 22-member Development Assistance Committee (DAC) of the Organization for Economic Cooperation and Development (OECD). The OECD, made up of developed, mostly Western nations, was established in 1961 with the goal of promoting economic growth, trade, and employment in its member countries and in nonmember countries to further the process of development. In the 1980s the official development assistance distributed by the DAC increased by about a quarter. But between 1991 and 1992 the disbursements rose by just 0.5 percent. Some argue that aid budgets around the world are ceasing to grow at all. Critics argue that aid has failed to reach the poorest of the world; they point to the fact that the ten countries that are home to two-thirds of the world's poorest people receive only one-third of world aid. Responding to these charges, governments are forging stronger partnerships and channeling increasing amounts of development aid through nongovernmental organizations, who have maintained a positive reputation for reaching and working with the "poorest of the poor."

Canadian International Development Agency (CIDA)
200 Promenade du Portage
Hull, Québec, Canada
(819) 953-6060
Marcel Masse, President

Since 1968, CIDA has administered Canada's development assistance with a wide range of programs supporting sustainable development in developing countries. CIDA's development policies are centered around four elements: environmental sustainability, economic development, political development, and social and cultural aspects of development, which are built into all programs and policies. The agency also responds to peace efforts, disasters, and consequences of conflicts. Increasing priority has recently been placed on issues of debt, environmental sustainability, the promotion of human rights, and democratic development. CIDA recently announced a strategy for Africa that identifies regional integration as a key to long-term sustainable development. Like USAID, the Canadian agency has also been confronted with institutional reforms of aid administration. In 1992, Canada allocated .46 percent of its GNP to overseas assistance. In 1995, the Canadian government announced that it would cut its development aid programs by 21 percent. One of the programs affected immediately was CIDA's well-reputed Development Education Program, which was eliminated in May 1995. Approximately 50 percent of CIDA's aid is allocated to bilateral assistance, 33 percent to international institutions, and 10 percent to programs of Canadian and international NGOs. CIDA was one of the first governmental agencies to recognize the potential of NGOs; as early as 1968 over 200 organizations were receiving funding from CIDA. CIDA concentrates its bilateral assistance to a limited number of countries selected on the basis of need, commitment to development, general Canadian interests, and geographical distribution of other donors' bilateral assistance.

Overseas Development Administration (ODA)
Eland House
Stag Place
London, SW1E 56H
England
(71) 273-3000

The ODA is part of the Foreign and Commonwealth Office and is responsible for the United Kingdom's development assistance programs. It aims to foster sustainable economic and social development and to safeguard the global environment. ODA has been one of the leaders in stressing good governance and pressing for higher standards in developing countries' political systems, public administration, and legal sectors. Emphasis is placed on poverty alleviation and private sector development. In 1992, 0.3 percent of the United Kingdom's GNP was allocated to development assistance.

Publications: British Overseas Aid (annual) and *Overseas Development* (4/year).

United States Agency for International Development (USAID)
320 Twenty-first Street
Washington, DC 20523-0056
(202) 647-4200
Brian Atwood, Administrator

USAID was created in 1961 with two purposes in mind: to respond to the threat of communism and to help poor nations develop and prosper. Since then it has been the U.S. government's primary administrator of economic and social assistance to developing countries. Charged with implementing programs which further American self-interest while demonstrating humanitarian concern, USAID uses international assistance as a foreign policy tool to effectively move nations toward free markets, free governments, and greater prosperity. During the period from 1992 to 1994, USAID funded programs totaling $16 billion, $11.7 billion of which was Development Assistance and Economic Support Funds which were provided to the developing countries of Africa, Asia, and Latin America. However, while the United States remains the largest donor in the DAC, it is among the lowest in terms of share of gross national product (GNP); in 1995 the United States contributed .13 percent of its GNP as compared to the 3 percent it contributed during the Marshall Plan.

USAID identifies three categories of countries where it provides assistance: "sustainable development countries," which receive an integrated package of assistance with clearly defined program objectives and performance targets; "transitional countries," which have experienced a national crisis, political transition, or natural disaster; and thirdly, countries where aid to nongovernmental sectors may facilitate the emergence of civil society, meet human needs, or influence a national problem with global implications. Aid to these countries focuses on population and health, broad-based economic growth, the environment, and democratization—all of which have transnational impact. Additionally, USAID carries out emergency humanitarian assistance; in

1994 it provided emergency assistance to over 50 countries, and emergency food to over 58 million people in 18 countries.

Today, USAID is faced with growing opposition and sharp budget cuts. In response to these attacks, it has taken strong measures to consolidate and adopt a more focused approach. It has closed 21 of its missions around the world, and the 33 goals which used to guide the agency have been replaced with four: (1) improving population and health conditions; (2) promoting economic growth; (3) protecting the environment; and (4) supporting democracy. In following these goals, USAID has concentrated its development resources in 41 countries. Highlights of its programs in these countries include assisting electoral tribunals in Latin America, South Africa, and Mozambique; providing market-strengthening assistance to the countries of Central America, which now have achieved positive economic growth; and providing large amounts of population assistance to 28 countries, which have reduced average family size from 6.1 children in the 1960s to 4.2 in 1992. An important element of USAID's strategy is forging partnerships—with other governmental agencies, nongovernmental organizations, indigenous groups, and universities. NGOs are increasingly contracted to carry out a substantial number of USAID's development programs and their role is securely positioned to grow; at the 1995 Social Summit, Vice President Al Gore announced that within the next five years nearly half of USAID's assistance would be channeled through private organizations rather than distributed directly to Third World governments.

Publications: Annual Report on Program Performance; Country Health Statistics Profiles; U.S. Non-Governmental Organization Directory; as well as strategy papers, issue briefs, evaluation publications, congressional presentations, and newsletters such as *Democracy Dialogue; Mothers and Children;* and *The Development Studies Program News.*

Multilateral Institutions

Aid contributed by several countries to an institution which then allocates the assistance to needy recipients is called "multilateral aid." The largest multilateral institution is the World Bank, but others that follow make substantial contributions in multilateral aid.

African Development Bank (ADB)
BP 1387, 01
Abidjan, Ivory Coast
Babacar Ndiaye, President

Founded in 1966, the African Development Bank promotes development projects for the economic and social advancement of its member states. In 1973, the bank established the African Development Fund, ADB's concessional arm, to offer "soft loans" to its neediest members. Today, unfortunately, the ADB is somewhat of a beleaguered institution; at the end of 1994 its arrears were almost four times the 1990 level, and donor countries have been holding back funds for the African Development Fund since 1992. Zaire and Liberia currently hold 80 percent of the bank's delinquent loans. Critics charge that the bank's efficiency has been crippled by poor management and lending policies. Unfortunately, there are no immediate signs for improvement; new loans continue to fall and the management struggles are not being easily resolved.

Asian Development Bank (ADB)
6 ADB Avenue, Mandaloyong
0401 Metro Manila, Philippines
(632) 711-3851

This development finance institution is engaged in promoting the economic and social progress of its members in the Asian and Pacific regions. The bank was established in 1966 by 31 member nations with the goal of filling the gap in external resources needed to build up the economies of the region's developing countries by providing technical assistance and lending funds. Twenty-nine years later, the goals remain the same, and while the region has experienced tremendous economic progress with a sharp increase in growth rates, per capita incomes, and life expectancy, there is still a great need for the assistance provided by this institution. Today, membership has grown to 55 members, 38 of which are from the Asia-Pacific region, and 4 developing country members (Hong Kong, Taipei, China, and Korea) have graduated from the ranks of borrowing countries. The bank identifies four areas on which it concentrates its activities: the development of the private sector, agriculture, infrastructure, and energy and industry. In 1992, it adopted a Medium-Term Strategic Framework that defined its objectives to include the improvement of the status of women, population planning, management of natural resources, reduction of poverty, and economic growth. Recently the bank has been successful in forming closer ties with NGOs and taking a more participatory approach to projects. With the largest concentration of the world's poor people living in the Asia-Pacific region, the ADB will continue to play an important role in the development of this area.

Publications: numerous books, periodicals, studies, reports, and occasional papers.

Caribbean Development Bank (CDB)
P.O. Box 408
Wildey, St. Michael
Barbados

The CDB was established in 1970 with the aim of contributing to the economic growth and development of its member countries in the Caribbean. Composed of 20 members (all 18 of the Commonwealth Caribbean countries plus Britain and Canada), the bank promotes its members' economic cooperation and integration with particular attention to the needs of the lesser-developed members. The bank helps finance specific projects in the fields of agriculture, fisheries, livestock, tourism, mining, and others, with priority given to regional projects. Its 1988 operating budget was $6.8 million.

Publications: The bank's Technology and Energy Unit issues a variety of information such as bibliographies, reports, studies, and the *TEU Newsletter.*

Inter-American Development Bank (IDB)
1300 New York Avenue, NW
Washington, DC 20577
(202) 789-5925

Established in 1959, the IDB aims to accelerate the economic and social development of its member countries in Latin America and the Caribbean. The main functions of the IDB are to promote investment of public and private capital in the region, to use the region's own capital and mobilize additional funds for economic and social projects, to help member countries make better use of their resources while fostering foreign trade, and to offer technical assistance in designing and implementing development plans. Twenty-eight of the bank's 46 members are in the Western

Hemisphere; the bank encourages nonregional membership as it fosters closer relations with Latin America. At the end of 1993, IDB's cumulative lending and technical cooperation was $65 billion, 38 percent of which was allocated for physical infrastructure such as energy, transportation, and communication. IDB identifies five critical areas as its priorities for the 1990s: social reform, productive and technical modernization, strengthening of the private sector, restructuring of the state, and support for more involvement of all members in decision making.

Publications: Annual surveys on socioeconomic progress in Latin America, loan announcements, monthly newsletter, occasional papers, proceedings of annual meetings, and statistical tables.

International Monetary Fund (IMF)
700 Nineteenth Street NW
Washington, DC 20431
(202) 623-7000
Michael Camdessus, Managing Director

While the International Monetary Fund is neither a bank nor a development agency, it is a crucial player in the world of finance in the global South. The IMF is closely tied to the World Bank (see following entry), not only in its goal of providing member states with financial assistance, but also in its membership; membership of the World Bank is conditional upon membership of the IMF. Like the World Bank, the IMF was also established at the Bretton Woods conference in July 1944. The effects of the Depression and the abandonment of the gold standard created an urgent demand for a stable international monetary system. In response, Harry Dexter White and John Maynard Keynes proposed a system which would provide for the unrestricted conversion of one currency into another, eliminate restrictions and practices such as competitive devaluations, and establish a clear and unequivocal value for each currency. They called for a permanent cooperative organization to supervise this system, and in 1945 the IMF began operations in Washington, D.C., with 39 members.

Today the fund is made up of 179 member countries who have pledged to cooperate to promote stability and maintain a productive global economic environment. A guiding principle of the IMF is that a fundamental condition for international prosperity is an orderly monetary system that encourages trade, creates jobs, expands economic activities, and raises living standards throughout the world. To this end, it provides short-term loans to member nations experiencing temporary balance-of-payment difficulties. Applicants must agree to IMF measures: usually devaluation of exchange rates; anti-inflationary programs (such as control of bank credit, higher interest rates, control of wage rises, dismantling of price controls); and greater hospitality to foreign investment. Although the fund is probably best known for the billions of dollars it pumped into the system during the debt crisis of the 1980s, the majority of its members continue to regard it primarily as a supervisory institution that facilitates and advises members on the formulation of their economic policies. The IMF also maintains an extensive program of technical assistance through staff missions to member countries in the areas of central banking, balance-of-payment accounting, taxation, and other financial matters.

The majority of the IMF's lendable resources comes from members' quotas or capital subscriptions. All members contribute relative to their own economic size, and the more a member contributes the more it can borrow in times of need. Quotas also determine the voting power of the member, which obviously results in a concentration of power reserved for the wealthiest nations of the world, an arrangement that has been the focus of controversy and criticism. Critics also argue against the fund's tendency to apply standard, often austere remedies, such as structural adjustment policies, irrespective of a country's circumstances.

The IMF counters these criticisms by pointing out that developing countries as a group represent about 40 percent of total voting power, giving these countries veto power over major decisions. The fund also argues that while its policies do generally display common features such as efforts to control government spending and assess exchange rate policy, the fund's recommendations are made on a country-to-country basis and in the end, it is the governments that must decide how the adjustment effort is distributed among the various categories of public expenditure and across the various social groups.

Publications: A wide range of financial and monetary studies, including reports of operations, periodicals, books, and reference works. A few examples are: *Balance of Payments Statistics; Finance and Development; Government Finance Statistics Yearbook;* IMF Staff Papers; *IMF Survey* (23 times a year); and *World Economic Outlook.*

The World Bank
1818 H Street
Washington, DC 20433
(202) 477-1234
James Wolfensohn, President

The Bretton Woods talks of July 1944 have been called the "most ambitious economic negotiations the world has ever seen" (*The Economist*, 9 July 1994). Out of these talks came the establishment of three institutions that would change and redesign the international economic order: the World Bank, the International Monetary Fund (IMF), and the General Agreement on Tariffs and Trade (GATT).

The World Bank is officially composed of five distinct institutions: the International Bank for Reconstruction and Development (IBRD), the International Development Association (IDA), the International Finance Corporation (IFC), the International Centre for the Settlement of Investment Disputes (ICSD), and the Multilateral Investment Guarantee Agency (MIGA). While these five institutions have the common objective of raising the standards of living in developing countries, the IBRD and the IDA are most commonly referred to as the World Bank.

The goal of the IBRD is to make loans and provide economic development and reconstruction assistance for developing countries. The bulk of the IBRD's funds are raised by borrowing in the international capital markets. Additional capital is derived from member countries' subscriptions in capital shares, calculated on the basis of the country's quotas in the IMF, which reflect the country's relative wealth. In addition to providing loans, the IBRD also provides technical support to projects; however, it does not take direct responsibility for project development and implementation. Instead, projects are designed and implemented by government agencies or private entities; NGOs are often contracted to implement projects where they are seen to have comparative advantage. IBRD is governed by a board of governors, composed of representatives from each of the member countries. The IDA's role is similar to the IBRD's, but it concentrates on the poorest countries of the world, providing "soft loans": interest-free loans which do not require the repayment of principal to begin until ten years after signature of the loan agreement. Since its earliest days, the World Bank has been involved in providing technical assistance, as well as assisting in the reconstruction and development of member countries by facilitating the investment of capital for productive purposes. The bank also has a sound reputation for its research, both basic and applied, on virtually every aspect of development.

In recent years, however, the bank has been the focus of mounting criticism from Third World representatives who argue that poorer countries have been ignored and even damaged by World Bank policies. Critics also accuse the bank of caring more about issuing loans than about how the money is spent. In response, the bank underwent substantial reorganization in 1987 to improve its efficiency and responsiveness, resulting in a shift in focus to "basic needs" rather than the big technological projects with which it had previously been identified. The bank has made a concerted effort to improve the quality of lending and now funds more small-scale development projects with 45 to 50 percent of its resources going to sub-Saharan Africa. However, the issue of lending may soon become less relevant; the bank's traditional project-financing role is gradually being replaced by world capital markets. Many developing countries are turning away bank project loans because private loans, which are investing tens of billions of dollars into these countries' infrastructures, are cheaper. This may provide the bank with greater flexibility to pursue social and sustainable development projects. One step in this direction is the bank's recent focus on "non-income" aspects of development in areas such as environment, social welfare systems, education, and primary health care.

Publications: Annual Review of Project Performance Results; ICSID Annual Report; World Bank Annual Report; World Bank Atlas (annual); *World Bank Catalogue of Publications; World Bank Economic Review* (3/year); *World Development Report* (annual); and staff working papers.

UN Agencies

"We the peoples of the United Nations are determined to save succeeding generations from the scourge of war, which twice in our lifetime has brought untold sorrow to mankind . . ." reads the Preamble to the Charter of the United Nations. Established on 24 October 1945, the UN is organized under six main organs: the General Assembly; the Security Council; the Economic and Social Council; the Trusteeship Council; the International Court of

Justice; and the Secretariat. All of these branches are dedicated to preservation of, or struggle for, global peace. However, in recognizing that peace is impossible without social and economic development, the General Assembly created 17 specialized agencies which today work around the globe on various aspects of the development process. These independent international agencies are linked to the UN system by a treaty or international agreement and coordinate their work through the UN Economic and Social Council. One of the UN's principal goals continues to be to "cooperate in solving international economic, social, cultural, and humanitarian problems." Four-fifths of the UN budget is allocated to economic and social development. The UN also hosts a number of conferences which address the global problems affecting development, such as the Environment and Development Conference of 1992, Population and Development in 1994, Social Development Conference in 1995, and the Advancement of Women Conference also in 1995. The agencies listed below reflect the UN's ongoing commitment to global development.

Food and Agriculture Organization (FAO)
Via delle Terme di Caracalla
00100 Rome, Italy
(396) 579-3434

The FAO, founded in 1945, was the first UN specialized agency established after World War II with the primary goal of achieving world food security. The four main tasks with which the FAO is involved are: to carry out a comprehensive program of technical advice and assistance for the global agricultural community; to collect, analyze, and disseminate information; to advise governments on policy and planning; and to provide a neutral forum where governments and experts can discuss food problems. FAO represents the world's farmers to member governments and to the international community, in addition to working alongside those farmers in thousands of agricultural projects in the Third World each year. Technical assistance is provided through its field projects in developing countries which strengthen local institutions, provide training, and develop new techniques to increase crop production. FAO's well-known Global Information and Early Warning System issues monthly reports on the world food situation and establishes national surveillance systems based on nutritional and socioeconomic indicators. "Let there be bread" is the

FAO's motto, and to that end it has made significant progress in the areas of soil erosion, designing pest control programs, and perfecting breeds of local crops. Emergency food assistance is also provided through the World Food Programme, which the FAO cosponsors. FAO receives the majority of its funding from the World Bank, as well as from its 158 member governments. FAO originated World Food Day in 1981, an awareness-raising event, which is celebrated each 16 October. In 1993, nearly 140 countries celebrating World Food Day focused around the theme "Harvesting Nature's Diversity."

Publications: Food Outlook (monthly); *Production Yearbook* (annual); and *The State of Food and Agriculture* (annual).

International Fund for Agricultural Development (IFAD)
Via del Serafico 107
00142 Rome, Italy
(396) 54591
Idriss Jazairy, President

One of the outcomes of the 1974 World Food Conference was the establishment of the IFAD. The principal goal of IFAD is to mobilize financial aid in the form of concessionary loans for agricultural programs, thus helping to finance rural development projects and agricultural production. The bulk of IFAD's resources are available in soft loans, repayable over 50 years without interest to the poorest of the developing countries. IFAD is the only UN agency with the single mandate to promote progress by and for the rural poor. The loans are designed to diversify and improve food production systems, with priority given to small-scale farming initiatives.

The United Nations Children's Fund (UNICEF)
3 United Nations Plaza
New York, NY 10017
(212) 326-7000
Carol Bellamy, Executive Director

Founded in 1946 to extend massive relief to Europe and China in the aftermath of World War II, UNICEF became a permanent agency in 1953. Its mission is to improve the lives of children and youth of the developing world by providing community-based service in primary health care, water supply, formal and nonformal education, nutrition, and emergency operations. One of UNICEF's principal goals has been to reduce infant mortality rates by attacking the major causes of preventable death and disease. Its work is focused on the following development sectors: water supply, nutrition, social services for children, formal and nonformal education, planning and project support, and basic health care. In addition to long-range development work, UNICEF is also active in providing emergency assistance and relief aid. UNICEF is funded primarily through contributions from its 41 member governments, but it also raises money through the sale of greeting cards, making it the only UN agency to receive funds from the general public. In 1965, UNICEF was awarded the Nobel Prize for Peace for its work on behalf of the world's children and the way its work has promoted peace throughout the world. UNICEF also participated in the drafting of the Convention on the Rights of the Child, and was key in the organization of the 1990 World Summit for Children. Landmark successes include the eradication of smallpox, and recently, with the World Health Organization, the achievement of their ten-year goal of immunizing 80 percent of the world's children, an effort that is now saving some 3 million lives each year.

Publications: Annual Report; Facts about UNICEF (annual); *The Progress of Nations* (annual); and *State of the World's Children* (annual).

The United Nations Development Programme (UNDP)
One United Nations Plaza
New York, NY 10017
(212) 906-5000
James Gustave Speth, Administrator

At the forefront of the UN's development efforts is the UNDP, the world's largest multilateral grant development assistance organization providing "a greater variety of services to more people in more countries than any other development institution" (*Annual Report*). The UNDP promotes faster economic growth and higher standards of living by supporting projects in agriculture, health, housing, public administration, industry, trade, and other fields in 175 countries. The UNDP does not actually implement these projects, but rather funds one of the UN's executing agencies to do so, such as the African Development Bank or UNICEF. UNDP is the largest source of technical assistance to developing countries and

87 percent of its resources are allocated to the world's poorest nations. All projects are undertaken in partnership with the governments and people of developing countries; the majority of UNDP staff are locally recruited nationals. In 1986, the UNDP established a Division for Women in Development, and later that year established a Division for Non-Governmental Organizations. It also administers a number of special-purpose funds, such as the UN Development Fund for Women (UNIFEM), which has supported innovative activities benefiting women since 1985. Recently the UNDP identified three priority goals within the sustainable human development framework: strengthening international cooperation for sustainable development; building developing countries' capacities for sustainable development; and helping the United Nations to become a powerful, unified force for development. The UNDP's budget of roughly $1 billion (1994) is funded by annual contributions from member governments of the United Nations.

Publications: Annual Report; Choices (3/year); *Cooperation South* (quarterly); *Decade Watch* (quarterly); *Human Development Report* (annual); *Mini Report;* and *World Development* (6/year).

United Nations Environment Programme (UNEP)
P.O. Box 30552
Nairobi, Kenya
(254) 333-930
Elizabeth Dowdeswell, Executive Director

The UNEP was established in 1972, following the UN Conference on the Human Environment in Stockholm, Sweden, where the Declaration on Human Environment and the Action Plan offering recommendations for governments and international organizations to protect life, control contamination, and improve settlements were adopted. The UN mandated the UNEP to coordinate and provide policy guidance for sound environmental action and to promote environmental law and education throughout the world. Governed by a council with representatives from 58 countries, the UNEP works closely with numerous other UN agencies, governments, and NGOs. Its main concerns are climate change, desertification control, water resources, forests, pollution, oceans, human settlements, and renewable sources of energy. The UNEP is well known for its coordination of Earthwatch, an international surveillance network composed of the Global Environment Monitoring System (GEMS), the Global Resource Information Database (GRID), and INFOTERRA, a computerized referral service to sources in over 130 countries for environmental information. The UNEP played a significant role in the preparations for the 1992 UN Conference on Environment and Development in Rio de Janeiro, Brazil.

Publications: Annual Report of the Executive Director, State of the Environment Report (annual); *Environmental Data Report; Environmental Events Record* (12/year); and *Our Planet* (4/year); as well as studies, reports, and technical guidelines.

UN International Research and Training Institute for the Advancement of Women (INSTRAW)
Avenida Cesar Nicolas Penson 102-A
P.O. Box 21747
Santo Domingo, Dominican Republic
(809) 685-2111

This autonomous body was established in 1976 under the auspices of the UN to analyze and identify new methods for enhancing women's contributions to development, and also to assist in making the development process more attuned to the needs of women. Working through existing networks of women's organizations and research institutions, INSTRAW places priority on establishing national focal points for their work. A large part of INSTRAW's work is dedicated to improving statistical information on women for use in development planning and to ensure that women are taken into account in programs related to food strategy, industrial production, and technological change. INSTRAW's work with women covers a wide spectrum, including women and environment, women and AIDS, and women and energy. INSTRAW is funded solely from voluntary contributions from governments, nongovernmental organizations, and philanthropic institutions.

Publication: INSTRAW News (4/year).

World Food Programme (WFP)
Villa delle Terme di Caracalla
00100 Rome, Italy
(396) 579-3030

Jointly sponsored by the UN and the FAO, the World Food Programme is the largest source of food-in-development assistance in the UN system. Established in 1963, WFP's main objective is to provide food to support development and to mobilize and deliver emergency food in times of crises. Using food supplies as an incentive to participate in development activities such as construction and reforestation, WFP's "food-for-work" strategy is well known and has been replicated by many NGOs. Save the Children and Oxfam are among the many NGOs who are active in local distribution of WFP food aid. WFP is primarily operational; it assists countries in preschool and school feeding programs, and conducts projects in forestry, soil erosion, and land rehabilitation, as well as assisting in the coordination of large-scale relief operations. Funding for WFP comes from donor countries, the Food Aid Convention, and the International Food Reserve.

Publications: Annual Report and *World Food Programme Journal* (6/year).

World Health Organization (WHO)
20 Avenue Appia
CH-1211 Geneva 27
Switzerland
(22) 791-2111
Halfdan Mahler, Director General

WHO was established in 1948 with the objective of the attainment of all peoples of the highest possible level of health. WHO operates through six regional committees: the Americas, the Eastern Mediterranean, Europe, the Western Pacific, Southeast Asia, and Africa. "Health for All by the Year 2000" is WHO's primary goal, and to this end it focuses on the promotion and development of comprehensive health services. Program activities include: the improvement of environmental conditions, control and prevention of disease, development of health services, biomedical research, and the implementation and planning of health programs. Directing and coordinating the world's health network programs, WHO facilitates technical cooperation among nations to promote research and establish standards in various fields. Much of WHO's work has concentrated on the successful eradication of smallpox, the eradication of the major tropical diseases, and immunization of all children against six of the major childhood diseases. In recent years, WHO has been involved in spearheading the fight against AIDS. WHO's 1990–1991 budget was roughly $653 million.

Publications: Bulletin of WHO (6/year); *Public Health Papers; Reports on the World Health Situation* (approximately every 6 years); *Technical Report Series; World Health* (10/year); *World Health Forum* (quarterly); and *World Health Statistics Annual.*

Nongovernmental Organizations (NGOs)

Nongovernmental organizations (NGOs) have been active in the field of development longer than any of the large, multilateral institutions. Many of the larger organizations profiled in this chapter were founded after World War II when the devastation of that war created an urgent demand for relief and welfare assistance in Europe. After Europe's rehabilitation, NGOs' attention shifted to the demands for assistance coming from the Third World. During the 1950s and 1960s, numerous new organizations were created with the goal of attacking the causes, as well as the symptoms, of poverty, and NGOs as a whole began to replace their feeding centers and refugee camps with long-term development projects. It quickly became evident that the most efficient means to ensure sustainable change was through working closely with indigenous groups. Church-affiliated NGOs were best positioned to initiate these North-South partnerships. With heightened awareness of the importance and effectiveness of these Southern NGOs, many Northern organizations broadened their mandates to include not only the technical and financial support of their Southern counterparts, but also to engage in advocacy or education work at home.

The scope of NGOs' work stretches wider every year, often facilitated by increased funding from their national governments. In fact, in the past 25 years support for NGOs from governments and multilateral agencies has increased tenfold. This large show of support is by no means undeserved. NGOs have proven their unique ability to achieve those goals often missed by the large multilateral agencies and governmental programs. However, this assistance has proven to be somewhat of a double-edged sword. The advantages are obvious—larger budgets mean more resources and ostensibly, the ability to reach more people. But this support is not without its costs. Indeed, many NGOs refuse government funding, fearful that government monies will erode operational independence. Organizations such as Oxfam argue that if NGOs were to become dependent on government assistance, there would be a growing temptation to plan projects based on the interests of the governments, often at the expense of the interests of the Third World citizens that need aid the most. Being tied to government assistance could also hamper an NGO's freedom to look critically at governmental actions and advocate for more responsible foreign policies. Some argue that the loss of autonomy for NGOs, caused by government aid, results in projects that are less responsive and less accountable to the poor.

Funding issues aside, the strengths and successes of Northern and Southern NGOs abound. Their abilities to reach the poorest segments of populations, to provide low-cost services, and to use adaptive and innovative technologies have enhanced their role in development at a time when the more established institutions are facing heated accusations of mismanagement and waste. NGOs are posed to take center stage in the development arena; not only are they increasing in number, budget size, and scope, but the multilateral and governmental institutions are becoming more and more willing to hand over the reigns to this community with the stronger track record. Already NGOs collectively contribute more funds to the Third World than does the World Bank. The history of development organizations reflects one of the greatest attributes of the NGO community: its ability to learn from the past and to listen to those who have the greatest stake in development—the citizens of the Third World. For the past three decades NGOs have changed as the world has, and they show every indication of continuing to evolve to meet the needs of this changing world.

Northern NGOs

The United States has the world's largest concentration of nongovernmental organizations. This section profiles many of the well-known U.S.-based agencies, as well as a number of European organizations, while the following section takes a look at their important partners in the South. Only those organizations which are engaged in development work overseas are listed here. Patricia L. Kutzner's *World Hunger: A Reference Handbook* (ABC-CLIO,

1991) is an excellent source of information about NGOs active in the research, policy advocacy, and analysis of development.

AFRICARE
440 R Street, NW
Washington, DC 20001
(202) 462-3614
C. Payne Lucas, President

AFRICARE was founded in 1971 by African and American leaders in response to the drought and famine in West Africa. Its efforts are concentrated in rural Africa, where projects such as the development of water resources, increasing food production, and the delivery of health services are in place. The agency is active in 21 countries throughout Africa, with field offices offering emergency assistance in 16 countries. Their development programs include maternal and child health care in Niger, small vegetable gardening in Senegal, Niger, and Mali, and wells construction in Niger, Chad, Somalia, and Zambia. The U.S. government is AFRICARE's largest source of income.

AFRICARE relies on the manpower within the host country to conduct its projects, thereby avoiding the expense of an overseas staff while helping African leaders develop skills as administrators of development projects. An AFRICARE team is sent into the field to evaluate and identify needs, then representatives from the national, regional, and local levels are brought together to discuss programs. Before any program begins, an accord is signed with the national government, and after each transfer of funds, AFRICARE's field staff evaluates the project before further funding. AFRICARE prides itself on its ability to cultivate good relations with government officials, many of whom have had histories of conflict with other European and American development specialists. Another source of achievement is AFRICARE's strong connection to the African-American community in the United States, including a large roster of prominent celebrities who assist with public awareness efforts. U.S. government grants constitute the bulk of AFRICARE's funding: In 1991 total revenue was roughly $15 million, $6 million of which came from the U.S. government.

Publications: A Handbook for Community Treatment of Onchocerciasis and fact sheets.

American Friends Service Committee (AFSC)
1501 Cherry Street
Philadelphia, PA 19102
(215) 241-7150
Kara Newell, Executive Secretary

The American Friends Service Committee was founded in 1917 by American Quakers to provide conscientious objectors to World War I with a constructive alternative to military service. Today, AFSC carries out programs of service, development, justice, and peace. In 1947, the AFSC, with the British Friends Service Council, received the Nobel Peace Prize for its "silent help from the nameless to the nameless." Their work in international relief, development, reconciliation, and peace education reflects an emphasis on peace, and the agency is known for its ability to work on both sides of a conflict in reconciliation efforts. AFSC has assisted in conflicts throughout the world through refugee resettlement, famine relief, rehabilitation, and development. Its development projects emphasize small community enterprise and self-reliance, and are designed to be phased out within a few years. Project activities include assisting in the improvement of water and sanitation systems, constructing schools and houses, assisting in the development of new crops, and supporting nutrition and health education programs. Active in over 25 countries, AFSC's total revenue in 1991 was $25.5 million. Approximately 25 percent of the AFSC program budget is devoted to peace and disarmament activities around the world.

Publications: Beyond Détente: Soviet Foreign Policy and U.S. Options; Bridges: Quaker International Affairs Reports (6/year); Compassionate Peace; International Program Bulletin (3/year); Quaker Service Bulletin (3/year); South Africa: Challenge and Hope; The Sun Never Sets; and Two Koreas—One Future.

American Jewish Joint Distribution Committee (JDC)
711 Third Avenue
New York, NY 10017
(212) 687-6200
Milton A. Wolf, President
Michael Schneider, Executive Vice President

Established in 1914, the American Jewish Joint Distribution Committee serves as the overseas arm of the American Jewish community, sponsoring programs of relief, rescue, and reconstruction, and fulfilling its commitment to the idea that all Jews are responsible for one another. Support for JDC comes primarily from the United Jewish Appeal (UJA). For the past 80 years, JDC has worked to meet Jewish needs around the globe and has been concerned primarily with health and welfare issues within the global Jewish community. JDC has been part of the U.S. government's program of food assistance to the former Soviet Union, and also provides nonsectarian disaster and development assistance worldwide through its "Open Mailbox" campaigns. In 1993, 40 percent of JDC's revenue was allocated for Israel, where their current priorities include addressing the needs of the most disadvantaged populations, such as Ethiopian Jews and disadvantaged groups among immigrants. In Latin America, JDC provides technical assistance to train lay leaders and is helping to strengthen community organizations. As part of JDC's International Development Program, they are involved in such activities as assisting Rwandan refugees, developing an urban project in China, and providing medical services in Armenia. Total operating expenses for 1993 were just over $58 million.

Publication: Annual Report.

Catholic Relief Services (CRS)
209 W. Fayette Street
Baltimore, MD 21201
(410) 625-2220
Kenneth Hackett, Executive Director

Catholic Relief Services is the primary relief and development agency of the Catholic Church in the United States. CRS's work is "guided by the Gospel of Jesus Christ as it pertains to the alleviation of human suffering," and assists communities on the basis of need, not creed, race, or nationality. Active in 47 countries, CRS focuses on both emergency relief and development. All of its regional offices work in the following areas: civil conflict response, natural-resource management, food and medical assistance, development, and human rights. Among CRS's programs are a village banking project for women in Guatemala, a tree-planting project in Tanzania, and a seed replication project in Rwanda. Its emergency response work includes providing food, medicine, and blankets. The majority of its food aid is donated by the U.S. government; CRS is the largest distributor of U.S. government surplus food. Africa is CRS's largest regional office in terms of financial resources, with programs in 29 countries focusing on areas such as nutrition, loans for small businesses, civil conflict response, and training of peace negotiators. In 1992, *Money Magazine* ranked CRS third in its annual listing of relief and development agencies for its low overhead, which was 5.8 percent in 1992. Total revenue for CRS in 1992 was $290 million, 38 percent of which was spent on development assistance.

Publications: Annual Report; Big Picture: An Introduction to International Development; and *Issues* (12/year); as well as action kits and Postcards from The Field.

Christian Children's Fund (CCF)
2821 Emerywood Parkway
P.O. Box 26484
Richmond, VA 23261
Paul McCleary, Executive Director

The Christian Children's Fund is one of the oldest and largest nongovernmental organizations engaging exclusively in child sponsorship programming. CCF activities include subsidizing schools, day-care facilities, residential facilities, and other institutions that assist children in 40 countries around the world. CCF does not accept federal funds and does not work in the area of disaster relief. CCF program implementation involves their field staff identifying a village that has asked for assistance, collecting the names and basic information about the children in the community, and photographing them. This information is sent back to international headquarters, where a sponsorship kit for each child is prepared. CCF received over $75 million in 1992 for sponsorhip programming; total revenue was $105 million.

Publications: Annual Report and *CHILDWORLD* (6/year).

Church World Service & Witness (CWS)
475 Riverside Drive
New York, NY 10115
(212) 870-2257
Lonnie Turnipseed, Executive Director

Church World Service is the international relief and development agency of the National Council of Churches in the United States, and has been working to address the needs of its partner churches overseas since 1946. Focusing on disaster relief, development, and refugee assistance, CWS works through a network of indigenous church NGOs in over 70 countries worldwide. CWS activities include enabling women in Bangladesh to establish a credit cooperative, working with the rural poor of Bolivia in building fish ponds, and supplying medicines and equipment to train health workers in rural Vietnam. Recently CWS projects have de-emphasized food and material aid and placed more efforts on supporting local NGOs and facilitating network building and information exchange among them. In 1994, CWS's total expenditures were $48.6 million, with 16.6 percent allocated to self-help development projects and 27 percent to refugee services.

Publications: Annual Report; Harvest (3/year); Make a World of Difference (curriculum); and *Monday* (weekly, on refugee issues).

Cooperative for Assistance and Relief Everywhere (CARE)
151 Ellis Street, NE
Atlanta, GA 30303
(404) 681-2552
Philip Johnston, President
Peter D. Bell, Chairman

CARE was founded in 1945 by 22 American religious, relief, civic, labor, and service groups as a cooperative emergency relief organization to provide assistance (and the well-known "care packages") to the people of war-torn Europe. Today, CARE International is a confederation of 11 national CAREs: Australia, Austria, Canada, Denmark, France, Germany, Italy, Japan, Norway, the United Kingdom, and the United States. CARE works in more than 53 countries in Africa, Asia, Latin America, and the former Soviet Union and Yugoslavia, sponsoring relief and development projects. Its mission is to help the developing world's poor in their efforts to achieve social and economic well-being through both emergency relief aid and development programs in such fields as agriculture, small business support, population, and health and nutrition. In 1993, CARE immunized 1.7 million mothers and children, helped 75,825 small businesses start and expand, and reached 2.4 million people with AIDS prevention programs. Assisting CARE in its efforts is the U.S. government and the United Nations; CARE received almost 600,000 metric tons of agricultural and other commodities from the UN and the U.S. government in 1993. CARE's 1993 total expenses were $438 million, and it received 42 percent of its revenue from the U.S. government.

CARE's program policy involves signing an accord with the host government before entering and implementing any program in that country. The host government must allow entry for CARE commodities duty free, must arrange and pay for inland transportation of those goods, and must protect CARE against legal suits and entanglements while operating in that country. The country must also agree not to intervene by redirecting contributed goods away from those recipients designated by CARE, thereby helping to avoid the problem of confiscation of supplies, which plagues many NGOs working in corrupt countries.

Publications: CARE: A Profile; CARE and the Environment: Strategies for the 21st Century; CARE catalog; CARE films; CARE World Report (quarterly); GlobeTrek (a curriculum for children); and *What and Where of CARE.*

Cultural Survival
11 Divinity Avenue
Cambridge, MA 02138
(617) 495-2562
David Maybury-Lewis, President

Founded in 1972, Cultural Survival works with tribal people and ethnic minorities in efforts to assist them to make accommodation on their own terms with states and international economic and political systems. Among its programs are: sustainable resource management projects with indigenous peoples in Brazil, Chile, Peru, Colombia, Panama, Ecuador, Mexico, and Namibia; handicrafts promotion; and medical care. Cultural Survival's research on the causes of the 1984–1986 Ethiopian famine is one of the largest and most systematic pieces of research on the topic.

Publications: Cultural Survival Quarterly; and books, including *Politics and the Ethiopian Famine, 1984–1985* (1986).

FOOD FOR THE HUNGRY, Inc.
7729 East Greenway Road
Scottsdale, AZ 85260
(602) 998-3100
Tetsunao Yamamori, Director

Active in 22 countries, FOOD FOR THE HUNGRY provides food and material aid for victims of disasters and implements development projects promoting self-reliance. Community Development, Water Resource Management, and Income Generation (loans for small business projects) are the organization's program areas. They are also active in agricultural initiatives, such as crop improvement, training centers, and support for reforestation programs. Hunger Corps, FOOD FOR THE HUNGRY's volunteer program, places volunteers for two to four weeks in poor communities and then requests that they advocate for the needs of the poor upon their return to the United States. Like CCF, above, FOOD FOR THE HUNGRY has a child sponsorship program. They also have a Spiritual Education Program involving ministers who conduct Bible studies and evangelical programs. Total revenue in 1992 for FOOD FOR THE HUNGRY was over $28 million, which included government grants, gifts in kind, and general contributions.

Publications: Annual Report and *Feeding the Hungry* (12/year).

Heifer Project International (HPI)
P.O. Box 808
Little Rock, AK 72203
(501) 576-6836
Jo Luck Cargile, Executive Director

The Heifer Project began in the late 1930s when Dan West, an Indiana farmer, volunteered to distribute relief supplies to hungry families in Spain during the Spanish Civil War. West saw the provision of "handouts" as degrading and futile, and wanted to replace the distribution of powdered milk with cows. The first shipment of heifers was sent in 1944. Since then HPI has been providing heifers, bulls, sheep, goats, pigs, poultry, honeybees, and rabbits to people in 107 countries. Today HPI works in 35 countries, including the United States. Its programs are focused on rural development, and specifically on food production and livestock projects. HPI's small-scale projects benefit needy farmers by providing animals adaptive to available resources and training in animal care and management. Another important program component is the teaching of environmentally sound, sustainable agriculture practices. Roughly half of HPI's program funds are allocated for the purchase of livestock (usually purchased near the project area to help the local economy), while the other half provides training and management. To ensure sustainability, recipients must be willing to pass on the gift by providing livestock to others. Church-related groups and individuals are responsible for roughly half of the Heifer Project's budget.

Publications: Exchange (24/year) and *Sharing Life* (quarterly).

InterAction
American Council for Voluntary International Action
1717 Massachusetts Avenue NW, #801
Washington, DC 20036
(202) 667-8227
Julia Taft, President

InterAction is the nation's largest coalition, encompassing 116 U.S. private voluntary organizations engaged in international humanitarian efforts. InterAction was established in 1984 to enhance the effectiveness of its members, fostering partnership, collaboration, and "the power of this community to speak as one voice as we strive to achieve a world of self-reliance, justice, and peace." To this end, InterAction advocates for the Private Voluntary Organization community to Congress, government agencies, funders, and the general public. It also assists its members by offering workshops, committees, and an Annual Forum where members are brought together with representatives from government, international agencies, and developing countries. InterAction is funded by private donations and grants from the Carnegie, Rockefeller, and Ford Foundations. Together, InterAction members receive more than $1.5 billion each year in private contributions and handle over $600 million in government funding, mostly in the form of commodities. InterAction's diverse membership includes agencies involved in disaster relief, refugee assistance and resettlement, long-term development, and development education.

Publications: Hope for the World's Hungry; InterAction Member Profiles (annual); and *Working Together: NGO Cooperation in Seven African Countries;* as well as additional books, InterAction newsletters, and reports.

International Institute of Rural Reconstruction (IIRR)
475 Riverside Drive, Room 1035
New York, NY 10115
(212) 870-2992
John Rigby, President

This international organization, incorporated in the United States with headquarters in the Philippines, works to improve the quality of life of the rural poor in Africa, Asia, and Latin America. IIRR's motto—"not relief, but release"—reflects the activities with which it is involved, such as a project to promote environmentally sound agriculture in semiarid areas of southwest India; integrated farming systems; and intensive gardening, soil fertility management, and off-season growing. IIRR also provides research and training. IIRR was the recipient of the 1995 Alan Shawn Feinstein Award for the Prevention and Reduction of World Hunger.

Publications: Annual Report; IIRR Report (2/year); and training kits.

International Orthodox Christian Charities (IOCC)
711 W. 40th Street
Suite 306
Baltimore, MD 21211
Alexander Rondos, Executive Director

International Orthodox Christian Charities was established in 1992 as the international humanitarian agency of the Standing Conference of Canonical Orthodox Bishops of the Americas (SCOBA). IOCC represents a unified orthodox Christian humanitarian response to the needs of the poor, either in response to emergencies or long-term socioeconomic development needs. IOCC funds and supports only projects that meet certain essential criteria, such as the caveats that projects must be carried out with or through an indigenous development organization, and project design must demonstrate a clear capacity for management. Overseas offices are set up only when the Orthodox hierarchy of the country in question has made a request. Funding comes from donations from Orthodox Christians and from foundations, governments, and multilateral agencies. The 1993 budget was over $3 million, with 75.3 percent going toward disaster and emergency relief. IOCC is currently active in the former Yugoslavia where an emergency relief program is under way, as well as a war trauma counseling program. IOCC is also assisting in the development of an Orthodox orphanage in Mexico, and has established a Caribbean Fund for programs throughout the Caribbean islands, such as small enterprise programs.

Publications: Annual Report and awareness materials for Sunday schools.

International Rescue Committee (IRC)
386 Park Avenue South
New York, NY 10016
(212) 689-0010
Robert DeVecchi, President

Founded in 1933, the objectives of the International Rescue Committee are to provide emergency relief, public health, medical, and educational services, as well as resettlement assistance for refugees and other displaced persons. All IRC projects are related to refugees and displaced persons; agricultural self-help projects are focused on long-term refugee integration, and emergency operations coordinate and oversee the flow of relief supplies for refugees. IRC's primary, technical, vocational, and literacy education programs are offered to Liberian refugees in Guinea, Afghan refugees in Pakistan, and Cambodian refugees in Thailand. IRC also trains refugee community health workers in primary health care and works to strengthen local health services. IRC is very active in resettlement efforts, providing processing assistance, counselling, job placement, and financial assistance for refugees admitted to the United States. Program countries include Nicaragua, Bosnia, Croatia, Bangladesh, Somalia, and many others. U.S. government contracts provided IRC with $21.5 million in 1992, with total revenues at $53 million.

Publication: IRC Worldwide Newsletter.

International Voluntary Services (IVS)
1424 16th Street, NW
Suite 204
Washington, DC 20036
(202) 387-5533
Don Luce, Executive Director

Founded in 1953, International Voluntary Services works in partnership with local communities, governments, donors, and other development agencies to alleviate hunger and inequality in the world. Skilled technicians in the fields of agriculture, environment, small enterprise development, AIDS prevention, and others are recruited to fill posts at the request of host governments and institutions. IVS works in over 30 countries around the world where its volunteers respond to requests to reinforce the strengths of local NGOs by transferring skills and technology. Program activities include improving crop and livestock production through advice and training in horticulture, animal husbandry, community development, and village-level health programs.Total revenue received in 1992 exceeded $1 million.

Publications: Developments (6/year) and *IVS Reporter* (2/year).

League of Red Cross and Red Crescent Societies
Case Postale 276
1211 Geneva 19
Switzerland
(22) 345580
Enrique de la Mata Gorostizaga, President of the General Assembly

This is the international federation of the 114 national Red Cross and 23 Red Crescent Societies. The league emphasizes its efforts around disaster relief, organizing and coordinating international relief for disaster victims and refugees, and promoting national disaster preparedness plans. In addition, the league advises national societies on development of their services in health, social welfare, education, and training programs.

Publications: Annual Review; The League (quarterly); and *Transfusion International* (quarterly).

Lutheran World Relief (LWR)
390 Park Avenue South
New York, NY 10016
(212) 532-6350
Kathryn Wolford, Executive Director

Lutheran World Relief works on behalf of the Evangelical Lutheran Church in America and the Lutheran Church-Missouri Synod by providing support for 155 development and relief projects in more than 35 countries. Most of LWR's resources are allocated for projects in Africa, where environmental protection and restoration projects are under way, as well as AIDS awareness and education, refugee assistance, and literacy outreach. In Latin America, LWR is engaged in assisting such projects as a women-run poultry business in Bolivia. In Asia, LWR funded 72 projects in 1994, providing flood relief, clean water, village sanitation, and support for integrated development. LWR works via its network of bilateral or multilateral relationships with local indigenous NGOs or government agencies and selects projects that promote agriculture, economic self-reliance, empowerment of women, employment, justice, the environment, and health care. Fifty-one percent of LWR's revenue comes from church body support; total receipts for 1994 were $19 million.

Publication: Annual Report.

Medicins Sans Frontièrs (MSF)
8 rue St. Sabin
75011 Paris, France
Chantal Firino-Martell, Executive Director

MSF, or Doctors without Borders, was founded in 1971 and is the world's largest emergency medical organization. Made up of physicians and other medical professionals, MSF works on medium-term programs in nutrition, immunization, sanitation, and public health. MSF works with UN agencies and local officials in its Disaster and Emergency Relief Program, conducting medical programs, surgery, and water distribution efforts. The Medicine and Public Health Program sets up or repairs local health care systems, and supplies food, basic hygienic services, and vaccinations. Migration and Refugee Services sends medical professionals to refugee camps where, in addition to providing medical care, the staff also works on the rehabilitation of hospitals and dispensaries. MSF was the first NGO allowed to assist Kurds in northern Iraq after the Gulf War, and it continues to monitor health systems in the region. The agency also had an important role in the 1984 Ethiopian famine; its vocal opposition to the government's enforced villagization program, which was claiming hundreds of lives, resulted in its expulsion from the country.

Publication: MSF International Newsletter (quarterly).

Mennonite Central Committee (MCC)
21 South 12th Street
P.O. Box 500
Akron, PA 17501-0500
(717) 859-1151
John Lapp, Executive Secretary

The Mennonite Central Committee is the service, development, and relief agency of the North American Mennonite and Brethren in Christ churches. Peace has consistently been the driving force behind MCC projects, reflecting their philosophy that "development [is] a new word for peace." Active in 54 countries, MCC programs are in the fields of community development, education, health, food production, and peace and reconciliation efforts. MCC places strong emphasis on mediation and efforts to eliminate violence, calling peacemaking their "driving force." This emphasis has been constant since MCC's founding in 1920 and is a reflection of the Mennonite Movement's 200-year commitment to peace. Among the MCC's development projects are a rural savings and credit program and a chicken vaccination program. All of their programs stress local participation and local leadership training. Contributions from the general public make up 45 percent of MCC's income.

Publications: Extending the Table: A World Community Cookbook; MCC Contact, Intercom (12/year); *MCC Magazine* (4/year); and *Washington Memo* (6/year).

Oxfam America
26 West Street
Boston, MA 02111
(617) 482-1211
John C. Hammock, Chairperson

Oxfam is one of the largest international agencies that funds self-help development and disaster relief projects around the world. Oxfam America is one of seven autonomous Oxfams and was formed in response to the Bangladesh famine in 1970. Oxfam grants support local groups working in 28 countries, including the United States, to increase food production or economic self-reliance. Oxfam is unique in that it does not accept money from any government and relies solely on partners throughout the United States for funding (87 percent of its revenues in 1992 came from families and individuals), giving the organization what it considers to be its greatest strength: autonomy. Tied to no government, no ideology, and no single or large source of funding, Oxfam has been able to develop a variety of styles of operation around the world and has been able to build relationships with nations and organizations independent of U.S. foreign policy considerations. Its disaster relief work focuses on advocacy and education.

Publications: Fast for a World Harvest Kit (annual); *Oxfam America News* (3/year); and many books and project reports.

Partners of the Americas
1424 K Street, NW
Suite 700
Washington, DC 20005
(202) 628-3300
William S. Reese, President

Partners of the Americas works to establish relationships and foster inter-American friendship while promoting long-range economic and social development in Latin America. Founded in 1964, the agency pairs American states with regions or countries of the Caribbean and Latin America in order to carry out grass-roots projects in such areas as agriculture, health, conservation, and small business development. The development projects are designed to allow for the exchange of ideas in science, technology, and culture between universities in the United States and those in Latin America and the Caribbean. Some of Partner's programs include occupational training for handicapped youth in Brazil and vocational training and job placement in El Salvador. Partners's 1991 budget was just over $10 million.

Publication: Partners (6/year).

Project Concern International (PCI)
3550 Afton Road
San Diego, CA 92110
(619) 279-9690
Daniel Shaughnessy, Chief Executive Officer

Formed in 1961, the goal of Project Concern International is to assist people in developing countries participate in the process of their own development, especially in the area of health care. PCI works in partnership with local communities, nationally and internationally, to provide basic, low-cost health care services. Projects focus on disease prevention, training of volunteer health workers, and the establishment of comprehensive local health systems. PCI family planning programs provide information in keeping with local culture and tradition, emphasizing activities such as birth spacing, breast feeding, and the distribution of contraceptives. With a 1991 budget of approximately $11 million, PCI operates such programs as the development of nutrition centers and the establishment of Maternal/Child Health and Child

Survival programs in eight countries in Latin America, Eastern Europe, and Asia. PCI works in conjunction with the host countries' governments on health care training and delivery systems, which will one day be self-sustaining and replicable throughout the country.

Publication: Concern News, OPTIONS Newsletter.

Save the Children
54 Wilton Road
Westport, CT 06880
(203) 221-4000
Charles McCormack, President

Save the Children is one of 25 independent members of the International Save the Children Alliance, which is one of the world's largest consortia of private, nongovernmental child assistance organizations. The mission of Save the Children has been the same since its inception in 1919: to create a better quality of life for needy children. The agency is active in 40 countries with programs focusing on women and children. Save the Children's programs focus on the following areas: education; economic opportunities, especially for women; health care initiatives that center on families and communities; and emergency response. One program that has received significant praise is the Ecole du Village program, a community-based and village-supported educational system carefully synchronized with the agricultural seasons. Both the UN Education, Science, and Cultural Organization (UNESCO) and the UN Development Programme have cited this program as an outstanding innovation. Funding for Save the Children comes from such sources as the Office of U.S. Foreign Disaster Assistance and the UN High Commission for Refugees, as well as public contributions and sponsorships. In 1992, total revenues exceeded $93 million, and expenses were $94 million. For several years *Money Magazine* has ranked Save the Children as one of the top ten best-run international relief and development organizations, based on their percentage of funds directed to program services (83 percent, from 1983 to 1989).

Publications: Annual Report; Footprints; Impact (2/year); and Strong Beginnings (education booklet), as well as fact sheets.

TechnoServe
49 Day Street
Norwalk, CT 06854
(203) 838-6717
Edward Bullard, President

TechnoServe was founded in 1968 with the goal of improving the economic and social well-being of the poor in Latin America and Africa through the provision of management training and technical assistance to community-based agricultural enterprises. These self-help enterprises include ranches, farms, cooperatives, savings and credit co-ops, and technical and business service companies, and are generally worker-owned. TechnoServe has developed and copyrighted a unique cost-effectiveness methodology which measures both the immediate and long-term benefits and sustainability of their work. Their efforts are concentrated in areas with high unemployment and poor health, usually in the agricultural sector. TechnoServe is currently active in 11 countries in Latin America, Eastern Europe, and Africa.

Publications: Cost-Effectiveness in the Nonprofit Sector; FINDINGS research series; Post-Secondary Development Education kits; *Sector Studies;* and *TechnoServe Newsletter* (2/year), as well as audio and visual documentaries.

Unitarian Universalist Service Committee (UUSC)
130 Prospect Street
Cambridge, MA 02139
(617) 868-6600
Richard Scobie, Executive Director

The Unitarian Universalist Service Committee was founded in 1939 to assist victims of fascism escape from Europe before and after World War II. Since its founding, UUSC has worked to support projects in the United States and the developing world to promote health care, education, leadership development, family planning, human rights, and other initiatives that help freedom and justice to flourish. UUSC's work places a strong emphasis on women's role in development. Their projects often focus on maternal health, child and youth health, food production and water resource development, and vocational education. UUSC also works on emergency relief projects, though priority is placed on building partnerships with local NGOs. UUSC self-help projects in 10 countries (in Latin America, Africa, and Asia) employ only local workers—UUSC does not place any staff or volunteers to work on its overseas projects. UUSC is an associate of the Unitarian Universalist Association, but receives no operating support from the association, nor does UUSC accept any funding from the U.S. government, and is funded instead by public donations and grants from foundations.

Publications: A Journey to Understanding; El Salvador Study / Action Packet; *High Hopes, Harsh Realities: The Challenge of Development in Central America; Introductory Guide to Africa; Service Community News;* and UUCC Philippines reports.

Voluntary Service Overseas (VSO)
317 Putney Bridge Road
London, SW15 2PN
England
(81) 780-2266

Voluntary Service Overseas was founded in 1958 with the goal of providing opportunities for volunteers with skills to make a practical contribution in a less developed country. Skilled volunteers are posted for two-year contracts in the following fields: agriculture, technical trades, education, health care, and social and business development. The United Kingdom government funds approximately 83 percent of the VSO's activities. The agency stresses the point that volunteers are never placed in a post that prevents or discourages a national from filling it, and volunteers are sent in response to the request by local governments or indigenous (or international) NGOs. There are currently over 17,000 volunteers working in over 55 countries around the world.

Publications: Annual Report and *Orbit* (in-house magazine). VSO also has a publishing unit which issues a number of books on a range of topics.

Volunteers in Technical Assistance (VITA)
1600 Wilson Boulevard
Arlington, VA 22209
(703) 276-1800
Henry Norman, Executive Director

The goal of Volunteers in Technical Assistance is to make available to individuals and groups in developing countries a variety of information and technical resources aimed at fostering self-sufficiency. VITA uses state-of-the-art communications technology in disseminating information to developing countries through a network of volunteer scientists, engineers, and business managers. Among the resources VITA provides are: needs assessment and program development support; consulting services; information systems; and training and management of long-term field projects. VITA's activities concentrate on agriculture, food processing, renewable energy applications, water supply and sanitation, housing, small business development, and information management. VITA recently developed a global communications system for developing countries called VITACOM, which consists of a satellite system, short-wave packet radio systems, and an electronic message delivery system that uses existing telephone networks. This communication system assists with disaster mitigation; prevention and response; health education and information; and administrative and logistic support. VITA is funded by the U.S. government, foundations, public contributions, and grants.

Publications: Development News (electronic bulletin board) and technology books and manuals.

World Neighbors
4127 NW 122 Street
Oklahoma City, OK 73120
(405) 752-9700
(800) 242-8387
James S. Brackett, Executive Director

World Neighbors, founded in 1951, is a nonsectarian agency that works to establish and assist self-help programs to eliminate hunger, disease, and poverty in Africa, Asia, and Latin America. In 1994, World Neighbors was active in 21 countries, with 87 development programs. Their overseas development strategy is based on over 40 years of experience at the grass-roots level, and aims to strengthen the community's ability to maintain, multiply, and sustain results as well as evaluate and document these results. Projects involving the development, testing, and extension of simple technologies are active throughout the world, such as in Nepal where gravity-flow water systems have cut water collection time in half and supply clean water for 1,140 people. World Neighbors is supported by private donations (constituting 50 percent of their income) and has a firm policy against accepting U.S. government funding. Program priorities are food production, community-based health, family planning, water and sanitation, environmental conservation, and small business development. A primary goal of World Neighbors is to create long-term programs which promote self-reliance and local participation. Another World Neighbor goal is to foster a sense of partnership between people of North America and those in Asia, Africa, and Latin America through study-visits to their program partners around the world.

Publications: Neighbors (quarterly) and *World Neighbors in Action* (quarterly, in English, Spanish, and French), as well as a training materials catalogue.

World Vision
919 West Huntington Drive
Monrovia, CA 91016
(818) 357-7979
Robert A. Seiple, President

World Vision was established in 1950 by evangelical leader Dr. Bob Pierce. While World Vision is a Christian organization, it does not maintain formal relations to any denomination. The key organizing principle for World Vision is the belief that material assistance and Christian evangelism should accompany one another, a principle not adhered to by most of the other Christian agencies, such as CRS and CWS (see above). World Vision's key objectives, as stated in its *Annual Report*, are: providing emergency aid; ministering to children and families (mainly through their child sponsorship program); strengthening leadership (including Pastors' Conferences and Christian outreach projects); developing self-reliance; reaching the unreached; and mission advocacy. In 1993, World Vision was involved in 5,568 projects in 97 countries worldwide. World Vision spends 12.3 percent of its budget, which was $263 million in 1993, on fundraising—producing and airing television programs and radio commercials, placing newspaper and magazine advertisements, and sending direct-mail appeals. In return, 1993 contributions from individuals, corporations, churches, and foundations totalled $146 million, or 56.6 percent of their total revenue.

Publications: Christian Leadership Letter; Cups of Cold Water: Caring for People in Need (adult church group curricula); *Newsbriefs* (weekly); *Reclaiming the Garden: Caring for an Environment in Crisis; Together* (quarterly); and *World Vision Magazine* (6/year).

Southern NGOs

When Northern NGOs began to realize that effective development would not be achieved by importing Northern ideas, technology, and volunteers to the Third World, Southern NGOs became the focus of much attention. Initially regarded primarily as merely a development instrument through which to channel aid money, the diversity, creativity, and effectiveness of the organizations were soon recognized and the role of these NGOs rapidly expanded.

Southern NGOs have been growing at an even faster rate than their Northern counterparts. The Overseas Development Institute in London identified over 25,000 grass-roots organizations in the Indian state of Tamil Nadu alone. In Mozambique and Kampuchea local NGOs, not official aid institutions, are the main development partners of the government. In Bangladesh and India they have had a significant impact in forcing through legislation concerning minimum wages, feudalism, and labor conditions. In Latin America, indigenous NGOs have been a channel for public concern when their governments have remained silent. Southern NGOs have been especially effective in challenging socially or environmentally damaging programs pursued by their own governments.

Responding to immediate local needs, Southern NGOs are engaged in an enormous range of activities, from community-based sewing cooperatives to regional entrepreneurial assistance. The diversity of Southern NGOs defies generalization; perhaps the only common characteristic that binds this vibrant community is that these NGOs are born of and reflect the culture of the people they aim to assist. Listed below are just a few of the more well-known, larger NGOs, which are often tauted as the South's "success stories."

All Pakistan Women's Association (APWA)
Pakistan

One of the largest Southern NGOs, the All Pakistan Women's Association was established in 1949 to assist the total involvement of women in the process of development and to take measures to restore women's legal rights. Priorities are placed on education, health, training in income generation, and vocational skills. APWA spearheaded national campaigns in education and health, establishing over 70 institutions of higher and primary education, and hospitals and health clinics which benefit over 250,000 women and children annually. APWA has 61 provincial branches and five affiliates, making it a national force capable of mobilizing huge numbers of volunteers.

Bangladesh Rural Advancement Committee (BRAC)
Bangladesh

BRAC is one of the largest NGOs in the global South, managing projects in 1,746 villages in 18 of Bangladesh's 64 districts. BRAC was developed in 1972 as a small relief organization providing services to refugees in the wake of the war of liberation, primarily focusing on construction projects to generate wage labor for the landless. Gradually, the relief-oriented approach was replaced with longer-term objectives such as health care and nonformal education. In 1976, BRAC began to focus primarily on the landless poor, with special emphasis on women. It provided credit and was successful in establishing a string of retail outlets to market crafts and textiles produced by rural artisans. By 1980 BRAC's reach had broadened, both geographically and in focus, as it sought to test the ability of the landless poor to use their own resources. Many groups proved successful in securing government land, in bargaining for higher wages, and even winning public office. However, the achievements proved to be short-lived and it was determined that external support was necessary due to the political and economic disadvantage experienced by the landless poor. BRAC has been very successful in attaining funding from a worldwide consortium; in 1991 BRAC's budget was $20 million. Today, BRAC's four main programs are: the Development Program which organizes villagers and facilitates income-generating projects by providing credit and working with government organizations; the Credit Project, a self-sustaining banking operation; Health Programs, such as the Child Survival Program; and the Primary Education Program. BRAC's initiatives in education have been highly successful; in 1985 it started 22 experimental village schools—by late 1989 the program had expanded to 2,500 schools, with attendance rates at over 95 percent.

Centro para el Desarollo Social y Economico (DESEC)
Bolivia

Established in 1963, DESEC (Center for Social and Economic Development) promotes rural development through the creation and consolidation of peasant organizations. DESEC coordinates the activities of a group of organizations throughout Bolivia working in the field of rural development, and offers them technical assistance in agricultural production.

Committee for the Fight for the End of Hunger (COLUFIFA)
Senegal

A famine in the Casamance region of Senegal in 1984 spurred the creation of this community self-help organization. COLUFIFA's approach is to respect and rely upon local traditions and a sense of community to feed the people in the area, and aims to eliminate hunger in the villages of the Casamance region by the turn of the century. Instead of relying on state or foreign aid, COLUFIFA created collective food banks and granaries—and received no outside funds between 1985 and1990. Striving for self-sufficiency, it commercialized agricultural products and, with the revenue, created a credit system called the Mutual Help Fund, which gives loans to needy members at low interest rates. COLUFIFA also provides training about nutrition and health. In 1994, it was awarded the Alan Shawn Feinstein Award for the Prevention and Reduction of World Hunger. Today COLUFIFA has over 15,000 members and is often requested by peasants in neighboring countries for assistance in organizing similar committees.

Development Alternatives with Women for a New Era (DAWN)
Brazil (Headquarters)

The 22 founding members of DAWN sought to define the issues of development from "the vantage point of women." Recognizing that the UN Decade for Women had fallen somewhat short of its targeted goals, this network of Third World women activists and researchers established DAWN in 1984. DAWN analyzed the nature of the economy into which the Decade for Women sought to integrate women, and asked "shall we integrate women or shall we restructure development?" DAWN has been most influential in revealing the extent to which women's issues are economic issues, and cannot be ignored when talking about development. With the assistance of the Norwegian Agency for International Development, DAWN published a book that would politicize the role of women in development in time for the International Women's Conference in Nairobi: *Development, Crises and Alternative Visions: Third World Women's Perspectives*, edited by Gita Sen.

Grameen Bank
Bangladesh

This project is perhaps the most well known of all the "development success stories." Established in 1976 by a university professor with the sole purpose of providing credit to the poor, the Grameen Bank has become a model for microenterprise programs. It was the first bank to offer loans, which had to be repaid within one year, to self-formed groups of landless poor. The bank allocates a capital sum to each group and the group allocates two members who will receive the loan. The bank will not issue any other members loans until the first two members have started their weekly repayments. These strict rules have yielded a repayment record of 97 percent. By 1983 the bank had extended its operations to a national level, and the following year received more than $25 million from the International Fund for Agricultural Development to assist its expansion to a targeted 500 branches. Beneficiaries of Grameen Bank loans have used these funds for the development of such enterprises as weaving, pottery, cycle repair, rice husking, and garment manufacture. The bank has been especially successful in providing loans to women; in 1991, 95 percent of its housing loans went to women. Today, the Grameen Bank receives requests from countries around the world, including the United States, for help in training community or village bankers and in adopting other components of the Grameen model.

Green Belt Movement
Kenya

The Green Belt Movement originated in 1977 from a project of the National Council of Kenyan Women. The principal aim of the movement is to work in cooperation with women's organizations in opposing deforestation. The Green Belt Movement's goal is "to improve the environment, and in the process, raise public awareness about the basic role of our natural environment at the family, regional, and national level." Almost all of the movement's financial resources come from the North, while local contribution occurs in the form of labor and some voluntary services. As of 1988, the Green Belt Movement had created 600 tree nurseries and grown 10 million, mostly indigenous trees, involving over 50,000 women and children.

Instituto de Educacion para el Desarollo Rural (INEDER)
Bolivia

INEDER (the Educational Institute for Rural Development) was created in 1973 and is active with farmer unions throughout Bolivia. The goal of INEDER is to improve the standard of living for farmers through socially organized production. Focal points are increased production and organization through training and information exchange. INEDER helps organize and coordinate networks in which grass-roots organizations, the local civil government, state development projects, churches, and other NGOs work together to define a development plan for the region. INEDER's program areas include: farming and animal husbandry, fostering of popular peasant organizations, promotion of women, rural radio, agricultural education, health, and research. INEDER faced significant obstacles in its early years due to a repressive dictatorial government which prohibited political activity in rural areas. Today, INEDER describes its fundamental aim as being "to contribute to the macroeconomic and political change of society."

Kaira District Dairy Cooperative
India

The Kaira Dairy Cooperative was formed during the 1960s in Gujuarat, India, to help women and the landless acquire milch stock. The cooperative introduced technological innovations in animal feeding, and gradually was able to invest in a factory producing a wide array of milk products on a national level, known today as the Amul Dairy. When in the mid-1970s the European Economic Community (EEC) offered the government of India surplus dairy products as food aid, the leaders of the Kaira Dairy cooperatives saw how this could sweep away the market they had built up. They quickly mobilized and negotiated with the government to reconstitute the EEC's dairy products as whole milk and then use the income from the sale of this milk to finance dairy production throughout India based on the Kaira model.

Mouvman Peyizan Papaye (MPP)
Haiti

MPP (Creole for Peasant Movement of Papaye) was established in the early 1970s out of a meeting of peasant farmers who had gathered together with the hope of achieving greater cooperation and dialogue. The farmers articulated their needs, which were not being met by the government, and decided to form a grass-roots organization in attempt to meet those needs. They established a small, agricultural collective, the MPP, in 1973. By the late 1980s, MPP enterprises engaged more than 12,000 peasants in cooperative processing and distribution of crafts and produce. Among the activities with which the MPP is involved are raising small livestock, honey production for local use and export, grain storage, and credit and marketing programs. Additionally, educational and environmental programs offset the region's high illiteracy rates and the erosion of croplands. During the 1991 military coup, the MPP offices were destroyed, assets stolen, and members attacked. With the recent return of a fragile peace to Haiti, the MPP began to restore seed and tool reserves, though its future, like the country's, remains uncertain.

Sarvodaya Shramadana Movement (SSM)
Sri Lanka

The Sarvodaya Shramadana Movement is one of the oldest and most successful rural development movements in the world, and is the second largest force, after the government, working for rural development in Sri Lanka. Begun in 1958, SSM is aimed at community development through community ownership, self-help, cooperation, and grass-roots organization. The Sarvodaya approach to development stresses the ideas of self-fulfillment and nondependence; the word *sarva* means "all," and *udaya* means "awakening." In the 30 years of its existence, SSM has mobilized over two million people in community development projects. The movement is based on the notion that sustainable development can take place only when poor people participate in a project from its inception on. The principles of simplicity, concern for others, and self-reliance guide the movement as it focuses on training villagers who, after training, return to their own villages to work. SSM receives funding from multilateral and governmental institutions, including UNICEF and USAID.

Self Employed Women's Association (SEWA)
India

SEWA was created and registered in Ahmedabad, India, as a trade union of self-employed women workers in 1972. Most of SEWA's members were construction laborers or street vendors—women who had no economic security and no access to credit other than through local moneylenders. SEWA addressed the multiple needs of these women by setting up its own bank, which provided loans at 12 percent interest. This allowed the women to increase their daily incomes and gave them the security to defend their rights against unfair fines and other marginalizing practices. In 1989, SEWA's bank had 25,000 savings accounts, $1 million in working capital, and a 96 percent repayment rate on its loans. SEWA's work with women has been modeled throughout India, and it also offers legal aid, maternity protection, productivity training, and child care.

Society for Promotion of Area Resource Centers (SPARC)
India

SPARC was established in 1984 in reaction to the Bombay State government's order for the clearing of thousands of "pavement dwellers" living on the streets without providing any alternate arrangements. SPARC's efforts have focused on fighting these attempted mass evictions and securing better and permanent sites on which the pavement dwellers could erect their homes. While SPARC has not won any significant resettlement yet, it has been successful in mobilizing the pavement dwellers, especially women.

Women's Organization of Independencia (WARMI)
Peru

Independencia, an impoverished suburb of Lima known as the "poverty belt," is home to this small, grass-roots group of women who operate an extensive network of community kitchens. In a country where inflation is over 1,000 percent and malnutrition is rampant, this group represents a glimmer of hope. The organization's members donate their time and talents to cooking in over 80 community kitchens, where meals are sold at cost or given to those who cannot pay. The kitchens also offer very basic health care. In 1990, Rosa Escalante de Amicama, a founding member of WARMI, received the Alan Shawn Feinstein Award for Public Service.

Selected Print Resources

The variety of references included in this chapter reflects the breadth of perspectives and disciplines relative to the field of global development. From specialized academic journals to how-to manuals for practitioners, this chapter provides information on development-related resources for a wide audience. The first section of the chapter focuses on periodicals and journals, published both in the United States and in the global South. Publications regarding development education are listed because they generally tackle more than pedagogical strategies; they tend to be a very good source of information about substantive core issues. Also included are publications that do not focus squarely on development but on those issues which are intricately tied to it, such as ethics, peace, refugeeism, and other issues.

Following the periodicals section is a listing of annual reports, statistical references, and occasional papers. The final two sections of the chapter focus on landmark monographs and introductory texts, including important articles within these categories. The landmark monographs section includes both early influential texts that framed the development debate and those texts which, in recent years, have challenged those pioneering

265

arguments and changed the terms of the debate. Also included in this section are less theoretical, but equally important, works which provide the historical backdrop to development, and influential texts written for the development practitioner.

Because the "landmark" texts are often specialized to a degree that makes them somewhat inaccessible for the lay reader without a background in development studies, and because the number of publications that concentrate on specific aspects of global development is growing rapidly, it is becoming more difficult to identify those introductory texts that discuss the subject of development more broadly. With this in mind, an annotated list of introductory books and articles is included that provides the reader with an excellent foundation for further study and a useful complement to the landmark texts.

Periodicals and Journals

Africa News (2/week)
Africa News Service
720 Ninth Street
Durham, NC 27720

The frequent publication of this newsletter provides the advantage of covering very current information about events in Africa. Each issue is generally divided into four sections: health, conflict, development, and economics. The interdependence of Africa and the United States is illustrated in many of the articles. Information about recently published books on Africa is included occasionally.

Afrique et Developpement/Africa Development (4/year in French and English)
Africa Development
CODESRIA, BP 3304
Dakar, Senegal

Published by the Council for Development of Economic and Social Research in Africa (CODESRIA), this journal is a forum for the exchange of ideas among African scholars from a variety of disciplines. The major focus is on issues central to the development of African society and offers the valuable perspective of Africans studying the conditions in their own lands. This bilingual journal offers an even distribution between English and French material, and covers such subjects as economic policies, class differences, and the division of labor.

The Ahfad Journal: Women and Change (2/year)
4141 North Henderson Road
Suite 1216
Arlington, VA 22203

Although predominantly concerned with the Sudan, this journal provides Islamic women's perspectives on issues of women as both beneficiaries and agents of development, with a heavy concentration on the subject of women's work in the developing world. Articles range in topics from case studies of women tea sellers to book reviews pertaining to the role of women in development.

Asian Action: Newsletter of the Asian Cultural Forum on Development (4/year)
Asian Cultural Forum on Development (ACFOD)
P.O. Box 26
Bungthonglang P.O.
Klongchan, Bangkapi
Bankok 10242, Thailand

ACFOD, a nongovernmental organization that aims to further the movement of "integral development" in the Asian and Pacific regions, publishes this quarterly newsletter. Short articles, human rights alerts, and investigative reports are featured in each issue. Sample articles include "Internal Refugees in the Philippines" and "Maori Struggle for Self-Determination."

Bridges: Quaker International Affairs Reports (6/year)
American Friends Service Committee (AFSC)
1501 Cherry Street
Philadelphia, PA 19102

These reports, written by AFSC representatives in the field, contain news and analysis from the perspectives of grass-roots leaders, government officials, and ordinary people in the developing world. The reports are designed to be a tool linking "grass-roots leaders and academics, [and] policymakers and those affected by policy." Issues covered include the search for solutions in Somalia and democracy in Thailand.

Caribbean Affairs (4/year)
Trinidad Express Newspapers, Ltd.
35-37 Independence Square
Port of Spain, Trinidad

Tackling issues of trade, debt, and politics in the Caribbean, this journal features a wide editorial range from serious thinkers in the Caribbean Basin. Contributors include scholars, journalists, and politicians. The goal of the journal is to inform readers of the issues affecting Caribbean countries and to encourage and assist in development, progress, and change within the region. The theme of a recent issue was Caribbean migration.

Central America Update (6/year)
Latin America Working Group
P.O. Box 2207
Toronto, Ontario M5S 2T2
Canada

Published jointly by the Latin America Working Group and the Jesuit Centre for Social Faith and Justice, this newsletter offers editorial analysis of U.S. or Canadian foreign policy toward Central America. The North American Free Trade Agreement (NAFTA) and the women's movement in Central America are among the topics covered in the *Central America Update.* Short reports and commentary on a wide range of issues accompany the editorial content.

Choices: The Human Development Magazine (3/year)
United Nations Development Programme (UNDP)
One United Nations Plaza
New York, NY 10017

This magazine, published by the UNDP, contains articles on a variety of development-related topics such as population growth, the informal work sector of Peru, and conservation efforts in Colombia's Pacific Frontier. Articles are written by UNDP staff, journalists from around the world, and politicians. The April 1995 magazine focused on the proceedings from the World Summit for Social Development.

Cultural Survival Quarterly (4/year)
Cultural Survival, Inc.
53A Church Street
Cambridge, MA 02318

This quarterly aims to educate the general public and policy-makers on the challenges facing indigenous groups. Short, informative articles focus on the interaction between indigenous populations of the developing world and encroaching industrialized societies of the developed world. Emphasis is placed on recent global developments, and most of the articles deal with issues of rights and enfranchisement. Each issue also features a list of resources, maps, letters to the editor, and reviews of books and audiovisuals.

Development (4/year)
Society for International Development
1401 New York Avenue, NW, #1100
Washington, DC 20005

Each issue of *Development* is organized thematically around such broad topics as "New Perspectives on Development" and "Reflections on World Solidarity." Contributors to the journal are academics and activists working in the international development community. The diversity of the writers' backgrounds assures that the articles speak to a wide audience. Article topics include grassroots action, human rights, and the world economy. The magazine is also published in Spanish, under the title *Desarollo.*

Development and Change (4/year)
28 Banner Street
London, EC1Y 8QE
United Kingdom

Sage Press publishes this interdisciplinary journal in the United States, which seeks to advance new, nonideological solutions to underdevelopment. Topics related to rural development, regional planning, education, and the role of multinational corporations are all discussed in this publication. The articles tend to be quite technical with a strong empirical basis.

Development and Peace (2/year)
Hungarian Peace Council
V. Szechenyi rkp 6
P.O. Box 1395
Budapest, Hungary

The editors of this publication succeed in demonstrating how development issues are an integral part of peace studies and activism. The journal is "devoted to economic, political, and social aspects of development and international relations." Each issue combines feature articles on a variety of topics with a number of substantive book reviews. Sample articles include "The External Indebtedness of Latin America" and "Interrelations between Militarism, Arms Race, and Economic Development."

Development Dialogue: The Record of Change in Southern Africa (12/year)
Development Media Publishing
102 Samora Machel West, Belvedere,
Harare, Zimbabwe

This newspaper features articles and opinion pieces on a variety of issues related to development in the ten countries of the southern Africa region: Angola, Mozambique, Namibia, Zimbabwe, Swaziland, Malawi, Tanzania, Zambia, Botswana, and Lesotho. The articles, written by field correspondents posted in the capital cities throughout the region, cover such topics as the development of a new crop in Zambia, and indigenous environmental initiatives in Zimbabwe. Environmental issues are covered extensively.

Development in Practice: An OXFAM Journal (3/year)
Oxfam U.K. and Ireland
274 Banbury Road
Oxford, OX2 7DZ
United Kingdom

This journal of "objective assessments of the experience of non-governmental development agencies provides a forum for the exchange of ideas and information among policymakers and field staff, both North and South." An excellent introduction to NGO activity, it contains articles on such topics as conflict, gender, and development training. Evaluation and analysis of Oxfam's, as well as other development organizations' activities, is also offered, providing suggestions for alternative approaches.

Development Policy Review (4/year)
Blackwell Publishers (U.S. publishers)
238 Main Street
Cambridge, MA 02142

The Overseas Development Institute, based in England, publishes this development policy journal. Focusing primarily on economic issues, the review stresses the activities of markets and consumers. Recent issues have focused on "Environmental Values and Their Implications for Development" and the role of public policy in the realm of economic development. Written primarily by academics, this journal is intended for an advanced audience interested in specific fields within development.

Ecoforum (6/year)
Environmental Liaison Centre International (ELCI)
P.O. Box 72461
Nairobi, Kenya

ELCI's goal is to facilitate networking on environmental and sustainable development issues. One of the tools to do this is *Ecoforum*, which is distributed to over 7,000 nongovernmental organizations and individuals in 100 countries. *Ecoforum* focuses on such issues as desertification and sustainable development. Readers are also updated on the activities of the United Nations Environmental Programme. The magazine is available in English, French, Spanish, and Arabic.

Economic Development and Cultural Change (4/year)
University of Chicago Press
5801 S. Ellis Avenue
Chicago, IL 60637

This is a scholarly and somewhat specialized journal that deals with development economics and anthropology. The impact of demographics on market forces in the Third World is a primary focus of the journal; population research and policy studies are another area of attention. Sample articles include: "Marriage

Markets, Labor Markets, and Unobserved Human Capital: An Empirical Exploration for South-Central India" and "Maize of the Ancestors and Modern Varieties: The Microeconomics of High-Yielding Variety Adoption in Malawi."

Ethics & International Affairs (1/year)
Carnegie Council on Ethics and International Affairs
170 E. 64th Street
New York, NY 10021

This annual journal examines the application of ethics to various key international problems from a variety of perspectives. Frequent contributors include Alberto Coll and J. Bryan Hehir. The 1995 issue featured essays on such topics as "Humanitarian Intervention: Three Ethical Positions" and "The United Nations and Global Security." Each issue contains a review essay and a listing of recent books in ethics and international affairs.

Global Pages: Voices from around the World (4/year)
Immaculate Heart College Center (IHCC)
425 Shatto Place, Suite 401
Los Angeles, CA 90020

This quarterly provides readers with global perspectives on a variety of issues, from democratizing education in Brazil to elections in South Africa and Mexico. Each issue highlights a different geographic area. The publication reflects IHCC's mission: to "integrate perspectives from various disciplines and explore how different histories and cultural values affect perspectives on and solutions to world problems." Each issue also contains curriculum suggestions and recommended resources.

Global Perspectives (4/year)
Center for Global Education
Augsburg College
731 21st Avenue South
Minneapolis, MN 55454

The Center for Global Education (CGE) was founded to help North Americans "think more critically about global issues so that they might work for a more just and sustainable world." To this end, one of the center's programs is the publication of *Global Perspectives*, which contains easy-to-read articles written primarily by CGE staff on a variety of issues, such as the consequences of economic and political violence for children. Book reviews and information about the center's travel opportunities are also featured regularly.

Hunger Notes (4/year)
World Hunger Education Service
P.O. Box 29056
Washington, DC 20017

Now in its twentieth year, this quarterly aims to present the facts concerning hunger and poverty both in the United States and in the Third World. Most issues focus on one topic in depth, often using a case study to illustrate the point, such as with Kerala, India, used as a case study of sustainable development. Excerpts of important development-related texts are included, and book reviews and resources are also featured regularly. The fall issue of *Hunger Notes* is always an "all-review" issue, containing up to 25 reviews of new books on hunger, development, and social change written by a panel of professionals in the field.

Hunger TeachNet (4/year)
Interfaith Hunger Appeal
475 Riverside Drive, Suite 1630
New York, NY 10115

This quarterly published by Interfaith Hunger Appeal (IHA) is targeted for educators teaching about development. Articles focus on pedagogical and substantive issues, as well as highlighting case studies from IHA's partner agencies' development projects. Each issue is organized around a different theme, such as linkages between the environment and development and gender and development. Book reviews are a regular feature, as are proceedings from IHA-sponsored curriculum development events.

Ideas and Information about Development Education (4/year)
International Development Conference
1875 Connecticut Avenue NW, Suite 1020
Washington, DC 20009

Ideas and Information about Development Education is a valuable networking tool written for an audience of development educators. This quarterly reports on conferences and educational initiatives by nongovernmental organizations and educational institutions and features articles on such issues as the future of foreign aid. Each issue contains an annotated guide to resources on development and environmental education, compiled by the American Forum for Global Education.

IDS Bulletin (4/year)
Institute of Development Studies
University of Sussex
Brighton BN1 9RE
United Kingdom

The *IDS Bulletin* is designed to bridge the gap between major professional journals and newspapers. Intended for an audience of students, planners, fieldworkers, and administrators, the *IDS Bulletin* is organized into four sections: Perspectives, Principles, Practice, and Prescription. An especially noteworthy issue of the *IDS Bulletin* was the January 1993 issue (vol. 24, no. 1), which was dedicated entirely to the theme of good government. Perspectives on the conditionality of aid in the context of Africa were featured, as well as an analysis of the World Bank's and the U.S. government's positions on the need for better governance in developing countries.

INSTRAW News: Women and Development (4/year)
INSTRAW Information Unit
Avenida Cesar Nicolas Penson 102-A
P.O. Box 21747
Santo Domingo, Dominican Republic

This quarterly, published by the International Research and Training Institute for the Advancement of Women (INSTRAW), "promotes networking on women in development issues at a global level." INSTRAW was established by the UN in 1980 and is involved with women in development issues across a broad spectrum, from women and AIDS to women's involvement in the economic and social sectors. The quarterly is published in English, Spanish, and French and contains feature articles on such themes as "African Women: Coping with Economic Crisis" and "Women in Management." Resource suggestions and editorial essays are also featured.

Journal of Asian and African Studies (4/year)
EJ Brill
P.O. Box 9000
2300 PA Leiden
The Netherlands

This journal presents scholarly accounts of society in the developing nations of Africa and Asia, with an emphasis on pure research for "the reconstruction of societies entering a phase of advanced technology." This scholarly, sophisticated journal is appropriate only for a somewhat advanced audience. Sample articles include "Family Structure and Age at Marriage: Evidence from a South Indian Village" and "The Upgrading of Squatter Settlements in Tanzania."

The Journal of Developing Areas (4/year)
Western Illinois University
900 West Adams Street
Macomb, IL 61455

This useful introduction to the current debates on underdevelopment emphasizes the goal of humanizing abstractions of the development process, such as debt, employment, and the environment. Not only are the more traditional studies of development published here, but also studies resulting from a range of disciplines, from music to philosophy. Recent articles focused on such topics as wage determination in Uruguay, the Indian forestry, and technology adoption in Swaziland.

The Journal of Development Planning (4/year)
Two United Nations Plaza
New York, NY 10017

These papers of the United Nation's Committee for Development Planning focus on the effective implementation of the UN's international development strategy. This specialized journal serves as a policy guide to foster economic and social cooperation between developing countries, and identifies problems and solutions involving economic relations between North and South. Each issue includes roughly ten articles divided into two sections: Policy Articles and Viewpoints.

The Journal of Development Studies (6/year)
Frank Cass and Company Limited
Gainsborough Road
London, E11 1RS
United Kingdom

This journal of economic studies of the developing world is written for a learned audience. Labor issues and trade are frequent areas of focus, and emphasis is often placed on farmers and other agriculture workers. Generally, the articles involve deep analysis of a specific topic, though each issue has at least one article on a broader theme, such as "Issues in Trade, Adjustment, and Debt" and the effects of the GATT agreement on developing countries.

The Journal of Modern African Studies (4/year)
Cambridge University Press
40 West 20th Street
New York, NY 10011

This journal provides an overview of the continent of Africa, including politics, religion, and conflict. The main emphasis is on people and policies, not necessarily development. The journal is written with both the political scientist and practical politician audience in mind. Academics do the bulk of the writing, although development practitioners are frequent contributors. The March 1995 issue included articles such as "The Life and Death of South Africa's Peacekeeping Force"; "Continuity and Change in Franco-African Relations"; and "The UN and the Resolution of Conflict in Mozambique."

Journal of Third World Studies (2/year)
Association of Third World Studies (ATWS)
P.O. Box 1232
Americus, GA 31709

Each issue of this self-described "provocative scholarly periodical" contains three to five academic articles, as well as a collection of shorter papers, book reviews, and review essays. The journal is an important aspect of the ATWS's work in coordinating the interest and activities of "persons who perceive the imperative need for improved understanding of Third World peoples, problems, and issues." Among the issues covered in this journal are human rights, agriculture, and industrialization in sub-Saharan Africa.

Latin American Perspectives: A Journal of Capitalism and Socialism (4/year)
Sage Publications
2455 Teller Road
Newberry Park, CA 91320

This self-styled "Marxist-oriented and anti-imperialist" journal focuses on the political economy in Latin America. Each issue presents a different window theme—for example, "The Ecological Crisis of Latin America"—and the articles focus on a specific aspect of economic interaction and exploitation. A variety of political viewpoints are published, "as long as they are braced by cogent arguments, are grounded in Latin American reality, and are written to be comprehensible to a wide audience."

NACLA Report on the Americas (5/year)
North American Congress on Latin America (NACLA)
475 Riverside Drive, Room 454
New York, NY 10115

After nearly 30 years of publishing this magazine, NACLA has earned a sound reputation for presenting well-documented critical analysis of the political economy of the Americas. Each issue focuses on a single cover theme, with four or five articles analyzing the topic in depth. Past issues have focused on indigenous peoples of Latin America, proposed market solutions, or on specific countries, such as Cuba and Peru. Feature articles are accompanied by short book reviews and letters to the editor.

New Internationalist (12/year)
P.O. Box 1143
Lewiston, NY 14092

This colorful monthly magazine reports on issues of world poverty and inequality, focusing on the relationships between rich and poor nations. Topics of recent issues include the arms trade, the role of the United Nations, and the media. Its goal is "to bring to life the people, the ideas, and action in the fight for world development." Each issue covers a different theme and includes articles, a country profile, recommended resources, and photographs or illustrations.

Peace Review (4/year)
Lynne Rienner Publishers
1800 30th Street, Suite 314
Boulder, CO 80301

Peace Review is a multidisciplinary, international journal of research and analysis focusing on the underlying issues and controversies of the promotion of peace throughout the world. The essays are short, free of academic jargon, and intended for a wide readership. The focus is generally on the cultural and political issues surrounding conflicts between nations and peoples. Distributed to over 40 countries, the journal examines such topics as political economy, refugees, and development.

Population and Development Review (4/year)
The Population Council
One Dag Hammarskjold Plaza
New York, NY 10017

Theoretical articles, case studies, and editorials focus on the interrelations between population and development, and provide a forum for the discussion of related issues of public policy. A variety of topics are covered in this publication, such as the political economy of fertility and the usefulness of gross national product as a yardstick of development. The March 1995 issue focused on social demography and identified characteristics of cultural norms for family size, such as son preference in Korea and the one-or-two child policy in Vietnam.

South: Emerging World Review (12/year)
South Media and Communications Ltd.
128 E. 37th Street, #4R
New York, NY 10016

Formerly entitled *South: The Business Magazine of the Developing World*, this news magazine offers updates on current events in the developing world region. Topics range from AIDS to poverty, and the economic implications of such issues are discussed throughout. Articles are not exposed to great scrutiny, though the various aspects of development are clarified by the report of daily events in the developing world. Once a year the editors publish a chart with information about the top 300 companies from the Third World.

South Asia Bulletin (2/year)
Duke University
Department of History
Durham, NC 27708

The focus of this publication is on the social and economic issues of contemporary South Asia. Written for an audience of Asian-studies professionals and academics, the articles cover such issues as contemporary politics and critical perspectives on class, caste, and state in South Asia. Each issue contains six to eight articles, as well as reports from other publications, texts of selected documents, statistical tables, and book reviews.

Studies in Comparative International Development (4/year)
Transaction Publications
Department 4010
Rutgers University
New Brunswick, NJ 08903

This resourceful journal introduces a range of disciplines to the field of development. Articles exploring the current research into development problems are balanced with articles analyzing the effectiveness and application of development policies. The range in focus is evidenced by such sample articles as "Modernist Discourse and the Crisis of Development Theory" and "Grass-Roots Development Where No Grass Grows: Small-Scale Development Efforts on the Peruvian Coast."

The Third World Quarterly (4/year)
New Zealand House
80 Haymarket
London SW1Y 4TS
United Kingdom

This quarterly is published by the Third World Foundation for Social and Economic Studies, which works to advance the development of Third World nations through advocacy, research, and seminars. This publication, which reflects a strongly Marxist perspective, focuses on the roots of underdevelopment, specifically in recent colonial experiences. Topics covered include neo-liberalism in Latin America and Third World conflicts.

Third World Resources (4/year)
464 19th Street
Oakland, CA 94612

Key development and relief organizations and their print and audiovisual resources are listed in this useful quarterly, which complements the *Third World Resource Directory*, updated biannually. Each issue has a comprehensive guide to organizations focusing on a particular region of the developing world. Reviews of printed and audiovisual materials are also included.

TransAfrica Forum (4/year)
545 6th Street, SE
Suite 200
Washington, DC 20004

This is the publishing arm of the well-known Washington lobby group of the same name. Its mission is to offer "independent and differing perspectives on political, economic, and cultural issues affecting black communities globally." As such, the journal examines not only African governments, but also the socioeconomic development of Africans worldwide. The *Forum* emphasizes U.S. involvement in African affairs, and features such articles as "Abandoning Structural Adjustment in Nigeria" and "Premises, Promises, and Paradoxes: U.S. Policy toward the Black World."

Voices from Africa (1or 2/year)
UN Non-Governmental Liaison Service
866 United Nations Plaza, Room 6015
New York, NY 10017

The UN Non-Governmental Liaison Service, which specializes in development education and facilitates dialogue between development nongovernmental organizations and the UN system, publishes this magazine. Like the Liaison Service's goal, the magazine strives to assist development practitioners and researchers to share their work and ideas with a broader audience. Each issue is centered around a common theme—for example, the role of women in development written by African women. The most recent issue, published in November 1994, focused on sustainable development.

WIN News (4/year)
Women's International Network
187 Grant Street
Lexington, MA 02173

This quarterly is dedicated to news and networking on women's issues around the world, and is written by and for "women of all backgrounds, beliefs, nationalities, and age groups." Topic headings such as "Women and the UN" organize features, news items, and resource suggestions. Additionally, reports from around the world are organized geographically: Africa, Asia and the Pacific, Europe, and the Americas.

World Development: The Multi-Disciplinary International Journal Devoted to the Study and Promotion of World Development (12/year)
Pergamon Journals
Headington Hill Hall
Oxford, OX3 0BW
United Kingdom

Solutions to problems such as poverty, malnutrition, and environmental degradation are explored in this long-established multidisciplinary journal. Each issue contains 10 to 15 articles on such topics as trade and payments imbalances and the lack of popular participation in economic and political life. The articles tend to be somewhat specialized and targeted for a learned audience.

Annual Reports and Occasional Papers

Alan Shawn Feinstein World Hunger Program. *The Hunger Report*. Brown University, Providence, RI.

This annual publication provides updated information on the condition of world hunger. Each report builds a Hunger Profile, a multidimensional assesment for the world as a whole, which takes into account variables such as food shortages, food poverty, and food deprivation. Other issues which receive attention include foreign aid provisions and policies, the global refugee situation, and proposals for eliminating hunger in the future. The 1994 *Report* presents the proceedings from the program's annual Hunger Research Briefing and Exchange, as well as proceedings from the fall 1994 conference in Thailand.

Bergesen, Helge Ole, and Georg Parmann, eds. *Green Globe Yearbook.* Oxford University Press, New York, NY.

First published in 1992, this annual examines the activities of the international community in solving environmental and development problems and the obstacles that stand in the way of effective international solutions. An easy-to-use reference guide identifies major international agreements on the environment and development, including pollution and sustainable forestry. The first part of the report is made up of a selection of analytical papers focusing on the difficult transition from principles to implementation from a variety of perspectives. Nongovernmental and intergovernmental organizations active in this field are also identified.

Bread for the World Institute. *Annual Report on the State of World Hunger.* Silver Spring, MD.

Since 1990, Bread for the World Institute has published their well-known "hunger reports," which not only provide statistics on global health, economic indicators, and poverty and hunger, but also focus on a different window theme each year. The 1994 report focused on the politics of hunger and looked at a range of responses to hunger, from churches' outreach responses to advocacy work. The 1995 report examined the causes of global hunger, including a summary of the latest trends affecting hunger worldwide. Regional hunger updates are also included, as are statistical tables and charts.

————. **Occasional Paper Series.** Silver Spring, MD.

Bread for the World publishes these occasional papers usually two to three times a year. The papers focus on a specific topic or region within the context of hunger and development, such as the Horn of Africa or the Politics of Hunger. The most recent paper, published in May 1995, focused on "The Future of Foreign Aid." Arguing that U.S. foreign aid is at a crossroads, the paper presents a brief background on the U.S. foreign aid program, examines sustainable development as an approach for restructuring aid, and identifies programs within foreign aid which work for sustainable development.

Brown, Lester, et al. *State of the World.* W. W. Norton, New York, NY.

The Worldwatch Institute has published this annual report on international environmental problems since 1983. This internationally acclaimed series examines the state of the environment, where progress is being made, and where the greatest threats lie. The 1994 report recommended actions to safeguard our environment, including strategies to save the world's forests, alternatives to dangerous chemicals, and government policies that improve the status of women. The report is published in 27 languages and is relied upon for the most authoritative environmental information available.

Dahl, Jens, and Alejandro Parellada, eds. *IWGIA Yearbook.* International Work Group for Indigenous Affairs, Copenhagen, Denmark.

This annual report of the International Work Group for Indigenous Affairs assesses the state of the rights of indigenous peoples throughout the world. A formal report on IWGIA's activities comprises Part One of the report, while reports from the public record on indigenous affairs make up Part Two. The texts of reports, documents, and formal declarations relating to indigenous rights make up the final section. Each edition focuses on a different topic; the 1991 edition focused on sustainable development.

Human Rights Watch. *Human Rights Watch World Report.* New York, NY.

This annual survey monitors human rights in 68 countries, identifying global trends and pressing human rights issues. The 1994 *Report* provided an overview of each regions' most significant human rights events. Country profiles include information in the following categories: human rights developments, the right to monitor, U.S. policy during the Clinton administration's first year, and the work of Human Rights Watch's regional divisions (Africa Watch, Americas Watch, Asia Watch, Helsinki Watch, and Middle East Watch).

Overseas Development Council (ODC). *Policy Essay Series.* Washington, DC.

This essay series provides a forum for the discussion of U.S.–developing country relations from a variety of perspectives. Opinions, predictions, and policy ramifications are discussed in a short, easy-to-read format. A recent series focused on the issue of conditionality and aid, discussing such questions as whether the development community can apply conditionality for the goal of poverty reduction, and the effects of multiple aid conditionalities. All of the essays assume that conditionality is only one of a broad range of approaches in promoting noneconomic policy reforms in the developing world. In their U.S.–Third World Policy Perspective Series, the ODC published papers on "Strengthening the Poor: What Have We Learned?" and "Poverty, Natural Resources, and Public Policy in Central America."

Sivard, Ruth Leger. *World Military and Social Expenditures.* World Priorities Inc., Washington, DC.

Each year Ruth Leger Sivard presents an annual accounting of the use of world resources for social and military purposes. Comparing military costs with social needs, Sivard exposes the competition for resources between two kinds of priorities. Each report contains data on the scale and spread of militarization, as well as the human costs of this militarization. World maps reflect such information as unmet human needs and the global spread of arms and armed forces. One hundred forty-two countries are ranked by their military and social indicators.

United Nations Children's Fund (UNICEF). *The State of the World's Children.* Oxford University Press, Oxford, UK.

This annual report on the progress and the challenges of achieving well-being for the children of the world presents a combination of statistics and data, and reports on a variety of topics relevant to children's lives. Data on enrollment in primary schools, deaths and causes, and immunization progress and projections are updated annually. Panels throughout the report offer analysis and discussion on such issues as the effect of AIDS on children and education initiatives taken in Bangladesh. The 1995 report assessed the progress made since the 1990 World Summit for Children and found that in the countries where UNICEF is active, malnutrition had been reduced, immunization levels had been maintained or increased, and the lives of 2.5 million children had been saved. This recent report also served as an important contribution to the 1995 World Summit for Social Development.

United Nations Development Programme (UNDP). *Human Development Report*. Oxford University Press, Oxford, UK.

In 1990, the UNDP set out to measure development using indicators other than the typically used economic indicators. The result was the first *Human Development Report*, which looks at knowledge, political freedom, and community participation, as well as the standard economic indicators in measuring development. As such, this is the only report that analyzes the human dimension of development and examines how growth in national production translates, or fails to translate, into human development; in short, it identifies people, not figures, as the center of development. In addition to analytical articles, the *Report* also ranks over 130 countries in order of their human development index. The 1994 *Report* concentrates on the new challenges brought about by the end of the cold war, outlining a new design for development cooperation, identifying early warning signs of breakdowns in diplomacy, and suggesting a concrete agenda for consideration at the 1995 World Summit for Social Development.

U.S. Committee for Refugees (USCR). *World Refugee Survey*. Washington, DC.

USCR defends the rights of refugees, asylum seekers, and displaced persons worldwide. Their annual survey documents the conditions faced by refugees, and advocates for fair refugee policy. The *Survey* is divided into three sections: feature articles, statistics and country reports, and a directory of organizations providing assistance for or information about refugees. The 1994 report contained five feature articles covering such topics as the situation in the former Yugoslavia and the use of antipersonnel mines. Statistics provide information on the number of uprooted people worldwide, including internally displaced populations.

World Bank. *The World Bank Atlas*. Washington, DC.

The World Bank Atlas presents maps, tables, and charts on a variety of statistics that measure development in over 200 countries. Key

social and economic information is organized under three headings: People, Economy, and Environment. Introductory texts explain the role that each theme plays in world development. New
topics such as infant mortality rates, net primary school enrollment, and size of the female labor force have been added to recent
editions. Data in the Enivronment section include figures on deforestation, energy consumption, and oil consumption as they
relate to gross domestic product. Text is in English, Spanish, and
French.

————. *World Development Report.* Oxford University Press, Oxford, UK.

This annual report contains the World Bank's well-known World
Development Indicators, which provide comprehensive information on the main features of social and economic development. In
addition to the Indicators, the report also offers economic projections for developing countries, information on social sector policies, and discusses the international factors affecting the Third
World. Each report focuses on a different topic such as population
(1992) and health (1993). The 1994 report examined the role and
importance of infrastructure for development, exploring the links
between infrastructure and development and suggesting ways for
developing countries to improve the quality and provision of
infrastructure services. The 1995 report focuses on "Workers in an
Integrating World" and explains how changes in the world economy affect the lives and expectations of workers around the world.
The demand for labor, the functioning of markets, and the factors
that influence labor supply are all covered in this latest report.

————. *World Tables.* Johns Hopkins University Press, Baltimore,
MD.

Current economic, demographic, and social data for 160 economies are updated annually in this report published by the World
Bank. Historical time series based on the bank's collection of data
on its member countries are organized by topic and by country,
covering 1973–1993. The topical pages report GNP, GDP, domestic
savings and investment, imports and exports, and other economic
indicators. The data for member countries are presented on four-
page tables, with data on GNP per capita, population, origin, and
use of resources. The *1995 World Tables* is the last edition to be

published conventionally; future publications of extensive time series data will be obtainable only on CD-ROM.

World Health Organization (WHO). *The World Health Report: Bridging the Gaps.* Geneva, Switzerland.

This new annual report on the global-health situation documents the causes of ill-health and death for each age group throughout the human life span, around the globe. The major causes of death and ill-health are ranked, and a discussion on the ways they can be prevented follows. The report also covers such issues as the causes of infant mortality and the repercussions of ignorance on the projected toll of the AIDS pandemic. Facts and figures presented in the report are balanced with analysis of questions regarding the impact of technology on health and the effects of ill-health on people's lives.

World Resources Institute (WRI). *World Resources.* Oxford University Press, New York, NY.

This series provides accessible, accurate information on the conditions and trends in the world's natural resources and in the global environment. First issued in 1988, the reports represent the collaborative efforts of the UN Environment Programme, the UN Development Programme, and the World Resources Institute. The 1994–1995 report focuses on people and the environment in support of the 1995 UN International Conference on Population and Development. Natural-resource consumption trends and their environmental consequences, population growth, and environmental degradation are among the issues highlighted in this issue. Each volume provides detailed analysis of a different region where environmental and natural-resource issues are especially relevant; China and India are analyzed in the most recent report. Part III of the report provides data on basic conditions and trends, and recent developments in each of the major resource categories, such as agriculture, water resources, and climate.

Worldwatch Institute. *The Worldwatch Papers.* Washington, DC.

The Worldwatch occasional papers series features breakthrough research reports on environmental issues. The first report was published in 1975, and subsequent titles include: "Environmental Refugees: A Yardstick of Habitability," "Women's Reproductive

Health: The Silent Emergency," and "Guardians of the Land: Indigenous Peoples and the Health of the Earth."

Landmark Monographs

Bauer, P. T. *Dissent on Development: Studies and Debates in Development Economics.* Cambridge, MA: Harvard University Press, 1971.

Bauer examines and challenges many of the notions held sacred by dependency theorists regarding development and poverty. This book of essays concentrates on disputing four common perceptions relative to the causes of underdevelopment. Bauer argues that there is not a vicious circle of poverty that perpetuates itself in mutually reinforcing circles, and he disputes the argument that rich countries caused the poverty and inequality in developing countries. He also challenges the notion that development depends on monetary investment, arguing that markets and trade are much more efficient tools of development. Foreign aid also comes under attack in this book; Bauer argues that aid should not be the responsibility of governments, but rather should be left to charitable organizations. Instead of providing aid, governments should assist underdeveloped countries by reducing the barriers to trade and investment.

Boserup, Ester. *Woman's Role in Economic Development.* New York: St. Martin's Press, 1970.

Much of the study and debate about women's roles in development have been stimulated by the publication of this book, which was a fundamental text for the UN Decade for Women. Boserup was a pioneer in putting women and development into the international context by revealing the human dimension of economic development and of development policy issues. She argues that population density provides the means necessary to develop and sustain technological change in agriculture, which in turn alters the work assignments of men and women. In examining the changing gender relations as societies move from shifting cultivation to intensive farming systems, Boserup identifies shifting cultivation as a female farming system, typified by Africa, and plow cultivation as a male system, typified by Southeast and South Asia.

Chambers, Robert. *Rural Development: Putting the Last First.* Essex, UK: Longman Scientific and Technical, 1983.

The central argument in this book is that rural poverty is unseen or misperceived by outsiders. Chambers contends that rural people's knowledge is rarely appreciated or acknowledged, and thus he sets out to challenge, or "reverse," the preconceptions dominant in rural development. The key "reversal" that Chambers advocates is for rural development practitioners and social scientists to put the wishes of the rural poor first, and in doing so additional reversals will follow, such as reversals in learning and in management. Chambers also analyzes the biases that impede outsiders' contact with the rural poor and examines the wealth of knowledge that exists within the indigenous rural community. In short, Chambers proposes a methodology for both practitioners and theoreticians working in the field of rural development that is based on respect and deference, rather than the paternalism that had dominated the methodology in the past.

Charlton, Sue Ellen M. *Women in Third World Development.* Boulder, CO: Westview Press, 1984.

"Women and development" is now a much-used phrase and a discipline critical to understanding development more broadly. Charlton facilitates this understanding with this work, which addresses the role of women in development within a historical and political context. Asking such questions as "who controls development?" and "does development help or hurt women?" Charlton addresses the specific implications of development for women. Part 2 of the book analyzes issues in research on women and links this to public policies. This analysis is then applied to three somewhat controversial case studies—the green revolution, cash crops, and the infant formula debate. The final section of the book surveys alternative development strategies and looks at the agencies involved in development work. Each chapter concludes with suggested supplementary readings, and tables and figures provide useful data throughout the book.

Clark, John. *Democratizing Development: The Role of Voluntary Organizations.* West Hartford, CT: Kumarian Press, 1991.

As development policy advisor to Oxfam U.K., Clark is an apt analyst of sustainable development and the role of nongovernmental organizations (NGOs). Arguing that voluntary organizations should not simply assist the poor in the fulfillment of basic needs, Clark stresses the need for NGOs to empower those they are trying to help and assist them in affecting changes that will render NGO assistance itself obsolete. The historical and potential role of voluntary organizations is explained, as well as the successes and failures experienced by Northern and Southern organizations alike. Clark points out that the most successful organizations have been those with the "ingredients of just development," or DEPENDS: Development of infrastructure, Economic growth, natural resources base Protection, and Democracy and Social justice. This DEPENDS approach has been credited with providing practical guidance for voluntary organizations that aim to reshape local and global development.

De Soto, Hernando. *The Other Path: The Invisible Revolution in the Third World.* New York: Harper & Row, 1989.

A bestseller in Latin America since it was first published, this book has altered the way in which Third World economies and political alliances are perceived. Lima, Peru, serves as the case study for examining the revolutionary world of the informal marketplace and the origins of social injustice and economic failure. Combining detailed analysis of how the economic underground operates with stirring political analysis, de Soto explodes a number of commonly held myths, such as the notion that the economic liberalism written into most Latin American constitutions is the cause of the inequalities and backwardness of those countries, and the belief that the traditions of mestizos and Indians are incompatible with entrepreneurship and competition. The first part of the book examines the operation, growth, creativity, and challenges faced by the black marketeers, while Part 2 looks at the political environment in which they work. Evidenced by the book's huge success and influence, the example of Peru obviously mirrors that of most developing nations.

Fanon, Franz. *The Wretched of the Earth.* New York: Grove Weidenfeld, 1963.

Written over 30 years ago, this book continues to be one of the most powerful articulations of the rage felt by the Third World against imperialism. Fanon, a leading spokesman of the Algerian war of independence, chronicles the role of violence in effecting historical change in the developing world. Analyzing the strengths and weaknesses of national consciousness, Fanon warns his readers against the disappearance of African culture and the dangers of Western culture. Fanon proposes that after generations of suffering from colonial violence, the people of the Third World should "heal" by exacting revenge; he writes that "violence is a cleansing force. It frees the native from his inferiority complex and from his despair." The colonized from Africa, Asia, and Latin America must unite to achieve revolutionary socialism, argues Fanon, "or else, one by one, we will be defeated by our former masters."

Frank, Andre Gunder. *Capitalism and Underdevelopment in Latin America.* New York: Monthly Review Press, 1967.

Frank, one of the most well known of the dependency school theorists, argues that capitalism is responsible for the under-development of Latin America. In this book he uses Brazil and Chile as case studies for this hypothesis. Opening with a reinter-pretation of the history of Latin America, Frank traces the under-development of Chile back through four centuries of capitalist development. The "Capitalist Development of Underdevelop-ment in Brazil" is also examined, as are the effects of capitalism on Brazilian agriculture. Frank's analysis centers on the metropolis-satellite structure of the capitalist system, as he argues that under-developed countries are part of the capitalist world system. As a result, he proposes that the only way for these underdeveloped countries to overcome the shackles that exploit them is to break out of the capitalist system entirely.

Freire, Paulo. *Pedagogy of the Oppressed.* New York: The Seabury Press, 1970.

Freire has revolutionized the way we think about education and revealed the political implications inherent in various methodolo-gies of teaching and learning. In this book Freire analyzes and critiques the dominant form of education, the "banking concept," wherein teachers view their students as empty receptacles passively waiting to be filled by someone else's knowledge. The alternative Freire proposes is dialogical: Both participants, teacher and student, are learners and teachers and education thus becomes "the practice of freedom." Freire's vision of education calls for radical self-awareness, which clearly has political implications, especially in the developing world when this consciousness raising involves opening one's eyes to massive inequality and oppression.

Goulet, Denis. *The Cruel Choice: A New Concept in the Theory of Development.* Lanham, MD: University Press of America, 1985.

Goulet, a pioneer in the field of development ethics, wrote this book with the goal of "thrust[ing the] debates over economic and social development into the arena of ethical values." Goulet's theoretical analysis is centered on the concepts of vulnerability and existence rationality, and the strategies proposed focus on democratic planning, technical cooperation, and the creation of value change. Three principles guide Goulet's ethical strategies for development: that the abundance of goods cannot define the good life, global solidarity is needed for development, and optimum participation in decision making is vital. Goulet points out that development processes are cruel and necessary, and that the benefits of development are often alienating rather than liberating. However, Goulet argues, if development policy is met with ethical priorities the goals of development hold greater promise of being realized.

Hamilton, John Maxwell. *Entangling Alliances: How the Third World Shapes Our Lives.* Washington, DC: Seven Locks Press, 1990.

Hamilton vividly displays how "interdependence has replaced independence" in this follow-up to his well-received *Main Street America and the Third World* (1986). Looking at three developing countries—the Philippines, Kenya and Costa Rica—Hamilton illustrates the process of interdependence and the tangle of connections it creates. The economic, cultural, and environmental ties that connect, in either a liberating or confining way, citizens in this country with those of developing lands are illustrated through the examples of the global data entry business in the Philippines, the Costa Rican rainforest, and the tourism industry in Kenya. The perspectives from citizens from developing countries are also heard in commentaries by journalists throughout the book.

Hellinger, Douglas, et al. *Aid for Just Development*. Boulder, CO: Lynne Rienner Publishers, 1988.

This highly acclaimed report takes a critical look at U.S. foreign aid policies and reveals how the development efforts of the global South have been affected by Northern aid. The authors argue that U.S. aid has resulted in a widening gap between two societies in the South; aid has rarely, if ever, corresponded to local needs and has created an institutional infrastructure in the Third World that has little relation to local reality. In addition to pointing out the shortcomings of aid policies, the report suggests fundamental changes in development assistance structures and proposes a true partnership with the people of the South. The authors identify the Inter-American Fund and the African Development Foundation as two institutions which, with changes, could form the core of an effective development assistance structure. The World Bank and USAID are also critically examined and recommendations for improvement offered. The report's appendices offer a strategy for popular involvement in regional development planning, guidelines for collaboration between major donors and Third World NGOs, and suggested criteria for the selection of projects for funding.

Independent Commission on International Development Issues. *North-South: A Program for Survival*. Cambridge, MA: MIT Press, 1980.

The international leaders who in 1980 set out to examine and offer recommendations for improving North-South relations viewed the upcoming two decades as "fateful for mankind." This report highlights four areas where emergency action is called for: the creation of a global food program to stimulate world food production; a global energy strategy; an increase in financial flows for the stability of national economies strained by debt; and reforms for broader participation in international financial institutions and more balanced conditions for trade. Little attention is given to the role of foreign aid; instead the commission argues for structural economic changes promoting development. While the report certainly issued a warning, the underlying message was that the dangers threatening the world could be averted. However, in the words of the commission's chairperson, Willy Brandt, "The shaping of our common future is much too important to be left to governments and experts alone."

Kaplan, Robert. "The Coming Anarchy," in *Atlantic Monthly.* February 1994, 44–76.

In this stirring, well-known article Kaplan predicts a gloomy future caused by widespread environmental scarcity and decay, crime, disease, overpopulation, and tribalism, all of which are "destroying the social fabric of our planet." Looking closely at West Africa as an example of these frightening realities, Kaplan warns that "we ignore this dying region at our own risk." He identifies four interdependent and mutually supportive conditions which are threatening places such as West Africa today, and the rest of the world in the immediate future: environmental scarcity, cultural and racial conflict, geographic destiny ("the lies of mapmakers," as Kaplan calls it), and the transformation of war. Anarchy, Kaplan argues, is imminent, and while the Western world may passively turn a blind eye to the regions of the world where this is proving to be true, the implications of this violence will not be confined to distant lands for long.

Korten, David. *Getting to the 21st Century: Voluntary Action and the Global Agenda.* West Hartford, CT: Kumarian Press, 1990.

This influential book has brought about a reappraisal of the role of NGOs in development and of the development process itself. Critical of the conventional "growth-centered" development strategies, Korten perceives development as becoming a "big business preoccupied more with its own growth than with the people it was originally created to serve." In response, he proposes a new development vision, one that is people-centered, provides equity-led sustainable growth, and has its base in the voluntary sector. The grass-roots voluntary sector, which the author describes as a distinctive institutional sector, has displayed the creativity and vision that are now vital to the development process. In reviewing the lessons of the 1980s, Korten describes the decade as one of crisis, denial, and opportunities. The opportunities that now lie ahead involve creating a development agenda for the 1990s that calls for a system transformation where mutual empowerment is the goal and the emphasis on growth is replaced by an emphasis on people, ecology, and society.

Lipton, Michael. *Why Poor People Stay Poor: Urban Bias in World Development.* Cambridge, MA: Harvard University Press, 1976.

The most important class conflict in the world, contends Lipton, is between urban and rural classes. Lipton argues that there is an urban bias affecting development policies that has resulted in the improvement in living standards for urban populations but not for rural ones. Taking the position that the development of mass agriculture is a necessary precursor to widespread development, Lipton strongly advocates for the investment in high-yielding mass rural development. This book, which has been the subject of heated debates and analysis, defines the concept of urban bias and provides evidence of its manifestations, such as disparities in welfare and earnings and unbalanced shares in capital.

Meadows, Donella, et al. *Limits to Growth: A Report for the Club of Rome's Project on the Predicament of Mankind.* New York: Universe Books, 1972.

The Club of Rome commissioned the authors of this book to investigate the long-term causes and consequences of growth on population, capital, resource consumption, and pollution. The results of the study created an international furor. Critics from all sides interpreted the report as a gloomy predictor of doom. The authors defend their work by arguing that they were offering choices at a time when wise choices were critical. The report answers the questions: What will happen if the world population growth continues unchecked? What will be the environmental consequences if economic growth continues at its current pace? And what can be done to ensure a human economy that provides for all and fits within the limits of the Earth? The authors argue that while the report certainly issued a warning, it also contained a message of promise—that it is possible to alter growth trends and establish a condition of ecological and economic stability with basic material needs for all.

Twenty years later the authors set out to update the *Limits to Growth* for its reissue and found that human society had reached a new position relative to its limits. The physical limits to human use of material and energy, which were identified in *Limits to Growth* as being decades away, had by 1992 been passed. In short, the resource and pollution flows "had grown beyond their sustainable limits." Instead of updating their report, the authors wrote *Beyond the Limits* (Post Mills, VT: Chelsea Green Publishing, 1992). The conclusions they had drawn 20 years before were reworked, emphasizing that a sustainable society is still possible, but that significant reductions in material and energy flows are absolutely necessary, as well as a drastic increase in the efficiency with which materials and energy are used. The publication of *Beyond the Limits* did not cause nearly the stir its predecessor had. Instead, it quietly joined the growing ranks of important publications calling for sustainable, environmentally sound policies.

Minear, Larry. *Humanitarianism under Siege: A Critical Review of Operation Lifeline Sudan.* Boulder, CO: Lynne Rienner Publishers, 1993.

Operation Lifeline Sudan, launched in April 1989, was made possible by an agreement between the UN, the government of Sudan, and the Sudan People's Liberation Movement/Army to allow humanitarian assistance to pass through the war-torn regions. In an age of growing widespread violence, which has simultaneously increased the need for humanitarian assistance and made it more difficult to provide, this report stands out as a valuable guide for operating within such a context. Minear provides the historical background to the conflict in Sudan and reviews the Lifeline's work on a month-to-month basis. He also explores the issue of sovereignty and discusses how it both accommodated and obstructed humanitarian action. Minear's book is a useful tool for practitioners and scholars alike interested in overcoming the complexities of providing humanitarian assistance within the context of war.

Murdoch, William. *The Poverty of Nations: The Political Economy of Hunger and Population.* Baltimore, MD: John Hopkins University Press, 1980.

Exposing the connections between rich nations' actions and the persistence of poverty, as well as the connections between population growth, inadequate food supply, and poverty were among the motivations behind the writing of this book. Critical of previous approaches to the problems of hunger and overpopulation, Murdoch set out to address these issues, interpret current research, and propose solutions. He analyzes food and population problems in a nontechnical, assessable way, focusing on high fertility and various aspects of food production. Arguing that agricultural development must come before economic development, Murdoch analyzes the internal structures of modern dual economies that support the emphasis on exports and foreign exchange.

Poverty, according to Murdoch, is maintained by the internal political structure of developing countries and by their relationships with rich, industrialized nations. While richer nations certainly do not have the ability to solve the Third World's problems of hunger and overpopulation, Murdoch will have achieved what he set out to do if readers recognize the connections revealed in this book.

Nash, June. *We Eat the Mines and the Mines Eat Us: Dependency and Exploitation in Bolivian Tin Mines.* New York: Columbia University Press, 1979.

This anthropological study of the Bolivian tin miners is regarded as a classical analysis of how the international economic order externally controls, though not necessarily consumes, the lifestyles of those it employs. Bolivia is second in world production of tin, with the lowest indices in per capita income, literacy levels, and life span, and the tin miners are the most revolutionary segment of the Bolivian working class. How these two realities intersect is the subject of this book. Nash explores the ideology of the miners, including their political, social, and cultural definitions, and describes how their belief system affects their work and their lives.

Pearson, Lester, et al. *Partners in Development: Report on the Commission on International Development.* New York: Praeger Publishers, 1969.

In 1969, the Commission on International Development, chaired by former Canadian Prime Minister Lester Pearson, was requested by the World Bank to "study the consequences of 20 years of development assistance, assess results, clarify errors, and propose the policies that will work better in the future." Fourteen experts from various fields and nine different countries made up the commission, and consensus was reached in advocating strongly for more foreign assistance to developing countries. Among the recommendations made were for: the creation of a framework for free and equitable international trade, increased volume of aid, a better partnership between rich and poor nations, a stronger multilateral aid system, and the revitalization of aid for education and research. In today's quasi-isolationist environment, the commission's findings might be considered obsolete and naive. However, this report offers an important insight into the path that development assistance has taken during the past half-century.

Rodney, Walter. *How Europe Underdeveloped Africa.* Washington, DC: Howard University Press, 1981.

Rodney's historical analysis of Africa and the devastating results of its contact with Europe provide a compelling explanation for the continent's current underdevelopment. Rodney begins his analysis with a discussion of the definitions of development and underdevelopment and the dialectical nature of their relationship. He goes on to describe how Africa developed up to the fifteenth century, before the coming of the Europeans, illustrating this development with the examples of Ethiopia and Egypt, among other countries and kingdoms. Africa's contribution to European capitalist development during the pre-colonial period is also examined as the author exposes the roots of African underdevelopment. The coming of colonialism and imperialism is described in detail, with special attention given to the horrors of the slave trade. One of the European rationales for colonialism was to bring an end to the slave trade, and Rodney reveals the hollowness of this argument as he points out that colonialism enabled the enormous expatriation of African surplus, and dealt Africa the most damaging loss of all—the loss of power. Rodney's aim, however, is not simply to expose the Europeans as oppressors and Africans as victims. He argues that the cause of Africa's underdevelopment is the imperialist system and those who manipulated that system, including African accomplices. Rodney set out to examine the past in order to understand the present, and while his historical analysis ends with the end of the 1950s, he proposed solutions for the future, among them a "radical break with the international capitalist system."

Rostow, W. W. *Stages of Economic Growth: A Non-Communist Manifesto.* Cambridge, MA: Cambridge University Press, 1960.

Written over three decades ago, this manifesto continues to spark debate and controversy. Finding Marx's solution of linking economic and noneconomic behavior inadequate, Rostow identifies five stages of economic growth through which modern economies "evolve." The first stage Rostow identifies is the society when it is still "traditional" and prescientific; the second stage occurs when the traditional society is challenged, usually by foreign commerce or conquest, and the opportunities for fundamental change arise. The third stage, which Rostow calls the "great watershed in the life of modern societies," occurs with the development of political power and the recognition of economic growth as a primary objective. Modern technology begins to be applied to a few leading sectors during this stage and society is at the "take-off" point. Drive for maturity marks the fourth stage, in which economic growth spreads to a wide range of activities and society enters the international economic order. The fifth and final stage, which Rostow labeled "the age of high mass consumption," occurs when the economic benefits are distributed throughout society and living standards rise steadily. Rostow's theories have been analyzed, criticized, and by many, discredited; however, they continue to represent an important voice in the development debate.

Sen, Amartya. *Poverty and Famines: An Essay on Entitlement and Deprivation.* Oxford, UK: Oxford University Press, 1981.

This study, launched by the International Labour Organization in 1969, is revered today as one of the most important and path-breaking studies of the causes of starvation, and especially of famines. Sen argues that the traditional analysis of famines that focused on food supply is flawed. Instead, he develops the "entitlement approach," which focuses on issues of ownership and exchange. He goes on to apply this approach to various case studies, such as the Great Bengali Famine of 1943, the Ethiopian Famine of 1973–1974, and the famines in the Sahelian countries in the 1970s. The measurement and characterization of poverty is also critically examined, using the approaches common to economics, sociology, and political theory. Sen succeeds in presenting a technical economic analysis that is accessible to a wide audience; most of the book's economic jargon is reserved for the appendix, where exchange entitlement and poverty measurement are analyzed and examined.

Sen, Gita, ed. *Development Crises and Alternative Visions.* New York: Monthly Review Press, 1987.

Development Alternatives with Women for a New Era (DAWN), a network of Third World feminists, was formed with the goal of creating alternative frameworks and methods to attain the goals of sustainable development free from all forms of oppression. This book is DAWN's "platform document"—"a small step in a much longer process," and was written collaboratively the year before the third UN conference marking the Decade for Women. Bringing together issues of development, social and economic crises, the subordination of women, and feminism, the authors challenge many of the assumptions that came out of the UN Decade for Women. The key assumption, that increasing women's participation and improving their shares in resources are sufficient to effect dramatic improvements in living conditions, is shown to be drastically flawed. Sen and her collaborators argue that women's socioeconomic status worsened rather than improved during the Decade for Women. The reasons for this are explained as the authors show how women's experiences with economic growth are determined by class and gender, and have been since colonial times. The devastating effects of structural adjustment programs are also revealed, as are the links between development policies and current crises. The final chapter of the book proposes strategies and methods to overcome these crises and evaluates the strengths and weaknesses of different types of organizations.

Sheahan, John. *Patterns of Development in Latin America: Poverty, Repression, and Economic Strategy.* Princeton, NJ: Princeton University Press, 1987.

This study focuses on three sets of issues: the persistence of degrees of inequality within Latin America; the nature of economic relations between Latin American countries and the rest of the world; and the close association between market-oriented economic systems and political repression. Sheahan looks at the economic problems common, though not unique, to Latin America, such as poverty, employment, external trade, and industrialization, and examines the various patterns of response by different countries. Early industrialization and violent reaction in Brazil and Argentina are contrasted with the middle-road economies of Mexico, Costa Rica, and Colombia. Two revolutionary alternatives, Cuba and Peru (under Velasco), are also examined and compared with the Marxism and militant monetarism of Chile. The final section of the book explores the connection, which has been in place since the 1960s, between changes toward more market-oriented economic strategies and greater political repression. The role of the United States is also considered as Sheahan raises the question "How are U.S. national interests related to poverty, dependence and repression in Latin America?"

Shiva, Vandana. *Staying Alive: Women, Ecology and Development.* London: Zed Books, 1989.

Shiva's involvement with women's struggles for survival in India led to the writing of this book, which reveals how rural Indian women are arresting the destruction of nature and working toward its regeneration. The dominant development paradigms are, according to Shiva, intrinsic to violence, to nature, and to the marginalization of women. Shiva traces the historical and conceptual roots of development, exposing how Western patriarchy has subjugated the more humane assumptions of economics and created a "crisis of poverty rooted in ecological devastation." She also describes the world of Indian women, from their spirituality and beliefs to their daily activities, and shows how women's movements identify the environment as a living force (*prakriti*) and themselves as partners with it. Analyses of the destruction of the rainforests, the food crisis, and the water crisis also reveal the important and healing role of women's initiatives in countering these crises.

World Commission on Environment and Development. *Our Common Future*. New York: Oxford University Press, 1987.

In 1983, the World Commission on Environment and Development was given the task of studying the global environmental and development problems and formulating realistic solutions. In *Our Common Future*, the commission proposes a "global agenda for change" focusing on the policy areas of population, food security, species and ecosystems, energy, industry, and urbanization. The report also addresses the need for international management and cooperation regarding "the global commons"—the parts of the planet that fall outside national jurisdiction: the oceans, outer space, and Antarctica. Excerpts from speeches made by the various delegates are also included, bringing a personal voice to the urgency of the report's proposals and prognoses.

Introductory Works

Berg, Robert, and Jennifer Seymour Whitaker, eds. *Strategies for African Development*. Berkeley: University of California Press, 1986.

The Commission on African Development Strategies was created to study Africa's long-term development and how U.S. policy can best support it. The papers in this book, also sponsored by the Council on Foreign Relations and the Overseas Development Council, are the result of one of the commission's studies. The essays offer policy and sectoral strategy guidelines and provide analysis of the continent's colonial legacy, its resources, education, and debt, among other issues. The papers are categorized under six headings: managing African economies; the people and the land; agriculture; industry; human resources; and Africa and the world economy. The 18 sector-focused studies yield consensus on a number of issues, such as the necessity of debt relief, the serious threat of population, and the need to strengthen technical, institutional, and human infrastructures. The views on African development expressed here mirror, for the most part, those held by the World Bank, and the contributors are mainly academics or World Bank staffers, such as Chandra S. Hardy, Dunstan Spencer, Jane Guyer, and Lloyd Timberlake.

Davies, Miranda. *Third World—Second Sex,* vol. 2. London: Zed Books, 1987.

The voices of women from the developing world are heard in this collection of interviews and articles. Davies organizes the essays and articles under seven thematic headings: Women, Politics, and Organization; Women at War; Education; Media; Health; Work; and Violence and Sexploitation. The activities of women in these various spheres are described, as well as their thoughts, perceptions, and aspirations. Underlying all the articles is the message advocating the value of international networking and solidarity, and the recognition of these women's vitality and strength. Among the women introduced in this volume are Virginia Vargas, who ran for Parliament in Peru in 1985 and witnessed and shaped the growing role of women's participation in the electoral process, a South African trade organizer, and women in the Guatemalan resistance movement. The book also contains a substantial resources section.

DeSilva, Donatus. *Against All Odds: Breaking the Poverty Trap.* London: Panos Publications, 1989.

This unique book counters the heart-wrenching images of the Third World given to us by Western media. Written and photographed entirely by Southern journalists, this book brings the message that "against all odds" change and development are occurring in the South, and the agents of change are the citizens themselves. The spirit behind nine development projects throughout the world is captured on these pages, from women street dwellers in Bombay building low-cost housing to marginalized farmers in Zambia increasing agricultural production. The projects, which were selected independently by the journalists, are objectively critiqued and provide a real, living example of what development can look like.

Erb, Guy F., and Veleriana Kallab. *Beyond Dependency: The Developing World Speaks Out.* New York: Praeger Publishers, 1975.

The Overseas Development Council, recognizing that too often development policies are made solely by U.S. experts and analysts, issued this collection of essays written by authors from developing countries as a companion volume to their *Agenda for Action* series. The contributors address such issues as high growth rates, the concept of security, international economic systems for trade, finance, investment, food production, and the environment. The first part of the book looks at the internal and external changes necessary to bring about a more equitable interdependence between rich and poor nations. The next section reviews the major issues facing countries in both the North and the South, and then goes on to discuss the issues shaping the current debate between developed and developing nations. The final section of annexes presents a number of the major statements and declarations that document the North-South debate of the mid-1970s.

George, Susan. *A Fate Worse Than Debt.* New York: Grove Weidenfeld, 1990.

The human costs of the world financial crisis are exposed in this illuminating analysis by Susan George, who is not an economist and considers the debt crisis to be "too serious to be left to financiers and economists." George draws the connections between debt and the prevalence of poverty and destruction of the environment. The first part of the book analyzes the actions and motivations of the "players" behind the debt crises—the International Monetary Fund (IMF), the banks, and the "world power structures"—and exposes how these players profited as a result of the crisis. Using case studies from Africa and Latin America, George examines the economic model imposed on the Third World and reveals how debt has affected people and the planet. The final section asks "Now What?" and offers suggestions from diverse perspectives, such as the IMF, the North, the South, and the author herself. George succeeds in explaining the debt crisis in very comprehensible, nonacademic terms, and in so doing makes the realities of it all the more acute.

"Poor Man's Burden: A Survey of the Third World," *Economist,* 23 September 1989, 2–58.

Although this survey was published almost six years ago, it remains an excellent and relevant introduction to development economics and the state of the Third World. Reviewing the lessons that have succeeded and failed in development since the 1950s, the article's main argument is that governments do have a role in development: a role that allows markets to work and supports private enterprise. The survey examines various countries in the global South, from the "dragons" of success to the failures of such countries as Peru and Ghana. Each case study supports the main hypothesis that economies succeed when governments do not intervene, but instead "let prices work."

Tinker, Irene, ed. *Persistent Inequalities.* New York: Oxford University Press, 1990.

This overview of past and current debates that have challenged assumptions about development provides an excellent introduction to the field of women in development. Contributors to this volume include both practitioners and theoreticians from developing and developed countries. The perspectives vary, even contradict one another, yet all include advocacy as part of their underlying goal. The first section focuses on the politics of women in development and reviews such issues as women's organizations worldwide, the interrelations between supporters of the UN Decade for Women and of global feminism, and the socioeconomic impact of export industries set up by multinationals. The second section focuses on intra-household dynamics and includes an essay on food allocation by Amartya Sen. The final section "challenges patriarchy" with perspectives from India, West and East Africa, and the Caribbean.

Selected Nonprint Resources 7

The library or bookstore is no longer the sole destination for people seeking information on global development. Instead, the options include pressing "play" on a VCR and turning on a computer. This chapter is an introduction to the resources available beyond the printed page. The first part of this chapter explores the vast array of available audiovisual resources, while the second part introduces readers to the extensive resource options available through computer databases, software, and the Internet.

Audiovisual Resources, Distributors, and Guides

Listed below are a number of films that focus on various aspects of development—from the role of women to the relationship between the environment and development. This briefly annotated selection includes films for all audiences—academic, lay, and young adults—and covers a range of formats from "talking heads" documentaries to African-made feature films. The distributors for all films listed here are included in the following section, along with additional distributors and their addresses. The final section is a brief listing of audiovisual guides and directories.

Films

Arab Women at Work
Type: VHS
Length: 27 min.
Date: 1990
Producer: United Nations Development Programme

This film shows the many activities, old and new, in which Arab women are engaged, by following them from the office, to farms, and to the home. Experts suggest what can be done to ease the burdens unique to women. Accompanied by a 32-page booklet.

Borrowed from Our Future
Type: VHS
Length: 20 min.
Date: 1989
Producer: United Nations Development Programme

An overview of basic environmental issues is presented here, including population growth, food security, biodiversity, energy, changing climate, urban growth, and rural development. The film shows how the United Nations Development Programme works with governments to promote sustainable development in Ethiopia, India, Morocco, and Bolivia.

Choices for the Next Century
Type: VHS
Length: 37 min.
Date: 1991
Producer: United Nations Development Programme

Inspired by the UNDP's Human Development Report, this film uses Botswana as an example of the positive consequences brought about when a government grants its citizens freedoms and invests in their education and welfare.

The Debt Crisis: An Unnatural Disaster
Type: VHS

Length: 28 min.
Date: 1993
Producer: Friendship Press

This lively video features animation, skits, music, interviews, and film footage from across the Caribbean to show the origins and growth of the region's debt. The links between international financial institutions and burdens on the Caribbean people, such as high prices, low wages, and declining health and education systems are all exposed. The film does not offer ready-made solutions, but instead encourages discussion about the debt problem. A study guide is included.

Dialogue on International Development
Type: VHS
Length: 20 min.
Date: 1989
Producer: Bullfrog Films

This film tackles questions relevant to any development discussion, such as the importance of social justice, the accountability of development practitioners, and methods of evaluation. Discussion participants represent Canadian governmental and nongovernmental organizations.

Documental World SHARE
Type: VHS
Length: 15 min.
Date: 1993
Producer: World SHARE/Guatemala Video

In 1986, representatives from World SHARE conducted a feasibility study for a community assistance program in Guatemala. Today, SHARE has become a leading NGO in Guatemala, working with over 40 local indigenous agencies. This video shows how it is the community that organizes, plans, and implements programs in technical assistance and support and forcefully makes the point that development ultmately happens at the grass-roots level.

Environment under Fire: Ecology and Politics in Latin America
Type: VHS
Length: 28 min.

Date: 1988
Producer: Environmental Project on Central America; also available from Church World Service

This video explores the issues behind the environmental crisis in Central America along with potential solutions, and looks closely at the links between environmental degradation and poverty. Top Central American and United States environmentalists provide further perspectives. The destruction of the rainforest, as well as other environmental hazards, are vividly documented. Included with each video is information on the work of the Environmental Project of Central America (EPOCA).

Femmes aux Yeux Ouverts (Women with Open Eyes)
Type: VHS
Length: 52 min.
Date: 1994
Producer: California Newsreel (in French with English subtitles)

This film, produced by Togolese filmmaker Anne-Laure Folly, presents portraits of contemporary women in four West African countries: Burkina Faso, Mali, Senegal, and Benin. The film asks What role are women playing in Africa's current movement toward democracy? A journalist, a health worker, a businesswomen, and others discuss this question and reveal how African women are speaking out and organizing around five key issues: marital rights, sexually transmitted disease, female genital mutilation, women's economic role, and political democracy.

Finzan: A Dance for Heroes
Type: VHS and 35mm
Length: 107 min.
Date: 1990
Producer: California Newsreel (in Bambara with English subtitles)

This film tells the story of two Malian women's rebellion and their struggle to control their own lives. A painfully realistic portrayal of village society tragically unable to free itself from the past, *Finzan* dramatically illustrates how the customs which bind the community together also drive out these women. An effective meditation, not only on the discontinuities sometimes inherent in the development process, but of the particular vulnerabilities of women in development as well.

Fragile Mountain
Type: VHS
Length: 60 min.
Date: 1989
Producer: Sandra Nichols Productions

The hills of the Nepalese Himalayas are fast approaching their capacity to support human life. Rapid population growth and overgrazing of livestock and deforestation have resulted in soil erosion and flooding. This video visits communities in the Nepalese hills and shows the innovative community efforts under way, including feeding livestock with harvested grasses, planting trees, and using solar power instead of firewood.

Growing Up in the World Next Door
Type: VHS and16mm
Length: 59 min.
Date: 1989
Producer: Bullfrog Films

Three teenagers, from Nepal, Kenya, and St. Vincent, are interviewed at the age of 12 and again at age 18. They describe their goals and each one explains how they were troubled in some way by an international development project.

Images
Type: VHS
Length: 20 min.
Date: 1992
Producer: U.S. Committee for UNICEF

This video takes a candid look at the images portrayed by the media and international organizations of the Third World. It discusses the possible bias in the media against the developing world, and questions whether relief and development agencies play up or exploit tragedies for their own purposes, such as raising funds. A study of various UNICEF educational and fund-raising campaigns is also included.

Invisible Workers
Type: VHS
Length: 20 min.
Date: 1988
Producer: Martha Stuart Communications (in Gujarati with English voice-over)

This video introduces the Self-Employed Women's Association (SEWA), a well-known Indian self-help cooperative. The video shows the many ways that SEWA members are engaged in home-based production, and how SEWA has succeeded in providing literary training and support services and forming trade groups.

Kume Kuch: From Sun-Up
Type: VHS
Length: 28 min.
Date: 1987
Producer: Maryknoll Films

In their own words, Tanzanian women describe their daily work-filled schedules and their cash income initiative, a beer-brewing collective. This film portrays the strength and intelligence of these women and is an inspiring depiction of the common bonds of motherhood and sisterhood.

Local Heroes, Global Change
Type: VHS (in four parts)
Length: 60 min. each
Date: 1989
Producer: Church World Service

A four-part television series, first aired on PBS-TV, *Local Heroes* examines the assumptions about development, power, learning, and interdependence. The series succeeds in making the complex issues of international development relevant on a individual level while focusing on such issues as the role of women in rural development, international trade, the experience of citizens taking control of their destiny, and the connections between the global North and South. The series presents a new look at the developing world through the eyes of the people overcoming poverty and creating positive change.

Love, Women and Flowers
Type: VHS

Length: 58 min.
Date: 1988
Producer: Women Make Movies (in Spanish with English subtitles)

More than 60,000 women work in the flower industry in Colombia where they are exposed to dangerous pesticides and fungicides, many of which have been banned in the developed world. The group of women interviewed for this video speak about their frequent illnesses caused by this exposure, and about their lives more generally. A poetic and moving film that has relevance both for women's studies and environmental studies.

The Money Lenders: The World Bank and International Monetary Fund
Type: VHS
Length: 85 min.
Date: 1992
Producer: Richter Productions

This film offers a critical perspective on the financial power and policies of the two major financial institutions. Five case studies examine the various activities of the World Bank and the IMF in developing countries. It also features interviews with senior officials from the two institutions, as well as with economists, labor organizers, and ordinary citizens of the Third World.

My Life, Our Struggle
Type: VHS
Length: 43 min.
Date: 1979
Producer: Third World Newsreel (in Portuguese with English subtitles)

This film is the story of group of women in São Paulo, Brazil, who led a community struggle to achieve their basic necessities, such as child care, nutrition, and jobs. It reveals important insights on how Third World women can successfully organize.

Nyamakuta: The One Who Receives. An African Midwife
Type: VHS
Length: 32 min.
Date: 1989
Producer: Filmmakers Library

A traditional African midwife narrates her own story and provides an intimate look at the lives of Third World women.

The Politics of Food
Type: VHS (in five parts)
Length: 20 min. each
Date: 1987
Producer: Church World Service

The Politics of Food is a five-part series that illustrates how food distribution and hunger are tied to politics and business. Program segments are: *The Food Machine,* which introduces the global effects of agribusiness; *The Hunger Business,* which explains how the ways in which agricultural products are traded affects wealthy nations and poor ones; *A Question of Aid,* which compares Bangladesh and Kerala, India, to show alternative approaches to development; *The Avoidable Famine,* which reveals how changes in farming methods affected the economy and society of Sudan; and *Sharing the Land,* which shows how the rapid industrial expansion in Brazil did not "trickle down" to the majority of society.

The Poverty Complex
Type: VHS
Length: 24 min.
Date: 1992
Producer: Church World Service

This video looks at the underlying causes of poverty and hunger, as well as offering potential solutions. The role of the World Bank and International Monetary Fund are also explored, and the Human Development Index (HDI), the new yardstick for measuring progress, is further explained.

Producing Miracles Everyday
Type: VHS
Length: 23 min.
Date: 1990
Producer: Adobe Foundations

This documentary portrays the thriving informal economy of Latin America, showing Latin Americans of all ages using their resourcefulness to create their own employment and income.

A Quiet Revolution
Type: VHS
Length: 60 min.
Date: 1988
Producer: Cinema Guild

This film introduces viewers to the importance of liberation theology in Latin America by showing the efforts of the Christian Base Communities to solve their problems of hunger, poverty, and political oppression. Three communities in Brazil, Ecuador, and Peru are examined, as well as interviews with community activists and religious leaders, including the "father of liberation theology," Gustavo Gutierrez.

Raiz de Chile/Chile's Roots
Type: VHS
Length: 50 min.
Date: 1991
Producer: Icarus Films

Chile's two largest indigenous groups are introduced in this film: the Aymara, who live in the Andes of northern Chile, and the Mapuche, who live in the middle region. The film explores the connections between the groups' customs and practices and the outside world. Through interviews of Aymara and Mapuche, viewers learn of their passionate ties to the land, their contributions to contemporary Chilean society, and the efforts to maintain their communities in the face of encroaching modernization.

Sango Malo: The Village Teacher
Type: VHS
Length: 94 min.
Date: 1991
Producer: California Newsreel (in French with English subtitles)

Sango Malo is a valuable look at the realities of a Cameroon village and the innovative efforts of a young teacher and his conflicts with his headmaster's Eurocentric curriculum. The film presents a powerful argument for populist education as a key component of "human-centered" development.

Seeds of Promise: The Critical Roles of Third World Women in Food Production

Type: VHS
Length: 18 min.
Date: 1988
Producer: OEF International

Designed for use by community organizations and educational institutions, this video introduces viewers to the critical roles of women as primary food producers in the developing world. Women in El Salvador, Honduras, and Senegal are shown in various income-generating activities. The video comes with a guide and 28-page booklet by Dr. Jane Jaquette.

Spaceship Earth: Our Global Environment

Type: VHS
Length: 25 min.
Date: 1990
Producer: Video Project

Aimed at a seventh- to twelfth-grade audience and hosted entirely by young people, this video illustrates the interdependence of the world's human, natural, and technological systems. By examining environments around the globe, it focuses on the issues of deforestation, global warming, and ozone depletion.

Ta Dona—Fire!

Type: VHS and 35mm
Length: 100 min.
Date: 1991
Producer: California Newsreel (in Bambara with English subtitles)

This pioneering Malian film is among Africa's first environmental features. Focusing on the themes of modernity and tradition within the context of rural development in Mali, the film tells the story of a young agricultural expert's quest for a secret Bambara herbal remedy. The film premiered at the Pan-African Film Festival in February 1991, where it won the award for best first feature.

Voices for Development

Type: VHS
Length: 20 min.

Date: 1990
Producer: Catholic Relief Services

This video introduces viewers to the concept of international development and explains the reasons why Americans, and Catholics in particular, should care about supporting development efforts.

What Is UNICEF?
Type: VHS
Length: 27 min.
Date: 1991
Producer: UNICEF, distributed by PDR Productions

This video explores five different issues facing the children of the world today by interviewing children about their lives and how they perceive the lives of children in the developing world. Scenes from around the world are portrayed, and the information is clear and comprehensive.

Where Credit Is Due
Type: VHS
Length: 69 min.
Date: 1990
Producer: National Film Board of Canada, distributed by
            Indiana University Audiovisual Center

This three-part series examines the issue of women's access to credit in the African context. The film tells the story of a woman who inherited her mother's stall at the market in Nairobi, Kenya, and how, with the help of a loan from Women's World Banking, an innovative credit program, she is able to expand her business and offer goods to the luxury hotels of the capital. A touching and effective argument for the necessity of providing women with access to credit.

With These Hands
Type: VHS and 16mm
Length: 33 min.
Date: 1987
Producer: Church World Service

This film presents the life stories of three women from Burkina Faso, Kenya, and Zimbabwe. Interspersed throughout the film are various graphics revealing such statistics as the percentage of food grown in Africa by women (75 percent) and the level of spending by the UN on projects for women (less than 1 percent). The film argues that the lack of support for Africa's women farmers may be a major cause of food shortages.

Audiovisual Distributors

Africa Family Films
P.O. Box 1109
Venice, CA 90291
(213) 392-1020

American Friends Service Committee (AFSC)
Film Library
1501 Cherry Lane
Philadelphia, PA 19102
(215) 241-7000

Bullfrog Films
Oley, PA 19547
(800) 543-FROG

California Newsreel
149 Ninth Street
Suite 420
San Francisco, CA 94103
(415) 621-6196

Catholic Relief Services (CRS)
Global Education Office
209 West Fayette Street
Baltimore, MD 21201
(410) 625-2220

Church World Service (CWS)
Audiovisual Library
P.O. Box 968
Elkhart, IN 46515
(219) 264-3102

The Cinema Guild
1697 Broadway, Suite 506
New York, NY 10019-5904
(800) 723-5522

Eco Media Private Ltd.
P.O. Box 8594
Thiruvanmiyur PO
Madras 600 041
India
(44) 41-48832

EcuFilm
810 12th Avenue
Nashville, TN 37203
(800) 251-4091

Friends of the United Nations Environment Programme
2013 Q Street, NW
Washington, DC 20009
(202) 234-3600

Icarus Films Inc.
200 Park Avenue South
Room 1319
New York, NY 10003
(212) 674-3374
(Exclusive distributor of the "Africa Film Library")

**Indiana University
Audiovisual Center**
Center for Media and Teaching Resources
Indiana University
Bloomington, IN 47405-5901
(812) 855-8087

Maryknoll World Production
Media Relations
Maryknoll, NY 10545
(800) 227-8523

**Mennonite Central
Committee**
Resource Library
21 South 12th Street
Akron, PA 17501
(717) 859-1151

OEF International
Development Education
Program
1815 H Street, NW
Suite 1100
Washington, DC 20006
(202) 446-3430

PDR Productions
219 E. 44th Street
New York, NY 10017
(212) 986-2020
(Distributor for all UNICEF films)

Third World Newsreel
335 West 38th Street
New York, NY 10018
(212) 947-9277

**United Nations Children's
Fund (UNICEF)**
Radio, TV and Film Unit
3 United Nations Plaza
New York, NY 10017
(212) 326-7290

**United Nations Development
Programme (UNDP)**
Division of Public Affairs
Room DC1-1910
One United Nations Plaza
New York, NY 10017
(212) 906-5301

U.S. Committee for UNICEF
331 E. 38th Street
New York, NY 10016
(212) 686-5522

The Video Project
5332 College Avenue
Suite 101
Oakland, CA 94618
(800) 475-2638

West Glen Communications
1430 Broadway
New York, NY 10018
(212) 921-0966

Women Make Movies
225 Lafayette Street, #207
New York, NY 10012
(212) 925-0606

World Bank Film Library
1818 H Street, NW
Washington, DC 20433
(202) 477-8350

Guides to Audiovisuals

African Studies Centre. *Africa on Film and Videotape: A Compendium of Reviews.* East Lansing: Michigan State University, 1982.

Lists over 750 reviews of films and videotapes on Africa available in the United States. Indexed by topic, country, and language.

Burton, Julianne. *The New Latin American Cinema: An Annotated Bibliography of Sources in English, Spanish and Portuguese, 1960–1980.* New York: Smyra Press, 1983.

Cyr, Helen. *The Third World in Film and Video, 1984–1990.* Metuchen, NJ: Scarecrow Press, 1991.

Continuation of the 1976 publication *A Filmography of the Third World.* Includes videocassettes as well as 16-mm films. Most films listed were made during the 1980s. Information is presented under geographical categories organized by continent and area, with brief annotation.

Media Network. *In Her Own Image: Films and Videos Empowering Women for the Future.* New York: 1992.

Contains critical reviews of 82 films and videos that explore a wide range of issues facing women in developing countries, as well as in the United States and Europe. Includes ordering information and addresses and phone numbers of film distributors.

Schmidt, Nancy. **"Films by Sub-Saharan African Women Filmmakers (A Preliminary Filmography)."** *African Literature Association Bulletin,* vol. 18, no. 4, 1992.

Television Trust for the Environment. *Moving Pictures Bulletin: The Quarterly Guide to Films on Development and Environment.* London, U.K.

Magazine published four times per year; includes articles, photographs, and film and video listings.

Computer Resources

This section offers an introduction to the abundance of computer resources available today—from databases and software to wide-area networks. While computer users have an increasingly wide variety of network choices, such as America Online and Prodigy, this chapter focuses on the Internet because it is the largest and most used. Additionally, the chapter concentrates on the World Wide Web, rather than alternative browsers, such as Gopher and File Transfer Protocol (FTP) sites, for similar reasons and because the Web provides access to virtually everyone on-line.

Global Networks

The Internet is the largest of the global networks and is expanding the entire concept of information retrieval, exchange, and communication. The Internet was developed in 1969 by the U.S. Department of Defense as a method to connect various radio and satellite networks and allow scientists to communicate and share information. Other networks soon developed and became linked by using common communication protocols. One of the most important of these new networks was the NSFNET, commissioned by the National Science Foundation, which was responsible for creating five supercomputer centers at major universities, thus making the resources of the network available for academic research for the first time. Today, the majority of four-year colleges are connected, as well as most local libraries. The range of resources available on the Internet grows every day and includes mailing lists, on-line libraries and databases, e-mail access, and the World Wide Web.

Mailing Lists

Electronic mail (e-mail) is still the best-known and most popular application on the Internet. Listserv is the Internet's e-mail handling program. It provides mechanisms that allow users to contribute to named mailing lists that distribute messages to all subscribed members. There are a number of mailing lists geared for an audience interested in global development issues—and, like most aspects of the Internet, the numbers are growing. Mailing lists usually have free subscriptions, and the range in quality of discussions emerging from the list can vary enormously. Listed below are the addresses of a few discussion groups that might appeal to this book's audience, but bear in mind that new lists are created on a daily basis.

Canadian Association for the Study of International Development

To subscribe, send the following message "subscribe casid-l yourname" to listserv@mcgill1.

The Environment in Latin America Network

This discussion group focuses on the diverse ecosystems that are the site of intense political and economic struggles in Latin America. It also undertakes such tasks as coordinating a series of papers for conferences (such as the Latin American Studies Association meeting of fall 1995). To subscribe, send the following message "sub ELAN yourname" to listserv@csf.colorado.edu. Further information on this group is also accessible through the CSF's page in the Web.

International Development Network. To subscribe send the following message "subscribe auidn-l yourname" to listserv@listserv.american.edu.

International Political Economy Network

This discussion group is also hosted by CSF and features discussion on such topics as NAFTA, international debt, democracy, and governance. Also publishes on-line draft articles and syllabi. To subscribe send the following message "sub IPE yourname" to listserv@csf.colorado.edu.

Studies in Women and the Environment

This international discussion group, hosted by Communications for a Sustainable Future (CSF), is a forum for the exchange of information and ideas in the field of women's studies and environmental concerns. Grass-roots activism, legislative action, and upcoming events are all discussed at this site. To subscribe, send the following message "subecofem yourname" to listserv@csf.colorado.edu.

SOC-SUMMIT

The Social Summit list, sponsored by the UN Development Pro-gramme, facilitates a broad discussion of such issues as alleviating poverty, expanding employment, and enhancing social integra-tion. To subscribe send the following message SUBSCRIBE SOC-SUMMIT to listservconfer.edc.org.

THRDWRLD

This list is sponsored by the Association of Third World Studies for the academic, diplomatic, and development communities. To subscribe send the following message "SUB THRDWRLD your-name" to thrdwrldgsuvm1.gsu.edu.

Because new groups are created with such frequency, printed directories are out-of-date before they even reach the shelf. The best way to find a list that fits your interests and needs is on the Internet itself: Send a message that reads "list global" for a com-plete listing of all global groups on the Internet.

Usenet is another software program, similar to listserv, that enables users to participate in the more than 14,000 discussion or news groups currently on-line. The program allows users to read messages and post responses in any discussion area. Unlike list-serv, newsgroups do not require special subscriptions, and there-fore messages are stored on the Internet host where the newsgroup is located, not on a subscriber's computer.

The World Wide Web

The World Wide Web is the newest information service and has quickly become the predominant method for accessing the In-ternet. Based on a technology called "hypertext," the Web is per-haps the most flexible and easy-to-use tool for discovering the Internet. Hypertext is a way of representing information with built-in references, commonly known as "links," to related infor-mation. It is the Web's capacity to facilitate "roaming and brows-ing" that has contributed to its staggering growth; in 1991, at the end of its first year of existence, there were some 500 Web sites, but by February 1995 the number was close to 5 million. For those climbing aboard the "information superhighway," the Web is, for now at least, the most popular way to establish a presence on the Internet.

The Web is truly democratic; there is no hierarchical or centralized system to the way in which it is organized. Any individual, company, or governmental agency can create their own home page (Web site) and make it accessible. Listed below are the addresses (URLs) and brief descriptions of a number of Web sites relevant to development studies. A number of these sites are gophers rather than Web sites, but all are accessible through the Web.

African Studies Program WWW
URL: http://www.sas.upenn.edu/African_Studies/AS.html

This database, established in 1994 at the University of Pennsylvania, includes information on African studies programs and resources around the world, such as articles, audiovisual resources, governmental documents, and information on grants, fellowships, and job opportunities. E-mail address: aadinar@sas.upenn.edu

Alliance for a Global Community
URL: gopher://vita.org/11/int/interaction/alli

This gopher document, accessible through the Web, provides a detailed description of the Alliance and why its work is important. The 115 Alliance member organizations are listed and agency descriptions (including non-Alliance members) are categorized as follows: governmental organizations, U.S.-based organizations, regional and national NGOs, and indigenous or local NGOs. Additionally, the Alliance Newsletter is published on-line. The site also includes the Alliance's 1994–1995 calendar of events, news clips, a glossary, and a number of 12-page articles on such issues as the successes of microenterprises and immunization efforts. Introductory articles on hunger, the environment, and education are also published on-line and provide excellent overviews of these topics. E-mail address: alliance@interaction.org

Communications for a Sustainable Future (CSF)
URL: http://csf.colorado.edu

CSF is the collective effort of a number of scholars dedicated to enhancing computer networking on global themes. In addition to hosting a wide range of discussion groups or listservs, CSF also publishes a wealth of information on its Web site. The CSF home pages provide further information and mail archives for their lists (some of which are noted above). Additionally, its IPENet site offers retrievable documents regarding the global political economy indexed thematically and geographically. CSF's newest link, the electronic bookstore and review of books, is still being developed and will soon sell on-line books from a range of publishers as well as publish current book reviews. E-mail address: gonick@csf.colorado.edu

Consultative Group on International Agricultural Research (CGIAR)
URL: http://www.worldbank.org/html/cgiar/HomePage.html

The CGIAR, jointly sponsored by the World Bank, FAO, UNDP, and UNEP, supports international research centers in 12 developing countries which are looking into ways to harness modern science for the sustainable development of agriculture in the developing world. This home page, also accessible through the World Bank's Web site, provides detailed information on the CGIAR, including press releases and the full text of their newsletter, published three or four times per year. A directory and further information of CGIAR's 16 research centers is accessible, as well as proceedings from meetings and a link which provides detailed analysis and information of one sector of CGIAR's activity: food crops relative to technological development. E-mail address: dlucca@worldbank.org

Development Information Service Online (DEVLINE)
URL: http://www.ids.ac.uk

Hosted by the Institute of Development Studies in Sussex, England, DEVLINE provides information on economic and social development and the relationships between rich and poor countries. The following services are available: IDISDB, an on-line catalogue and journal article database of more than 80,000 monographs, serials, and periodicals from the British Library for Development Studies; EGUIDE.DB, a compilation of electronic information sources on development studies; PEOPLE.DB, a listing of development studies specialists; and COURSES.DB, a listing of development studies courses in the United Kingdom. Updated annually. E-mail address: d.beer@sussex.ac.uk

Envirolink Network
URL: http://envirolink.org:/start_web.html

This is the largest on-line environmental information service in the world, reaching over 550,000 people in 98 countries. This home page features access to environmental information services and environmental resources for teachers and students, including a listing of all schools, elementary to higher education, which have access to the Internet. The page also contains an Enviroarts gallery, which displays an ecclectic collection of visual arts, poems, and the like. E-mail address: admin@envirolink.org

HungerWeb
URL: http://www.hunger.brown.edu/hungerweb/

A project of the Alan Shawn Feinstein World Hunger Program at Brown University, HungerWeb aims to facilitate the free exchange of ideas and information about sustainable development. The Web site is organized with four audiences in mind: researchers, advocates/activists, teachers and trainers, and fieldworkers. Policy documents, information on teaching resources, and current information on various development crises or programs are among the resources available at this site. As with most Web sites, access to other relevant home pages is also possible, such as ISA, the Internet Non-Profit Center, and the UN's home pages. E-mail address: whpweb@brownvm.brown.edu

IISDnet
URL: http://iisd1.iisd.ca/

The International Institute for Sustainable Development (IISD) is a nonprofit organization established by the governments of Canada and Manitoba to promote sustainable development. Their home page collects information regarding sustainable development activities, initiatives, and projects around the world. Resources available through IISDnet include: *Linkages,* a clearinghouse for information on past and upcoming meetings relevant to development; the Youth Sourcebook on Sustainable Development; and the Earth Negotiations Bulletin. Information about IISD's activities and publications is updated monthly. E-mail address: reception@iisdpost.iisd.ca

Institute for Global Communication (IGC)
URL: http://www.igc.apc.org/

IGC, the U.S. member for the Association for Progressive Communication, runs five computer networks—PeaceNet, EcoNet, ConflictNet, LaborNet, and WomensNet—which link over 11,000 members in 133 countries. The IGC home page provides further information on each of these networks, as well as subscription information and instructions for participating in on-line conferences. Also on the home page are biographies of IGC staff, board, and volunteers. IGC's bimonthly newsletter is published on-line, and news and featured articles are available and updated frequently. A complete listing of on-line conferences is accessible, indexed by subject area. E-mail address: igc-info@igc.apc.org

InterAction
URL: gopher://vita.org/11/intl/interaction/iact

This Web-accessible gopher document provides detailed information on InterAction: its role, mission, and activities. The 160 member organizations are listed, as well as InterAction's newsletter highlights and situation reports. Background information to various crises throughout the world is published on-line, with information about the agencies responding and updated situation reports. Advocacy information is also provided: how to lobby, talking points in support of foreign assistance, and more. Also accessible are recent speeches delivered on the subject of foreign aid: for example, Brian Atwood's remarks on foreign aid, given to the Center for National Policy. E-mail address: ia@interaction.org

International Service Agencies (ISA) Online
URL: http://www.charity.org/

An annotated listing of 55 premier North American voluntary organizations working to alleviate poverty throughout the world. Many of the development organizations listed in the Organizations chapter of this book are listed here, including Catholic Relief Services, CARE, and AFRICARE. Organizations are indexed according to their focus: children, education, hunger relief, medical care, refugee/disaster assistance, or economic support. Each organization has a 1–2 page description, and donation information is also provided by ISA. E-mail address: isa@dgs.dgsys.com

OneWorld Online
URL: http://www.oneworld.org

This "world-wide conversation on development" was launched publicly in January 1995. The site was developed by OneWorld Broadcasting as a meeting place where people who care about development can exchange ideas and information. Regular features on the page include emergency news, feature stories on development from around the world, conference reports, resources, and TV and radio schedules pertaining to programming about development. E-mail address: oneworld@bbcnc.org.uk (an archive of mail received via e-mail is also available at this site).

Praxis—International and Comparative Social Development
URL: http://caster.ssw.upenn.edu/~restes/praxis.html

This is an excellent reference guide to a broad range of national and international data regarding social and economic development. Dr. Richard Estes of the University of Pennsylvania, who developed this site, offers access to an array of archival resources for teachers and students interested in development and also for those interested in international social work resources. This 32-page site provides links to a wealth of home pages, including international organizations, development studies information services, maps, and government resources. E-mail address: restes@caster.ssw.upenn.edu

United Nations Development Programme (UNDP)
URL: http://www.undp.org/

A wealth of information about the UN agencies, especially the UNDP, is available at this site. The UNDP statement of purpose and governing structure is available, as well as descriptions of program activities and copies of current press releases. Current information about the UN, including a defining description, General Assembly documents, and official documents and proposals from UN summits are all available on-line. Additionally, comprehensive links to other UN agencies and related organizations are accessible. Also on hand is a listing of WWW servers worldwide and environment-related information. In recognition of its fiftieth anniversary, the UN has set up a page to link Internet information on any of the local UN activities around the world. E-mail address: jdsouza undp.org

US Agency for International Development
URL: gopher://gopher.info.usaid.gov/

This is a gopher document, though it is accessible through the Web. The database includes an agency-wide overview, information on USAID development efforts, congressional presentations, strategy papers on economic growth, speeches on stabilizing population growth, and resources and publications. Main files include: Why Foreign Aid?; Agency-Wide Overviews; Supporting Broad-Based Economic Growth; Protecting the Environment; Promoting Democracy; and Documents and Publications. E-mail address: gopher-admininfo.usaid.gov

Volunteers in Technical Assistance (VITA)
URL: gopher://gopher.vita.org/

VITA works to assist developing countries through the provision of information services and technologies. This home page offers further information about VITA's mission, goals, and activities worldwide. VITA's current annual report is published on-line, and their publications catalogue is updated regularly. Additionally, VITA publishes on-line *DevelopNet News*, a monthly publication, which is available at the following address: gopher://gopher.vita.org/11/intl/dnn. E-mail address: vita@vita.org

World Bank
URL: http://www.worldbank.org//

This site provides easily accessed information about the World Bank—what it is, how it is structured, and information about its programs worldwide. Detailed publication information is also provided, including the capacity to order resources on-line. A new policy on disclosure brought about the establishment of the Public Information Center (PIC), which makes previously restricted documents available to the public. This Web site provides information about the PIC, including information on documents and ordering information. The Operations Evaluation Department, an independent evaluation unit, is also accessible, with information on the bank's lending policies and processes. Various sectors of the bank also have their links here, such as the Finance and Private Sector Development and Human Resource Development sectors. Additionally, information about current research the bank is engaged in is also at hand, such as the Living Standard Measurement Study and the Economic Growth Study. E-mail address: services@worldbank.org

World Health Organization (WHO)
URL: http://www.who.ch/

As well as providing useful information about WHO, this site offers current information and data on health situations throughout the world, such as the Ebola virus and the AIDS epidemic. Major WHO programs are described, such as the Division of Communicable Diseases and the Division of Drug Management and Policies. Also accessible is the Statistical Information System list of databases, as well as numerous discussion spaces, such as that of the WHO Nursing Board. WHO's publications and ordering information are updated regularly. E-mail address: postmasterwho.ch (Additionally, the entire e-mail directory for WHO staff is accessible.)

World Neighbors
URL: http://www.halcyon.com/fkroger/wn.html

This home page for the well-known international development organization offers information about the agency, as well as descriptions of their projects arranged by country. Articles on various development issues, such as women in development, are published on-line, and information on how to visit project sites is also provided. Helpful links to other development studies information sites are listed, as is the World Neighbors resource catalogue. E-mail address: fkroger@halcyon.com

A new Web site comes on-line somewhere in the world every 20 seconds. As a result, one of the most helpful Web sites to be familiar with is one that will itself help you navigate the Web. Yahoo is an example of a well-known search engine that looks for documents based on titles and key words. Yahoo's URL is: http://www.yahoo.com/. The Web's explosive growth makes using an on-line search tool much more effective than consulting printed directories.

On-Line Databases

The largest on-line bibliographic company in the United States is Dialog Information Services, which offers the Knowledge Index, launched in 1981. Dialog provides access to over 450 on-line databases and over 45 CD-ROM titles. Most of the databases listed below are available on the Knowledge Index. Another on-line database company is BRS/After Dark, a low-cost, menu-driven service offering over 130 databases, many of which are also offered by Knowledge. Dialog is accessible through the Internet by using the Web; the URL is: http://www.dialog.com/

AGRICOLA
U.S. Department of Agriculture
Beltsville, MD

Established in 1970, this database contains over 2.5 million citations of periodical articles, government reports, theses, and technical reports on topics such as: agricultural economics, agricultural production, animal sciences, and food technology. A vital, comprehensive source for rural development studies. Information is updated monthly. Available on: Knowledge Index, BRS, BRS/After Dark, and DIMDI, as well as on CD-ROM.

Central America Update
Latin American Institute
University of New Mexico
Albuquerque, NM

An electronic current events news analysis bulletin produced as part of the Latin American Data Base (LADB) at the University of New Mexico, *Central America Update* includes reports and analyses written by LADB staff from U.S., European, Asian, and Latin American news service sources. Covers political, military, economic, social, and cultural developments in Central America. Information updates twice a week. Available by subscription from Bitnet or NewsNet.

Economic Literature Index

This database includes journal articles and book reviews from 260 economic journals and approximately 200 monographs per year. Information is updated quarterly. Available from Knowledge Index.

Enviroline

Includes articles from over 3,500 journals covering all areas of environmental concern. Updated ten times per year. Available from Dialog Information Services.

National Newspaper Index

Features front-to-back indexing of the *Christian Science Monitor, New York Times,* and the *Wall Street Journal,* and includes all articles, editorials, letters to the editor, reviews, etc. Additionally, it covers both national and international stories written by staff writers of the *Washington Post* and the *LA Times.* Updated monthly. Available from Knowledge Index.

Software: Compact Disks and Diskettes for Personal Computers

Adjustment in Africa. Washington, DC: World Bank, 1995. $14.95

A 3.5" double-density diskette for use on personal computers with a hard drive, at least 512K of RAM, and MS-DOS 2.1 or higher. The statistical data from the World Bank's *Policy Research Reports* Series, the disk contains the most recent available data as well as the data used in writing the *Reports.* Allows users to view single items, construct and view a table on-screen, or export the data for use in other programs. The diskette should be used in conjunction with the printed report, as the text of the report is not included.

Compact International Agricultural Research Library, Basic Retrospective Set 1962–1986. Washington, DC: World Bank/Consultative Group on International Agricultural Research (CGIAR). $495.00

This set of 17 CD-ROM disks, produced by CGIAR, provides a comprehensive library of agricultural research. It includes the complete text, images, and catalogue records for some 1,350 titles originally published by CGIAR's agricultural centers worldwide. Also included are over 50,000 monochrome images such as graphics and photographs. Among the research areas covered is that of helping developing countries to formulate and carry out effective agriculture and food policies, and building links between institutions in developing countries and other elements of the global agricultural system. Translated into 11 languages. System requirements: IBM-compatible computer with at least 550K of memory and standard CD-ROM drive. Also available in Macintosh format, delivered on HyperCard stacks called DataStacks.

DAC Aid Performance. Washington, DC: OECD Publications and Information Center. $265.00

The statistical data included on these diskettes cover the flow of financial resources from the individual members of the Development Assistance Community (DAC) to developing countries and multilateral organizations over the past 20 years. Data are also given on Official Development Assistance and total flows as a percentage of Gross National Product (GNP), population, and GNP deflators of DAC countries. Diskettes are 3.5" or 5.25", double-sided, and formatted on both sides.

Earth Summit on CD ROM. New York: United Nations Publications. $495.00

Contains over 40,000 pages of information on the Earth Summit proceedings, including AGENDA 21, the Global Partnership for Environment and Development, Official Statements, National and Regional Reports, the Prep-Coms, and UNCED Research Papers. An easy-to-follow manual is included. System requirements: 386 PC or higher, 4MB RAM and 1.5MB available on hard disk. Software must be DOS 3.3 or higher, Windows 3.0 or higher, and Microsoft CD-ROM Extensions 2.0 or higher.

Social Indicators of Development 1995. Baltimore, MD: Johns Hopkins University for the World Bank. $26.95

This 3.5" double-density diskette provides the latest social data for 191 economies, including estimates of fertility, mortality, illiteracy, access to health care, and shares of Gross Domestic Product (GDP) for selected social expenditures; 87 social and economic indicators are also included. System requirements: IBM-compatible personal computer with a hard disk, at least 512K RAM, and MS-DOS 2.1 or higher.

Statistical Yearbook on CD-ROM. New York: United Nations Publications. $249.00

The *Statistical Yearbook* presents an overall, comprehensive description of the world economy, its structure, major trends, and recent performance—for all countries and areas of the world. Includes over 140 tables of systems in image form as well as database format. Data available as of 1 September 1992. System requirements: 386 PC or higher; 4MB RAM; 5MB available on hard disk;

512K free memory, and 1MB of expanded memory. Also must have DOS 3.3 or higher.

UN EARTH Version 1.0 The United Nations: What It Is and What It Does. New York: United Nations Publications. $95.00

UN EARTH is a convenient, user-friendly, PC-based package of two diskettes produced to provide information from many sources of the United Nations system. Information can be retrieved by country, organization, region, politico-economic grouping, or globally. Booklet included. System requirements: 12MB of hard disk and at least 500K of memory.

World Data 1994: World Bank Indicators on CD-ROM. Washington, DC: World Bank. $275.00

This is the most comprehensive set of statistical data the World Bank has ever produced. Features over 700 time-series indicators of World Bank national accounts and data for over 200 economies, covering the period from 1960 through 1992. The product includes data sets from *World Tables*, *World Development Tables*, and *Social Indicators of Development*, as well as the full text from *Trends in Developing Economies*. The data are updated annually, and the CD is accompanied by a 24-page guide. System requirements: 512K memory and MS-DOS version 2.1 or higher.

World Development Report on CD-ROM, 1978–1995. Washington, DC: World Bank. $375.00 (annual renewal $95.00)

This CD-ROM product presents all 18 *World Development Reports* published by the World Bank, together with the *World Development Indicators 1995*. Going back to the first report issued, which focused on Development in the International Economy, this series brings the reader up to the current report, *Workers in an Integrating World*. An easy-to-use search engine makes this a valuable, accessible resource. System requirements: Windows 3.1; a minimum of 4MB RAM and a 386 or faster; and a CD-ROM drive to MPC level 1 specifications.

World Resources Data Base Diskette. New York: Oxford University Press. $99.95

This reference tool contains all of the vital economic, population, natural resource, and environmental statistics found in the print edition of *World Resources,* plus 20-year time-series for many variables. Each diskette pack includes a comprehensive user's manual and 3.5" and 5.25" high-density, IBM-compatible disks. System requirements: IBM-compatible personal computer with a hard disk and at least 512K RAM.

Glossary

absolute poverty The income level below which a minimally nutritionally adequate diet plus essential nonfood requirements are not affordable. World Bank president, Robert McNamara, coined this term to describe "a condition of life so degraded by disease, illiteracy, malnutrition and squalor as to deny its victims basic human necessities."

adult literacy rate Percentage of persons age 15 and over who can read and write. The adult literacy rate is one of the indicators used to measure human development.

AFSC *See* American Friends Service Committee.

Agricultural Trade Development and Assistance Act Known also as the Food for Peace Act, this law provides food aid to selected countries as relief or at reduced cost. Passed in 1954, billions of dollars of food aid have been shipped under the act, which has achieved important humanitarian ends, but has also been widely criticized for its negative economic effects on donor nations and local food producers. Public Law 480 is the short name for the act.

American Friends Service Committee (AFSC) AFSC is one of the oldest relief and development agencies, founded in 1917 by American Quakers. It is currently active in over 25 countries.

Association of South East Asian Nations (ASEAN) ASEAN was established in 1967 to foster and encourage economic support, social progress, and cultural cooperation in the Southeast Asian region.

asylum Legal protection granted to refugees from another country.

balance of payments The difference between a country's receipts and payments. Balance of payment consists of two main accounts: a current account, which includes balance of trade, and a capital account, which includes investments. A balance of payments deficit occurs when a country's payments exceed receipts.

Basic Human Needs approach A strategy adopted in the 1970s that focused development assistance on those programs that directly met the basic needs of the poorest segments of a population. Basic needs were identified as: sufficient nutritious food and clean water, adequate shelter, protection from disease, and elementary education.

bilateral aid The transfer of funds, goods, and/or services directly from one government to another.

Brady Plan The plan unveiled in 1989 by U.S. Treasury Secretary Nicholas Brady as a possible solution to the international debt crisis. The plan called for shared responsibilities and benefits designed to renew economic growth and stability among debtor countries.

Brandt Commission Officially known as "The Independent Commission on International Development," the commission was established in 1977 to study the global issues arising from the disparities between North and South. Chaired by former West German chancellor, Willy Brandt, the commission published two reports: *North South: A Program for Survival*, in 1980, and *Common Crisis North-South: Co-operation for World Recovery*, in 1983.

Bretton Woods Conference Negotiations held in Bretton Woods, New Hampshire, in 1944, attended by 45 states and leading world economists to design the postwar economic order. The goals were to ease the reconstruction of Europe and to foster international trade and economic integration. The talks called for the creation of what today are often known as the "Bretton Woods Institutions": the World Bank, the International Monetary Fund (IMF), and the General Agreement on Tariffs and Trade (GATT).

Brundtland Commission The informal name for the World Commission on Environment and Development, which was established in 1983 by the UN General Assembly to propose long-term strategies to deal with global environmental problems. The commission was chaired by Norwegian Prime Minister, Gro Harlem Brundtland, and in 1987 published the report, *Our Common Future.*

Canadian International Development Agency (CIDA) CIDA is the official governmental agency mandated to administer Canadian development assistance.

capital flight The transfer of capital by the economic elite of Third World countries to safe havens in developed countries. The wealth is converted to foreign exchange, and thus implies a loss of resources that could have been nationally invested. Capital flight is very hard to measure because much of it is secret or illegal.

CARE One of the world's largest humanitarian nongovernmental organizations, CARE was founded in 1945 and today assists over 30 million people in more than 53 countries with relief assistance and development planning. When it was first founded in 1945, the acronym CARE stood for "Co-operative for American Remittances to Europe"; however, as the scope of the agency's work extended beyond war-torn Europe, CARE came to stand for "Co-operative for Assistance and Relief Everywhere."

carrying capacity The term used by ecologists to describe the ability of an ecosystem to support life.

cash crop An agricultural product grown for the purpose of being sold, usually in international markets, rather than for consumption as in subsistence farming. Typical cash crops include tobacco, cotton, coffee, and cocoa.

Catholic Relief Services (CRS) Founded in 1943, CRS is one of the largest relief and development organizations in the world and is currently active in 79 countries.

Church World Service (CWS) CWS was founded in 1946 and is the collective expression of 32 U.S. Protestant and Orthodox denominations' commitment of development and assistance in the Third World.

CIDA *See* Canadian International Development Agency.

commodity Articles and goods traded on the international market. Commodities are primary goods that come directly from the ground without the added value of industry—agricultural goods or mineral products that are mined or extracted from the earth—and they often comprise the bulk of developing nations' exports. Commodity goods are distinguished from industrial or finished goods that are mostly produced by the more developed economies and are subject to a wide variation of price, leaving Southern economies vulnerable to market shifts.

community development The promotion of the process through which people gain an understanding of the socioeconomic conditions in which they live, define their own needs, and discover the means of meeting them. On a local level, community development focuses on grassroots initiatives and self-help schemes.

concessional terms The conditions of a loan that provide lower interest rates and/or longer payback periods than do commercial loans. The International Development Association (IDA) is the World Bank's concessional loan associate, offering loans to the poorest developing countries.

conditionality A set of techniques used by aid donors to encourage policy reforms in developing countries by tying the provision of aid to the sought-after reforms. The concept of conditionality is controversial in that it implies coercion on the part of wealthier nations or institutions. Recipient countries are often required to adopt such policies as reducing government spending or ending human rights violations.

CRS *See* Catholic Relief Services.

CWS *See* Church World Service.

DAC *See* Development Assistance Community.

Debt crisis The emergency in the world's financial system in the 1980s and 1990s is called the international debt crisis. Western banks and multilateral institutions lent aggressively to Southern nations in the 1970s, and when these debts could not be repaid in a timely manner, the solvency of banks and the finances of Southern governments was called into question. To receive further funds, Southern governments were asked to adopt structural adjustment policies. As a result, social services, health care programs, and food security measures were cut throughout the South.

debt forgiveness The cancellation of all or part of the obligation to pay a debt.

deforestation "The permanent depletion of the crown cover of trees to less than 10 percent" is the official UN definition. The term is commonly used to describe the destruction of forest or woodlands, mainly by logging, overgrazing, or clearing. The threat of deforestation is most severe in tropical forests, particularly in South America.

dependency theory One of the principal paradigms of development that argues that Third World underdevelopment is caused by the patterns and interests of developed countries. Based on historical analysis that looks at the long-term effects of colonialism, dependency theorists argue that developing countries have always been dominated by the needs of advanced capitalist states and made dependent on the markets of developed countries. Development, according to this theory, can only occur when the capitalist relationship is broken, either by revolution, independence from a capitalist system or through the creation of a new international economic order.

desertification The creation of dry, desert-like conditions due to natural changes in climate or human mismanagement. The man-made causes of desertification are overcultivation, overgrazing, deforestation, and poor irrigation.

devaluation The lowering of the value of a country's currency relative to the currency of other countries. Devaluation can be the unintended result of trends in the international currency market or a governmental policy required under the terms of a structural adjustment program.

developed countries The term used to describe countries with relatively high per capita incomes. Today, developed countries are also characterized with high productivity, low illiteracy rates, low birthrates, strong infrastructure, and market economies.

developing countries The approximately 130 countries in Africa, Asia, and Latin America where all or some of the following characteristics are found: The majority of the population is living in poverty; there is little or no industry; and there are high birthrates, low life expectancies, malnutrition, and poor housing. Most developing countries have economies based on the exportation of raw materials. *Developing countries* is often used interchangeably with "less developed countries," "Third World countries," and "the global South."

Development Assistance Community (DAC) Development Assistance Community of the Organization of Economic Cooperation and Development (OECD) was established in 1961 as a 17-member committee to provide a forum for donor governments to consult and cooperate with each other on aid policies.

development banks International banks that provide loans and technical assistance to developing countries to help in their development. The banks typically raise funds on international markets and through member-country contributions. Examples include the Inter-American Development Bank and the Asian Development Bank.

drought A prolonged period of dry weather often worsened by human actions. Droughts are sometimes caused by a shift in climate brought on by deforestation.

ecofeminism Theory that draws a parallel between dominance and violence toward women and dominance and violence toward the environment. Ecofeminism argues that development is flawed because it is based on patriarchal Western paradigms that stress control over nature and over women.

economic development An increase in a country's economic growth rate, or Gross National Product, caused by the more efficient use, production, and distribution of resources, goods, and services.

export-led growth Governmental policies that emphasize the production of finished goods for export. Countries that followed this strategy include Japan, South Korea, and Singapore, all of which experienced extraordinarily rapid growth rates. In Japan, elements of export-oriented growth included early and successful land reform, massive education programs, and the promotion of labor-intensive export industries.

family planning   Planning that is geared to achieve a desired number and spacing of births. It usually implies efforts to limit births, though it also means efforts to induce pregnancy.

famine   A widespread lack of access to food. Before the publication of Amartya Sen's *Poverty and Famines*, it was widely believed that famine was caused by a sudden deficiency in food supplies. Sen has effectively revealed the social and political roots of famine, in proving that famines are caused when a section of a population loses access (or entitlement) to food.

FAO   *See* Food and Agriculture Organization.

food aid   Assistance or aid in the form of commodities, such as cereals, wheat, oils, and milk powder, given to a developing country by a donor government.

Food and Agriculture Organization (FAO)   Founded in 1945, FAO is a specialized agency of the UN that works to raise levels of nutrition and standards of living by improving production and distribution of all food and agricultural products. FAO also monitors the world food situation through its Global Information and Early Warning System.

food security   The state of being assured a supply of food adequate to sustain growth and life. Food security can be achieved by direct access to agricultural lands, by income sufficient to purchase food on the market, or by social policies that guarantee food to all in times of shortage.

foreign aid   The provision of either loans or outright contributions (funds or services) from one government to another, either directly (bilateral) or through an intermediary institution such as the World Bank (multilateral). The Development Assistance Community (DAC) stipulates that grants or loans must be below current market rates to be considered aid. Foreign aid can also include emergency assistance.

free trade   Trade that is not subjected to any restrictions, such as quotas or tariffs.

GATT   *See* General Agreement on Tariffs and Trade.

GDP   *See* Gross Domestic Product.

General Agreement on Tariffs and Trade (GATT)   GATT is a multilateral trade agreement that came out of the Bretton Woods agreements of 1944 with the goal of liberalizing world trade. It promotes the equal treatment for all trading nations, negotiated tariff reductions, and the elimination of import quotas.

GNP   *See* Gross National Product.

Green Revolution The term used to describe the development of high-yielding strains of wheat, corn, and rice in the Third World that resulted in an upsurge in production, specifically in Mexico and India in the late 1960s.

Gross Domestic Product (GDP) GDP is the total value of goods and services produced by an economy in a given year.

Gross National Product (GNP) GNP is a broad measure of an economy's performance. It measures the total value of all goods and services produced by a nation in a given year plus income residents receive from abroad, minus similar payments made to nonresidents who contribute to the economy. The term *per capita GNP* refers to the gross national product of a nation divided by its population.

Group of 77 The 77 developing countries that formed a coalition at the first meeting of the United Nations Conference of Trade and Development in 1964. Today the term is generally applied to the caucus of all developing countries in the United Nations.

Human Development Index The ranking, formulated by the United Nations Development Programme (UNDP), based on health conditions, literacy, and access to goods and services. The three indicators used in the index are: income per capita, converted according to purchasing power; adult literacy rate; and life expectancy. The UNDP revealed that a high ranking on this index is not necessarily associated with high average incomes.

human settlements The term used to refer to both housing and the surrounding environment.

hunger A condition in which people lack the basic food intake to provide them with enough energy and nutrients to allow them healthy, productive lives. There is no universally accepted definition of hunger, though recent research indicates that hunger is a function of poverty and disempowerment rather than of food scarcity.

IBRD *See* World Bank.

IDA *See* International Development Association.

IFAD *See* International Fund for Agricultural Development.

IMF *See* International Monetary Fund.

Imperialism The political and economic domination of distant nations, the dominating country being called the *imperial power*. Imperialism is usually associated with European overseas expansion between 1500 and 1900, when Spain, France, England, Germany, and other countries controlled many parts of today's global South. Native cultures were often suppressed by the imperial power, and the occupying powers sometimes subjected indigenous peoples to enslavement and exploitation. Also called *colonialism.*

import-substitution Government policies, common in the 1950s, that encouraged the domestic production for domestic consumption of goods that were being imported. This was a strategy for improving a country's balance of payments and increasing its self-sufficiency. The strategy also advocated the imposition of quotas and tariffs to keep foreign goods out. Some countries even made it illegal to import any product that could be made at home. Countries that adopted import-substitution policies include Chile (during the 1960s) and India (during the 1960s and 1970s).

indigenous peoples Ethnic groups who have resisted assimilation and extermination by nonnative cultures and who have maintained the integrity of their culture and way of life. The UN estimates that there are approximately 300 million indigenous people. Other terms to describe indigenous people include Indians, aborigines, autochthonous peoples, and natives or "first nations."

infant mortality rate The annual number of deaths among children under the age of one, per thousand live births.

informal economy Part of the economy that is not recognized by the government, also referred to as the "black market." It operates parallel to the official economy, and arguably contributes greatly to the country's balance of payments, national income, and employment.

infrastructure The basic facilities and services that are essential to the functioning and development of an economy, such as transportation, communications systems, and water and power facilities. Infrastructure can also refer to social infrastructures such as schools, health facilities, and housing.

internally displaced people People forced to flee their home communities due to "refugee-like" conditions, but who remain within the country.

International Development Association (IDA) IDA was established in 1960 as the concessionary arm of the the International Bank for Reconstruction and Development (IBRD). It provides loans to the lowest-income countries (countries with annual per capita income of about $800 or less) on more favorable terms than those offered by the IBRD. Loans, or "credits," have a service charge but are interest free and allow a ten-year grace period. *See also* World Bank.

International Fund for Agricultural Development (IFAD) IFAD was established in 1977 as the only UN institution that focuses exclusively on agricultural projects for the poorest farmers in the developing world.

International Monetary Fund (IMF) The IMF was established in 1945 to promote stability in the international monetary system. The IMF offers loans on the condition that the receiving country adopts a plan that takes measures to correct the deficit. However, the IMF is not primarily a lending institution, rather it is an overseer of its members' monetary and exchange rate policies.

land reform The reorganization of the existing system of land ownership to bring about a more equitable division of ownership, use, and control of the land. It is often considered one of the most important prerequisites for development.

Least Developed Countries (LDC) LDC is the designation given by the UN to those countries which fulfill the following criteria: gross domestic product of less than a certain figure (in 1989 the figure was $300); manufacturing represents less than 10 percent of Gross Domestic Product (GDP); and an adult literacy rate of less than 20 percent. LDCs are sometimes referred to as "Fourth World" countries. Of the 47 nations officially labeled LDCs, 31 are in Africa.

Lutheran World Relief (LWR) The relief and development organization that represents the Lutheran Church-Missouri Synod and the Evangelical Lutheran Church. LWR is known for its effectiveness in establishing partnerships with local, indigenous development efforts.

LWR *See* Lutheran World Relief.

macroeconomics The study of an entire economic system in terms of goods and services produced, total income earned, and overall level of investment and employment. An example of a macroeconomic indicator is change in gross domestic product.

maldevelopment The term used by theorists advocating alternative development policies to describe those aspects of development which have had an extremely negative effect on developing economies. Megaprojects, such a dam-building, that dislocate populations and worsen social inequality are often cited as examples of maldevelopment.

malnutrition Physical and/or mental health impairment caused by the failure to achieve nutrient requirements. Malnutrition can be caused by inadequate food intake or by a shortage or imbalance of key nutrients.

Malthusian theory A population theory originated by Thomas Malthus (1766–1834) who argued that population was growing faster than food production, thus if fertility is not controlled, disasters such as famines and wars will act as natural population restrictors. Today, Malthusian theory is considered a pessimistic assessment of population growth that too heavily emphasizes birth control programs.

market economy An economy in which decisions on allocation of resources, production, investment, and distribution are made by supply and demand. Usually, market economies are based on a system of private ownership.

Marshall Plan The informal name for the European Recovery Program launched by the United States in the aftermath of World War II. The plan dispensed over $13 billion between 1948 and 1952 and is widely hailed as a key factor in Europe's rapid return to economic security.

MCC *See* Mennonite Central Committee.

Mennonite Central Committee (MCC) One of the oldest non-governmental organizations, formed in 1920 for domestic and international programs in emergency relief and development.

microeconomics The study of a portion of an economy, such as a consumer group, commodity, or industry, and the distribution of production and income among them.

modernization theory This theory of explaining the origins of poverty and underdevelopment argues that the underdevelopment of the Third World is caused by developing countries' lag in transforming themselves from traditional societies to modern ones. It argues that developing countries need only to follow the steps taken by industrialized nations to develop.

multilateral aid Contributions from several countries to an international, intermediary institution, such as the World Bank, that then allocates the aid to recipient countries.

nationalization The process of government takeover of previously private business. While nationalization of key industries was a popular development strategy several decades ago, most economists now believe that market forces manage businesses better than governments, and so today nationalization is disfavored generally.

New International Economic Order (NIEO) The proposals made by the Group of 77 in 1974 for restructuring the international economy and redressing the economic imbalances felt by developing nations.

Newly Industrialized Countries (NICs) These are the nations whose economies are no longer primarily agricultural and whose export base typically includes more industrial (or secondary) products than commodities. Many of these nations have industrialized with aggressive export-led strategies. Examples of NICs are South Korea and Taiwan.

NGO *See* Nongovernmental organization.

NICs *See* Newly Industrialized Countries.

Nongovernmental organization (NGO) NGOs are independent, non-profit charitable organizations involved in aid giving and regional development. The term *PVO*, which stands for "Private Voluntary Organization," is interchangeable with NGO and is used more frequently in the United States.

North-South   The term used to describe the economic division of the world between the developed countries of Europe, North America, and the Far East, and the developing countries of Africa, Asia, and Latin America.

ODA   *See* Official Development Assistance.

OECD   *See* Organization for Economic Cooperation and Development.

Official Development Assistance (ODA)   Defined by the Development Assistance Committee (DAC) as "grants or loans undertaken by the official sector with the promotion of economic development and welfare as the main objectives." These are funds provided to developing countries and multilateral agencies. The funds must be concessional, contain a grant element of at least 25 percent, and be administered with the prime objective of promoting development.

OPEC   *See* Organization of Petroleum Exporting Countries.

oral rehydration therapy   Simple, low-cost treatment for diarrhea consisting of salt, water, and sugar. Diarrhea drains the body of fluids and nutrients, causing dehydration, which is the largest single killer of children.

Organization for Economic Cooperation and Development (OECD) Made up of most of the world's developed and industrialized nations, the OECD's purpose is to further economic growth and to encourage cooperation among its members.

Organization of Petroleum Exporting Countries (OPEC)   OPEC was established by major oil exporting countries in 1961 and acts as a cartel to promote the joint economic interests of its members.

Oxfam America   One of seven autonomous Oxfams around the world, the original being the Oxford Committee for Famine Relief, founded in England in 1942. Oxfam America funds self-help development and disaster-relief projects in Africa, Asia, and Latin America and does not accept funds from any government.

Pearson Commission   A commission headed by former Prime Minister Lester Pearson of Canada in 1967 to review and propose strategies for international development assistance. The commission published their report *Partners in Development* that called for donor governments to set a target for overseas development assistance at 0.7 percent of gross national product (GNP).

population density   The number of people per unit area of land.

poverty line   An official measure of poverty defined by national governments.

primary health care   Low-cost, simple health services that include family planning, a clean water supply, sanitation, immunization, and nutrition education. The focus is on disease prevention and detection rather than treatment.

privatization The process of government divestiture of publicly held companies. While in past years, governments often acquired key industries in the belief that central planning could ensure just development, most economists now believe that market control of business is the best means of ensuring growth. Hence, many nations have privatized key industries, raising public revenues by selling businesses to private concerns.

protectionism Trade barriers imposed to restrict the inflow of imported goods from another country. Import-substitution strategies often call for the imposition of tariffs and/or quotas on imports to curtail foreign competition and supposedly to insulate the economy from external influences and potential crises.

Public Law 480 *See* Agricultural Trade Development and Assistance Act.

recession A period of reduced economic activity, marked by a decline in productivity and employment that if prolonged can lead to a depression. A recession is defined by two consecutive quarters of decline in major economic indicators.

refugee A person outside his/her home country who has a well-founded fear of persecution if he/she were to return because of race, religion, nationality, political opinion, or membership in a particular social group. The countries that have generated the largest number of refugees in recent years are Afghanistan, Mozambique, and the former Yugoslavia.

relief Assistance offered to ameliorate short-term crises caused by natural disasters, such as eartquakes and floods, or by war and civil unrest. Relief is often offered in the form of food and shelter.

repatriation Sending refugees and other migrants back to their home countries.

resettlement Permitting refugees to remain in an asylum country on a permanent basis.

rural development Activities designed to raise the economic and social standards of rural populations. Rural development usually includes land reform, agricultural improvements, water supply, health care, education, training, and environmental rehabilitation. The majority of the world's poor live in rural areas.

Sahel The semi-arid zone south of the Sahara, from the Atlantic coast of Mauritania and Senegal to Sudan and Chad. The Sahel was struck by devastating famine from 1968 to 1974 and continues to be the region most threatened by drought and desertification.

social indicators Statistics that measure the social welfare of a population. The principal social indicators are the adult literacy rate, population increase rate, mortality rate, and average life expectancy. Other indicators include school enrollment ratios and access to water.

structural adjustment A cluster of policy prescriptions dedicated to liberal, free-market economics. Structural adjustment programs demand that governments spend within their means, keep exchange rates competitive, let markets determine prices, withdraw from regulation and subsidy, and privatize industries that had previously been nationalized.

subsidy A payment by a government to producers or distributors to either ensure the economic viability of an industry or prevent an increase in prices.

subsistence farming Small-scale agriculture practiced by an individual or families to provide for immediate food needs.

sustainable development Described by the Brundtland Commission, sustainable development is "a process of change in which exploitation of resources, the direction of investments, the orientation of technological development, and institutional change are made consistent with future as well as present needs." Development is defined as the satisfaction of human needs and aspirations.

Third World This term was originally coined in the 1950s by a French economist to describe those countries that rejected alignment with both the "First World" of the West and the "Second World" of the East. While the political, nonalignment connotations of the term remain, it has taken on a broader meaning. Today, *Third World* refers to all developing countries and encompasses all of Latin America, Africa, except South Africa, and all of Asia, except Japan, Singapore, Hong Kong, and Israel. The term *South* is also used to refer to countries of the Third World.

UNCTAD *See* United Nations Conference on Trade and Development.

UNDP *See* United Nations Development Programme.

UNEP *See* United Nations Environmental Programme.

UNICEF *See* United Nations Children Fund.

United Nations Children Fund (UNICEF) UNICEF works around the world to improve the lives of children in developing countries by providing community-based service.

United Nations Conference on Trade and Development (UNCTAD) UNCTAD was created in 1964 to facilitate international trade and promote trade as "the primary instrument for economic development."

United Nations Development Programme (UNPD) The world's largest source of grant funding for development cooperation that promotes higher standards of living, faster economic growth, and environmentally sound development.

United Nations Environmental Programme (UNEP)   UNEP is mandated by the UN to coordinate and provide policy guidance for sound environmental action throughout the world.

United States Agency for International Development (USAID)   USAID is the official government agency responsible for administering U.S. overseas development assistance.

USAID   *See* United States Agency for International Development.

WFP   *See* World Food Programme.

WHO   *See* World Health Organization.

women in development (WID)   The branch of development studies that investigates the economic and social roles of women in the global South. WID grew out of the scholarship of the 1970s that brought to light women's substantial, yet unrecognized, contribution to Southern economies.

World Bank   Comprised of five organizations: the International Bank for Reconstruction and Development (IBRD); the International Development Association (IDA); the International Finance Corporation; the Multilateral Investment Guarantee Agency; and the International Centre for the Settlement of Investment Disputes. The IBRD is the main lending organization, providing loans and technical assistance to countries with a relatively high per capita income. The IBRD raises its funds on the international markets and is owned by its 177 member countries. The IDA offers loans, or "credits," to those countries that cannot afford IBRD loans.

World Food Programme (WFP)   WFP is the largest source of food assistance, sponsored jointly by the Food and Agriculture Organization (FAO) and the United Nations.

World Health Organization (WHO)   WHO was founded in 1948 with the mandate to assist people to reach the highest possible level of health.

Index